Russia's Energy Policies

National, Interregional and Global Levels

Edited by

Pami Aalto

University of Tampere, Finland

Edward Elgar
Cheltenham, UK • Northampton, MA, USA

Published by
Edward Elgar Publishing Limited
The Lypiatts
15 Lansdown Road
Cheltenham
Glos GL50 2JA
UK

Edward Elgar Publishing, Inc.
William Pratt House
9 Dewey Court
Northampton
Massachusetts 01060
USA

A catalogue record for this book
is available from the British Library

Library of Congress Control Number: 2011932886

ISBN 978 1 84980 029 7

Typeset by Cambrian Typesetters, Camberley, Surrey
Printed and bound by MPG Books Group, UK

Contents

List of figures   vii
List of tables and boxes   viii
List of contributors   x
Acknowledgements   xiv
List of abbreviations   xvi

PART I A NEW APPROACH TO RUSSIA'S ENERGY POLICY

1. Introduction   3
    Pami Aalto
2. How are Russian energy policies formulated? Linking the actors
    and structures of energy policy   20
    *Pami Aalto, David Dusseault, Markku Kivinen and
    Michael D. Kennedy*

PART II THE NATIONAL LEVEL

3. Public and business actors in Russia's energy policy   45
    Markku Kivinen
4. Russia's East and the search for a new El Dorado: a comparative
    analysis of Russia's Kovytka, Sakhalin-2 and Chaiadinskoe
    greenfield projects   63
    David Dusseault
5. Environmental sustainability of Russia's energy policies   92
    Nina Tynkkynen and Pami Aalto

PART III THE INTERREGIONAL LEVEL

6. Russian foreign policy and energy: the case of the Nord Stream
    gas pipeline   117
    Hanna Smith
7. Russia's central and eastern European energy transit corridor:
    Ukraine and Belarus   136
    Margarita M. Balmaceda

8.   Russia's energy policy in the Far East and East Siberia   156
      Shinichiro Tabata and Xu Liu

PART IV   THE GLOBAL LEVEL: RUSSIAN ENERGY IN A WIDER
          PERSPECTIVE

9.   'They went East, they went West...': the global expansion of
      Russian oil companies   185
      Nina Poussenkova
10.   Russian energy dilemmas: energy security, globalization and
      climate change   206
      Michael Bradshaw
11.   Conclusion: learning about Russian energy policies   230
      Pami Aalto

References   239
Index   267

Figures

1.1 Russia's main production areas, as well as oil and gas pipelines
     (towards Europe)   8
2.1 Social structurationist model of energy policy formation   39
6.1 The Nord Stream natural gas pipeline   121
8.1 Crude oil pipelines in the Eastern regions of Russia   165
8.2 Natural gas pipelines in the Eastern regions of Russia   170
8.3 Japan's imports from Russia   173
10.1 Russia's annual GDP growth 1996–2009, per cent   220
10.2 Trends in Russia's greenhouse gas emissions and energy
     intensity 1990–2008   225

Tables and boxes

4.1	Decision-making axes in the energy sector	67
4.2	Variations in socio-economic and political rent distribution	68
4.3	Structural dimensions observed in East Siberia and the Russian Far East	72
4.4	Case regions and associated structural dimensions I: Irkutsk	75
4.5	Case regions and associated structural dimensions II: Sakhalin	76
4.6	Case regions and associated structural dimensions III: Sakha	77
4.7	Regional socio-economic development priorities and approaches	79
4.8	The structurationist model applied to Kovytka, Sakhalin-2 and Chaianda	84
4.9	Results of the structural analysis in political/institutional and financial/socio-economic contexts	86
4.10	Rent distribution for Russia's public sector	87
5.1	Potential of non-traditional renewable energy sources in Russia	99
Box 5.1	Regional potential of non-fossil fuels in Russia	100
7.1	Pricing of Gazprom's gas to selected FSU states, in US dollars per thousand cubic metres, 2005–10	138
7.2	Average gas sale prices by Gazprom to domestic, CIS/Baltic and European markets (excluding export taxes and customs duties), 2003–06, in US dollars per thousand cubic metres	142
8.1	Crude oil production in East Siberia and the Far East, 1970–2030	157
8.2	Natural gas production in East Siberia and the Far East, 1970–2030	158
8.3	China's imports of crude oil, in million tons	161
8.4	Japan's imports of crude oil	162
8.5	Korea's imports of crude oil, in million tons	163
8.6	Japan's imports of LNG by country	171
8.7	Korea's imports of LNG by country, in million tonnes	172
8.8	Economic development of the Russian Far East and Sakhalin, as a percentage of the previous year	174

8.9   Oil pipeline tariff of Transneft, in roubles per 100 tkm   177
9.1   Lukoil involvement in foreign upstream projects during the
      1990s   190
10.1 The Russian energy nexus   217

Contributors

Pami Aalto is Jean Monnet Professor in the School of Management and Director of the Jean Monnet European Centre of Excellence, University of Tampere, Finland. He has worked at the interface of international relations, political geography, psychology and sociology; and in interdisciplinary fields such as energy research, post-Soviet studies and European studies. He is co-editor (with V. Harle and S. Moisio) of *International Studies: Interdisciplinary Approaches* (Palgrave, 2011) and *Global and Regional Problems: towards an Interdisciplinary Study* (Ashgate, 2011); (with H. Blakkisrud and H. Smith) *The New Northern Dimension of European Neighbourhood* (CEPS, 2008); editor of *The EU-Russian Energy Dialogue: Europe's Future Energy Security?* (Ashgate, 2007), and author of *European Union and the Making of a Wider Northern Europe* (Routledge, 2006) and *Constructing Post-Soviet Geopolitics in Estonia* (Frank Cass, 2003).

Margarita M. Balmaceda (MA and PhD in Politics from Princeton University) is Professor of Diplomacy and International Relations, Seton Hall University and Associate of Ukrainian Research Institute at Harvard University. In 2010–11, under an EU Marie Curie Fellowship in partnership with the University of Helsinki, she has been conducting a project on 'Getting energy from Russia to Europe: domestic political conditions in the energy-poor transit states and risks to energy transit', an area of research she has developed through, among other publications, her books on *The Ukrainian–Russian–Central European Security Triangle* (Editor, CEU Press, 2000), *Energy Dependency, Politics and Corruption in the Former Soviet Union* (Routledge, 2008) and (forthcoming) *The Politics of Energy Dependency: Ukraine, Belarus and Lithuania Between Domestic Oligarchs and Russian Pressure, 1992-2010*. In 2011–12 she will be a Senior Fellow at the Krupp Institute for Advanced Studies in Greifswald, Germany.

Michael Bradshaw is Professor of Human Geography in the Department of Geography at the University of Leicester, UK. He is also Honorary Senior Research Fellow in the Centre for Russian and East European Studies at the University of Birmingham, UK, and a Visiting Senior Research Fellow at the Oxford Institute for Energy Studies. In 2007 he received the Back Award from the Royal Geographical Society (with the Institute of British Geographers) in recognition of his research on applied aspects of economic transformation in the post-socialist world. From 2008–11 he was the recipient of a Major Research Fellowship funded by the Leverhulme Trust to work on the relationship between energy security, globalization and climate change. From this research, a book will be published entitled: *Global Energy Dilemmas: Energy Security, Globalization and Climate Change* (Polity Press, 2012).

David Dusseault is currently a Post-doctoral Research Fellow at the Aleksanteri Institute, University of Helsinki. Previously, he held the post of Acting Professor for Russian Energy Policy at the Department of Social Policy, University of Helsinki. His research interests focus primarily on the political economy of the oil and gas sector and their subsequent influence on socio-economic development and modernization policies of producing states. His recent publications include book chapters 'The legacy of the oil industry in Tomsk oblast: contradictions among socio-economic development, political legitimacy and corporate profits' (Springer, 2011), 'The impact of Nord Stream, South Stream on the gas transit via Ukraine and security of gas supplies to Ukraine and the EU' (Turku School of Economics, 2009), as well as policy briefs on Russian energy politics in the Baltic Rim Economies. On-going research projects include energy sector development from different perspectives, 'The political economy of Azerbaijan's energy sector: looking beyond the contract of the century' and 'Walking with giants: navigating the domestic energy sector with Russia's energy minors'.

Michael D. Kennedy is Professor of Sociology and International Studies at Brown University, where he explores the relationship between knowledge practices and global transformations. Beginning with studies of intellectuals and professionals in East European social movements and systemic change, for example *Professionals, Power and Solidarity* (Cambridge University Press, 1991) and *Cultural Formations of Postcommunism* (University of Minnesota Press, 2002), Kennedy now works on how transformations in the communicative capacities of intellectuals and their institutions articulate alternative futures around extensions of democracy, peace, and sustainability with particular places in mind. His most recent publications have addressed the public university, area studies and energy security in these terms.

Markku Kivinen is Professor and Director of the Aleksanteri-institute, Finnish Centre for Russian and East European Studies, University of Helsinki. Previously he has been Professor of Sociology at the University of Lapland and Visiting Professor at the University of Michigan. He has published widely on Russia and on transition in Russia and in the West. His research interests comprise social theory, power, inequality and cultural structures. His most recent books are *Progress and Chaos: Russia as a Challenge for Sociological Imagination* (Kikimora, 2002) and (co-edited with K. Pynnöniemi) *Beyond the Garden Ring: Dimensions of Russian Regionalism* (Kikimora, 2002). Professor Kivinen directs the Eurasian Energy Group of the Aleksanteri institute.

Xu Liu is a research fellow in the Slavic Research Center, Hokkaido University, Japan, and is currently studying Russia's energy and environmental policy and energy cooperation in Northeast Asia. He earned two bachelor's degrees from Peking University, one in Russian Literature and the other in Economics, and has studied at Tsukuba University and Hokkaido University; he later received his PhD from Hokkaido University. He is a regular contributor to the opinion corner of the Economic Research Institute for Northeast Asia (ERINA) and has published papers related to Russia's energy policy in academic journals and industry magazines, including 'Oil development and environmental problems in the Eastern part of Russia: a case of the construction of the Eastern Siberia–Pacific Ocean pipeline', in the volume *Russian and East European Studies* (JAREES, 2008).

Nina Poussenkova is senior researcher in the Institute of World Economy and International Relations (IMEMO), Russian Academy of Sciences, where she heads the Forum 'Oil and Gas Dialogue'. She has formerly worked for the Russian consulting company Center for Foreign Investment and Privatization; Salomon Brothers and Lazard Freres investment banks; and as a project manager and expert for WWF Russia, and Project Director at the Carnegie Moscow Center. She has published extensively on Russian energy issues, energy companies and environmental questions. Together with Lev Tchurilov, the last Minister of the Oil Industry of the Soviet Union, and Isabel Gorst, she wrote *Lifeblood of Empire: A Personal History of the Rise and Fall of the Soviet Oil Industry* (PIW Publication, 1996). Her most recent publications include *Lord of the Rigs: Rosneft as a Mirror of Russia's Evolution* (James Baker Institute for Public Policy publications, Houston, 2007), *Russian Companies in the 21st Century: Towards Competitive Corporate Citizenship* (WWF-Russia, 2007), and 'Russia's future customers: Asia and beyond', in *Russian Energy Power and Foreign Relations* (Routledge, 2009).

Hanna Smith is a researcher at the Aleksanteri Institute, University of Helsinki, Finland, and is an expert on Russian foreign policy, as well as domestic policy trends affecting Russia's foreign relations. She holds degrees from Sweden and the United Kingdom in Russian language, history, politics and foreign policy as well as international relations. In 2001–02 she was a visiting researcher at the University of Birmingham and in 2006 at the Finnish Ministry of Foreign Affairs. Having worked in numerous academic and policy-oriented projects, her publications include the edited volumes *Russia and its Foreign Policy – Influences, Interests and Issues* (Kikimora, 2005); *The Two-Level Game: Russia's Relations with Great Britain, Finland and the European Union* (Aleksanteri Institute, 2006); (with O. Kuusi and P. Tiihonen), *Russia 2017: three scenarios* (The Committee of the Future, Parliament of Finland, 2007); *Challenges of Russia* (Ministry of Defence of Finland, 2008) and (with P. Aalto and H. Blakkisrud) *The New Northern Dimension of the European Neighbourhood* (Centre for European Policy Studies, 2008), as well as numerous articles.

Shinichiro Tabata is Professor in the Slavic Research Center, Hokkaido University, Japan, and a contributing editor of *Eurasian Geography and Economics*. He has an MA in sociology. He has published widely on energy economics and the Russian economy, including the edited volume *Dependent on Oil and Gas: Russia's Integration into the World Economy* (Slavic Research Center, Hokkaido University, 2006). He has contributed to the journal *Eurasian Geography and Economics* on such topics as oil and gas export revenues, the Stabilization Fund, comparison between Russia and Saudi Arabia and the impact of global financial crisis on the Russian economy.

Nina Tynkkynen is a post-doctoral researcher at the School of Management, University of Tampere, Finland. Her research interests focus on international environmental politics and environmental aspects of energy policy. She has published on Russian environmental politics and cooperation, including her doctoral dissertation *Constructing the Environmental Regime between Russia and Europe: Conditions for Social Learning* (Tampere University Press, 2008), and articles for example in *Environmental Politics*.

Acknowledgements

This book is the result of collaboration on the study of Russian energy policy and its theoretical modelling that was started in 2006, with Pami Aalto, David Dusseault, Markku Kivinen and Michael Kennedy among the key driving forces. Since 2007, the core team behind this book has held several workshops and seminars in the Aleksanteri Institute, University of Helsinki, Finland, under the auspices of the Institute's Eurasia Energy Group. Two meetings were also organized at the University of Michigan's Center for Russian, East European and Eurasian studies and hosted by Kennedy.

Hanna Smith, Margarita Balmaceda and Mikko Palonkorpi also provided valuable input to many of those meetings and discussions, while several other members of the Aleksanteri Institute's staff and associated researchers took and continue to take part in some of the activities, among them Jeremy Smith. The core group also presented its work at the Russian International Studies Association conference in 2006 and the Nordic International Studies Association conference at the University of Southern Denmark in 2007, at the Association for the Advancement of Slavic Studies conference in Boston, 2009, where Robert Legvold proved a characteristically able and perceptive discussant, and the Aleksanteri Conference 'Fuelling the Future: Assessing Russia's Role in Eurasia's Energy Complex', in October 2010, among many other events. We continue to be most grateful to the organizers and participants of these events for the opportunities to obtain valuable feedback and to engage with stimulating audiences.

The idea for the present book grew gradually through the progress of the joint work and meetings, and was made the main objective of the collaborative work in the framework of the Academy of Finland project 'Russia's energy policy and its external impacts' (Kivinen, 2008–11). Later, Aalto's project 'Energy policy in European integration' (Academy of Finland, 2011–14, no. 139686) provided further academic and administrative support for the joint work. The more policy relevant side of the development work was greatly enhanced by smaller projects producing policy memos on Russian and Russian-European energy politics to the Ministry of Foreign Affairs in the course of 2006, and a related project funded by the Ministry on 'The new Northern Dimension and the possibility of an energy partnership – cooperation between Finland and Norway' (2007–09), coordinated by Aalto and Smith.

The contributors to this book held a book workshop in Helsinki in May 2010 to discuss draft papers. Between June and September the same year, Aalto made a memorable study visit with his family, as a Foreign Visiting Fellow in the Slavic Research Centre, Hokkaido University. This helped decisively to prepare the groundwork for the book and also included presentations in Hitotsubashi University, Tokyo, and Korea University, Seoul. The visit was kindly and ably hosted by Shinichiro Tabata, with the most hospitable presence and local help of Tomoko Tabata, Mika Osuga, Sachiko Yamashita and David Wolff, and the rest of the extremely helpful staff and associated academics within the institute. In the editing phase Sarah Naundorf offered valuable commentary and technical help at the University of Tampere, and Virginia Mattila worked efficiently with language revision.

On a more personal note, along those many discussion partners and critics encountered during the course of the numerous project events and occasions in Europe, Russia and North America, only some of which were mentioned above, the editor would like to thank those Japanese and Korean audiences with whom he had the pleasure to interact while working on this book in the Slavic Research Center in Hokkaido in 2010. For a scholar coming from Russia's European neighbourhood and where Russia is sometimes equated with its northwestern provinces, looking at Russia and its energy resources from the perspective of Asia's established and emerging powers with quite different regional cooperation interests with it, as well as reservations, was truly enlightening. These experiences confirmed that not only are there numerous facets of Russian energy policies as argued in this book, but also several viewpoints – empirical, theoretical and geographic – from which to study Russia and energy politics.

Abbreviations

APEC	Asia-Pacific Economic Cooperation
BP	British Petroleum
BRIC	Brazil, Russia, India and China
CEO	chief executive officer
CIS	Commonwealth of Independent States
CPC	Caspian Pipeline Consortium
DEA	Danish Energy Agency
EBRD	European Bank for Reconstruction and Development
EEZ	exclusive economic zone
EIA	Energy Information Administration
ENGO	environmental non-governmental organisation
ESPO	East Siberian Pacific Ocean pipeline
EU	European Union
FSU	Former Soviet Union
GDP	gross domestic product
GHG	greenhouse gases
GRP	gross regional product
IEA	International Energy Agency
IFI	international financial institution
IGO	intergovernmental organization
INGO	international non-governmental organization
IOC	international oil company
IPE	international political economy
IR	international relations (discipline)
LNG	liquefied natural gas
MEP	Member of the European Parliament
NATO	North Atlantic Treaty Organization
NOC	national oil company
NGO	non-governmental organization
NSGP	Nord Stream Gas Pipeline
OPEC	Organization of Petroleum Exporting Countries
PM	prime minister
PSA	Production-sharing agreement
SKV	Sakhalin-Khabarovsk-Vladivostok gas pipeline

SMEs   small and medium size enterprises
UNDP   United Nations Development Programme
WTO   World Trade Organization
WWF   World Wide Fund for Nature
YKV   Yakutiia-Khabarovsk-Vladivostok gas pipeline

PART I

A new approach to Russia's energy policy

1. Introduction

Pami Aalto

RUSSIAN ENERGY OLD AND NEW

Russian energy policy is a key issue in global energy policy, and energy policy is crucial for Russia. To adequately account for these wide-ranging interrelationships, this book examines Russia's energy policies on several levels. These range from the *national* level, where both Russia's national energy policies and its federal and regional politics related to energy come into play; the *inter-regional* levels, where Russia's energy sales and relations with several European regional energy markets, Eastern European transit states, the Caucasus, Central Asia and Asia are addressed; and the *global* level, where Russian energy supplies and their political, economic, environmental and other implications are critical.

The co-presence of several levels on which Russian energy policies are formulated, coupled with the reciprocal linkages between them, implies that the subject of Russian energy is as complex as it is crucial. This complexity has made Russian gas and oil in particular, together with the proceeds from the export of these goods and the associated politics, a frequent and divisive topic in scholarly analysis and policy commentary. Terms portraying Russia as an 'energy superpower', 'energy giant', 'petro-state', or more critical references to its allegedly 'coercive energy policy', 'energy imperialism' or 'energy blackmail' are part of this debate. At the other end of the debate we find references to a 'natural resources-dependent third world-style economy' and to a possible 'Dutch disease' or 'resource curse' in Russia, coupled with observations of personalized, non-transparent and even partly corrupt management of the state's resource base. In addition to these foreign policy and economics-oriented images others abound.

Where do all these terms and images come from? The diverse commentary on Russian energy at the global level is underwritten by the soaring price of oil from long-term lows in 1998 of some US$10–15 per barrel. The price leap towards US$140 per barrel by 2008 helped to lift Russia out of its post-Soviet economic decline and made it one of the emerging powers within the framework of the loose grouping of the BRICs (Brazil, Russia, India and China). The global financial and economic crisis of 2008 caused prices to slump again, severely affecting Russia's energy dominated and oil price-linked economy, before they reached what for Russia is a very sustainable level of US$70–80 per barrel in 2010, and topped US$100 per barrel in spring 2011. At the regional level of Russian-European relations, a significant part of the interest in Russia's energy springs from Europe's heavy dependence on Russian supplies. This helped to fuel alarmist reactions to the conflicts and disruptions in the supplies that have become almost an annual event since 2006. Some of the problems originate in disagreements on energy supply prices and transit fees between Russia and two Eastern European key transit countries mediating a large share of that energy traffic, Belarus and Ukraine. In addition, we find disputes about transit pipelines and other politicized energy conflicts in former Soviet territory, as well as tensions in energy relations with certain EU Member States (see Orttung and Øverland 2011). At the national level, a further source of newsfeed is how energy companies rise and fall in Russia's federal and regional power games, and where foreign energy majors have experienced both successes and dramatic losses, with new energy provinces and energy 'oligarchs' or 'oil barons' riding on energy proceeds.

Apart from that multilevel, yet familiar, oil and gas fuelled agenda of Russian-European and Russian-Eurasian energy relations, towards the end of the 2000s enough has happened to suggest different accounts as well. The most familiar of these is how Russia has become an increasingly important energy supplier to its fellow BRIC member China, as well as to the Northeast Asian economic giants Japan and South Korea. Of these new customers China became the world's biggest energy consumer in 2009, surpassing the USA for the first time in a century. This new market conquest is making Russia a player in Asia with a weight not seen since the dissolution of the Soviet Union in 1991. Russian energy companies have also established partnerships with other energy producers in Asia, Africa and the Americas.

Simultaneously, at the global level energy policies are subject to pressures to turn towards renewable sources of energy while states and international organizations also call for increasing energy efficiency and for energy savings. These calls are motivated by climate change concerns and expectations of increasing difficulties in accessing adequate fossil fuel supplies and acceptable prices, especially among western industrialized countries (for example, Scrase and McKerron, 2009; Kjarstad and Johnsson, 2009). Although this 'green' turn underlines the role of domestically available renewable resources and a set of new energy strategies, thanks to its vast potential in this sphere Russia can be part of that emerging greener energy agenda as well. Russia's participation is in fact crucial for a successful response to global climate change due to its large exports of fossil fuels, high greenhouse gas (GHG) emissions and energy intensive economy. Russia is absolutely central to the implementation of the Kyoto protocol regulating GHG emissions globally and to achieve a new treaty after the present agreement expires in 2012 (see for example Novikova, Korppoo and Sharmina, 2009; see also Chapters 5 and 10 of this volume).

In this book we will approach Russia's energy policy as a multilevel and complex sphere, developing further the scholarship on energy policy proceeding from similar starting points (for example Aalto, 2007; Prontera, 2009; Strange, 1994; cf. Güllner, 2008). From this multilevel and complex nature, it follows that in practice there is no single Russian energy policy despite serious attempts to create one, most notably under the auspices of Russia's energy strategy until 2030 (Government of the Russian Federation, 2009a). Rather, we posit *several energy policies* ranging from the various forms of energy at issue, and varying between associated industries and different geographical regions of Russia and its multiple export directions (cf. Wenger, 2006, p.17). In order to develop informed analyses of the Russian policies we use fieldwork material and experience, and local sources alongside existing research, documents and statistics.

We examine Russian energy policies with reference to Russia's established energy agenda where it is Europe's main fossil fuels supplier, and a major energy policy actor within the Commonwealth of Independent States (CIS) on the territory of the former Soviet Union, and where it is extending its fossil fuel supplies globally, especially towards Asia. In addition we will touch upon the new 'greener' energy agenda where Russia faces the increasingly significant climatic and environmental aspects of energy. The tensions between Russia's 'old' and the 'new' energy agendas are further highlighted by the global financial and economic crisis since late 2008, which momentarily reduced the demand for Russia's fossil fuel exports. While reluctant to belittle the importance of the new energy agenda, or the effects of the global economic crisis, we want to accentuate how neither of these two factors is likely to render irrelevant the well-established fossil fuels energy trade linking Russia with Europe and the CIS any time soon (cf. Aalto, 2011a). In the interests of a realistic, comprehensive and forward-looking analysis of Russia's energy policies we study the established and new agendas in parallel while paving the way for the development of a new theoretical approach (see Chapter 2). To specify the distinctive contributions we intend to make, it will be useful to next take stock of existing research.

WHAT DO WE KNOW ABOUT RUSSIAN ENERGY POLICIES?

Scholarly and policy analysis of Russia's energy policies is a small industry in its own right. It includes major academic works, only a few of which are theoretically informed; edited books and case studies mostly concentrating on empirical analyses of events past and present; and extends to high-cost consultancy reports on highly specific and technical aspects. Owing to the extent of this work it will only be possible to here outline what we (roughly speaking) know today.

The vast majority of work on Russian energy policies available in English concentrates on the country's fossil fuels sector and its exports. If we also include publications in Russian, we find scholarship on trends in the new energy agenda and as ecological issues in energy production (*Energeticheskaia politika*, 2009), Russia's role in global climate change politics (Korppoo et al., 2006), and energy efficiency and renewable energy resources in Russia (*Energeticheskaia politika*, 2008a; b; Øverland and Kjærnet, 2009). There is also research on the coal, electricity and atomic energy sectors in Russia. Although these sectors are still predominantly oriented to meeting Russia's domestic development needs, they also have important interregional and global implications which for practical reasons have been excluded from the scope of our book (see for example Bushuev and Troitskii, 2007).

The Energy Resource Base and Production

The literature on Russian fossil fuels often correctly posits that sector as the foundation for Russian energy policies. Research on Russia's energy resource base and production in disciplines such as geology, engineering and economics, including economic geography, is often ably summarized in the publications of organizations like the International Energy Agency (IEA) representing leading (western) industrialized states, or the Energy Information Administration (EIA) in the USA. This body of work has examined the nexus between the abundance of Russia's fossil fuels and the limits of its technical and economic exploitation. As such it gives us some idea of the limits of the possible and helps us to avoid the excessive voluntarism of some of the commentary in the international policy and academic communities (see below).

Oil sales have generated the majority of Russia's energy export revenue and the country's renewed wealth, although in the 2000s gas has become almost equally important (Bradshaw, 2009a, pp. 4–5). The geologist John Grace exposes the difficulties in assessing Russia's resource base by noting how the Russian oil industry for two decades after the collapse of the Soviet Union adhered to Soviet standards in analysing reserves – the so-called $A + B + C_1$ system that is slightly different from the western energy companies' system differentiating between proven, probable and possible reserves. Of these, Grace set proven reserves at 68 billion barrels in 2003. This is close to many widely accepted figures, and enough to sustain production at the high volumes of that time for some 22 years. Proven reserves imply a 90 per cent certainty that they exist, are technically recoverable and economic to produce under prevailing conditions. This makes Russia's reserves the biggest outside the Organization of Petroleum Exporting Countries (OPEC) and seventh biggest globally. Often this is seen to account for some 5–10 per cent of global reserves. Probable and possible reserves would add up to a further 32 and 33 billion barrels, resulting in the range usually given in Russian estimates of some 100 to 150 billion barrels. The Russian calculation system allegedly overestimates the prospects of technical recovery and disregards the pricing effects conditioning the economic worth of those reserves (Grace, 2005, pp. 5, 178–83).

Arild Moe and Valery Kryukov (2010, p. 313) conclude Russia's reserve-to-production ratio as being more or less sustainable during the 2010s and for half a decade thereafter. Yet in their opinion the overall trend should cause concern for Russian actors and their customers. Discussing the 'exploration crisis' in Russia, they note how, regardless of technical improvements in the new millennium, using western partner companies' expertise and techniques to totally exhaust the remaining potential of the big fields discovered and originally developed during the Soviet era has only deferred the problems. The new fields intended to replace the Soviet-developed fields are smaller, heterogeneous and more demanding in their geological characteristics, many of them plagued by harsh climactic conditions with little or at best emerging infrastructure (such as in eastern Siberia), or are further north from the current major production areas in West Siberia and Timan-Pechora (see Figure 1.1; also Figure 8.1). Reduced investments in exploration as a result of the financial crisis have worsened the long-term outlook for Russia's oil industry, which now needs high prices to sustain production and may be unlikely to maintain the high volumes of the late 2000s (Jaffe and Olcott, 2009).

In the sector of natural gas the outlook is better. However, similar reservations regarding the reliability and compatibility of the widely discrepant calculations of reserves and production capability need to be factored in. The $A + B + C_1$ formula puts the proven natural gas reserves at 48 trillion cubic metres as of January 2008, accounting for some 23 per cent of global reserves; and expected overall resources at 164 billion cubic metres (Government of the Russian Federation, 2009a, pp. 8, 39). The IEA (2009, p. 51) gives a figure of 45 trillion cubic metres of proven reserves, the biggest of which are located in western Siberia close to the Ural mountains. Prospective production regions exist further northwest to the Barents and Kara Seas, while less than a tenth of eastern Siberia – Russia's emerging fossil fuels production area – has been explored with up-to-date techniques (Poussenkova, 2009, pp. 134–5) (see Figure 1.1; also Figure 8.2).

Russia's natural reserves make it for gas what Saudi Arabia is for oil – home to by far the biggest deposits. However, Jonathan Stern warns us how

Notes: The current major fossil fuel producing regions in west Siberia, Timan-Pechora, Volga-Urals and the Caspian region are marked by medium dark grey colour. Prospective production regions in the Kara and Barents Seas, and South Turgay are marked by light grey colour.

Source: Energy Information Administration, 2009.

Figure 1.1   Russia's main production areas, as well as oil and gas pipelines (towards Europe)

> Given the size, complexity and uncertainties ... nobody should be confident of stating that future gas availability will or will not be sufficient to cover the country's internal requirements and external obligations over the next decade and beyond, even if they had conducted detailed research... (2009a, p. 10)

With this warning Stern goes on to note how Russia's domestic gas consumption (where the majority of production goes), and its exports to Europe and the CIS, in that order of volumes, have in the past few decades relied on the super-giant fields in the Nadum-Pur-Taz region of Western Siberia. These fields are 65–75 per cent depleted and output is sharply declining (Government of the Russian Federation, 2009a, p. 40). By cutting demand by 10–15 per cent in Russia and its main markets, the global economic crisis of 2008–09 helped to curb the feared effects of a possible gas squeeze ensuing from the depletion of main production fields and low investment in new production. Gazprom's roadmap for the next 20–30 years is to bring online compensating production in the Yamal peninsula and the neighbouring Ob-Taz Bay region in the country's northwest by late 2012 and subsequently in Shtokman in the Barents Sea (Stern, 2009a, pp. 2, 4–7). This is complemented by the Eastern gas programme developing Eastern Siberian and Sakhalin Island's resources for domestic use and for exports to Asia, mostly in liquefied natural gas (LNG) format (see for example Bradshaw, 2009a, pp. 7–11).

The considerable amount of research on Russia's pipeline infrastructure has noted how the majority of the country's energy exports flow to Europe through Belarus, Ukraine, and other central and eastern European transit states. While the exploitability of the material resource base is affected by available technology and prices, when speaking of pipeline politics we must add to these the need for long-term contracts to help pay for the pipelines, together with consumer demand; legal frameworks ranging from supranational to national; and diplomatic ties between producers, transit countries and consumers. Variance in these factors accounts for pipeline projects being started, but also abandoned, rerouted and the building consortia reformed. Such fluctuations abound in Russia's pipeline projects (Nies, 2008, p. 7).

For example, the Russian and German-led consortium for building the Nord Stream pipeline along the Baltic Sea (the first track to be completed by the last quarter of 2011; see Chapter 6) and the South Stream project along the Black Sea (scheduled for completion by 2015; see also Figure 1.1 and Dusseault, 2010a) respond to the problems experienced with the ageing transit pipelines of the central European route that have so far carried the bulk of that traffic. In particular Belarus and Ukraine are seen as unreliable transit states that should be bypassed in the future (see Liuhto, 2009). These two new pipelines, along with many oil transit projects, are reorienting Russia's European transit towards northern and south-eastern Europe (Aalto, 2009) (see also Figure 1.1).

Another front to compensate for Russia's transit bottlenecks in oil exports is opening up in north-eastern Asia with the completion of the East Siberian Pacific Ocean (ESPO) pipeline from Taishet in the Irkutsk oblast to Kozmino Bay in the Pacific (see Chapter 8; also Figure 8.1). For Asian partners this will compensate for the gradually diminishing production in East Asia and help to diversify the region's Middle Eastern imports. Yet soaring gas production costs in eastern Siberia are delaying Russia's gas supply projects (Motomura, 2008, pp. 68–78). In this context Russia's new gas projects seem in the mid-term to be limited to supplies of LNG from Sakhalin Island that started in small volumes in 2009 with technical support from international companies (see Figure 8.2).

Research on Russia's plentiful peat and its huge renewable resources – in which peat is often controversially included in Russia – has pointed out that together with domestic coal burning and nuclear energy expansion, increasing the share of these resources in domestic energy provision will release more oil and gas for export. Russia's renewable resources include hydropower, solar power, wind power, geothermal power, tidal power and biomass (see Chapter 5; also Kulagin, 2008; Øverland and Kjærnet, 2009).

Natural Resource Economics, Energy Economics and Business Studies

Natural resource economics and energy economics, together with the applied field of business studies boast a well-defined research programme built on economic theories and with close connections to the study of Russia's resource base. Scholars investigate issues such as how energy prices, market developments and various energy rents (received and then paid to transit states and domestic actors) impact on Russia's energy companies, the state, its economic basis and society. One debate within this literature revolves around whether Russia's resource use has created a sort of 'Dutch disease' (for example Fetisov, 2007; Roland, 2006). Booming income from energy exports as prices went up after 1999, together with Russia's own higher production, caused a rise in the exchange rate of the rouble. When money generated through energy sales is pumped into the domestic economy, the strong currency prompts consumers to buy more imported goods because they have suddenly become more affordable. This feeds higher inflation and undermines domestic manufacturing, which faces competition from cheap imports and a punitive exchange rate. From this Marshall Goldman (2008, pp. 12–13) develops a thesis of a 'Russian disease' where energy proceeds trigger field ownership disputes and compromises democratic development.

While many cite Norway and the USA as among the few countries to make resources a blessing rather than a curse, the work of Clifford Gaddy and Barry Ickes (2010) stands out in this context. Alongside many others, they note how heavily dependent the Russian economy is on oil prices (see for example Hanson, 2009a; Sutela and Solanko, 2009). Until 2009, oil prices also largely determined the prices in Russia's gas contracts, in a system where gas prices were tied to a basket of replacement fuels consisting of oil and oil products. However, in 2009 the market entry of cheap LNG prompted many of Russia's European customers to violate parts of their contracts and pay penalties. Since then the long-term future of the oil–gas price linkage has been under pressure. Its precise future depends on market conditions (Stern, 2009b, p. 12). Given that up to two thirds of Russia's export earnings and some 40 per cent of its budget come from oil and gas sales (Hanson, 2009a; Liuhto, 2010, pp. 9–24), it follows that oil prices inevitably also affect the Russian state as a whole.

Against this background Gaddy and Ickes posit natural resources not as a curse but a blessing to Russia and something from which it *must* benefit. They note how the annual sales of companies in the *non*-oil and gas sector have followed annual average oil prices since 1999. In the midst of the financial crisis, the shares of these companies plummeted more dramatically in the Russian RTS stock market than oil and gas shares did. Had Russia diversified its economy more prior to the crisis, as advocated by many analysts to avoid the Dutch disease, the negative impact on gross domestic product (GDP) would have been even greater (Gaddy and Ickes, 2010, pp. 285–90). In the first half of 2009 the absolute decline in GDP was 10.4 per cent compared to the same period in 2008. In some manufacturing sectors the drop was more than 30 per cent (Tabata, 2009a, p. 692).

On this basis Gaddy and Ickes argue that diversification would not have made economic sense and that prior to the crisis Russia benefited enormously from its competitive advantage of abundance of natural resources, and that this is likely to continue. The problem rather is that in Russia's case the proceeds ensuing from energy exports are misused in a 'resource addiction' to maintain Soviet-era domestic production structures in the interests of social and political stability. Unlike that addiction, they argue that Dutch disease was mostly avoided by building a large petroleum fund divided up into the Reserve and National Wealth funds (see Gaddy and Ickes, 2010, pp. 290–2). In April 2011 the former stood at US\$26 billion and the latter at US\$91 billion; while by spring 2010 the overall reserves were already on an upward trend again at US\$460 billion (see Ministry of Finance of the Russian Federation, 2011a; b; Liuhto, 2010, p. 51; Medvedev, 2010).

Energy Diplomacy, Energy Security and the Geopolitics of Energy

Economic analysis of sorts is often combined with a focus on energy diplomacy, energy security or the geopolitics of energy in research conducted in fields like contemporary history, political science and international relations (IR), and area studies (such as Finon and Locatelli, 2008; Perovic et al., 2009; Wenger et al., 2006). These three literatures represent internally highly diverse pursuits sharing empirical themes rather than theoretical frameworks. Many authors do not even articulate any sort of background theory (for example Baev, 2008, p.155). Often these studies respond to the policymaking needs of actors such as the USA, its energy import needs and global power balance calculations; or security of demand in Russia's main energy markets; or the security of supplies within the European Union (EU) or its Member States. Here the divisive nature of energy policy becomes apparent. For large energy importers like the EU and the USA, energy security means security of supplies at acceptable prices. For large energy exporters like Russia, it means stable demand and good prices in its main markets. For energy transit countries it implies a constant flow of transit rents and leverage over the countries of origin. In each case it is usually underlined that in order to understand Russia's energy diplomacy, we must pay attention to both economic and political factors.

Many studies focus on EU–Russia energy diplomacy or Russian–Eurasian energy politics for the simple reason that on those fronts there is a lot to study due to the many political bodies and business relationships mediating between them (for example Balmaceda, 2008; Romanova, 2007; Stulberg, 2007; see also Chapter 9). Several disputes can also be pointed out between these actors in the 2000s (Orttung and Øverland, 2011, p. 78). In terms of theorizing the interplay of political and economic considerations in Russia's external energy relations, Adam Stulberg's (2007) work has the highest research programmatic ambitions. He draws upon realist and liberal IR theories on the role of power and interdependence respectively, and the literature on 'soft power' for exploiting relative advantages in the sphere of energy policy, in order to influence the other party's options and choices made. Combining these perspectives with the insights of prospect theory on how policymakers are risk-acceptant when facing probable losses, and risk averse when thinking of gains, he develops a theory of 'strategic manipulation'. The first condition for Russia to be able to manipulate its energy customers' decision-making is that it wields market power in the targeted country. Second, Russia must be able to line up its statecraft and energy companies together into a united front. With this framework Stulberg examines Russia's energy relations with Central Asian states. He finds that Russian decision-makers are not always highly cognizant of how precisely to best affect the target countries' perceived risks and opportunity costs. Russia's ability to 'manipulate' is highly variable from country to country and depends on whether what is at issue concerns oil, gas or nuclear politics.

In a more mono-theoretical IR approach that uses a neo-classical realist theory, and which also is close to applications of traditional geopolitical frameworks to energy politics, Anita Orban (2008) partly supports Stulberg's emphasis on the compatibility of power play and market power, and his finding of Russia's diversified impact upon its energy customers. At the same time Orban partly contradicts Stulberg's assumption of relationships of interdependence between Russia and its customers or 'targets', by speaking of Russia's 'energy imperialism'. She assumes that Russia's primary motive in its neighbourhood is to increase its power and that the most effective means to that end is expanding its politico-economic presence in the energy sphere. These aims are conditioned by the Russian leaders' perceptions of the country's role in the balance of power and the resources available to the Russian state. From her East and Central European case studies she finds Russia to have been most successful in Slovakia and Hungary. The analysis concludes with various policy recommendations for the USA, Central and Eastern Europe and the EU, on how to limit Russia's influence. Most of these suggestions are diversification projects away from Russian energy. Somewhat remarkably, as many of the proposed projects and measures are relatively expensive or do not make direct economic sense, they undermine the emphasis on the balance between political and economic considerations. Hence from the starting point of the interplay of economic and political considerations we arrive at a geopolitically tuned 'to-do' list for Russia's energy customers. Alongside such steps to overcome Russia's alleged 'energy imperialism' we find calls to 'end Russian leverage' (Baran, 2007) and characterizations of Russia's 'coercive energy diplomacy' (Larsson, 2006a) which is a 'danger to Europe' (Smith, 2006, p.1). More moderate accounts term Russia 'a key regional player with global ambitions' (Perovic, 2009, p. 9), with limited leverage over its main energy customers in Europe (Closson, 2009).

These examples show how much of the research on energy security and the geopolitics of energy is geared towards wider questions of the nature of international relations or linked to nation or bloc-specific foreign policy goals. These are important considerations for policymakers and policy analysts, in particular, in that they pertain to wider questions of balance of power and demand-supply patterns (see Lesage, Graaf and Westphal, 2010), but they do not represent the primary concern in this book. Here these issues are contemplated from the perspective of the formation of Russia's energy policies, conditioned by processes at the national, interregional and global levels. In general, energy security is a wider theme whereas energy policy and its formation is a more specific *and* more fundamental problem. Without understanding the content and formation of energy policies it is meaningless to speak of energy security.

The Federal and Regional Politics of Energy

In order to look inside the black box of energy policy formation processes within the Russian Federation, we also wish to contribute to the small but important body of literature on the federal and regional politics of energy between Moscow and Russia's energy provinces. This literature accentuates the role of resource use in regional development and centre-periphery relations in Russia; and in some cases highlights the personalities, corruption, intrigue and the overall murky conditions of decision-making. The overall gist of the literature relates to deficiencies in the functioning of institutions in Russia (for example Buccellato and Mickiewicz, 2009; Dusseault, 2010b; Orttung, 2009; Tkachenko, 2007).

At this point some general patterns begin to emerge. First, each of the works discussed represents particular approaches, or at best combines two. At the same time the bulk of the scholarship available is interested primarily in producing mere empirical knowledge that frequently ends up lagging behind events, lacking any predictive value, quickly losing its import and lacking adequate linkage to other works. This clearly does not help in developing energy policy research or the academic study of Russian energy. Second, earlier studies of Russian energy policies clearly represent a multidisciplinary endeavour where work in several disciplines is used in an additive sense, when scholars combine perspectives with one another (see Long, 2011). Third, although, for example, economic and political perspectives are frequently combined in this way, research in the more theoretical sense remains fragmented along disciplinary lines, as is typical of multidisciplinary work. In particular scholars in economics operate in a relatively insular discipline (Jacobs and Frickel, 2009, p. 49). For their part some political scientists ignore or downplay underlying economic, geologic and infrastructural realities. Fourth, most scholars produce work mainly for their own audiences. The situation is even more dire in the highly specialized area of energy law, where most of the research (and the demand for it) pertains to the EU, not Russia. All this leads to a lack of an overarching framework to indicate a suitable slot for each body of work to generate more holistic and/or synthetic knowledge of Russia's energy policies. Importantly, this is not simply a feature of the study of Russian energy policy, but of the study of energy policy in general.

As a solution to some of these problems we propose a comprehensive and synthetic analytical model of the formation of Russia's energy policies which can subsequently be applied to any other cases as well. All contributors to this book were asked to think how looking through that model, or individual aspects of it, would influence their work, and to relate their respective discussions to that model as much as possible. In this way we aim to provide an analysis of the levels and complex dimensions underwriting Russia's energy policies, and of their interrelationships, in order to make it is easier to relate the individual contributions to one another; to see what aspects of the puzzle of Russian energy are addressed in each individual piece and what is left out; and what is the totality of the puzzle that ultimately should be covered. In this book, we can naturally only address a part of that big puzzle. We invoke earlier research, documents, statistics, news material, and whenever possible complement these conventional sources with interviews and field experiences. Many of the contributions to this book build on extensive site visits and discussions with energy industry insiders and governmental regulators over several years, not all of which can be recorded here. Sources both in Russian and other relevant languages in other regions crucial for Russian energy are used.

WHAT WILL WE SAY ABOUT RUSSIAN ENERGY POLICIES?

The existing approaches yield useful information but represent a relatively fragmented whole despite their multidisciplinary connections, which connote some mutual communication and factual supplementation of one another's findings and perspectives. For this reason, instead of merely pursuing the classificatory approach used in the literature survey above, in this book we prefer to think anew. Consequently in the next chapter we propose a new analytical model covering the whole field of Russian energy policy formation, reserving a place for each of the approaches surveyed while simultaneously opening up new lines of enquiry (for this type of an approach to knowledge generation, see Laudan, 1977).

The new analytical model provides a shared theoretical platform and organizational device for all chapters to this book. Most chapters link up with only certain aspects of the model as their aims are narrower than the model's relatively comprehensive approach to processes of energy policy formation; some take the model to the centre of investigation; some add further perspectives necessary to set the formation of Russia's energy policies into the wider context of global energy politics. In this sense the model allows for different angles from which to consider energy policy, and serves as a device structuring research efforts. It thus becomes partly a 'menu-for-choice' and partly a springboard for further studies.

The model is built around the idea that energy policy actors – states, bureaucracies within them, energy companies, international financial institutions, and so on – need to make sense of their policy environment in order to create viable policies. To do so they adopt different cognitive frames guiding their policy choices. With the help of these frames they assess the various dimensions of their policy environment: resource geographic, financial, institutional and ecological. In more theoretical terms, these four dimensions represent the structure in which energy policy actors operate and which they have to navigate more or less successfully. As a result we arrive at a structurationist model of energy policy formation where both actor agency and the conditioning structures have a role, and where various energy political events may occasion changes in the ways in which the actors assess their policy environment (see Chapter 2).

In the second part of the book Markku Kivinen's chapter focuses on the national level of energy policy formation by analysing the different frames guiding the choices of political and business actors in Russia. He argues that after the demise of the Soviet interdependence frame, which accentuated the role of cheap energy deliveries and shared energy infrastructure in sustaining the Soviet bloc and the Soviet Union, the business frame, with an accent on profits, has become predominant in Russia. Yet to an extent it exists in parallel with the often mentioned 'energy superpower' frame, which for its part accentuates the role of political gains in the energy business. Overall, however, the business frame is a more solid description of the cognitive frames of

Russian actors. Kivinen illustrates his argument with expert interviews, and presents a set of hypotheses for further study on tensions between the interests of the Russian state, the various interests groups within its bureaucracy, and within and between oil and gas companies in Russia. In this way he further concretizes our research agenda where energy policy formation is studied as a dynamic process fed by historically changing frames guiding the actors and the formation of their different (occasionally converging but also often diverging) interests and associated struggles (see Chapter 3).

David Dusseault takes the examination further into Russia's federal and regional energy politics by examining energy policy actors and their policy environments in Russia's new and emerging Eastern oil and gas provinces, where energy projects are in different cycles of production: in the Irkutskaia administrative region (oblast) (in particular the Kovytka gas field); the Sakha Republic (Chaiadinskoe gas and oil field); and Sakhalin Island in Russia's Far East (Sakhalin-2 oil and gas projects). He finds that in the 2000s Russia's federal institutions have strengthened their grip in all three cases in relation to other actors. This nevertheless only poses a bigger task for the Russian government and Russian institutions in general to manage the challenges inherent in these projects across the resource geographic, financial and institutional dimensions, and distribute the revenue or rent generated from the projects across political, economic and social groups in the country. Such wider interests than energy policy proper are significant for the development needs of these peripheral regions. So far only in Sakhalin is production well under way, and consequently there is solid evidence of regional interests being realized. In the other two cases the legitimacy of the energy projects rests on a similar outcome (see Chapter 4).

Nina Tynkkynen and Pami Aalto take up the role of environmental sustainability in Russia's energy policies at the turn of the 2010s. First of all they note how the Russian understanding of environmentally sustainable energy differs from that widely used in the West. Again, here too it pays to study the national level of energy policy formation even when what is at issue is a supposedly global concern with 'borderless' environment and climate change. While Russia has a lot of potential to improve its energy efficiency and possesses abundant renewable resources for developing a more environmentally sustainable and less fossil fuel-based energy policy, several other features currently prevent such a perspective from becoming more widespread in the country when viewed along the resource geographic, financial, institutional and ecological dimensions. Some new policies are concomitantly formulated supporting an 'ecological' or 'renewable energy superpower' frame in Russia, to steal some space from the fossil fuels-based 'energy superpower' framing that to an extent coloured the 2003 energy strategy in Russia but waned in the new strategy of 2009 (see Chapter 5).

In the third part of the book we use aspects of the theoretical model to examine the interregional level, or the interaction between Russian energy policy actors, Russia's transit states and its energy customers in the country's adjacent regions. These case analyses include Russia's foreign energy policies in the case of the Nord Stream gas pipeline project linking Russia's key northern European energy customers to the new resources in the Yamal peninsula and Shtokman fields in the Barents Sea. Looking at the institutional dimension of energy policy formation, in this chapter Hanna Smith finds several different interests that drive the Russian, German and other parties involved in this project which has towards the 2010s become increasingly multilateral (again) after a brief bilateral format. This includes various energy security interests pertaining to supply, demand, or security of transit (depending on actor); profit interests; and political power interests. In addition, identity-based factors, or in this case feelings of *ressentiment* – a particular type of politics of past negative experiences, in particular for Ukraine and Poland – are important factors explaining why the pipeline had to be built bypassing these formerly so important transit states (see Chapter 6).

Margarita M. Balmaceda probes more deeply into the institutional dimension of Russia's foreign energy relations examining the gas disputes with Ukraine (1994–2010) and gas and oil disputes with Belarus (2000–10). In particular she highlights the central role of domestic institutional struggles on both sides and how interests groups on both sides, Russia and its transit states, are interconnected as they share in the same energy rents and are parts of the same value-added chains. This approach underlines how Russia and its transit states are not unitary actors; neither do they have unitary energy policies. Gazprom and the Russian state trade various types of economic and political gains between them, and the involvement of intermediary companies in foreign deals implies the co-presence of personal interests (see Chapter 7).

Shinichiro Tabata and Xu Liu examine the eastern shift in Russia's interregional energy relations. They show that this shift is driven by a need to replace the West Siberian large production base that is becoming depleted, with new resources in East Siberia and the Far East; and by an interest in diversifying Russia's export markets towards China, Japan and Korea and a wider social interest in promoting economic growth in Russia's Eastern regions. In their analysis of the ESPO oil pipeline from Irkutsk to Skovorodino and on to China and Russia's Pacific coast, they find the decision to construct the pipeline informed by strongly political frames, its two spur lines driven by a business frame of diversifying markets, and its final route conditioned by environmental considerations. At the same time, tax relief is given to the regions that in the future are set to supply oil to fill the pipeline. The policies adopted have helped to kick-start production in these regions, have increased exports to the

Far Eastern market and have also most markedly boosted regional development in Sakhalin, as also noted by Dusseault in Chapter Four. These fairly
impressive results notwithstanding, in their Eastern policies Russian actors are
constrained by the heavy tax burden, high transportation fees and insufficient
natural gas demand in the Far Eastern region. Both governmental actors and
companies are guided mostly by the business frame in the cases studied (see
Chapter 8).

The fourth part of the book moves the discussion into a wider context by
analysing the global environment of Russian energy policies. Nina
Poussenkova focuses on the relatively little discussed subject of how since the
1990s, Russian oil companies have been expanding their activities not only in
Russia's immediate neighbourhood in Europe, in the Caucasus and the
Caspian region, but also towards Asia and the Americas, for example. She
argues that the resource geographic, financial and institutional dimensions
have exercised variable impact on the oil companies' global expansion interests. After the centralized export policies of the Soviet era, in the 1990s access
to finance and making profits became more important, highlighting the benefits of internationalization for the most agile private companies such as Lukoil,
and Yukos, whose assets were later acquired by the fully state-owned Rosneft.
This was part of the process by which institutional actors – the state's representatives in particular – regained some of their positions in the 2000s. With
their re-entry, they in fact made the operating environment of energy companies more challenging. In several cases governmental involvement backfired
in the companies' global expansion plans. Yet by the 2010s the state-backed
Rosneft was gradually usurping Lukoil's leading position in Russian oil
companies' internationalization (see Chapter 9).

The global outlook is completed here by Michael Bradshaw's contribution,
which focuses on Russia's role in solving global energy dilemmas in the midst
of efforts to ensure energy security, responding to economic globalization and
climate change. These wider challenges make for a very uncertain and volatile
environment for Russia's modernization aims. Energy proceeds must play a
large part in achieving these aims because of their centrality to Russia's political economy – something that will not diminish in the near future. Russian
actors have reacted slowly to the global climate change debate. Although the
potential climatic and other consequences are now being assessed in Russia,
the country's leadership has at best taken an ambivalent attitude towards the
global institutional politics of managing change through the Kyoto process. In
contrast to the virtuous cycle of increasing energy efficiency and reducing
GHG emissions, Russia's energy sector faces severe financial and technological challenges in trying to develop the new oil and gas fields in its remote
regions where environmental conditions may be about to change drastically
(see Chapter 10).

Overall, as also discussed in the conclusion by Pami Aalto, we end up with the complex nature of the policy environment in which actors must formulate and implement their energy policies as specified in our model. In the conclusion the model's importance for learning about Russian energy policies is assessed. As part of that task it is also discussed how our analyses have helped to evaluate the hypotheses on public and business energy policy actors in Russia, which were suggested in Kivinen's chapter, and what remains to be done in future studies (see Chapter 11). We hope that the model we use here will generate further research – not only assessing the model's benefits and drawbacks, but also helping to develop detailed case studies and comparisons, and stimulating balanced analyses of Russia's energy.

2. How are Russian energy policies formulated? Linking the actors and structures of energy policy

Pami Aalto, David Dusseault, Markku Kivinen and Michael D. Kennedy

INTRODUCTION

In this chapter we discuss how energy policy actors in Russia formulate the policies that together form the multi-level and complex space of Russian energy politics. Such policy formation processes can be found on various levels ranging from the national to interregional and global levels, all of which are interrelated.

We start by outlining the main energy policy actors in Russia. Next, we discuss what interests they develop vis-à-vis the policy environments which they must assess and interpret in order to develop viable policies. In a more theoretical sense, those policy environments represent the structure of which the actors are part; to grasp the qualities of that structure properly, we discuss its various dimensions. We then elaborate how certain key events can induce actors to reorient their interests and correspondingly alter their perceptions of the policy environment, and ultimately, adjust their policies. In developing this model we account for how Russian energy actors position themselves in relation to each other, to foreign energy companies operating in Russia, Russia's energy transit states, other producer and consumer states, and with international institutions and organizations. We end up with a new synthetic, comprehensive and generic analytical model which we will call a social structurationist model of energy policy formation. The generic nature of the model means that it is applicable to any case of energy political agency although our main interest in this book will be in Russian energy policy actors.

The comprehensive nature of the resulting model accommodates important parts of the research agendas typical for many existing approaches to Russian energy policies discussed above (see Chapter 1). The model also makes it possible to use these approaches alongside each other within the same overarching framework. As such, the model makes interdisciplinarity a natural practice in energy policy research (see also Aalto and Korkmaz Temel, 2011) and helps to establish a more effective scientific division of labour than we have seen so far. Towards the end of the chapter we also take up more practical questions pertaining to the angles from which the model can be approached and used flexibly in empirical research. In this way we intend to establish a tolerant, yet well-structured framework for organizing research that will also be applicable to other contexts of energy policy formation beyond Russia.

ENERGY POLICY ACTORS IN RUSSIA

It is extremely important to acknowledge the diversity of energy policy actors in Russia. Russia is not a monolithic energy policy actor. For us this makes any casual, unqualified notions of an 'energy superpower' problematic from the start. Unless properly conceptualized such labels are more useful for making headlines than for analytical purposes (cf. Goldthau, 2008; Palonkorpi, 2009; Rutland, 2008). The complex task of managing Russia's diverse energy resources, and the different challenges each resource type and individual deposit pose, likewise dilute any references to uniformly and consistently pursued 'Russian energy imperialism'. In this spirit we will reject any over-powering, essentialist images of Russia. Instead we will proceed from an assumption that interdependence among energy producers, transit states and consumers is the defining feature of the energy markets in which Russian actors have to operate in order to benefit from their assets. Only in this way can Russia exercise any power. This is not to dispute that the precise degree of interdependence and relative power of actors varies historically and from one region and energy sector to another.

Russia is home to sizable fossil, nuclear and renewable energy resources, and is a large energy producer and exporter (see Chapter 1). But Russia is also an energy importer, a transit state and a large energy consumer (Dusseault, 2010c, p.146; see below). In a centralized state such as Russia the president is nearly always involved in some capacity in processes of energy policy formation, together with or through the presidential administration, the prime minister and the government (with its several ministries' energy questions), legislative assemblies and regional administrations (see Chapter 5; also Tkachenko, 2007). Yet in most cases it is not the president or government *per se* that bears the primary burden for the implementation and funding of any given energy projects or transactions. Ministries and governmental agencies assume important responsibilities for permits and strategic planning, but most of the action on the ground is handled by specialized energy and service companies. This means that in our analyses of Russian energy policies an element of political economy should always be present (see Strange, 1994).

And to take into account the wider social and developmental needs which the state and the companies must cater for in Russia, and the wider social systems in which they are embedded, there is also a strong case for speaking of the political sociology of energy (Aalto, 2007; Aalto and Westphal, 2007). When pushed further towards the historically developed cultural understandings and cognitive framings influencing the approach to energy questions, we could even speak of the cultural politics of energy (Kennedy, 2008; cf. Meulen, 2009).

With regard to our main focus in this book – oil and gas politics, and the challenges posed by the new greener energy agenda – Russian energy companies can be conceptualized in many ways. According to company type they can be divided, for example, into federal monopolies, regionally owned and privately owned companies. According to the sector in which they operate we can discriminate not only between gas, oil and hybrid companies but also between the upstream, value-added and downstream sectors (see Dusseault, 2010c, p.148). At the same time these categories are at best analytical. Many of the Russian companies have characteristics cutting across these categories. The situation also evolves through acquisitions and new business tracks being opened up.

Russia's gas giant Gazprom is often deemed a federal monopoly, more popularly a 'state within the state', or even with regard to its role in Russia's energy diplomacy, 'Russia's Ministry of Foreign Affairs for the 21st century' (Tkachenko, 2007, p. 184). First Deputy Prime Minister Viktor Zubkov chairs its board. Gazprom has monopolistic characteristics thanks to its dominant position in Russia's gas production, its effective network of Russia's domestic gas pipelines, and legally guaranteed control of gas export pipelines. This makes Gazprom the only Russian gas company capable of operating in the downstream sector. It has several holdings in eastern and central Europe in particular (Orban, 2008). In the CIS, however, its grip is loosening somewhat as the market there is recovering very slowly from the economic crisis that started in late 2008 and may in fact be shrinking in the middle term together with the gas imports available for Gazprom. Regional actors are developing more independent actor capabilities to compete with Gazprom. In January 2010 Turkmenistan completed a new gas pipeline to Iran which will eventually increase capacity to 20 billion cubic metres. At the end of 2009, a new pipeline was opened connecting Turkmenistan, Kazakhstan and Uzbekistan with China (see Pirani, 2009; p. 28; Pannier, 2009). Nevertheless, Gazprom continues its operations in Central Asia and enjoys leverage over European consumers who have an eye on direct access to non-Russian natural gas, which so far has only been possible through Gazprom's Soviet era pipelines.[1]

The federal monopoly position of Gazprom makes economic sense. It maximizes the economies of scale as production technology costs cause long-term average total cost to decrease as output expands. Due to the high cost involved, setting up two competing gas distribution systems would be uneconomical. From this angle gas distribution can be seen as a public good and Gazprom as a natural monopoly. Gazprom's monopoly position also comes from its specific function of collecting proceeds from the EU and CIS markets to sustain the domestic rent system (Meulen, 2009, pp. 838–9, 847–8).

Gazprom's federal monopoly position notwithstanding, the Russian government only owns 50 per cent plus one share of it. More than a fifth is owned by international investors and the company is listed on the stock market in Moscow and in New York through the American Depositary Receipt scheme (ADR). In fact, as an alternative to a federal monopoly, Gazprom could be termed a national champion, a privileged class which in the sphere of energy it occupies together with the 75 per cent state-owned Rosneft – whose shares are listed in London through the Global Depositary Receipt (GDR) scheme. In the Russsian government's auctions of the 2000s, most of the development licences for new fields that are set to account for Russia's emerging production in eastern Siberia and the Sakhalin were allocated to these two companies. The whole licencing procedure was reworked to enable their domination (Moe and Kryukov, 2010, pp. 320–4). They were also given preference by the state to buy assets from other Russian and international companies in the various operations since 2004 that have renationalized a large part of the fossil fuels business. In part this was a corrective to the poorly managed privatizations and production-sharing agreements (PSAs) of the 1990s which many regard as overly generous to businessmen – the then emerging 'energy oligarchs' – and the foreign companies involved (Bradshaw, 2009a, pp. 6–10).

Of the two national champions Gazprom is a global leader in the energy business, and is by far Russia's largest company in terms of market capitalization. It is also the most profitable one with net profits of US$32 billion in 2010. Although Gazprom's share of Russia's gas production dropped from 92 per cent in 1999 to 82 per cent in 2008, its production prospects are not bad. The projected rise in domestic gas prices owing to gradual marketization started in 2010 with a 15 per cent rise – is expected to support investments in new exploration (see Motomura, 2008, pp. 74–5; Stern, 2009a, p. 4; see also Chapters 7 and 10). Yet independent producers, most notably Novatek – which is 25 per cent owned by Gazprom – invested differently, acted more efficiently, and increased their production and relative share of Russia's output in the late 2000s. According to one projection, these companies can triple their production from the current 120 billion cubic metres in 2010 to more than 350 billion by 2025, with lower production costs than Gazprom (Henderson, 2010); in early 2011 the Russian government initiated procedures for opening pipeline access to these companies. Of the Russian oil companies, in 2009 Rosneft and TNK-BP also produced more gas than before (see Pirani, 2009, p. 29). While these factors are compelling Gazprom to improve its business at home, it is simultaneously globalizing its operations beyond its main markets in the CIS and Europe. It also developed an oil arm, Gazpromneft, by acquiring Sibneft in 2005, and subsequently moved into electricity, coal and other businesses including the Kyoto Protocol emissions trading mechanisms, media outlets and sports groups.

Rosneft is essentially a domestic oil giant which grew, during the 2000s, through acquisitions, auctions and preferential licencing. These deals included the fields of Yukos – the internationally and politically ambitious, and subsequently bankrupted private company – as part of the oil sector's renationalization. Although Yukos' CEO Mikhail Khodorkovsky was imprisoned in the process, several capable Yukos managers were appointed to Rosneft (Motomura, 2008, pp. 72–3; see also Chapter 3). Rosneft has bright prospects and is Gazprom's main competitor in the new production fields of Russia's Far East (see Chapters 3, 4 and 8). It is also aligned with the so-called *siloviki* faction of the Russian elite – Russia's Deputy Prime Minister Igor Sechin was the Chair of Rosneft's board until April 2011, when he had to step down following President Medvedev's ban on deputy prime ministers and ministers from having roles in the 17 state-owned companies.

Lukoil is Russia's leading and most international privately owned oil company. It is the second largest producer with profits of US$9 billion in 2010 compared to Rosneft's US$10.7 billion. Since the 1990s it has tried to adapt Western corporate structures, strategies and technologies to Russian conditions with at least some success. Despite its privately owned status it has always been acutely aware of federal priorities (Grace, 2005, p. 220). It is active both upstream and downstream, and was 20 per cent owned by the US firm Conoco-Phillips until 2010 when the latter started offloading its holding to raise cash, completing the process in February 2011.

Together Gazprom, Rosneft and Lukoil account for nearly a third of Russia's total exports. Between them Gazprom and Lukoil have invested US$35 billion abroad, which is double the combined foreign investments of the next ten Russian companies. They have also attracted 90 per cent of foreign investment in Russia's oil and gas sector – a large part of which, however, is repatriating Russian capital. These features make Russia's oil and gas business a highly concentrated yet internally divided group of actors (Liuhto, 2010, p. 18).

Of the big three companies Lukoil is facing the greatest pressures in Russia. Yet it is still likely to enjoy more muscle in the mid-term and has better long-term prospects than the next biggest, albeit much smaller, TNK-BP that is jointly owned by British Petroleum and the Russian Alfa Group (consisting of businessmen, sometimes dubbed 'oligarchs', such as Mikhail Fridman, German Khan and Viktor Vekselberg). Surgutneftegas is another sizable privately owned company. In terms of sales it is some two thirds of the size of TNK-BP. It is often characterized as being somewhat Soviet-style, but more recently its secrecy has given way to greater transparency (see Carbon Disclosure Project, 2009). It is soundly run and wealthy, but it sits on limited reserves and consequently has uncertain production prospects. Slavneft is far behind these big corporations, as are the regionally owned oil companies Tatneft and Bashneft (Grace, 2005, pp. 220–1; Liuhto, 2010, pp. 5–6; 10–12; 19; Motomura, 2008, p. 73). The independent actor capability of all these companies is limited by the fact that the Russian oil export and oil product pipeline network is controlled by Transneft, which is completely state-owned.

The overall trend in Russia's oil and gas business until 2010 was towards more state consolidation, restrictions for foreign ownership, intra-sector consolidation and increasing international investments by Russian companies (Liuhto, 2010, p. 5). Yet many analysts expect a continued global economic crisis to persuade the Russian state to keep the oil and gas business open to foreign minority investments, especially in the numerous technically challenging projects, or even carefully reopen these sectors; and in the gas sector to allow more of a role for independent producers. None of this will detract from the fact that the Russian state has, since Vladimir Putin's rise to power in 1999, taken a very active coordinating and supervisory role in the fossil fuels business which no company operating in Russia can afford to ignore (Tkachenko, 2007). Yet the Russian state is not a unified actor, something demonstrated by the competition between national champions and by the literature on Russia's federal and regional energy policies (see Chapters 1, 3 and 4). The Russian government (2009) foresees an investment need in its energy sector of US$2.4–2.8 trillion by 2030 which it cannot obtain from the domestic market. Consequently it tolerates the operations and continued involvement of foreign companies as minority investors, shareholders and technical partners in both onshore and offshore projects in Russia. They include American, European and Asian private companies and national champions, as well as international financial institutions (IFIs) and banks (see Chapters 6–10).

As for non-fossil fuel actors in the new energy agenda, Russian business actors are small but supported by sound expertise in engineering and basic research in relevant sciences (see Øverland and Kjærnet, 2009). Think tanks and research establishments abound in energy policy matters both old and new. But in a centralized state where energy projects are large and often dominated by national champions, where companies' transparency is imperfect yet improving (see for example Carbon Disclosure Project, 2009), and where information overall circulates poorly, the role of non-governmental organizations (NGOs) is bound to be limited. WWF Russia is one of the most active NGOs together with regional and international environmental organizations (see for example WWF Rossiia, 2008a; see Chapter 5).

ACTORS ARE DRIVEN BY INTERESTS THAT ARE PART OF THEIR WIDER SCHEMATA

Energy policy actors in Russia act on the basis of what they are pursuing, what they observe others to be pursuing, and what others actually do. In the course of this interaction actors respond to their observations and by their actions promote their interests within the observed limits of the possible. The *interests* of the actors are thus the key to understanding the driving forces of energy policy formation. Yet at the same time these interests are notoriously elusive to define. They are constantly influenced by the wider social, political and material contexts within which they are advanced. For this reason we suggest treating interests as embedded in wider *schemata*, or cognitive devices, with which actors operate. Schemata help actors to articulate their interests and map, or assign meaning to, and make sense of the surrounding policy environment (cf. Wendt, 1999, pp. 133–4).

To access the nexus of interests and schemata we proceed from the most concrete example of energy companies. In an ideal-typical depiction, energy companies operating in a market environment have an interest in making a *profit*. Here we should note that not all of the actual energy markets are ideal-typical ones. In the Russian case we speak of domestic markets with monopolistic features (gas), mono- and oligopolistic features (oil), and of liberalizing, unbundled markets (electricity) in addition to regional variation. Nevertheless in most of the cases the companies themselves seek to make a profit and the state wants to collect rents from those profits in the form of taxes. But since there are conflicting ideas on how best to achieve the biggest profits – what gains are available, where, how and what risks are involved – we must treat the profit-making interest as part of a wider schemata pertaining to the actors' ideas of the business environment and practices likely to realize the underlying interest. In the case of the profit-making interest and the associated business practices, that wider schemata is a relatively coherent cognitive device that we will call a *business frame*.

There are schemata with various degrees of coherence. Of these we will mostly concentrate on frames (see also below). In general, a frame is a relatively coherent form of scheme that in the sense of Goffmann (1974) establishes relatively clear-cut conditions for expectations and interaction. With a frame an actor can articulate coherently and decide on a suitable course of action. This makes it a clearly identifiable actor with well-formulated energy policy interests (see Fiss and Hirsch, 2005). A business frame is thus held by an actor purposefully pursuing profit, or benefitting from profit-making by collecting rents on the basis of *situational rationality*. This is about making decisions based on observations and assessments of the gains and risks of different options, by exercising subjective judgement on the prevailing structural conditions – including considerations of one's own resources, who the other actors are, what they have and what they want, how much, and to what extent those competing interests have to be taken into account. The resulting business frame is influenced both by the actor's own cognitive processes and the changing structures in which the actor is embedded (see Stulberg, 2007, pp. 43–4). The business frame therefore establishes the anticipated conditions for profiting financially. It can guide the actions of energy companies, IFIs, banks, governments, as well as intergovernmental organizations (IGOs) and supranational bodies.

A second type of schemata is often associated more exclusively with state actors and their presumed interests in seeking more *power*, most often defined as *influence*, through energy policy (for example Orban, 2008; Stulberg, 2007). In the Russian case this is also often linked to the interests of the *siloviki* and the country's military ambitions (Baev, 2008). Energy projects can in this way be assessed in terms of their capacity to increase Russia's absolute or relative influence. As the country is to a large extent energy independent, we mainly speak here of power-seeking through foreign energy exports. Yet at the same time it is clear that any given energy project will favour some Russian political, company or regional energy actors more than others and can actually dis-empower some, for example when new fields are opened and new pipelines are laid and traditional routes bypassed. Quite simply, investment in projects intended to enhance Russia's leverage over its energy customers and its more ambiguous international prestige will always empower some actors more than others. In this sense the power-seeking interest can only translate into a relatively ambiguous 'energy superpower frame' that politicizes energy projects but often remains conspicuously incapable of unifying all Russian actors (Kivinen, 2007; see Chapter 3). Variations of the energy superpower frame include a more general political power frame as well, and the more specific 'liberal empire' idea aired in 2003 by the CEO of Russia's then electricity monopoly RAO UES, Anatoli Tshubais, whereby Russia would dominate the CIS by economic means, the most important of which relate to energy.

Alongside these two chief interests and frames for Russian energy policies, there are also some signs of an embryonic interest in environmental security in Russia (Tynkkynen, 2008). This has yielded a *sustainability frame* guiding action focused on the minimization of the environmental side-effects of energy projects and combating the harmful effects of global climate change (see Chapters 5 and 10; also Aalto, 2011a). Such frames are admittedly better institutionalized among Russia's European partners such as the Norwegian Statoil (and French Total), in the Shtokman gas fields project in the Barents Sea, and its European energy customers, environmental NGOs and international NGOs (INGOs) (see Aalto and Tynkkynen, 2007; Bradshaw, 2009; WWF Rossiia, 2008). At the same time leading Russian energy policy decision-makers increasingly understand that energy business must not in the longer run totally compromise the country's sustainability. In such an instrumentalist account, the sustainability frame can hence be held to support the viability of the business frame in the long run.

Among Russia's European customers it is easy to find an *energy security frame* expressing an interest in guaranteeing security of supplies from Russia to downstream markets. In Russia's European markets this interest and the associated framing is driving some actors closer to Russia and some away from it owing to perceptions of overdependence (Aalto, 2009). In the Asian direction, by contrast, policies informed by energy security frames make Russian energy an additional security measure compensating for overreliance on the Middle East (cf. Chapter 8). Within Russia itself, at the national level, energy security frames relate to the interest in meeting rising domestic demand. By 2030 total primary energy supply needs are expected to be up to one and half times higher (Government of the Russian Federation, 2009a, p. 94). At the interregional level energy security frames relate to the interest in ensuring security of demand in the main export markets. Energy security frames in Russia thus prioritize very different matters from those among its energy customers.

There are also cases where actors rethink their energy interests. Among Russia's energy customers in Europe, this happened particularly towards the latter part of the 2000s. In these situations we speak of *sense-making* rather than of a clear-cut frame informing the articulation of energy policy interests. Sense-making implies a situation where actors lack a clearly formulated agenda and struggle to ascertain how an event or issue relates to their concerns. It thus 'stresses the internal, self-conscious process of developing a coherent account of what is going on' (Fiss and Hirsch, 2000, p. 31). Some of the widely reported events such as the Russian-Ukrainian gas disputes which temporarily halted supplies to Europe, the building of the Nord Stream gas pipeline, and other such contested projects in the 2000s forced many European governments to rethink their interests (see below; Chapter 6).

Finally, we should note that in Russia just as among its energy customers, different actors may hold on to different frames. This means that in Russia we find several co-existing energy policy frames. At the national level this may result in incoherent energy policies unless the frames support each other as, for example, the business frame and energy superpower frame in principle can do; and as an instrumentally upheld sustainability frame can in the long run support business frames. At the interregional and global levels different frames may seriously complicate energy relations and highlight energy conflicts. The analytical benefits of conceptualizing interests through schemata/frames are multiple. This conceptualization helps us to move beyond one-dimensional analyses by acknowledging the existence of different frames; to situate actors' interests in the wider context of how they assess the policy environment; and to acknowledge the role of knowledge, interaction, and the associated intended and unintended consequences (see below). Because of such a multitude of factors, at any given time in Russia, we find many energy policy processes and associated schemata at work simultaneously.

ACTORS DEVELOP INTERESTS AND SCHEMATA WITHIN THE CONFINES OF STRUCTURE

Excessively actor-centric conceptualizations of energy policy formation may take the form of either simplistic rationalism or excessive voluntarism. To avoid such extremes it is crucial to obtain a clear idea of the policy environment – that is, the structural conditions in which the actors operate and interact. Our main postulate here is that actors formulate their energy policy interests and wider schemata by observing and then assessing their policy environment. These assessments thus depend on what the actors know, or how well or ill-informed they are (Dusseault, 2010c, p. 166).

The role of information and knowledge has long been an important part of the research agenda of environmental politics (Ascher et al., 2010), as testified, for example, by its focus on epistemic communities (Shackley, 2001). We suggest that the role of information should be equally important in the sphere of energy, which manifests a comparable degree of complexity, spread over multiple levels (see Chapter 1), and where actors likewise suffer from not knowing enough when contemplating their policy options. Our theoretical assumption is that in most of the cases, and for most of the time, actors have incomplete information and can thus make what from a rigid rational choice perspective look like sub-optimal choices. This means that socially and culturally produced information and knowledge have a pervasive influence on energy policy formation, while that knowledge is too rarely critically examined (cf. Foley and Lönnroth, 1981, pp. 6; 16; 19–21; Prontera, 2009, pp. 6–7). The fact that relatively little information is pooled in energy policy interaction, compared to the international scientific panels found in the environmental sector proper such as the International Panel on Climate Change (IPCC), and that secrecy, misrepresentation and 'information wars' are part of the game, only aggravates the situation. Hence it follows that we should study how actors observe and assess their policy environments, and how in those processes they are guided by their policy frames. A further critical need is to think how and when the actors' assessments should be challenged by a critical and balanced analysis of these environments.

We will conceptualize the actors' policy environments in terms of structural dimensions. These have both social and material qualities. They both enable and constrain the actors. These policy environments straddle the resource geographic, financial, institutional and ecological dimensions of structure.[2] In other words, these four structural dimensions are to us analytical categories describing the policy environments faced by the actors. With this structural contextualization we make schemata socially formed cognitive devices mediating between actors and structure, both of which we think must be accounted for if the analysis of energy policy formation is to be adequate and realistic. The actors' schemata thus express what they think of the issues, problems and dilemmas we discuss under our four structural dimensions. For each dimension we will first describe the main issues and problems involved, and thereafter the typical actors and sources of expertise, including alternative perspectives that may be employed to understand that dimension; this is followed by a brief account of what schemata actors are likely to develop in order to approach the opportunities and constraints set by each dimension.

The Resource Geographic Dimension

The resource geographic dimension of structure marks issues that in Russia begin at the national level. It refers to the links between the use of the physical energy resources on the ground and their end use, the options for which Russian actors must assess. At the most basic level this includes considerations such as the finite and one-time nature of fossil fuel resources and the uneven distribution and access to resources which, of course, privileges Russian actors in general. But it also requires them to possess the technological means of production used to extract, develop and transport the resources. Moreover, moving from the national level to interregional and global levels, Russian actors encounter an extensive physical geography shaping the forms of transportation and distribution – the need to build and maintain pipelines, railways, ports and terminals, as well as storage facilities and distribution grids.

The actors that are typically found along this dimension include companies, natural scientific research institutions representing both basic and applied research, technical expert agencies of states, and international organizations. Their most knowledgeable experts are educated in the disciplines of geology, engineering (including the study of energy systems), as well as physical and economic geography (see Chapter 1). These experts concentrate on the material features of reality. The interaction between them and the social scientists interested in the wider implications of the physical resources and infrastructure is a challenge to arrange meaningfully (see Jacobs and Frickel, 2009, p. 49). This is problematic, given that this dimension is also of interest to economists and IR analysts who (should) regard it as a key background variable to their own specialized analyses. However, thinking through this dimension, the analysis of energy *policy* is not the primary consideration. Rather it is energy as a material and/or technologically produced good. Nevertheless the technologies used to produce and refine the extracted energy resources into marketable goods also have important social qualities in the form of social capital and technological expertise.

With an eye to the schemata developed by energy policy actors, assessments of the resource economic dimensions of structure should constitute the backbone of any frames developed by the actors. Thus this dimension should be central to any framing of energy political action irrespective of whether we are talking about the business, energy superpower, or any other frame. Actors failing to account for this inherently material foundation of energy policy as enshrined in the resource geographic dimension are bound to make poor policy choices.

The Financial Dimension

Energy projects can be financed by relying on national level means but they often require huge investments necessitating large consortia including a number of actors from Russia and beyond. Russia's extensive geography only highlights this multilateralizing feature. In this structural dimension we include all financial transactions, incentives and constraints pertaining to energy, and in the wake of the financial crisis that erupted in 2008 we take them to connote both material and social qualities. The importance of this understanding was demonstrated in 2008 when confidence and belief evaporated, intra-bank interest rates skyrocketed and credit froze, even to healthy companies in Russia and beyond.[3] The fluctuations and global speculation in currencies have likewise highlighted how money is not only intended to measure underlying economic relations and capacities, but centrally connotes the socio-culturally mediated estimates of value and reliability shaping those resources. Overall, in this financial dimension, we can include finite investment and exploration capital, and capital overall, the lack of which originally forced the Russian government to integrate the country's economy with regional and global markets (Meulen, 2009, pp. 847, 853); energy commodity pricing mechanisms on which Russia is heavily dependent (see Chapter 1); exchange rates, chiefly the relationship between the rouble and the US dollar; as well as the size and evolution of Russia's domestic and international energy markets.

The core actors along this dimension are business establishments such as investment banks, investors (who in Russia also include energy 'oligarchs'), states, regional blocs and IFIs. The best knowledge on these financial matters typically comes from academic and business analysts, and consultants educated in fields such as natural resources economics, energy economics and business studies (see Chapter 1). Each of these fields assigns varying degrees of rationality to the actors. Actors are assumed to mostly think rationally about the pricing and other economic mechanisms mediating the supply and demand for energy. In disciplines and fields like IR and international political economy (IPE) there would be ample opportunity to contribute to the study of these matters, but so far very few examples of those possibilities have materialized in general, or in the more specific context of Russian energy policies (however, see Stulberg, 2007; Tkachenko, 2007).

Actors viewing energy policy through the financial dimension constitute an ideal-typical case of market actors with a business frame. However, in a business where national champions and state companies produce most of the oil and gas today and sit on most of the reserves (in Russia just as elsewhere), the limitations of a pure business frame are evident as political institutions also enter the picture.

The Institutional Dimension

On the institutional dimension we encounter enabling and constraining factors at different levels. First, on the national level we can start with *informal* institutions. At their most profound they include informal customs and norms that change only slowly over decades and centuries (Meulen, 2009, p. 835). Thus the energy power of Russia comes with a long history of energy sector development (Goldman, 2008) conditioned by various layers of Russian social institutions, customs and habits – for example, making projects big and centralized. On a second layer we find tacit 'rules of the game' which highlight the role of insiders and the lack of transparency within the sphere of energy politics (Balmaceda, 2008; see also Pynnöniemi, 2008). The informal institutions question the formal rules of institutional politics. As for formal institutions, in the Russian context their weakness is often noted – the centralizing tendency since the 2000s notwithstanding – together with a lack of societal trust. This results in uncertainty over agreements and private property rights, for example, and makes the formal governmental institutions represented by the Putin-Medvedev tandem intervene forcefully to compensate for the lack of trust and prevent the free-riding enjoyed by energy oligarchs in the 1990s. In this way the Russian government achieves sub-optimal control whereby businesses like Gazprom feed the domestic economy and the rent system through tax payments (Meulen, 2009, pp. 843–48). In sum, on this national level of the institutional dimension, actors face and by their own actions reproduce both informal and formal institutions; at the same time their choices are conditioned by their own sectoral interests and decision-making capacities. Relations among regional and federal actors are also significant. Russian domestic actors are naturally advantaged as a result of their superior knowledge of these linkages.

In addition to the national level, energy policy actors in Russia encounter institutional processes originating in the interregional and international levels, especially when marketing Russian energy resources to neighbouring regions and further afield. These range from interstate and inter-bloc relations to the force of international agreements, regimes and formal institutions – and likewise to the conditioning effects of popular attitudes and international cultures of interaction. They may vary according to the setting – be it cooperative, competitive, or one of power politics (see for example Wendt, 1999; Buzan, 2004).

The actors on the various levels of the institutional dimension therefore include domestic public bodies conditioned by informal and formal rules, other consumer, transit and producer states and their representatives, IGOs, and INGOs. They are bodies which on different levels of analysis can regulate and allocate the financial resources required and organize the production, distribution and consumption of energy resources. In terms of how to approach these, institutional issues occupy a middle ground in the continuum from social to material aspects of energy policy. This puts a premium on approaches capable of grasping the social and political factors well. Hence we can refer to political science, IR and sociology; insights drawn from new institutional economics which in part at least draws upon and is connected to these fields; and energy law. But theoretically informed political science and IR approaches are currently grossly underused in energy policy research. It is even harder to understand why there has been so little interest among the IPE community in these institutional questions, although Susan Strange had already outlined a research agenda for this purpose a decade and half ago in 1994. In the Russian case, in particular, only a small part of applicable theory is currently used.[4] Thus while institutions and their interaction should in principle represent a major domain for energy policy analysis, owing to the underuse of relevant theories, our ability to properly grasp these varied processes has remained limited.

To the credit of existing research, the issues which in our model fall into the institutional dimension of energy policy formation are frequently linked together with those that are part of our financial dimension (for example Meulen, 2009; see Chapter 1). Examining actors in this way by linking the financial and institutional dimensions produces a fairly powerful approach. However, more mono-dimensional efforts whereby actors are examined along the institutional dimension only, risk producing much more skewed analyses. For example, there are geopolitically inspired studies concentrating on the institutional deficiencies (or lack of rules and regulation) of the interregional and global levels of energy policy. With their focus on how the increasing competition for fossil fuel resources raises the status of actors like Russia, these studies are in danger of overlooking financial arrangements and Russia's need to care for its client base, issues which are pivotal for Russian actors. In this way we end up with excessively narrow studies portraying Russia as a mere energy superpower although that on its own is a very limited perspective. Alongside these critical remarks on the need to combine dimensions, we wish to stress how the institutional dimension can be satisfactorily studied on its own by understanding that it connotes more than, for example, mere interstate power balance and how that is affected by regional and global energy balances. In short, the multilevel and complex character of energy policy formation emerges especially strongly in the consideration of the institutional dimension. Generalizing from only some of its aspects runs the risk of skewed analysis and poor policy advice.

The Ecological Dimension

The physical and material nature of energy issues also lends itself to another, quite different logic from that of the production and transport of resources discussed above along the resource geographic dimension. This additional dimension which Russian actors must increasingly note with the emergence of the new, greener energy agenda is evident in the environmental side-effects of energy production, transport and use, and the associated climatic consequences. Energy technology has a crucial role in the ecological dimension, as it does in the resource geographic dimension. But in contrast to what is customary in the oil and gas industry, the actors' concern here goes beyond ensuring full resource use. Rather it is to do everything with a minimal ecological footprint, which ultimately may mean less energy being used. Given the traditional link between energy use and economic growth – which is, however, not automatic and may be weakening – this may also mean that less economic growth is in fact needed globally. In this sense the logic of the ecological dimension runs at least partly counter to those of the resource geographic *and* financial dimensions. In other words, the self-evident policy priorities along these dimensions are questioned – exploitation of scarce and polluting fossil fuel resources (which in fact should be minimized); and the optimization of the profits and markets of energy companies (which in fact should be re-oriented to green energy).

Those actors who prefer to view energy policy issues through this dimension are likely to play a very different game from the engineers, oilmen, oil price speculators, energy bureaucrats and geopoliticians (geopolitical analysts and the policymakers implementing similar agendas), who straddle the resource economic, financial and institutional dimensions. Here we refer to environmental IGOs, INGOs and NGOs, representatives of states' environmental bodies, academics, other experts and activists. Yet, in common with some of the more traditional energy policy actors, they have an interest in the development, investment in and support for renewable technology industries – even if their underlying interests differ – and can also cooperate in the shaping of domestic and international institutional regulation of global environmental and climate policy issues. How these matters are best handled encroaches on the territory of a number of scientific communities. Most of the interested parties consider themselves to represent the multidisciplinary field of environmental studies and environmental politics.

These actors mostly cling to what we termed above the sustainability frame. This leads to varying degrees of criticism of the other competing framings that today continue to represent the mainstream within the sphere of energy policy. However, in the longer run it is to be expected that this ecological dimension will gain strength in Russia, too. There is considerable inertia, however, due to the 'lock-in' factors making actors path-dependent on fossil fuels; other solutions adopted today and tomorrow will also have consequences lasting for decades (Scrase et al., 2009, pp. 225–6).

CAN ENERGY ACTORS BE OVERTAKEN BY EVENTS?

We have so far suggested that some actors have a particular interest in and/or knowledge of certain dimensions of the policy environment (structural dimensions), and consequently develop cognitive frames guiding them to view energy politics in the way they think best enables the realization of those interests. The formulation of energy policies always constitutes a puzzle where the pieces of information the actors have are assembled together against the backdrop of each of the four structural dimensions of the policy environment – the totality of which no actor masters completely. The more meticulously and adequately the assembly or mapping of the policy environment is performed, within the constraints of time, the better the resulting policies should in principle be. The more the actors deliberate over the issues relating to the four structural dimensions, take into account the different levels cutting across them, and bring these knowledge sets together when mobilizing their resources, the better informed the policy choices should be. By contrast, decision-makers holding on to one frame alone may not produce very good results over time. How the assessments of the structural dimensions change over time, rationally or irrationally, is the remaining piece in the building of our analytical model.

In addition to actors, schemata and structural dimensions, we can now add the category of *events* to our conceptualization of the processes of energy policy formation. This takes into account how the sequence and combination of events can be central to the explanation of change. Here we revert to the issue of how observing Russian developments has resulted in new terms to describe its role in energy policy matters on different levels. In this context,

Russia is often viewed as the actor behind or causing events – it is a key actor in the conduct of global energy policies and according to geopolitical analyses, pursues assertive energy policies. Other actors such as the EU, and many of its Member States, allegedly with weaker energy policies, are viewed as reacting to Russian moves (Hoogeveen and Perlot, 2007). These views of Russia striking and others running in panic are decidedly prevalent in the energy superpower debate. Regardless of whether these views are correct, this hints at how examining events can help us to analyse interaction and power relations among actors.

We understand events as sequences of occurrences that may result in the reformulation of energy policies. They may prompt actors to accentuate a new dimension of energy policy formation at the expense of others, or eventually help them to learn to develop a fuller picture of the policy environment including all of its relevant dimensions. Events can induce actors to review the balance among the structural dimensions they deem relevant and re-examine what information they identify and highlight on each dimension. Such re-examinations can occur because the structural dimensions are multiple, as demonstrated in the four facets just introduced; transposable in the sense that, for example, physical resources and pipelines can be viewed in terms of geopolitical significance or investment consortia; and overlapping in the sense that they depend on each other as, for example, the development of technologies to exploit a physical resource presupposes financial investment (see Sewell, 2005, pp. 217, 227).

However, on their own, events do not make anything happen. They require active agency to make them significant. This is done with the help of schemata. In other words, we can suggest that schemata are maintained or re-made in response to events and that they have profound consequences for policy formation (Fiss and Hirsch, 2005, p. 30). At the same time schemata are deeply embedded in the four structural dimensions and their historically developed and current features.

The landmark case where events or activities with Russian involvement prompted Russia's energy customers to review their energy relationship with Russia was the Russo-Ukrainian gas conflict of 2005–06. At issue were transit fees for gas en route for Europe through the Brotherhood pipeline and gas prices to Ukraine and its debts to Gazprom/Russia. After the initial reactions within the EU critical of Russia, most subsequent assessments have put the blame jointly on Russia and Ukraine arising from their non-transparent, complex and highly rent-seeking energy trade relations (see Chapter 7). What we do know is that Ukraine was siphoning off the transit gas when its own supply volume was cut off by Gazprom. The episode left many EU Member States who were at the end of the pipeline suffering from considerably reduced gas supplies in a cold winter (Emerson and Gnedina, 2009, pp.1–4). When deliveries resumed a few weeks later at normal volumes, the same Russian gas, from the same old western Siberian fields, at approximately the same prices, had become much more threatening than before.

Another similar example of actors responding to events in which Russia is perceived to be the active party include the building of the Nord Stream pipeline from Russia to Germany (see Chapter 6). Yet it is also important to note the events that have compelled Russia to reframe its policies. These include the revolution in the use of unconventional gas in the USA and its repercussions in Europe, and the global economic crisis, which abruptly reduced the demand for Russian fossil fuels (Aalto, 2011a; see Chapters 1 and 10). In each case, the research task then becomes to analyse how actors observe and react to the event, and readjust their schemata if needed, with potential consequences for relations among producers, consumers and transit states. Again, events relate to questions of knowledge and to the need to re-examine what actors (think they) know.

THE SOCIAL STRUCTURATIONIST ANALYTICAL MODEL

Our resulting model of energy policy formation links the various energy policy actors in Russia with the four structural dimensions through which they will have to navigate. In so doing actors develop schemata that help them link their core interests with their salient policy environment – depicted in our four structural dimensions. We assume that in the case of profit-seeking interest, actors develop a business frame; that at least a partly competing interest in increasing influence in external markets can be articulated through an energy superpower frame or some of its variations; that concerns for environmental protection logically relate to the prevalence of a wider sustainability frame; and that questions of security of supplies and/or security of markets lead actors to think through energy security frames. Obviously there are also other frames mediating the processes of Russian energy policy formation. Moreover, when faced with unanticipated events, actors may make sense anew of the situation they are in and ultimately come up with new frames. All these processes can include interaction among several actors, over time, and both along and across the national, interregional and global levels.

We assume that what energy policy actors in Russia do and how they frame their choices within their salient policy environments have severe structural consequences in Russia and beyond. Some of the possible outcomes are evident, for example, in the images of Russia as an energy giant, energy impe-rialist, or a resource-cursed state. At the same time our model is designed to show why no single actor has a free hand in the interdependent world of energy policy formation. No actor possesses perfect information or controls all the structural dimensions, and normally no one enjoys full control over the schemata of other actors within energy chains extending to thousands of kilometres (see Stulberg, 2007). The biggest prospects of structural transformation or paradigm change exist in energy policy when we witness a change in the way in which the issues within the four dimensions are perceived by the actors, for example as a result of unanticipated events. The resource geographic dimension is typically not rapidly malleable although technological breakthroughs like the commercial exploitation of unconventional gas reserves have recently made new resources available, undermining the market power of Russian gas. Financial means also accumulate only slowly although the financial crisis of 2008–09, and the continuing credit and financial problems in the eurozone, have revealed how quickly business confidence can evaporate. Formal institutions are more readily malleable, although their informal institutional foundations are resistant to change. In the last few decades the ecological dimension has become more pivotal.

Mindful of these prospects of structural change and resilience, our model takes processes of energy policy formation as akin to processes of *structuration,* as suggested by the theory of Anthony Giddens (1984; see also Henriksen, 2010). With the concept of structuration, Giddens refers to how actors are enabled and constrained by the structural positions they occupy at a given time. Structuration refers to the processes by which actors actualize the resources available to them in the social and material dimensions of structure (Giddens, 1984, p. 33, ch. 1). Viewed in this way, what we can take as energy political structures, such as Russia's present fossil fuels-based regime and associated frames, signify the patterning of the conduct of actors and the processes that have preceded it. This makes it imperative to take into account both recognized and unacknowledged dimensions of action, as actors are not in possession of complete information. This means that energy political action has both intended and unintended consequences (ibid., ch. 1, 176).

Our model allows for causal analysis of these trajectories but does not suggest general explanations. As the frames or articulations of the four structural dimensions are variable over time and space, the causal mechanisms and combinations of these also vary case by case. In this sense our model is not a case-specific or empirically generalized causal model, but a generic and abstract model applicable to any case of energy policy formation, including various sets of actors (see Figure 2.1). At the same time the model has heuristic value in clarifying the complex environment of energy policy formation and action, and can be used to grasp how actors are linked to each other as they operate in the same policy environments. This means that the model also allows for descriptive analyses and can help to point at less acknowledged processes, themes and problems worth attention.

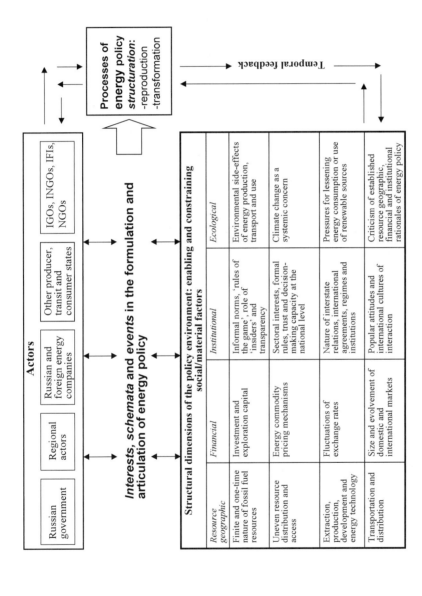

Actors

| Russian government | Regional actors | Russian and foreign energy companies | Other producer, transit and consumer states | IGOs, INGOs, IFIs, NGOs |

Interests, schemata and events in the formulation and articulation of energy policy

Processes of energy policy structuration:
-reproduction
-transformation

Temporal feedback

Structural dimensions of the policy environment: enabling and constraining social/material factors

Resource geographic	Financial	Institutional	Ecological
Finite and one-time nature of fossil fuel resources	Investment and exploration capital	Informal norms, 'rules of the game', role of 'insiders', and transparency	Environmental side-effects of energy production, transport and use
Uneven resource distribution and access	Energy commodity pricing mechanisms	Sectoral interests, formal rules, trust and decision-making capacity at the national level	Climate change as a systemic concern
Extraction, production, development and energy technology	Fluctuations of exchange rates	Nature of interstate relations, international agreements, regimes and institutions	Pressures for lessening energy consumption or use of renewable sources
Transportation and distribution	Size and evolvement of domestic and international markets	Popular attitudes and international cultures of interaction	Criticism of established resource geographic, financial and institutional rationales of energy policy

Figure 2.1   Social structurationist model of energy policy formation

METHODOLOGICAL IMPLICATIONS

The remaining question to be settled is how our analytical model of energy policy formation can be applied to empirical research. There are several possibilities. To start from the most demanding task, the whole chain from actors to schemata/frames and structural dimensions, and on to events and overall patterns of structuration of energy policy, can be analysed for any given country such as Russia, and for any given time, energy project or geographical direction. A comprehensive combination of these can also be provided. Such studies are likely to become lengthy reports or books. A less demanding task would be to analyse only the parts of the processes that the model allows us to account for. This is in fact what is done in most of the contributions to this book. Although we provide an in depth picture of Russian public and private, federal and regional level actors, the main frames guiding the formation of energy policy in the country, the most important geographical directions of Russian foreign energy policies, and the major energy projects in the 2000s and 2010s, it is clear that our model allows for more scope and depth than can be done in the confines of one book.

Actor-centric applications of our model can be interpretative or based on rational choice. In the more interpretive studies the analysis can start from the schemata/frames of the actors. This may include studies on how frames held by different actors evolve over time, and comparisons of how compatible or incompatible these frames are. These patterns then give us reason to speak of energy policy coherence in Russia, prospects of resource mobilization for promoting different interests, and prospects of cooperation on national and international levels (see Chapter 3). The prospects of an emerging frame such as the environmental sustainability frame in Russia can also be examined against the constraints and opportunities of the structural dimensions (see Chapter 5). More rational choice-attuned applications of the model, by contrast, can further theorize the cognitive processes of the actors in the different regions of Russia and analyse how they observe their policy environments in conditions of unequal distribution of information while attempting to maximize their interests (see Chapter 4; also Dusseault, 2010c).

Another strategy is to start from individual energy projects such as the numerous pipeline projects linking Russia at the interregional level with its energy customers. Alternatively, one can start from pipeline projects designed to bypass or sideline Russia (such as the EU-promoted Nabucco pipeline; see Dusseault, 2010a). In the context of an individual pipeline project the crucial events can then be examined in light of which actors were responsible for them, possibly analysing actors' interests in participating in those projects, or which actors in particular were forced to reformulate their frames; what dimensions of the policy environment enabled the documented events; and what dimensions caused events to unfold as they did. In these analyses the structural limits of the possible constraining the actors, and balance among the structural dimensions, can become pivotal. Analyses of this type can adopt either an explanatory or descriptive research strategy and can focus on actors on the supply or demand side, usually contrasting their structural positions and/or frames with each other (see Chapters 6–8).

Finally, the model can be used in the more general sense of thinking of global level structures and of how Russian governmental actors or Russian energy companies navigate through the dimensions of the policy environments as witnessed in global energy markets and politics. How and why do Russian companies seek to access fossil fuel resources outside Russia? Do they need financial backing from other actors? Do they prefer to cooperate on an informal or formal institutional basis at the international level? Do they keep agreements, and how do they respond to the activities of partner and competitors (for some of these aspects, see Chapter 9)? It is also possible to ask what kind of structural energy security challenges Russia encounters in general within the global environment when the state defends its position in global energy supply chains, in the context of economic globalization, and when climate change questions the very assets it has to offer (Chapter 10).

Regardless of the specific approach adopted, the purpose of our modelling in this chapter was to render the complexities of energy policy formation explicit. Complex matters have to be studied using complex models. At the same time our model is offered to help us identify relevant, well-defined problems for research while simultaneously keeping the big picture in sight. Theoretical modelling has little intrinsic value unless it serves practical purposes in a hugely important field such as energy policy in Russia and beyond. Pure practical studies, by contrast, have limited value on their own without a framework pointing out what role they play in the context of knowledge formation as a whole.

NOTES

1. However, some of the gas Russia has sold to the EU area has in fact for long been from Turkmenistan. Russia has been using Turkmen gas as a swing resource to augment its own production. For nearly the whole of the 2000s Russia bought Turkmen gas at a lower price than it sold to the EU. Only in 2009 were these Turkmen deliveries suspended owing to diminished demand. In 2010 Russia diversified its imports by also agreeing to buy gas from Azerbaijan, in addition to Kazakhstan, Uzbekistan and Turkmenistan. The bulk of the imports were still Turkmen gas, up to 30 billion cubic metres for a price tied to Gazprom's European sales prices; see CIS Oil & Gas (2010).

2. For related structural international political economy schemes – which are further developed here as part of our model – see Strange (1994) where the independent structural logic of ecology is not acknowledged unlike it is here; and Belyi (2003), who applies Strange's general framework to the European context. These studies also incorporate an 'energy security'

dimension which we think by contrast is a wider category and best kept analytically separate from processes of energy policy formation which we regard as primary.

3. This brought many Russian companies to their knees and forced them to request financial support from the state. Putin's government ultimately protected them from the creditors and the Russian Central Bank used its reserves to support the value of the rouble. From 3 October to 19 December the price of oil fell by 64 per cent and the rouble by only 6 per cent (Gaddy and Ickes, 2010, pp. 300–302).

4. For example within IR, liberalism would offer approaches to study the domestic and bureaucratic sources of Russian external energy relations and regime formation with its energy partners. The English School would help in better revealing the nesting of informal and formal institutions in Russia's external energy relations (Aalto and Korkmaz Temel, 2011).

PART II

The national level

3. Public and business actors in Russia's energy policy

Markku Kivinen

INTRODUCTION

In this chapter I analyse the contradictory interests of some of the most important public and business actors involved in the formulation and implementation of Russia's energy policies. To highlight these different interests – and the debates and conflicts their pursuit has caused throughout the post-Soviet era – I will anchor my discussion to the social structurationist analytical model introduced in this book (see Chapter 2). In particular, I will argue that the interests of energy policy actors are not given or inherent to them, but develop through historical processes of competition and interaction among them (cf. Wendt, 1999). These processes are discursive in nature, evident in the different ways in which actors articulate and frame their own interests in relation to those of the other players. By examining those processes we can outline how energy policy actors become institutionalized into the various public and private entities, and hybrid forms, in which we find them in a given historical situation (see Chapter 2). This is important because we often disagree on what types of actors actually are involved in Russian energy politics and what interests they are actually pursuing.

My discursive approach to the institutionalization of energy policy actors and interaction between them suggests that we need to consider not only the actors' intentions but also the wider discursive fields on the various levels of which they are part (cf. Chapter 2; Natorski and Surralles, 2008). This entails analysing the interaction between different actors and discourses (cf. Kivinen, 2002). In this interaction all actors are guided by the frames with which they operate and make sense of their own positions vis-à-vis their policy environments and the discourses therein. Moreover, we have to acknowledge how knowledgeable actors must interpret those environments not only in their original context but also in unexpected conditions (Aalto et al., forthcoming).

I have demonstrated elsewhere (Kivinen, 2007) the differences in frames of interaction between states in their energy policies. Here I evince six hypotheses on various public and private actors in Russia's energy sector and the interaction between them. My argument is that we should not create oversimplified assumptions on joint interests and frames of private and public actors in Russia. In this light, the popular suggestion 'what is good for Gazprom is good for Russia' is highly misleading as the issues in question are actually much more complex than that.

It must be acknowledged, however, that the conflicts of interests between various energy policy actors are not usually openly discussed in Russia. In order to obtain material to generate the hypotheses I conducted thematic interviews with experts, both Russian and foreign, on what in their view is actually taking place in the backstage of Russian energy policy – or in the course of the institutional games and other insider struggles among political and business actors in Russia. All the experts interviewed had long experience of dealing with the Russian energy sector: they were managers of major companies, business partners, and employees in ministries or academic institutions. The interviewees remain anonymous and are described only by the nature of their expertise. The interview material is complemented by material from earlier fieldwork on the processes of Russian energy policy formulation.

Finally, I wish to emphasize the exploratory nature of my effort. My intention is to generate hypotheses on this delicate matter that can then be tested and evaluated in further research. The hypotheses are proposed on a fairly general level and will prospectively help us to develop more specified hypotheses concerning interaction among energy policy actors in given historical situations. At the same time the hypotheses help us to contemplate the relevance of energy vis-à-vis Russian strategic choices and what role energy policy can play in addressing the fundamental problems of the country's overall societal development. For their part, the other chapters in this book offer some material for an initial evaluation of the hypotheses, which is tentatively attempted in Chapter 11; at the same time it is clear that many more studies will be needed to delve deeper into the 'black box' of Russian energy policies.

FRAMES OF ENERGY POLICY

In general terms we can find three frames guiding the historical transformation of Russia's energy policies from its Soviet legacy to the new Russia of the 2000s: the Soviet interdependence frame based on planned economy; the energy business frame; and the energy superpower frame which, however, largely remains at the level of aspirations rather than being a widely applied policy scheme (see also Chapter 2).

These three general frames are not completely mutually exclusive. Rather the transition from one to another can be characterized as a gradual replacement of, for instance, planned economy interdependency in the non-market environment of the Soviet era by a purely business frame during the 1990s. The idea of an energy superpower frame, for its part, emerged with the rise of oil prices towards the end of the century and the 2000s.

The Soviet interdependency prevailed in an environment in which all Soviet Republics had a common energy policy and shared the same infrastructure. There was only one actor in charge of policy formulation for exploiting each source of energy. At that time, just as today, the main sources were oil, natural gas, coal, nuclear power and hydropower (see also Chapter 5). That one actor was not a business enterprise but a ministerial structure within the planned economy. This constellation could not have been immediately replaced by the principles of market economy based on profit interests and world market pricing. Rather, we should suggest that in Russia there was a slow and gradual movement closer to a business frame in the conduct of energy policy. Some steps in the associated privatization process were extremely rapid. For instance, in the context of the 'loans for shares' programme, the state with a serious fiscal deficit in 1995 sold shares in major energy and other natural resources companies in return for loans provided by commercial banks. Huge private oil companies emerged almost out of the blue when the deals favoured insiders and concentrated ownership into the hands of what became known as 'oligarchs'; at the same time the programme laid the foundation for the exponential growth of these companies. However, the change at the microlevel was much more gradual and in corporate governance it is still ongoing (Dixon, 2008).

Following the Russian media and the political debate in the 2000s, there is no doubt that the energy superpower frame has been strongly present in the debates since then (Gorst, 2004; Kotkin, 2005; Olcott, 2004). There is good reason to suggest, however, that it is primarily a device used for the articulation of energy policy interests on the domestic political scene. It has a certain appeal to politicians who are hankering for the lost empire of the Soviet era. This is typical for example of Vladimir Zhirinovskii's Liberal Democratic Party of Russia (LDPR) (see for example Energetika, 2011). But from the business point of view the situation is far less clear. Would it not be natural to expect that businessmen in the energy sector – who are in charge of the actual operations of extracting, producing, transporting and selling the energy resources – are interested primarily in making profits for the company they represent? Nevertheless this pure business frame may be jeopardised by the importation of frames used in the political sphere. This would seem to raise the question of the extent to which the energy superpower frame is a real action frame. It may very well be a mere rhetorical horizon assembling diverse actors under apparently the same discourse, with no clear interest articulation and no real political coherence to lend credence to the term 'policy'.

The ambiguous connections and discontinuities between the business and energy superpower frames require us to take a closer look at Russia as an actor. Here we cannot overlook the structure of the Russian state as a federation of 83 federal subjects and divided administratively into seven federal districts. The state bureaucracy, for its part, consists of different federal level actors. It is evident that the President, the Presidential Administration and the Government of Russia are nearly always involved in major issues of energy policy. Several ministries, various technical agencies and legislative assemblies also play their own roles in energy projects. We characterize this as the bureaucratic politics of energy. At another level we must also comprehend the role of regional politics of energy (see Aalto and Westphal, 2007, pp. 4–5; Tkachenko, 2007; Dusseault, 2010b; see also Chapters 4 and 5 in this book).

There is no doubt there has been growing state control in the hydrocarbon sector up until the 2010s (see Chapter 2; also for example Bradshaw, 2009a; Goldman, 2008). But what does this really mean? What is state control all about? What kinds of organizations or institutional agencies are the Russian state owned firms such as Gazprom, Rosneft or Transneft? Are they really the predators that many Western observers argue (Baran, 2007; Smith, 2006)? Or have they been tamed during the era of the tandem leadership of Vladimir Putin as Prime Minister and Dmitry Medvedev as President since 2008, and the global financial crisis that followed and badly hit the Russian state and its energy businesses (see also Chapters 1 and 10)?

First of all it should be noted that the energy sector has been neither socialized nor renationalized. The balance between public and private actors is different in each segment of energy policy. The electricity sector is the most liberalized in Russia, with key legislation passed in 2001, 2003 and 2006. The unbundling and privatization of both the state-owned holding company RAO UES and the regional *oblenergos* was accomplished during the period 2003–07. Transmission lines were kept as a natural monopoly, while competition was introduced in generation and retail (Solanko, 2011, p. 27). In terms of the institutional dimension of the policy environment (see Chapter 2), the marketization reform that has been going on since then redefines the rules of the game, even though the government will continue to play a role in regulating prices.

In the oil sector in 2009, private companies such as Lukoil and TNK-BP provided 22 per cent of sector output. Slavneft, which is completely controlled by TNK-BP, produces a further 4 per cent. The state companies Rosneft, Gazprom and Gazpromneft account for 29 per cent. The rest is covered by locally owned companies such as Surgutneftegaz and Tatneft. It should be noted, in any case, that the share of Rosneft and Gazprom was on the increase, especially during the 2008 economic crisis (Liuhto, 2010, Appendix 2, cf. Suhomlinova, 2007). Furthermore, Transneft is a completely state-owned company that controls the oil export pipelines and thus the flows of oil and oil products. In the gas sector Gazprom accounted for 79 per cent of output. However, as Kari Liuhto has pointed out, the Russian oil and gas corporations are not the largest actors on the global energy scene (Liuhto, 2010, pp. 10–11, see also Appendix 3). Russian energy companies are mainly regional players, their main focus regions being Europe and Eurasia, even though they also conduct some energy extraction and trade operations with Russian political support with some Southern American, North African and Persian Gulf states (see Chapter 9).

However, the state seems to be an increasingly crucial agent in the oil segment of the industry. Yet the state's interests and the consequent policies on the development and modernization needs of the oil sector – and with it, and the proceeds it generates, the modernization needs of the whole state – are not clear-cut and simple. Neither are the rules of the game any more obvious to all actors concerned. Foreign companies especially have been puzzled at the back and forth movements of the authorities. In several cases they have been re-invited to Russia. It may even be the case that there is no one major actor in the whole process of the structuration of Russia's energy policy with a comprehensive understanding of the interests or policy priorities of all parties, or what to make of all those interests and priorities.

The best candidate to look for strategic coherence and capability to aggre-gate the various interests and priorities is to be found in the gas sector, as it is the most state-controlled sector. Therefore in the expert interviews we wanted to examine what kind of actor Gazprom is. Consequently, we begin our tenta-tive survey behind the scene of Russian energy policy formulation from a hypothesis concerning interest formation within Gazprom.

Hypothesis 1: Gazprom is not a coherent entity but a conglomerate of interests

Gazprom is a federal monopoly in the sense that it has a legally stipulated control over export pipelines and dominates Russian gas production and the domestic market (see Chapter 2). It should be kept in mind that much of Russian oil and gas production is from a small number of very large but mature fields. There has been little investment in the infrastructure or devel-opment of new 'green' fields. Since the early 1990s Gazprom has done rela-tively little to develop new fields (Heinrich, 2006; Perovic and Orttung, 2007), although efforts to develop the Yamal Peninsula and the resources of Sakhalin Island in cooperation with foreign companies would suggest some new open-ings (see Chapters 4, 6 and 8). Another key problem is how Russia handles its growing domestic energy consumption relative to its finite production capa-bilities and export commitments. Alexey Gromov from the Russian Institute of

Energy Strategy presented this dilemma in the form of a scenario where the lessening energy intensity of the economy will not be able to offset growing domestic energy demand in the forthcoming two decades. In other words, it will be difficult to reduce the energy dependency in the Russian economic structure (Gromov, 2011)

Yet as argued, Gazprom is only half owned by the Russian government, partly internationally owned, and is internationally a (stock market) listed company operating worldwide through its numerous subsidiaries. We have also argued that Gazprom could be termed a national champion together with the 75 per cent state owned Rosneft (see Chapter 2), but this definition for its part fails to do full justice to the company's transnational interests. Yet in energy policy, owing to its strategic nature, company actors are closely linked to their host states. Today, the bulk of global fossil fuel reserves is controlled by states or state-owned companies. In most cases they are expected to yield profits and pay taxes to the state – as is well testified by Gazprom's cash machine status for the Russian state and the high taxes it has to pay (see Chapter 8). For all these reasons we must accept that there is a complex inter-action between public and private actors in Russia's gas sector (cf. Guillet, 2007). This does not really make Gazprom as coherent an actor as is often supposed:

> Gazprom: it is not a company with one single mission; all sorts of things are happening all the time within it; it is a ministry that was transformed into an enter-prise and still does many things that are not related to entrepreneurship. (Finnish policy specialist)

One reason for this is the long-lasting legacy of the company's Soviet past. However, some parts of the ministerial structures had much closer contact with markets and conditions within market economies:

> On the one hand Gazprom is a ministry, on the other it is a firm. This contradiction is reflected in its operations. At one time Gazprom's marketing department consisted of a separate department of the Ministry of Foreign Trade. Today the enterprise born out of it functions internationally in London as well as in Paris – probably also in Rome – and it functions very effectively. (American manager)

A further national-level reason for the company's lack of alleged coherence is its character as a national company of a federation consisting of very different regions, and the internal governance of the company:

> Gazprom is a conglomerate of various regional interests and the common interest is constructed in the complex power struggle orchestrated by Alex Miller [the company's CEO – M.K]. (Finnish industrialist)

Even at the highest level of management, companies comprise different traditions. Gazprom is much more a conglomerate of different interest groups than Rosneft seems to be:

> Rosneft is run by the firm's director general and Minister Setchin, so two persons; a clear pattern in which the firm's board of directors is the same as the Council of Ministers. Gazprom's situation is more complex. Other members of the board of directors, not just Miller, have power of decision, so the vertical is not as clear as with Rosneft. (Russian energy specialist)

Finally, some experts note Gazprom's diverse interests outside the gas business proper in a situation where it faces several investment challenges to its core business:

> Russian state-run companies are inefficient at exploiting current projects and too debt ridden to start new ones. Gazprom's production has shrunk and it keeps on shrinking. Gazprom's interest is in buying its own airplanes (it has 170 of its own airplanes), leisure destinations abroad. Not many oil and gas investments would be needed, as long as the direction is right. (Russian economist)

> Gazprom is interested, among others, in satellite technology, because in Russia refining is so inefficient and crude oil gives a better price. (Russian energy specialist)

Hypothesis 2: Major state owned firms lobby within the state apparatus to define the rules of the game to suit their own interests

The main business actors competing heavily among themselves in Russia are Gazprom and Rosneft despite their shared national champion status:

> The rules of Russian energy policy do not originate from any general interests but more from lobbying battles. Igor Setchin is Rosneft's man and this is why they try to open the gas sector to competition. Rosneft and Gazprom do not have any common interests in this sense, freeing up the competition is exactly in Rosneft's interest. (Russian manager)

> When the leadership changed in 2002, after that no more connections to outsiders, the doors were shut and you cannot pass through the iron curtain. When Minister Sharanov voiced a few critical opinions he was replaced. In 2006, when Setchin became vice-prime minister, Gazprom's power diminished, however, while Rosneft's grew. Now the firms are competing and balancing each other. Within Gazprom there are different regional and other parts of the whole whose interests compete with each other. (Russian consultant)

Setchin was forced in spring 2011 to stand down from his position as Chair of Rosneft's board of directors as part of Medvedev's reforms to establish a distance between the government and the state's economic apparatus. Whether this has really changed the basic lobbying practice where each of the energy giants has its own patrons within the Russian government, remains to be seen. So far the experts argue that Russia's institutional structures are not optimally suited to deal with these pressures despite efforts to ensure adequate tax revenue from the energy sector:

> Putin has stated that the civilized level to be reached in the taxation of oil production, which has been reached; 90 per cent of the export price (which is 20–30 per cent overpriced) goes into the state's coffers and oil companies are the state's cash cows. On the other hand during Setchin's time energy exporters' taxation has been eased because the director of Rosneft understands the producers' concerns. (Finnish policy specialist)

With regard to developing the energy sector, Russian experts follow international examples as they did in connection with the privatization of the electricity sector (see Øverland and Kjærnet, 2009). When and how concrete steps could be taken remains an open question:

> Gazprom is too large to be interested in small gas fields. However, the problem is that organizing competition on the side of a huge state monopoly would demand some sort of state organization to supervise the competition. The Dutch have an interesting experience of this. An organization called Groningen functioned as the regulator of competition. The Russians could have a chance to follow this model. (Russian manager)

The Russian institutions give too much leeway to powerful individuals who are able to influence their functioning disproportionately. A lobbying process of this kind seems to lead to an ad hoc type of energy policy, as commented by a Russian manager: 'Ad hoc reigns. Twelve months ago Gazprom could do anything, now that Setchin is Minister of Energy Gazprom can be criticized but Rosneft can do nothing wrong'.

However, in comparison with the Yeltsin era, the institutions do have a tighter grip on energy policy – although the sector is not as efficiently organized to serve the wider social needs of the state as it is in Norway, despite collecting taxes at a higher rate (for the Norwegian model, see for example Al-Kasim, 2006):

> There is coherence in politics at least in the sense that ten years ago the state received only three per cent of the revenues from natural resources and the oligarchs together with the Kalmucks (the local oligarchs – M.K.) took the rest. Now the state receives many times more revenues. (American manager)

> Energy production-wise Russia does not differ from other countries, all in all the costs rise to 30 per cent a year. Taxation practice is where the countries differ; in

Russia profit is most taxed. The limit is 25 US dollars a barrel and after that 95 per cent of the profits go to the state. Taxation is the severest in Russia, if in Norway it is 91 per cent in Russia it is 95 per cent. Oil and gas are marvellous cash cows for the state. (American manager)

In Norway the state sector's role is in general quite similar to Russia's; only the rules of the game concerning enterprises are clearer. Norwegians have similarly kept the exploitation of natural resources under state control, but they have done it much more efficiently, we could learn from them. (Russian manager)

Companies in the non-fossil segment of energy policy have not managed very well in bringing their concerns onto the agenda of Russian institutional politics (see also Chapter 5). At the same time as the energy sector is diversifying into other industries and products in other countries and thereby creating new industrial successes, Russian companies remain specialized in the mere primary production of energy resources with very little oil refining, for example:

The challenge of Russian energy policy? The greatest challenge is to encourage saving and let go of fossils, to move to the 'postfossil world'. For example, the Finnish Vacon stock exchange listed company is doing well because it produces pumps that save energy. In the United States the trend is to develop energy efficient devices and cars and to increase regulation. In politics it has been questioned why rogue states should be supported endlessly just because of energy dependence. (Finnish policy specialist)

The experts interviewed regard Russian diversification plans in energy policy as too optimistic and predict that the basic energy mix will prevail during the next decade:

Russia's energy policy will not change within the next 15 years; oil and gas and mineral exports are all intertwined and the balance between them will prevail. And the energy mix will be preserved, the use of coal will not increase but it will still be used for heating houses. A new emission-free coal technology is being tested in the United States; it will take ten years before it is in use in Russia. And the plans for nuclear power plants are over-optimistic, it is realistic to expect only 50 per cent of the planned supplementary constructions to be executed. (Russian energy specialist)

After all everyone understands that diversification must be pursued. But it is unclear how it can be done concretely. Refining is unprofitable for the moment and development is directed at other fields. Only Lukoil and TNK are developing petrochemicals in addition to the rest. Gazprom, TNK (formerly Yukos) developed other fields. Gazprom might have a role in diversification, oil companies not. (Russian consultant)

Hypothesis 3: domestic pricing causes a major conflict of interests between energy companies and the state

In the energy dialogue between the EU and Russia the dual pricing system of natural gas was long a major stumbling block. The EU sees the system, which has differentiated prices for domestic consumers and for exports, as a trade barrier which gives Russian energy intensive industries unfair advantages over their EU counterparts. The Russian government, on the other hand, has long viewed lower domestic prices as one of Russia's natural competitive advantages. Many Russian industries are energy intensive to the extent that paying the world market price for energy would cause them fundamental problems. This is one reason for the delay in the original plan to abolish dual pricing in 2011 and instead opt for a more gradualist approach in price increases (see Chapter 5). When opting for such a cautious course the Russian government has evidently not only taken into account the effects of the global financial and economic crisis since 2008, but also the views of ordinary energy consumers who regard energy as a social good because their frame of expectations is still within the experience of planned economy or the Soviet interdependence model.

However, the dual pricing system is not in the interests of energy companies. They must view all these efforts to find compromises between different societal interests merely dysfunctional from the perspective of their business logic. Domestic prices are not expected to reach European levels before 2014–15 (Øverland and Kjærnet, 2009, pp. 12–13, 76–78). Although these conflicts of interests are not publicly discussed, in our expert interviews the political aspects are presented in a fairly straightforward way:

> In gas pricing there are different curbs for probable prices for the European Union, Ukraine and the home country. The plan for the domestic price curb was not followed due to political reasons, most of all due to Putin's support. (Russian consultant)

Contradictions between ministries and companies are discussed at a high level, without being brought up in public discussion:

> Gazprom speaks directly to the President and the Prime Minister. Bypassing the ministries it makes business directly with the President of Russia regardless of who is president. Gazprom says that ministries are selfish or take too big risks. (Russian energy specialist)

Domestic holding companies are used for controlling foreign firms. State interests, institutional interests and personal interests are intertwined in the process (see also Chapter 7):

The share of foreign capital is being reduced through domestic funds and holding companies. Through them the state's share in the economy will be strengthened. However the difference with the United States is that the state's hold also means obligations for firms. In the background of these obligations are above all the private interests that are constantly being intertwined with political and economic constraints. Uralsib is part of the mechanism through which the state's share of the economy will be strengthened. The director is from the security service. It is common that directors do not understand the substance but instead take care of political relations. (Russian consultant)

All these contradictory interests lead to unintended consequences – losses in the competitive advantages of Gazprom. Because of overpricing and its 'cash cow' role, the gas sector seems to be losing in the competition with other types of energy in nearby markets in Europe (see also Chapter 1): 'The price of gas is so high that consumers in Finland among others are switching to other energy sources. Gasum [the Finnish gas distributor 25 per cent owned by Gazprom – M.K.] sells with too high a price.' (Finnish policy specialist)

Hypothesis 4: more effective private and foreign companies are trying to strike a balance between high profits and high uncertainty over political risk

In the gas segment, Gazprom dominates but there are also more than 30 private companies. Independent firms hold licences for 20–25 per cent of Russia's explored gas reserves (Perovic and Orttung, 2007). And while Gazprom accounted for negative or zero growth, private producers accounted for basically all the growth in the gas sector in the last five years. In general these Western-style firms tend to be the most efficient and well-run companies with a clear source of competitive advantage in market economy terms. However, their competitive advantage along the financial dimension must be accompanied by political learning and flexibility along the institutional dimension:

Khodorkovskii tried to seize too much power for himself, which is when his allies turned their backs on him. What was important of course was the meeting of the President with the companies of the energy sector in early 2003. Khodorkovskii accused Rosneft of corruption because one small company had been bought clearly above value. Setchin and Putin were infuriated by this. (Russian manager)

In her analysis of the case of the imprisoned Russian oil tycoon Mikhail Khodorkovskii, and the eventual bankruptcy of his Yukos company, Sarah Dixon concludes:

There appears to have been a clash between what Sztompka would call the 'capacity for self-transcendence' and the 'capacity of social learning' (Sztompka, 1991,

p. 116). The former was represented by the creativity of Khodorkovskii and his ability to conceive new business formats, whereas the latter was represented by his unwillingness to learn from experience and to be shaped by the preceding historical process (Dixon, 2008, p. 212).

Yukos was demolished in a similar way as Rockefeller's Standard Oil was ordered to dissolve in the USA in 1909, on the basis that the business was against the public interest. However, other big private players are still fighting. The jointly Russian and British owned TNK-BP was for a long time very interested in developing the Kovytka project. Kovytka is the richest gas project in East Siberia with an annual production capacity estimated at 40–45 billion cubic metres. The field is estimated to have as much gas as Canada. TNK-BP owned a 62.4 per cent stake in Russia Petroleum, which operated the Kovytka project (Giannopoulos and Anglopoulou, 2006). In 2007 BP relinquished control of its majority stake in the Kovytka gas field to Gazprom. Even at that point BP gave the transaction a positive flavour arguing that it had formed an historic strategic alliance with Gazprom, the world's largest gas producer, to jointly invest in projects and swap assets around the world. Analysts were not impressed with the price paid for the stake in Kovytka, arguing that the valuation of its controlling stake was unattractive given the huge potential of the field and the US$450 million that TNK-BP had already invested in developing the asset. Before that BP had come under increasing pressure from the Russian government culminating in a threat to revoke the licence granted to Russia Petroleum. Russia's Ministry of Natural Resources repeatedly claimed the field had failed to produce enough gas to satisfy the original licence conditions. However, it had been unable to meet the production targets because of Gazprom's refusal to develop an export pipeline (see for example Kramer, 2007; Dixon, 2008, p. 213; cf. Chapter 4).

Kovytka was used as a showcase for how eventually the Russian state wants to control the rules of the game in the Russian gas business (Kivinen, 2007). The bankruptcy of Russia Petroleum in 2010 was a clear indicator of this in a long process of compromises between high profits and political risks. In a similar process Royal Dutch Shell surrendered control of its US$22 billion Sakhalin-2 project to Gazprom in December 2006 after the Russian government raised concerns over the environmental damage related to the project.

The experts interviewed emphasize the contradictory constellation of high risks and high profits in Russia:

> For BP, TNK has been its best investment in history, it has already got its money out of it. TNK is also large, 25 per cent of the whole production of BP. TNK is a success story and the regressive economic situation can be of benefit to it. BP has such large stakes in Russia that it cannot back down. TNK faces Gazprom as a tough

negotiator. For the moment the aim is to let go of its claims in order to maintain a chance for another sort of, larger participation in the future. Foreign and domestic companies are in the same situation. The TNK-BP quarrel was more due to the fact that Russian shareholders were fooled and because the company had no general director (Russian manager).

In her analysis of the organizational transformation in the Russian oil industry, Sarah Dixon outlines a general logic of corporate governance wherein a top-down approach to management is first replaced by a combination of top-down and more empowering approaches; in the third phase a fully empowering approach relies on innovation and enables sustainable competitive advantage to be created. She argues that Western-style companies could afford costly expatriates and training programmes to increase the pace of organizational learning. They would be the first to reach the third phase in corporate governance. This phase would not concentrate only on short term survival and would be already working without the Soviet top-down management style, opening up opportunities for long term strategic flexibility and competitive advantage. At the same time, the valuable resource base and high demand for oil allowed the local companies – Surgutneftegaz in Dixon's case study – to continue the old strategy of extensive growth even in a rapidly changing economic environment (Dixon, 2008, pp. 125–49).

In the interviews the differences between Western and Russian styles of corporate governance were put in a very straightforward way:

Unlike in Russian companies, here performance-based management reigns, mere lies in the CV will not take you far. Here the performance of the whole firm, team and the individual is measured with the Balanced Scorecard; the same system is not known in Russian companies. The Russian model is based on fear and bellowing leadership. Recruiting is challenging, added to which the secretary costs US$30,000 a year, the same as in Washington DC, except that this one does not know anything. But for those who strive forward, who are not looking only at money, TNK offers a learning environment. (American manager)

Hypothesis 5: strategic frames of action are defined by a complex combination of formal and informal rules of the game

Theorizing should proceed from an understanding of how rule compliance implies skills that can only be achieved through the practical experience of dealing with constraints. The formal rules of the game in the Russian energy sector have undergone dramatic changes starting with the rapid privatization of coal and oil in the Yeltsin era, to the renewed attempt at state control during the Putin regime. But in addition to focusing on constraints, I would also be inclined to agree with Alena Ledeneva (2007) that 'Rather than looking only at what does not work in Russia and why, one should concentrate on what does work and how. It is this practical knowledge of the rules of the game that makes one an expert in unwritten rules'.

According to Ledeneva, unwritten rules: are the know-how needed to 'navigate' between formal and informal sets of rules, and between rules and their enforcement; regulate the ways in which organizations and networks interact; and exist in all societies but predominate in those where enforcement and formal and informal rules are not synchronized and do not constitute coherent rules of the game. Ledenova argues that 'It might be tempting to think that unwritten rules are generally disadvantageous to the system. This is only true, however, if the rules of the game – formal and informal constraints and their enforcement – further the public interest and are beneficial to economic performance'. And she concludes: 'As this has not always been the case in Russia, the impact of unwritten rules is rather ambiguous' (Ledeneva, 2007, p. 7; cf. Ledeneva and Shekshnia, 2011).

The experts interviewed identify informal rules of the game on all levels of interaction:

> In order to function both keys need to be in order, to the Federation as well as to the local level. What is essential is that state authority cooperation stretches to all the phases of the value adding chain. The federation's political level is the most common one, then the ministry from where you receive licences, then pipes and Transneft, regions and oil refinement etc. Your relations need to be in order with all the actors: the centralized power, the mayor of Moscow, regional governors, the licence office, Transneft for exportation rights etc. There are costs at each step [everyone takes their share] (American manager)

> Sometimes regulations change overnight: in Ust-Luga a refinery was being negotiated when the order came that it was forbidden, meaning the taxation procedure had changed. (Russian energy specialist)

In a joint article, Ledeneva and Sheksnia (2011, p. 5) end up by criticizing the top-down logic of corruption. They call for a bottom-up perspective and for a shift of the focus from legal or moral prescription to a relational understanding of specific practices as 'strategies of coping' within the larger system. They argue that the main reason why it is so difficult to get rid of informal practices is that they are also somewhat functional for the economy. The informal rules perform the function of 'shock absorbers' for the system. Consequently they are context bound and always in flux. Informal practices adjust and readjust informal codes oriented to the past, and integrate them with future-oriented formal rules. In institutional terms the informal rules are functional for solving the problems posed by defects in the legal system and corporate culture.

As Dynkin and Sokolov (2002) argue, it seems that as a result of historical processes, the state and big businesses are the only actors capable of promoting modernization in Russia (cf. also Sakwa, 2004; Kuusi et al., 2007). Dynkin and Sokolov maintain that only integrated business groups have trained and qualified staff, managerial skills, leading technologies and financial resources. They mention eight such major groups: Lukoil, Interros, Siberian Aluminium and Sibneft, Alfa-group, Severstal, Yukos, Surgutneftgas and AFK-sistema.

In terms of formal and informal rules, the main question for Russian economic development now is the relationship between these actors and the state. Are Russian integrated business groups able to play a similar role in economic development as the South Korean *chaebol* or Japanese *keiretsu* (see for example Sakwa, 2004, pp. 191–206; Kuusi et al., 2007; Remes, 2007)? This issue is still open but most probably the state will play a dual role in this process. The government prescribes the formal rules for managing natural resources. On the other hand the state expects private firms to follow more or less informal rules as regards their role in reconstructing the infrastructure and diversifying economic activities. Energy companies must also be prepared to coordinate their activities with the government's foreign policy interests. Those failing to follow the informal agenda will most probably be purged by the selective use of formal rules. Whether a consistent modernization policy can be created on this basis is unclear.

Hypothesis 6: foreign policy discourses are neither identical to nor simply dominating the business interests

I have described elsewhere (Kivinen, 2007; cf. Monaghan, 2007) two scenarios for the relationship of energy and Russian foreign policy vis-à-vis Russia's main partners in Europe. For the EU the worst case scenario is that Russia diversifies its energy towards China and uses energy as a lever to construct a new alliance against the North Atlantic Treaty Organization (NATO). This new coalition would be based on cooperation under the auspices of the Shanghai Cooperation Organization, where Russia and China are key members, and a new military alliance in the territory of the Commonwealth of Independent States. Evidence of such a move can be seen in the increase in economic relations and trade, as well as the export of weapons (two thirds of all Russian weapons exported are bound for China and India). The volume of trade between Russia and Asia has risen rapidly, and according to the energy strategy document of the Russian government in 2009, Russia's energy exports to Asia will rise to around a fifth of the whole volume of energy exports (see Chapter 8). If the whole Russian economy diversifies towards the armaments industry this would in the worst case create a completely new kind of confrontation in Europe as well as globally.

The most positive scenario for Russian–European relations, by contrast, would be the enforcement of a normal business frame between Russia and its partners. This would also include a possibility to locate common interests. These could be developed on many levels if the politicians both in Russia and in Europe were to make an effort to avoid old-fashioned confrontation. At the time of writing, however, it seems that neither of these extreme scenarios is likely to be realized as such. With an eye on where the relationship between Russian and Chinese actors might be heading, one of the experts interviewed speculates on the prospects of rapprochement:

> The common game of economics and politics as well as profit-sharing is emphasized in these regions. In Eastern Siberia the effect of the Chinese is increasing all the time. If relations with Europe cool down Russia will develop its economy regardless, of which there are already signs. (Russian energy consultant)

However, other experts add that real cooperation between Russia and China is only in an embryonic phase as far as defence and energy are concerned:

> There are no real co-operation agreements; China sells fighter planes around the world without real co-operation agreements and against Russia's interests, China did not meet Rosneft half way at all and there is no agreement concerning the Yakutian gas fields. (Russian economist)

> It will take six to eight years from greenfields to gasoline pump. Simply for this reason Chinese markets cannot be an alternative. And if you follow the negotiations in Kovytka between the Russians and the Chinese they have been going on for 15 years and so far China has not given Russia any guarantees. South Korea might be a customer but they intend to use liquid gas. Sakhalin gives some flexibility to the Russians but it is used for domestic consumption as well. (American manager).

And the experts emphasize that Russia is far from being an omnipotent actor. The Russian economy is relatively open and thus vulnerable to political and economic risks. And within Russia a tension exists between economic policy and the needs of welfare development (see also Chapter 4):

> Russia's economy is very open but the citizens do not understand it. Russia is a more open economy than the United States or Japan, probably even more open than China. An open economy requires skilled politics from policymakers, among others about understanding the directions of currency and stock prices. It is stupid, like throwing a bucket of cold water on your neck, that in a recession situation the employer costs are increased by 8 percentage points (the influence to employer costs is 1/3). The increase was railroaded through without argumentation and without attaching it to any framework. There should be actions aiming at controlling an acute crisis. In this sense the needs of economic policy and society policy are in conflict. (Finnish policy specialist)

Nor is the EU is an omnipotent actor. The interdependency between the two actors is considerable:

The EU should focus on competition legislation and policy. It is not able to make energy policy. As far as foreign policy is concerned one should not take Russia's threats to close down the gas tap seriously – when Europe was in a state of fear we laughed. Russia cannot sell gas to Asia because the needed infrastructure is missing. (American manager)

Party ideologists try to maintain energy as a geopolitical weapon, economists say it is a weapon like a nuclear bomb. However, there is a lack of trust: Russia is afraid of Europe ceasing to buy: 'we are afraid of the client; we are afraid we will lose the client'. All in all Russia's energy policy is a defence policy where propaganda has a large share, and Scandinavia is the last that should be afraid of Russia. Of course we must understand that the political tap weapon cannot be used for gas but for oil it can; *OPEC can*. (Russian energy specialist; emphasis added)

CONCLUSION

Overall, the interviews conducted for this research suggest that the business frame is likely to dominate the formulation of Russian energy policies. There are no inevitable structural forces to support highly political energy super-power frames and the consequent more confrontational scenarios of energy diplomacy to materialize. The combination of profit interests and the business frame, and infrastructural and technological constraints that for their part obstruct the energy superpower frame, also create a very complex environment for Russian actors to make energy political choices.

We have already argued in this book that in energy policy analysis it is pivotal to acknowledge the diversity of actors including states and the blocs, regimes and IGOs they form. Yet, in this complex field transnational actors are equally important (Prontera, 2009, p. 16). They include transgovernmental coalitions and networks; energy companies with the technical competencies in charge of the actual implementation of energy infrastructure projects, including extraction, production, transport and distribution; IFIs that provide the funding and credit for these often very expensive undertakings; and international environmental and other NGOs. In my discussion of the Russian state and business actors in this chapter, I have among other things covered their relationships with some of the main transnational business actors and compared them to the latter as seen through the eyes of a group of energy policy experts.

The expert interviews underline the complexity of agency and contradictions in interest formation within and between the major actors. Structural constraints limit the rational formation of interests by strategic actors, but they do not directly define the time windows or wider interaction discourses that for their part structure the relations between the actors. We started with the assumption that the frame of business logic is gradually becoming more significant in Russia. However, this assumption seems to hold only on a very general level as an ideal type. In its concrete development and to put it into practice, several contradictions emerge and require analysis. For example, I have indicated that within Russian energy enterprises such as Gazprom, the private interests of individuals, departments and regions are intertwined in the definition of the strategic choices of the firm (see also Chapter 7). On the other hand, dependency on state authorities at all levels jeopardises rational business action.

As far as the Russian state is concerned we can draw three basic conclusions. First, the energy policy of the Russian government has to strike some kind of balance between the interests of the energy sector and the profitability of other industrial fields. Nor can the legacy of energy as a social good during Soviet times (as seen in the case of the Soviet interdependency frame) be cast completely aside by the political elite. Hence, a delay in raising the level of domestic prices of natural gas has proved a contradictory process. Second, analysis of the rules of the game in the Russian energy sector must focus more thoroughly on the lobbying process by big state companies. And third, the foreign policy aspect in Russian energy policy seems to be less significant as an overall driver than has generally been assumed (for the case of the Nord Stream gas pipeline, see, however, Chapter 6). In this last respect, the relationship between Russia and China remains one of the key open issues that could change the picture.

The Russian state has created a vision of its energy strategy until 2030 (Government of the Russian Federation, 2009a). In this programme virtually nothing is said about the contradictions and diversified interests which were tentatively hypothesized and discussed in this chapter. In order to analyse the actual developments in individual cases in more detail, we have to be able to look more closely at the real actors, their frames and processes of interest formation. The six hypotheses presented in this chapter should be seen as one step towards this kind of more concrete and realistic analysis.

4. Russia's East and the search for a new El Dorado: a comparative analysis of Russia's Kovytka, Sakhalin-2 and Chaiadinskoe greenfield projects

David Dusseault

INTRODUCTION: THE CHANGING CONTEXT

This chapter will analyse the regional politics of energy in Russia (see Chapter 1), especially vis-à-vis the eastern parts of the country where several new oil and gas fields will begin operation in the coming years and decades supplementing existing production. The regional focus is a welcome improvement on previous research, which has not fully accounted for how Russia's energy sector extends far beyond the much discussed macro-issues of global pricing and security of supply issues, posed respectively by geoeconomic and geopolitical schools of thought. Regardless of the focus such global level topics merit, to fully come to terms with the challenges posed by the further development of Russia's hydrocarbon base and the benefits to be derived from it, we need to examine competing actors and their interests in Russia, the extent to which the underlying structures are malleable, along with competing visions for the organization of the country's energy sector (Bradshaw, 2008).

Unlike the current macro-level assessments assuming that economic rent achieved from sales of Russia's hydrocarbons is simply pooled in the federal level coffers (Gaddy and Ickes, 2010), the proceeds from Russia's oil and gas trade play a far more complex role beyond enriching the country's political and economic elite and ensuring their legitimacy. As stated in Russia's energy strategy up to 2030, the exploitation of the country's energy sector is not an end in itself. Instead, the Russian energy sector is a means to provide economic rent and political legitimacy to underpin the wholesale development of Russian society at the national and regional levels while improving Russia's economic standing in global terms (see Government of the Russian Federation, 2009a, p.10). Accordingly, the 2030 strategy set out by the government back in 2009 does not represent a static policy formulation process. Russia's energy policy demonstrates an evolution of the perceptions and expectations of various groupings in Russia's leadership about the social, economic, and political costs and benefits derived from the further development of the country's natural endowments.

The daunting task facing policymakers, the private sector and society alike is how to coordinate the distribution and access to socio-economic and political rent from areas where raw resources are extracted. Then, public administration and business interests must determine how these resources are to be refined and shipped to global markets where commodities and value added goods are ultimately traded and consumed (Government of the Russian Federation, 2009a, p.10). Illustrative of this formidable undertaking is the change in policy trajectories between Russia's energy strategy up to 2020 and the subsequent strategy up to 2030 (adopted respectively in 2003 and 2009). While the 2020 strategy document emphasized increased extraction and export of raw commodities and value chain consolidation, the more recent 2030 strategy has added a domestic facet emphasizing issues such as additional refining capacity, gasification, increased power generation and domestic energy efficiency as a driving force for the socio-economic development of the Russian Federation (ibid.).

Several structural shifts may be responsible for the strategic shifts in Russia's energy policy. For example, in terms of what we have called the resource geographic and the financial dimension of energy policy formulation, the previously consolidated value chains that brought energy from Soviet fields to end consumers in Europe have been fractured along political lines with the dissolution of the Soviet Union and the reorientation of several East and Central European transit states (Dusseault, 2010a). At the same time Russia's hydrocarbon industry is moving eastwards, away from the maturing mega-fields of the Volga Basin and the West Siberian plain. This physical shift towards the east connotes new challenges on the ecological dimension: fields located in isolated taiga and subarctic climatic conditions, which are more susceptible to the possible effects of global climate change. Finally, in terms of developments along the institutional dimension (see Chapter 2), the political regimes that have coordinated the country's energy policy have adopted differing approaches. These have ranged from central planning under the Soviet regime to privatization of oil and coal production under Yeltsin in the 1990s, and the return of state influence in the oil sector in particular, resulting in an institutional hybrid regime under Putin's leadership from 1999 onwards and its continuation under Dmitry Medvedev's presidency since 2008 (see also Chapter 3).

Despite the policy implications induced by the changes above, improving our comprehension of the Russian energy sector cannot be achieved solely by tracing contextual shifts or homing in on interests associated with specific constituencies, public sector institutions or corporate bodies. Instead, this work intends to investigate to what extent the interaction of actor agency with various structural factors influences the development and implementation of Russia's energy strategy to 2030.

This chapter will therefore apply the social structurationist analytical model (see Chapter 2) at the regional level to three empirical cases located in Eastern Siberia and the Russian Far East.[1] In light of an empirical analysis, it is found that even while federal authorities have been able to regain control of or shield major oil and gas fields in the East from international investors, the task now facing Russian public officials is even more daunting: the organization of vast, underdeveloped economic value chains, the distribution of socio-economic and political rent to diverse domestic constituencies, and the simultaneous maintenance of supply along with profitability abroad.

In theoretical terms, this article concludes that even if various actors' core business and political interests in the energy sector are manifest (through profit and political legitimacy in the context of Russia's federal and regional development), maximization of said interests is subject to divergent socio-economic and political evaluations of energy as a commodity and can hardly be guaranteed under the prevailing structural dimensions characterizing the present policy environment. One of the main concerns centres upon the lack of policy coordination (institutional capacity) between the federal centre and the regions and among the regions themselves which is inherent in the Russian federal system.[2]

Therefore, the search for a new 'El Dorado' in which Russia succeeds in diversifying historically underperforming resource-based economies in Siberia and along the Pacific Rim may be a case of unrealistic expectations, coupled with inadequate understanding of the complexities inherent in the development of core production, distribution and regulatory components necessary for the integrated development of the Russian energy sector in the East.

FRAMING THE THEORETICAL PROBLEM: THE ISSUE OF SCOPE AND THE LACK OF INFERENCE

The energy sector represents a vast policy environment, as will be discussed in more detail below. Within it the scope of the value chains, the multilayered nature of institutions and the number of actors involved give rise to significant research design issues. Access to and the accuracy of data, the number of relevant observable cases, along with the fluidity of various contexts are the primary (methodological) challenges.

To demonstrate the difficulties inherent in developing a sound research design to address the Russian energy sector, it is possible to observe several axes of decision-making in the energy sector that make it problematic to generate explanatory power across the whole sector. These axes concern, for example, federal hierarchy or the set of institutions at any level of the Russian federal system (Moscow, the regions or localities); specific interests that drive a particular agenda set by a specific sector of the hydrocarbon industry (oil, natural gas or coal); geographical location along the economic value chain (upstream, value added or downstream); evaluation of a particular commodity (profit, legitimacy or services); sources of power generation beyond hydrocarbons; and the role of utilities in Russia (see Table 4.1).

For example, although the strategy until 2030 is a federal initiative, the policy manifests itself in a substantive manner at the regional and even local levels of the federal hierarchy through greenfield development (new oil, gas and condensate deposits), the expansion of related infrastructure (pipelines, power lines, roads and railways) and significant investment in value-added industrial assets (power stations and refineries) (Government of the Russian Federation, 2009a).

Such industrial ventures do not occur in a federal vacuum. Instead, these strategic projects are inherently nested in socio-economic development plans adopted by the regions themselves.[3] Subsequently, regional development is embedded not only in the implementation of federal energy policy, but forms a vital link in the economic value chains which extend to consumer markets abroad, and generates profit for the private sector and subsequently returns budgetary revenues to federal coffers through the implementation of the country's taxation system. These extensive value chains not only span the institutional dimension, but also the resource geographic dimension of energy policy formation, linking related industries ranging from extraction to refining and distribution of both raw materials (oil, gas and coal) and associated utilities such as heat and power production.

Seemingly crucial to all of these interconnected, yet fractured agendas is the basic issue of a commodity's value. One could argue that, depending upon the position at which actors are located within the various axes, the costs and benefits of the energy trade can be deemed predominantly social, economic or political interests that are inextricably linked (see Table 4.2). Far from being homogeneous, the roles and relationships resulting from the three interests groups counterbalance one another, while core maximization/minimization interests are contradictory.

Reading the table from left to right, the incongruities begin to emerge in terms of defining operational competencies, the forms in which rent is obtained and distributed, and strategic interest maximization developing among the various actors involved in Russia's energy trade. While the relationship between business and society (producer and consumer) as well as the rent flow shared with the public sector (payment of taxes and provision of

Table 4.1 Decision-making axes in the energy sector

Observable axes	Areas of agenda overlap and division			Sources of agency	Causes of variance
Federal hierarchy	Moscow	Regions	Localities	Institutional competency	Path dependency and lobbying
Hydrocarbon sectors	Oil	Natural gas	Coal	Business models	Nature of commodities
Location along the value chain	Upstream	Value added	Downstream	Business models	Economic rationality
Commodity evaluation	Profit (business)	Legitimacy (pol. admin.)	Services (society)	Core interests	Actors' interpretation of value
Sources of power generation	Hydrocarbons	Renewables/ alternatives	Nuclear	Budget and bureaucratic maximization	Path dependency and lobbying
Utilities	Electricity	Heat	Water	Consumer demand	Path dependency and lobbying

Table 4.2 *Variations in socio-economic and political rent distribution*

	Business	Public sector	Society	Maximization	Minimization
Business	–	Economic rent (taxes) and social rent (subsidies)	Economic rent (goods and commodities)	Economic profit and social rent	Political and social costs of business transactions
Public sector	Underwrites economic and political risks (legislation and enforcement)	–	Service provision (housing and education)	Political legitimacy and economic rent	Friction among business, political and societal actors
Society	Economic rent (goods and commodities)	Economic rent (taxes) and political rent (votes)	–	Access to goods and services	Costs of social and economic rent

public services) is more or less straightforward from the societal and business sector points of view, the public sector's role in maintaining cohesiveness among all actors is more complicated. In other words, the institutional dimension is key to policy cohesion. In the Russian case, public administrators are faced with the daunting task of deciding how rents from the regional resource economies will be employed to serve socio-economic development at the regional and local levels while simultaneously creating political legitimacy throughout the federal hierarchy.

This chapter subsequently argues that the main challenge to gaining more inference in the structuration of the Russian energy sector – that is, to understand and explain how associated mechanisms actually function in their full complexity – is in deciphering the distribution of a combination of social, economic and political costs and benefits to the relevant actors under the changing policy environment or set of structural dimensions they face, across all the axes identified (see Tables 4.1 and 4.2).

THEORETICAL APPROACH AND HYPOTHESIS: SOCIAL STRUCTURATIONIST ANALYTICAL MODEL

Owing to the problems in research design outlined in the previous section, this chapter posits that a more *holistic approach* must be taken to make further advances towards a better understanding of the processes by which Russia's energy policy is formulated. First, the conditions under which policy is created need to be explained in some detail. Only then can we begin to ascertain what actors are competing for and finally determine how realistic their strategic goals are in relation to the policy environment.

As pointed out in the introduction to this chapter, various circumstances under which Russia's energy strategy until 2030 developed have been significantly transformed. Subsequently, it can be hypothesized that these shifts have had a considerable influence over just how actors behave in the pursuit of their core economic, social and political interests. The social structurationist analytical model (see Chapter 2; also Aalto et al., forthcoming) asserts that the policy environment, in this case the Russian energy sector, is populated by numerous actors as well as several interlinked structural dimensions. The model emphasizes that the interplay among actors and observable structures is symbiotic in nature. However, conceptualizing such symbiotic interplay of agency and structure poses significant design problems.

Actors' pursuit of interest maximization does not take place in isolation from their competitors; and rarely do structures change in and of themselves owing to any sort of deterministic form of path dependency. The opaque nature of cause and effect contributes to the imperfect nature of information and frequently has unintended consequences for both structures and actors. Thus, under such unpredictable conditions, it can be maintained that policy outcomes are not zero sum results (full maximization or nothing) but can be perceived as successful to a lesser or greater extent.

Therefore, the ability of actors to maximize their political, social and economic interests in the Russian energy sector depends upon the degree of accuracy with which actors are able to interpret the ever-changing policy environment. As such, descriptive causality and subsequent explanatory power are gleaned by assessing the extent to which actors' expectations outlined in strategic policies maximize their social, economic and political interests in relation to the structural dimensions observed in the policy environment at that time (see Figure 2.1 in Chapter 2).

Just how accurately actors interpret signals from the policy environment can be conceptualized as follows: actors form policy *expectations* in regard to core political, social and economic interests based on their particular interpretation of the existing policy environment. Subsequently, acknowledging that both actor behaviour and the structural dimensions are inherently volatile over time, actors assess changes in the environment and *anticipate* the extent to which these changes may affect actors' ability to maximize their core interests. In the final phase of policy formation, actors then adopt concrete *contingency* or plans (in this case the Russian Energy Strategy to 2030 and regional development plans to 2020) that correspond both to their expectations and the anticipated risks derived from the morphing policy environment (Dusseault, 2010c).

A brief analysis of the variance in strategic priorities outlined in the 2020 and 2030 energy strategies of Russia clearly demonstrates the changes in expectations, risk assessment and also contingency plans due to shifts in the policy environment. The 2020 strategy visibly emphasized increased extraction and improved access to expanded downstream markets, which, plainly put, demonstrated the need for the federal authorities to increase the budgetary revenue derived from the export of the country's hydrocarbon resources entering the Kremlin's coffers. The focus of the 2030 strategy has shifted inwards, to the development of value added industries such as refining, improvements in energy efficiency, and the creation of a regulatory environment fostering a competitive market environment in the domestic energy sector (Government of the Russian Federation, 2009a, p 12).

In terms of the regional development strategies, most macro-policies are derived from or are in line with directives from the federal centre. However, owing to structural differences at the regional and local levels (the structure of economies and living standards in particular), variation in regional elites' own expectations, risk assessments and contingency plans can be observed in the long term. Within the energy sector itself, deviations are apparent when scrutinizing different levels of the energy chain. For instance, both Sakha and

Irkutskaia *oblasts* constitute vital links in the production, refining and transport links along the economic value chain outlined in the federal energy strategy until 2030 (Prezentatsiia, 2007). However, regional priorities differ. Whereas Irkutskaia *oblast's* electricity supplies are connected to the federal grid, Sakha's electricity is produced locally, especially for the isolated populations north of the regional capital Yakutsk. As expected, Sakha has put a great deal of emphasis on its socio-economic development plans for unifying at least some of its production while upgrading local plants to burn more sustainable fuels such as natural gas and renewables (Skhema, 2006).

Competing models for development also occur within the individual regional plans themselves. For example, within the strategic socio-economic development plan for Irkutskaia *oblast* two scenarios are presented for the region's future. The first scenario is based upon continuing exploitation of regional resource and industrial bases. On the other hand, the alternative scenario relies upon the creation of new clusters of economic activity including high tech industry and tourism (Strategiia, 2007).

The point here is that while these documents cannot replace real capital investments, regulatory changes, or even the construction of industrial assets symbolizing the tangible aspects of socio-economic development, strategies do demonstrate the different ways in which the policy environment is interpreted by decision-makers whose political legitimacy depends upon delivering social and economic rent to their own constituencies.

METHOD: COMPARATIVE CASE STUDY

In order to elucidate the processes of energy policy formation, three empirical case studies will be employed in this chapter. The cases are Irkutskaia *oblast*, in the Siberian Federal District, and Sakha Republic and Sakhalinskaia *oblasts*, both in the Far East Federal District. The empirical data for the case studies was compiled from various primary sources in Russian. Strategic documents from the federal level include the 2020 and 2030 energy strategies. In addition, regional development plans, produced either by the regional administrations themselves (in the case of Sakha and Sakhalinskaia *oblasts*) or policy think tanks (in the case of Irkutskaia *oblast*) were examined. In addition, socio-economic data and indicators for each of the regions were provided by the Independent Institute of Social Politics. Finally, industry specific data concerning the projects have been taken from Russian business press sources and companies.

The data collected from these sources are organized as follows. First, a general characterization of the East Siberian and Far East *okrugs* from the structural perspective is presented (see Table 4.3). Second, the three regions

Irkutskaia *oblast*, Sakhalinskaia *oblast* and the Sakha Republic (Yakutia) are described in greater detail (see Table 4.5). Third, the main socio-economic challenges and development priorities for each region are enumerated (see Table 4.6). Finally, the structuration model is applied individually to each of the greenfield projects on the territory of the three case study regions.

This multilayered approach will provide a detailed picture of how various dimensions form an interwoven policy environment at different levels of the federal system as well as at various points along the economic value chain. Next, the issue of actor agency within the policy environment will be addressed by examining the regional development plans. Finally, the major trends in terms of the challenges and risks facing regional and federal policy-makers will be discussed.

The three regions are all targeted for comprehensive energy sector development under the 2030 federal strategy as well as in regional development and corporate investment plans. The general structural dimensions for all three are similar on a macro geographical, environmental, socio-economic and institutional level (see Table 4.4). However, some discussion is warranted concerning

Table 4.3   *Structural dimensions observed in East Siberia and the Russian Far East*

Structural dimensions	Existing conditions
Resource geographic	Isolated, under-developed infrastructure system; significant underinvestment outside the rail sector (TSR/BAM); greenfields are distributed away from populated areas
Financial	Regions' economies dominated by pulp/paper, heavy, non-ferrous metal and hydrocarbon industrial conglomerates; with a substantial amount of production intended for export
Institutional	Public institutions are charged with coordinating socio-economic development from the perspective of socio-economically underdeveloped areas: rich in resources yet limited access to rent flows originating from regional resource base
Ecological	Harsh Eastern Siberian or Northern Pacific climatic conditions; large tracts of forested areas; environmentally sensitive areas; some of the most polluted regions in the Russian Federation

the structural dimensions themselves, interlinkages among the structural dimensions, and the knock-on effects these interlinkages may have on one another along with the influence structures may have on strategic decision-making on the part of the public administration.

Glancing at the general resource geographic, institutional and financial features which dominate in Eastern Siberia and Russia's Far East, regional administrators, business interests and society have significant, interrelated obstacles to overcome if they are to succeed in improving the living standards of the general population, the profitability of regional industrial operations and the political fortunes of the regional administrative elite. While all the regions have considerable natural resource wealth, the combination of structural features may inhibit actors' abilities to maximize the economic, political and social benefits to be derived from the energy trade.

For instance, in terms of the ecological dimension, exploitation of the hydrocarbon base entails industrial development: the moving of heavy engineering equipment into sensitive areas, and the construction of closed systems in which waste water, debris and even associated hydrocarbons are used either in the production process, recycled or stored for disposal at a later date to prevent damage to the surrounding environment.

Moreover, regarding socio-economic development, existing pollution from earlier industrial development has caused serious health problems in local populations. Improving access to health care services, cleaning up the existing pollution, and ensuring that further industrial development limits damage to flora and fauna are issues that need to be addressed by regional authorities and the private sector alike.

Such projects cost money and therefore improved access to economic rent on the part of the regional administration is a priority. Owing to the complexities of the Russian federal system, rent derived from resource rich regions does not always stay within the region itself (see Tables 4.4, 4.5 and 4.6). Taxation rates for hydrocarbon extraction are high with the majority of the proceeds pooled at the federal level and then earmarked for distribution among the country's 82 constituent units. Competitive federal grant mechanisms in the social and economic sectors along with corporate sponsorship can bridge some of the funding gaps in regions' development budgets.

One solution to the rent issue would seem to be regionally based companies being taxed at source, thus providing more revenue directly to regional coffers. However, owing to the structure of the energy business, major firms are registered in Moscow and therefore pay less tax to the regional authorities. Another solution seems to be the diversification of the energy trade into refining and value added industries based in the regions themselves, while still another approach is sponsoring other forms of business activity in the economy away from resource extraction.

However, regardless of the access to economic rent to fund any regional administration's regulatory activities and social service provision, the understanding and political will to enact and enforce environmental legislation is not guaranteed. Therefore the institutional capacity to distribute the costs and benefits of the energy trade among businesses motivated by profit, and society which prefers energy as a predominantly social good, is a significant issue to ponder.

As identified in Russia's energy strategy to 2030, Eastern Siberia and the Sea of Okhotsk have been targeted for exploration, extraction, transit, and export to markets primarily in Northeast Asia. Additionally, in the mid-term, further capital investments will be earmarked to build refining capacity in order to support related value added industries such as petrochemicals.

Initial estimates put reserves in Eastern Siberia and the Far East at 10 per cent of the oil and 14 per cent of the natural gas on the territory of the Russian Federation.[4] As a result, the greenfield projects in Irkutskaia *oblast*, Sakha Republic and Sakhalinskaia *oblast* are key elements in the development of the eastern component of Russia's energy strategy to 2030 (see Tables 4.4, 4.5 and 4.6).

A preliminary analysis of the policy environment in each of the three case regions highlights three issues to be examined in more detail in the following section. First, while each of the regions is endowed with substantial hydrocarbon reserves, these federal units are ranked as either weak resource-based (raw material extraction dependent in the case of Sakha and Sakhalin) or weakly developed (diversified, yet underperforming industry-based production in Irkutsk). This possibly indicates that intervening variables are at work (such as institutional capacity to distribute various forms of rent) when considering the relationship between resource endowments, economic growth and investment in social services such as education, healthcare, housing, transportation infrastructure and job creation.

According to ratings produced by the Independent Institute of Social Politics in Moscow, the gross regional product (GRP) per capita reveals the underperforming economies for each of these richly endowed regions (see Table 4.4; see also Tipy regionov, 2011). Irkutskaia *oblast's* rating of 77 categorizes the region as a weakly developed economy, while the ratings for Sakhalinskaia *oblast* (104) and Sakha Republic (Yakutia) (114) are slightly higher, but still do not make these regions economically robust.

Upon further examination of the regional ratings, it appears that despite their hydrocarbon wealth, Irkutsk, Sakhalin and Sakha do not compare favourably with other oil and gas producing regions in terms of socio-economic investment per capita. According to the investment index (Investitsii Tablitsa 8, 2009), only Sakhalinskaia *oblast* (at approximately three times the national average) has investments per-capita at the higher levels of the spectrum. However, in this respect Sakhalin does not match other fossil fuel producing regions such as

Table 4.4 Case regions and associated structural dimensions 1: Irkutsk

Resource geographic	Financial	Institutional	Ecological
Transit: ESPO and trunk lines (under construction); rail (year round) Value added: Petrochemical (oil and gas refining); utilities (gasification industrial/ individual consumers) Reserves: Oil: 232mt (est.) pre-peak (exploration and production); gas: 160bcm (est.) pre-peak (exploration and production); gas condensate: 232mt (est.) pre-peak production; Coal: 46mt pre-peak	GRP: 77 (weakly developed) Economy: Resource extraction/heavy and light industry/utilities generation Domestic markets: Raw commodities (oil and gas); refining (oil and gas); utilities (diesel, coal and gas (planned) Export markets: Western Pacific basin: oil (production) China: gas (planned) Rent flow: see federal system FDI: low	Federal system: Coordination and distribution of associated costs (taxes) and benefits (federal grants and funds) from the energy trade among various institutional levels (federal, regional local), corporate actors (state and private firms) and societal groups (industrial and individual consumers/ indigenous groups)	Climate: Continental (South) and borderline sub-arctic (North) Energy intensive; inefficient consumption; coal and hydropower based power generation; owing to Soviet era industrial development highly polluted region; gasification for power generation and industrial consumption planned

Sources: Dusseault (2010b); Renaissance Capital Research Portal (2011); 'Strategiia …' (2007).

Table 4.5   Case regions and associated structural dimensions II: Sakhalin

Resource geographic	Financial	Institutional	Ecological
Transit: pipelines (undersea and overland); rail (year round); tankers (LNG) Value added: Petrochemical (oil and gas refining/LNG); utilities (gasification industrial/individual consumers) Reserves: Oil: 896mt (pre-peak (exploration and production); gas: 671bcm pre-peak (exploration and production); coal: 20bt pre-peak-maturing	GRP: 104 (weak resource-based) Economy: hydrocarbon extraction/fishing industry Domestic markets: raw commodities (oil and gas); refining (oil); utilities (coal and gas) Export markets: Western Pacific basin: oil and LNG (production) South Asia: oil and LNG (planned) Rent Flow: see federal system FDI: high	Federal system: Coordination and distribution of associated costs (taxes) and benefits (federal grants and funds) from the energy trade among various institutional levels (federal, regional, local), corporate actors (state and private firms) and societal groups (industrial and individual consumers/indigenous groups)	Climate: Moderate monsoon Energy intensive; inefficient consumption; coal and diesel-based power generation; urban centres polluted due to emissions from older power plants; concerns surrounding present and future resource extraction operations; gasification for power generation and industrial consumption planned

Sources: Dusseault (2010b); Renaissance Capital Research Portal (2011); 'Sakhalin ...' 2009, 'Strategiia ...' (2008).

Table 4.6 Case regions and associated structural dimensions III: Sakha

Resource geographic	Financial	Institutional	Ecological
Transit: ESPO pipeline and trunk lines (under construction); rail (year round); river (seasonal) Value added: Petrochemical (oil and gas refining); utilities (gasification industrial/ individual consumers) Reserves: Oil: 300mt pre-peak (exploration and production); gas: 2.3tcm pre-peak (exploration and production); coal: 10bt (pre-peak-maturing)	GRP: 114 (weak resource-based) Economy: Highly diversified resource extraction/light industry/ utilities generation Domestic markets: Raw commodities (oil and gas); refining (oil and gas); utilities (diesel, planned); coal and gas) Export markets: Western Pacific basin: oil and LNG (production) South Asia: oil and LNG (planned) Rent flow: see federal system FDI: Low	Federal system: Coordination and distribution of associated costs (taxes) and benefits (federal grants and funds) from the energy trade among various institutional levels (federal, regional, local), corporate actors (state and private firms) and societal groups (industrial and individual consumers/ indigenous groups)	Climate: Subarctic Energy intensive; inefficient consumption; coal and diese-based power generation; urban centres polluted due to emissions from older power plants; concerns surrounding present and future resource extraction operations; gasification and hydropower planned

Sources: Dusseault (2010b); Renaissance Capital Research Portal (2011); Independent Institute of Social Politics (2001); Government of the Sakhalin oblast (2011) ...' (2011).

Nenetskii Avtonomnii *okrug* (at 14 times the national average). While investments in Sakha Republic increased during the period 2002–07, its level of investment is only 81 per cent of the national average, far below Sakhalin and the other fossil fuel producing regions. The investment ranking of Irkutskaia *oblast* is the lowest of the three cases at 30 per cent of the national average.

Second, the role of hydrocarbons in each regional economy is not necessarily central. Both Sakha Republic's and Irkutskaia *oblast's* energy sectors are nested within a more diversified economic context. While Sakhalin's hydrocarbons are the primary drivers of the region's GRP, the oil and gas industries in Irkutsk and Sakha are relative newcomers to the regional economy behind existing interests in heavy industry/metallurgy (Irkutsk) and mining (Sakha). This raises questions about the role of the energy sector in the strategic planning process at the regional level.

Finally, if the regions' hydrocarbons are indeed to be integrated into Russia's 2030 energy strategy, how is this to be accomplished from the institutional and social perspective? Russia's federal institutions face a cost-benefit distribution quandary which must be coordinated not only within the region itself but also among regions within provinces. The role of hydrocarbons in regional economies can be derived from the specific regional socio-economic development plans (see Table 4.7).

Before addressing the role of hydrocarbons in regional development plans, it is interesting to note that the general development priorities for each region are very similar (see Table 4.7). What is not clear is *why* each plan is so similar to the others. Perhaps the ability of the public administration to plan and implement complicated policy decisions, create the supporting regulatory framework to enforce the rules of the game, along with adapting to changing structural conditions has led to a 'one size fits all' development strategy. In other words, the plan for hydrocarbon development is clear, but the areas in which to invest remain unknown and the skills and information needed to make such investments are lacking.

Nevertheless, it is obvious that Irkutsk, Sakhalin, and Sakha plan to follow a similar path to promote socio-economic development. Hydrocarbons will play a prominent role in each of the regional plans. Exploitation of the hydrocarbon resources in the regions will provide the economic revenue to bridge the gap between the existing economy and a more diversified one in the future in the case of Sakha and Irkutsk, while the oil and gas industry lies at the very heart of Sakhalin's economic growth. However, where the cases differ concerns the degree to which the regional hydrocarbon industry can be relied upon as a driver of increased investment, economic diversification and social development. As will be shown below, the individual fields are at different stages of their development life spans. On the one hand, Sakhalin-2 is now at a high level of output with its resources destined for contracted markets. On

Table 4.7   *Regional socio-economic development priorities and approaches*

Case region	Development priorities	Approach
Irkutsk	Increase investment in regional economy; economic diversification away from traditional extraction industries; reversal of downward demographic trends (shorter life expectancy and outward flow of intellectual capital)	Continued exploitation of natural resource base (forests, hydropower); modernization of industries; expansion of the resource economy (mining and hydrocarbon extraction, refining, transportation); establishment of new and/or high tech forms of economic activity (tourism, aerospace, chemicals, and machine industry); and participation in national projects in housing, education, healthcare and infrastructure
Sakhalin	Continue investment in the regional economy; economic diversification away from traditional extraction industries; reversal of downward demographic trends (shorter life expectancy and outward flow of intellectual capital)	Expansion of the hydrocarbon extraction and refining industry; establishment of new areas of economic activity (bio-tech, construction materials and services); and participation in national projects in housing, education, healthcare and infrastructure
Sakha	Increase investment in regional economy; economic diversification away from traditional extraction industries; reversal of downward demographic trends (shorter life expectancy and outward flow of intellectual capital)	Continued exploitation of traditional natural resource base (diamonds and coal); expansion of hydrocarbon extraction refining and export industry; establishment of new areas of economic activity (metals mining, hydroelectric power); and participation in national projects in housing, education, healthcare and infrastructure

Sources: See 'Prezentatsiia ...' (2007); 'Skhema ... (2009); 'Strategiia ...' (2007); Struchkov (2009); 'O Strategii ...' (2008).

the other hand, with basic questions of legal status and the ultimate destinations for resources unresolved, increased production from Kovytka and Chaianda seems further off. Not only would significant delays in production timelines pose questions about the likely success of Russia's energy strategy until 2030, but they could also undermine the economic basis upon which regional development plans depend.

APPLICATION: KOVYTKA, SAKHALIN-2 AND CHAIADINSKOE

Each of the regions has gas and oil fields that are currently operational (Sakhalin-2/Sakhalinskaia *oblast*), or which have been earmarked for future development (Chaiadinskoe/Sakha Republic and Kovytka/Irkutskaia *oblast*). By applying the social structurationist analytical model to each of these projects individually (see Table 2.1 and above in this Chapter), the remaining part of this chapter seeks to operationalize, and then examine the interplay of the structural environment and agency within the political context (distribution of rent) and socio-economic context (resource-based development and economic diversification).

Kovytka

Kovytka is one of the Russian Federation's largest gas fields. According to estimates from TNK-BP, the field's reserves top out around 2 trillion cubic metres of natural gas and 83 million tonnes of gas condensate. Currently, the operating licence to develop the field's extensive reserves (granted in 1993 and due to expire in 2018) is under the control of Rusia-Petroleum. TNK-BP owns a controlling interest in Rusia-Petroleum (62.8 per cent), with OGK-3 holding a package of 25 per cent minus one share, and Irkutskaia *oblast* administration owning the remaining 10.78 per cent of the company's stock.

On 3 March 2011, Gazprom became the owner of Kovytka by buying out TNK-BP's share package in Rusia-Petroleum for a reported US$770 million. While Rusia-Petroleum may now be in the hands of Gazprom, the licence for further developing Kovytka remains to be reformulated. In terms of what the change in ownership means for the field, the timeline for the field's further development has now been deferred back to 2017 (RBK Daily, 2011).

The original development plans of Rusia-Petroleum envisaged Kovytka's gas (in volumes of 35–40 billion cubic metres from 2010–12) being exported to consumers in Northeast Asia with 20 billion cubic metres going to China (Chinese National Petroleum Corporation) and 10 billion cubic metres to South Korea (Korean Gas Corporation). In order to aid the transit of the gas to the Northeast Asian markets, Rusia-Petroleum considered the construction of the 550-kilometre Kovytka–Sajansk–Angarsk–Irkutsk pipeline (Ekspert On-line, 2010a).

Difficulties with Kovytka's development emerged on two fronts. According to the original development licence, Rusia-Petroleum contracted to provide consumers on the territory of Irkutskaia *oblast* nine billion cubic metres of natural gas annually. Unfortunately, deliveries to the region have only amounted to 2.5 billion cubic metres, far below the negotiated amount stipulated by the licensing agreement. Additionally, Gazprom saw the export of

Kovytka gas to Northeast Asia as direct competition to its own Eastern gas strategy (Gazprom, 2011). Owing to the inability of Rusia-Petroleum to meet its contractual obligations to consumers in Irkutskaia *oblast* and pressure for the field's licence to be reopened to competitive bidding by national energy firms such as Rosneft and Gazprom, the fate of Rusia-Petroleum and the development of the field's reserves were in doubt (Ekspert On-line, 2010a). As a result, the spectre of bankruptcy has loomed over Rusia-Petroleum.

In addition, any plan undertaken for Kovytka's further development has been hampered by lack of an extended value chain (infrastructure and consumers). For its part, Gazprom considers Kovytka's gas to be destined for export and gasification of the region (approximately two million consumers). In addition, the original plans to process the gas at regional refineries would be a preferable alternative from the regional perspective. As of 2010 the Kovytka project was frozen at a mere 41.7 million cubic metres a year of gas and 2100 tonnes of condensate production – by contrast, the initial TNK-BP estimates for 2010–12 were 35–40 billion cubic metres a year (Ekspert On-line, 2010b) (Table 4.8).

Sakhalin

Sakhalin's development has been a casualty of institutional competition over legal control of the region's wealth between the federal authorities in Moscow and international oil companies. In April 2007, Shell's majority stake in Sakhalin Energy, the parent company of the Sakhalin-2 project was surrendered to Russia's natural gas monopoly Gazprom (Sakhalin Energy at a Glance, 2006).

Legal wrangling over the 1990s production sharing agreements (PSA) and Russia's sub-soil legislation has involved federal and regional administrative elites and international companies.[5] Subsequent analyses of the project's institutional underpinnings, resource geographic characteristics, financial parameters and ecological costs clearly illustrate the ever changing complexities facing decision-makers in Russia's energy sector (see Rutledge, 2004).

Despite the challenges posed by the extreme climatic conditions, in physical terms, Sakhalin-2 is the largest integrated oil and gas recovery project in the world, and is earmarked to provide high quality supplies of oil and liquefied natural gas to the region's increasing consumer markets.[6] Both the domestic and international significance of such a huge undertaking is incalculable, not only in bottom line figures, but in terms of political prestige and its far-reaching socio-economic ramifications.[7]

Regardless of the obvious financial incentives for going ahead with the project, several further financial and institutional factors intervened and served to cloud Sakhalin-2's future. The structuring of the costs and benefits outlined in the 1994 PSA clearly favoured the international oil companies involved in the enterprise. From the outset of the project, the initial costs and risks associated with the field's exploration and assessment were covered by the Soviet state. However, the calculation mechanisms employed in the PSA place the bulk of the fiscal burden and risks associated with development, cost overruns and fluctuations in world oil and gas prices on the Russian state (Rutledge, 2004, p. 15). It can be argued that these cost overruns would be more than covered by the profits obtained by the Russian side from the sale of the project's oil and gas. However, these percentages were also tilted in favour of the international oil companies.[8] To make matters worse, the PSA was non-negotiable in the sense that after its term expired, the agreement was automatically renewed by clauses in the original PSA itself (ibid.).

The risks associated with such a large and complicated industrial undertaking located in an environmentally sensitive region were also underestimated by the operating company Royal Dutch Shell. Early on, the European Bank for Reconstruction and Development (EBRD) had positioned itself as a possible stakeholder in the project with the role of ensuring high environmental and industrial safety standards (EBRD, 2005). The authority that the EBRD might have brought to the project evaporated. According to the EBRD's environmental impact report on the Sakhalin-2 project, the undertaking was categorized as unfit for the purpose, with the document citing the adverse impact of intense industrial development on the region's indigenous population, along with the island's unique flora and fauna. EBRD funding for the project was scrapped altogether in January 2007 following Shell's loss of its controlling stock package to Gazprom (see EBRD, 2005; 2007).

Owing to both the EBRD ruling, along with mounting pressure on the part of the Russian federal authorities, ownership of Sakhalin-2 passed to Gazprom (50 per cent share) from the previous consortium of Royal Dutch Shell, Mitsubishi and Mitsui in 2006 (Bradshaw, 2010a). In 2008, Sakhalin-2 started year-round production activities, exporting to date 17.2 million tons of oil to Northeast Asia. Developments on the natural gas side of the project have seen the opening of Russia's first LNG terminal at Prigorodnoe with deliveries totalling 7.48 billion cubic metres (Bradshaw, 2010a).

To date, Sakhalinskaia *oblast* has greatly benefitted from the exploitation of the region's hydrocarbon resources. According to the Far East Federal *okrug*'s statistics, Sakhalinskaia *oblast* is the most productive regional economy in the *okrug,* as demonstrated by the *oblast*'s GRP of 500 000 roubles per inhabitant. The oil and gas industry has not only served consumers in Northeast Asia and the neighbouring regions of the Russian Far East, but contributed 19.3 billion roubles to the regional budget in 2009. Positive multiplier effects have been observed with improved employment opportunities for the local population, increases in foreign direct investment,[9] progress in economic diversification,[10] modernization of transport infrastructure, gasification of the utility sector on the southern part of the *oblast*,[11] and improvements in the housing stock[12] (Ekspert On-line, 2010d) (see Table 4.8).

Chaiadinskoe

The major producing fields in the Sakha Republic of 2010 were located along the south-western reaches of the Velui river valley towards the republic's border with Irkutsk *oblast*. This central cluster of fields which forms the basis for Sakha's growing gas industry is divided among the federal monopoly Gazprom (the Chaiadinskoe field with its 2 million tonnes of oil and 25 billion cubic metres of natural gas); the privately owned oil giant Surgutneftegaz (the Talakanskoe field with 6.5 million tonnes of oil and 790 million cubic metres of natural gas); the republic-owned Sakhatransneftegaz (the Otriadinskoe field with 100 million cubic metres of natural gas); and the joint stock company Taas-Iuriakh Neftegazdobycha (the Srednebotuobinskoe field with 4.5 million tonnes of oil and 430 million cubic metres of natural gas) (Struchkov, 2009).

In spring 2008, the operating licence for the Chaiadinskoe field was granted to Gazprom by the Russian Ministry of Natural Resources without the usual tendering process due to the strategic size of the field's deposits (*Vedomosti*, 2008a). However, in 2006, owing to the lack of gas deposits in western Sakha, the republican administration already looked to Chaiandanskii gas to bridge the gap in domestic demand (Ekspert On-line, 2006). Conversely, as far back as 2006, Gazprom saw Chaiadinskoe along with Kovytka as composing the core resource base for its Eastern gas strategy based upon export to consuming states in Northeast Asia (Gazprom Eastern Strategy, 2011).

Unlike the more consolidated policy environment observed west of the Urals, where resources, infrastructure and regulatory frameworks are well known, the planned development of Russia's energy sector in Sakha faces several daunting and interlinked challenges. Tensions between the Sakha administration and Gazprom surrounding the ultimate destination of Chaiandanskii gas demonstrate this rift (Ekspert On-line, 2008). There is a domestic component to the socio-economic needs of Sakha inherent in Gazprom's international gas strategy in the East. While Gazprom understands that it needs exports to derive revenue for its upstream operations, the company also realizes that the legitimacy of its business as well as the political system as a whole rest on providing social rent to the region's inhabitants in addition to affordable energy for domestic industry and individual consumers. Besides the company's gasification plans for Sakha, both Gazprom and the Sakha Administration have pledged to cooperate on regional education, employment and the expansion of social services, especially in the localities near the Chaianda field (Ekspert On-line, 2010b) (see Table 4.8).

Table 4.8 The structurationist model applied to Kovytka, Sakhalin-2 and Chaianda

	Policy env.	Actors	Policy	Maximization	Explanatory factors
Kovytka	Collapse of the Soviet economic, institutional and social fabric; re-establishment of Russian federal economic, social and institutional systems	National oil companies (NOCs) (Gazprom, Rosneft, Rusia-Petroleum), international oil companies (IOCs) (TNK-BP, CNPC, KGC), Russian government (federal authorities, Irkutsk Oblast regional and local administration)	Ownership allowing for IOC accruing maximum benefit/minimum risk at the expense of RF interests; renouncing of earlier agreement in favour of a re-tender and new ownership group (Rusia-Petroleum)	IOCs maximize economic profit while avoiding risks involved in upstream exploration and development; NOCs and RF improve access to rent flows and shift revenue from IOC to RF budget	The strengthening of Russian institutions, the rise in the world price of hydrocarbons, unrealistic agreements (gasification), poor project management (TNK-BP) and RF strategic natural resource legislation
Sakhalin-2		NOCs (Gazprom), IOCs (Shell, Mitsui, Mitsubishi), Russian government (federal, regional and local), IFOs (EBRD), ENGOs	PSAs allowing for IOCs accruing maximum benefit/minimum risk at the expense of RF interests; renouncing of earlier PSA in favour of ownership swap in NOCs and RF interests	IOCs maximize economic profit while avoiding risks involved in upstream exploration and development; NOCs and RF improve access to rent flows and shift revenue from IOCs to RF budget	The strengthening of Russian institutions, the rise in the world price of hydrocarbons, unbalanced PSAs, poor project engineering (Shell) and RF environmental legislation
Chaianda		Russian government (federal authorities republican and local administration); Gazprom	Fields deemed strategic are excluded from foreign ownership by RF legislation with licences granted at the discretion of federal authorities; field development licences are granted to NOCs within a broader strategic development framework	Strategic field development postponed indefinitely	The strengthening of Russian institutions, the rise in the world price of hydrocarbons, loss of political, social and economic rent from hydrocarbon trade abroad and RF strategic resources legislation

DISCUSSION: LESSONS LEARNED?

The successful application of the social structurationist analytical model rests upon the model's ability to provide insight into just how accurately actors are able to interpret the fluctuating structural dimensions and then translate their understanding of the policy environment into strategies to pursue their socio-economic and political interests (see Table 4.9).

In all three cases, descriptive causality can be ascribed to the strengthening of Russian federal institutions resulting in a redistribution of control over hydrocarbon assets away from international oil companies and, at least in the case of Sakhalin-II, back to Russian companies. While this institutional shift may provide national energy firms like Gazprom with a higher proportion of agenda control over how the fields' assets will be exploited (raw resource export, refining, utilities) and to which markets the oil, gas and condensate will be sent (Northeast Asia, East Siberia or the Russian Far East), the rent distribution challenge for Russia's public sector becomes much more salient (see Table 4.10).

Russia is a federal state. As such, Moscow's main domestic task is to be the nexus for the coordination and distribution of a finite amount of socio-economic rent among a highly diversified group of constituent units. Under the auspices of international oil company control of field development in the Sakhalin, for example, the consortium would have to pay economic rent to the federal government in Moscow to legitimize the project's continued operation (Mareeva, 2006). Under such circumstances, it would have then been up to the federal authorities to divide the rent as it saw fit. However, while this general scheme is still in place, the inclusion of Russian energy firms and their need to provide services to their domestic constituencies complicates the rent distribution matrix.

From the regional perspective, economic and social rent derived from projects such as Sakhalin-2, Kovytka and Chaianda should have a more immediate socio-economic impact (Ekspert On-line, 2010b). Extra-budgetary mechanisms established at the regional level such as the Sakhalin Development Fund (Sustainable Development Report, 2009) are tools with which the regional administration can shelter project proceeds from the federal tax collector while plugging revenue holes in regional and local service provision. Such mega-engineering projects are also seen as generators of long-term, skilled employment opportunities which all but dried up in Irkutsk, Sakha and Sakhalin following the collapse of the Soviet Union. Finally, all three projects are earmarked to become keystones for Gazprom's gasification programme for Siberia and the Far East. The introduction of natural gas into the regional energy mix will provide more sustainable fuel for utility generation for industrial and individual consumers while improving environmental conditions.

Table 4.9 Results of the structural analysis in political/institutional and financial/socio-economic contexts

	Expectations	Anticipation	Contingency
Political/institutional context	Consolidation of federal administrative system would allow greater access to rent flows from RF's natural resources and subsequently provide economic rent for socio-economic development and political legitimacy	Imbalanced distribution of rent between the federal centre and regions; lack of institutional coherence throughout the Russian federal system; sustainability of new institutional arrangement	Adoption of federal energy strategy regional socio-economic development plans; strengthening of taxation regime and environmental resource legislation; removal of international oil companies from control over strategic reserves; and awarding of strategic fields to national oil companies
Financial/socio-economic context	Increased access to economic rent flows would enable RF to stabilize financial situation, improve socio-economic conditions and diversify production away from natural resource base	Costs of Russian energy sector strategy and socio-economic development; efficiency of socio-economic rent distribution; level of services provided versus expectations on the part of the public and private sectors	Shifting of newly acquired economic rent from foreign companies to federal coffers; merging of national oil companies' business activities and socio-economic development priorities; distribution of economic rent for regional socio-economic development through federal grant programmes and other fiscal federal transfer mechanisms

Table 4.10 Rent distribution for Russia's public sector

	Gazprom	Public sector	Society	Maximization	Minimization
Gazprom	–	Federal/regional taxes and schools, hospitals, roads	Value added products and employment subsidized; utilities (heat and power) and services	Economic profit and social rent	Political and social costs of business transactions
Public Sector	Energy and socio-economic policy, economic legislation, co-ordination and enforcement	–	Socio-economic legislation, coordination, enforcement and housing, healthcare, infrastructure and education	Political legitimacy and economic rent	Friction among business, political and societal actors
Society	Labour, profit through consumption and public support	Economic rent (taxes) and political rent (votes)	–	Access to goods and services	Costs of social and economic rent

However, hydrocarbons and their associated value added derivatives have increasingly become economic goods since the collapse of the Soviet Union. Domestic consumers are facing the economic reality of reduced pricing subsidies on raw commodities such as natural gas with resulting price increases in the utilities sector. In addition, with domestic consumption set to increase through gasification, questions of scarcity arise when international demand is brought into the equation. All three projects are set to deliver supplies of piped gas or LNG to the growth markets of China, Japan and Korea. Nevertheless, regional administrators in Yakutsk are wondering publically whether or not there will be enough gas from Chaianda to supply both domestic demand and foreign supply contracts (Ekspert On-line, 2010b). While increased demand may be seen as a positive development for corporate profit interests and the government's revenue build-up, it would seemingly place higher demands on the part of society on both the public and private sectors to distribute the economic rent back in terms of improved employment opportunities, social service provision and improved living standards.

CONCLUSIONS

This chapter set out to examine the regional level complexities surrounding the development of Russia's energy sector in the East. The work posited that the Russian energy sector is not a money-making machine at the exclusive disposal of the Moscow elite, but is a rent distribution mechanism charged with providing the economic revenue to generate socio-economic development and political legitimacy throughout the Russian federal system. To this end, the social structurationist analytical model was applied to three case studies in which it was hypothesized that maximization of socio-economic and political interests in the energy sector was contingent upon actors' ability to accurately interpret the structures that make up the policy environment.

From the federal perspective, the empirical application of our analytical model showed that the strengthening of Russian institutions afforded federal authorities and Gazprom increased access to revenue flows derived from the development of the country's hydrocarbon resources in the Eastern parts of the country. The empirical data also illustrated that the energy trade in Russia has a key role to play in regional socio-economic development in resource endowed, yet underdeveloped regions such as Sakhalin, Sakha and Irkutsk. What remains unclear in this application of the social structurationist analytical model is just how realistic the regional plans for socio-economic development are within the existing institutional and financial contexts.

The challenge of coordinating various economic, social and political interests in the country's energy sector is huge because the demand for socio-economic development in the regions is obviously high, as evidenced by the lack of investment in the social sectors and the poor state of the regional economies. However, since the policy environment for exploiting the resources of both Kovytka and Chaianda is not yet well structured, it is difficult to determine the extent to which future revenue derived from the fields will benefit the regional economies outside the strategic confines of the regional development plans for increased investment in economic diversification and social programmes designed to reverse negative demographic trends. Regional elites in Sakha are still arguing with Gazprom over the volumes of gas to be provided by the company to the Republic's consumers. In Irkutsk, the balancing out of volumes destined for regional gasification along with export to foreign markets is an open question. In the case of Sakhalin, the development picture is somewhat clearer as, with the field at full production, regional elites have access to economic rent from the operation of the project through the extra-budgetary revenue such as the Sakhalin Development fund to plug holes in the regional development budget.

It seems that as long as basic issues of volumes, consumers and price remain unresolved, plans for socio-economic development based on the energy trade will be delayed. Yet the federal authorities along with Gazprom are not omnipotent in determining the country's energy policy.

Researchers tend to conceive of the Russian federal system as one in which federal elites, whether in the Kremlin or (corporate headquarters) in Gazprom, dominate the creation and implementation of strategies and policies. From a macro-analytic perspective this may well be the case. However, owing to the fundamental nature of the energy business, energy chains must be integrated in order for enterprises to maintain access to sustainable amounts of economic rent. So it is in the case of policymaking. As demonstrated in the case study analysis, Russia's hydrocarbons are connected directly to local and regional constituencies through the provision of economic goods or social services. As such, anything planned in Moscow should not only take into consideration, but is inherently dependent upon the economic, social and political expectations and capacities of regional and locally based actors in order for the whole federal system to remain solvent.

This being so, despite the publically held belief that Russian political, economic or social groups do not compete with one another, it is obvious from the analysis in this chapter that Russian actors do indeed vie among themselves over the distribution of socio-economic and political rent derived from the country's energy sector. Whether the competition is between the regions and Moscow, among the regions themselves, or Gazprom and the regional authorities, what are at stake here are the core interests of numerous actors positioned within a multilayered federal hierarchy. The legitimacy of that system rests on the ability of the actors to provide socio-economic or political rent to their own constituencies from various levels of a global economic value chain.

Taking the two previous points into account elucidates the challenges which the policy environment poses for decision-makers. Even if a major institutional shift such as re-introducing Russian energy firms as controlling partners is successful, as the cases demonstrate, such changes expose actors almost immediately to a new set of financial, institutional and resource geographic structural challenges. While the institutional shift may provide Gazprom and the Kremlin with increased access to massive revenue flows, questions now abound about their ability to effectively distribute the shifting socio-economic costs and benefits among various domestic and international constituencies under ever-changing structural circumstances.

NOTES

1. These two federal districts (*okrugi*) are composed of several types of constituent regions (*oblasti, avtonomnije okrugi* and *krai*). The Siberian Federal *okrug* consists of the Altai Republic, Altaiskii *krai*, the Buryat Republic, Zabaikalskii *krai*, Irkutskaia *oblast*, Kemerovskaia *oblast*, Krasnoyarskii *krai*, Novosibirskaia *oblast*, Omskaia *oblast*, Tomskaia *oblast*, the Republic of Tyva, and the Republic of Khakassia. For its part, the Far East Federal District is made up of Amurskaia *oblast*, Evreiskii Avtonomnii *okrug*, Kamchatskii *krai*, Magadanskaia *oblast*, Primorskii *krai*, Sakha Republic (Yakutia), Sakhalinskaia *oblast*, Khaborovskii *krai* and Chukhotskii Avtonomnii *okrug*.
2. Some governors such as Aleksandr Khlopotkin of Krasnoyarskii *krai* feel such coordination issues can be solved by competitive federalism, that is, regions competing amongst one another for federal subsidies to support regional economic modernization and social development. However, competitive federalism may cause regions to duplicate development trajectories in order to increase their budgets to the detriment of economic diversification. As a result, other officials like Deputy Prime Minister Aleksei Kudrin see the federal centre's role as the central coordinator for bottom-up regional development: the federal centre is not only an arbitrator, but determines the strategic path for the country's economic modernization, thus accomplishing the institutional groundwork for more horizontally integrated, diversified development at the regional level (see Ekspert On-line, 2011).
3. Owing to the hierarchical structure of the Russian federal system, development policies are produced at several levels, starting at the federal centre in Moscow and moving down through the districts and then the regions themselves. This nested development is amply apparent when federal policies are linked to district and then regional development projects in the energy sector. For more detail, see 'Proekt ...' (2009); 'Strategiia ...'; "Strategiia sotsial' ...' (2007); and 'Skhema ...' (2006).
4. According to some estimates, the resources of oil, condensate and natural gas (held) in the Far East equal 25 billion tons of oil, equivalent to 40 per cent of the total located along the Okhotsk shelf. Eastern Siberia and the remaining regions of the Far East have approximately 18 billion tons of oil and 25 trillion cubic metres of natural gas which in turn represents 20 per cent of Russia's total hydrocarbon reserves (see Ekspert On-line, 2007).
5. Duma members gain domestically by attacking the PSAs, which are perceived as exploitative. The sub-soil law, designed to define and delineate ownership over the country's natural resources, suffers from the same problem (see Bradshaw, 2006).
6. In terms of recoverable reserves, the Piltun-Astokhkoye and Lunskoye fields account for 133 million tonnes of crude oil and 634 billion cubic metres of free and cap natural gas; see 'Sakhalin Energy at a glance, p. 19).

7. For example, in 2006 Phase 2 of the project employed 20 000 people, 70 per cent of whom were Russian citizens. According to the project's annual report, the project will create 2400 permanent jobs on the island. Another indicator of the socio-economic benefits accruing from the project is that unemployment in Sakhalin *oblast* dropped to 1.5 per cent in 2006. See 'Sakhalin Energy at a glance, p. 18).

8. The PSA allowed the Russian state to collect oil revenues when the operating company recovered all its initial costs and a 17.5 per cent real rate of return. Once this level was met, the Russian government gained 10 per cent of revenues for two years and 50 per cent thereafter. Once the 24 per cent real rate of return threshold was reached by the operating company, the Russian side would receive the long term 70 per cent rate; see Rutledge (2004).

9. In 2009, the *oblast* accounted for US$5.8 billion or 67 per cent of foreign direct investment for the whole of the Far Eastern Federal Okrug (see Ekspert On-line, 2010c).

10. Besides investing in the value added sector of oil and gas refining, the *oblast*'s administration diversification plan for the region's economy includes investments in the cement, fish processing, tin mining and processing industries (see Ekspert On-line, 2010c).

11. By 2020, Gazprom intends to serve the utility needs of 120 000 of the *oblast*'s inhabitants through the company's gasification programme, in which 200 new gas-fired boilers will be installed in regional and local combined heat and power plants (see Ekspert On-line, 2010c).

12. Leading up to and following the world economic downturn in late 2008, the regional housing sector continued to boom with 70 0000 m^2 being constructed in 2007, 140 000 m^2 in 2008 and 167 000 m^2 in 2009 (see Ekspert On-line, 2010c).

5. Environmental sustainability of Russia's energy policies

Nina Tynkkynen and Pami Aalto[1]

INTRODUCTION

This chapter addresses the *environmental* sustainability of Russia's energy policies. Focusing mainly on national level developments in Russia, we will scrutinize in particular the role of energy efficiency, savings and renewable energy in the country. On this basis we will assess to what extent an 'environmental sustainability frame' (see Chapter 2) is emerging to guide the formation of energy policies in Russia (for the more global picture of Russian energy policies in the context of climate change, see Chapter 10).

The promotion of energy efficiency, savings and renewable energy is conditioned by both constraints and opportunities within the policy environment, including its resource geographic, financial, institutional and ecological dimensions. To fully account for these dimensions of the policy environment we will use primary data such as official documents, reports and statistics; and interviews with Russian energy policy actors and experts, as well as with Finnish experts and industry representatives familiar with energy sector cooperation with Russia, conducted in St. Petersburg, Moscow and various locations in Finland in summer 2009. As the environmental sustainability of Russian energy policy is an area on which relatively few studies are available in English, we will also make use of what to external observers may prove to be a surprisingly rich debate in Russia, referring in parallel to Anglophone studies by Western institutions and other research.

After this introductory section, the Russian national understandings of sustainable development and environmental sustainability of energy are discussed against the backdrop of the global debate on this subject. Second, we introduce the resource geographic, financial, institutional and ecological dimensions of the policy environment that constrain and/or enable the evolution of an environmental sustainability frame in the energy efficiency and renewable energy fields of Russia's energy policies. Finally, in the concluding section we argue that although energy efficiency and energy savings have become high priorities for Russia – while renewable energy is emerging on a smaller, regional scale – they are mostly framed in economic rather than ecological terms. This indicates how the environmental frame or 'greener' energy agenda is understood somewhat differently in Russia than its main markets in Europe, for example.

Underlying our discussion is the vast ecological footprint of energy in Russia. The extraction, production, transport and use of energy have negative environmental effects and side-effects. In broad terms, the environmental impacts of energy encompass climate change induced by greenhouse gas (GHG) emissions; local and regional air and water pollution; natural resource and ecosystem degradation; radiation hazards and risks of accidents and sabotage (IEA, 2002a). The United Nations Development Programme's (UNDP) report on energy and sustainable development sets the Russian situation in the wider context of economic and social consequences, characterizing it as 'energy and environmental malaise' (UNDP, 2010). For example, the energy sector accounted for 82 per cent of Russia's GHG emissions in 2008 (UNFCCC, 2010). In addition, over 50 per cent of air pollution, and more than 20 per cent of environmentally harmful waste waters originate in the energy sector (Government of the Russian Federation, 2009a, p. 19). The degree to which these environmental risks have been recognized and addressed, either by regulatory action or by tax and pricing structures, varies across Russia's regions (for example Aksenova, 2006; Oldfield, 2005).

Alongside the environmental effects of energy production, transport and use, the current Russian way to exploit energy resources is problematic. At the turn of the 2010s, around one per cent of Russia's energy mix was covered by non-fossil fuels (excluding nuclear power and large-scale hydropower). At the same time some 45 per cent of its primary energy consumption was wasted. Consequently Russia is among the world's least energy efficient countries (World Bank, 2008). The Russian economy relies heavily on the export of oil and natural gas, and domestic use of coal, but while deposits of these three major fossil fuels are plentiful in Russia (see Chapter 1), they are not inexhaustible. The global energy agenda is slowly shifting towards new energy policy solutions (for example Helm, 2007; Scrase and MacKerron, 2009), and due to changing markets in the long term and the domestic problems of a fossil fuels-based economy, it is clear that Russia eventually must adapt to these changes, too (see Aalto, 2011a).[2]

Inevitably, the Russian economy cannot be developed in an environmentally sustainable manner in the long run if there is excessive reliance on traditional energy resources and if there is no change in the way they are currently used (see also Chapter 10). In order to meet the environmental challenges posed by the energy sector, the main tasks include increasing energy efficiency and developing a strong renewable energy industry. A certain shift in Russian policy on these tasks, improving energy efficiency in particular, is discernible.

The new energy efficiency legislation approved by President Dmitry Medvedev in November 2009 aims to improve the energy intensity of GDP by 40 per cent during the period 2007–20 (Government of the Russian Federation, 2009b). Moreover, the Russian government announced its target to increase the share of renewables in electricity generation to 4.5 per cent by 2020 (excluding large hydropower stations) (Government of the Russian Federation, 2009c). In this chapter, we will show that in practical terms, important steps have been taken to realize Russia's rich potential in this field; however, these steps remain tentative in the face of the challenging policy environment that will be analysed below. To understand these challenges properly we will first consider what environmental sustainability actually might mean in the Russian context.

RUSSIAN UNDERSTANDINGS OF ENVIRONMENTALLY SUSTAINABLE ENERGY

The Brundtland Commission's report *Our Common Future* of 1987 introduced the concept of sustainable development, which entered the international environmental debate (WCED, 1987). Despite the contested definitions and extensive criticism that the concept has evoked (see for example Sachs, 1999), the idea of sustainable development has remained the central goal and guiding norm of international environmental and development politics for over two decades. Commensurate with the definition of sustainable development, sustainable energy in the Anglo-American literature is defined as the provision of energy in such a way that the needs of the present are met without compromising the ability of future generations to meet their needs. Sustainable energy has two main components: energy efficiency and renewable energy. Furthermore, the term includes the environmental side-effects of energy production, transport and use (Tester et al., 2005), which are largely bypassed here.

According to Lesage, Van de Graaf and Westphal (2010, p. 39) the three pillars of sustainable development – social, economic and ecological, are all inextricably linked and equally important to sustainability – and can, and indeed should be transposed to energy. The imperative for creating a sustainable energy regime is to ensure the justness, equality, reliability, affordability and sustainability of energy for all actors on the global level, and also for future generations. International energy agencies have developed indicators for sustainable energy development to measure and monitor changes and progress towards the achievement of sustainability objectives in each of the three respects: social, economic, and environmental (see for example IAEA et al., 2005). In this chapter, we focus on the environmental aspects of sustainable energy.

Russia and Sustainable Energy

The concept of sustainable development has provoked notable debate in the Russian scientific literature over its meaning and relevance in the Russian context. The main subject of that debate centres on the difficulties of translating the term sustainable development into the Russian language. For example, the term *ustoichivoe razvitie* is closer to notions of 'stable development' (for an English overview of the conceptual debate, see Oldfield and Shaw, 2002). Some authors have suggested that because of these translational difficulties, the concept of 'ecological safety' (*ekologicheskaia bezopasnost*'), widely used in Russian, would be a better rendering for 'sustainable development' (see Rytövuori-Apunen and Takkinen, 2000). Conceptual ambiguities notwithstanding, the notion of sustainable development and the related international environmental discourse have been incorporated into legislative and policy processes in Russia (Oldfield et al., 2003).

In Russian understandings of sustainable development, a key aspect is Russia's importance for the state of the environment globally (Oldfield, 2005, p. 72). In this context, an ecological superpower frame can be identified. The frame has recently emerged in Russian debates initiated by a group of Russian geographers (for example Kliuev, 2002; Kontratev et al., 2003), in relation to Russia's role in international environmental policies, and global climate policy in particular (Tynkkynen, 2010). The frame captures the idea that the superpower status of Russia could be based on its natural resources and ecological reserves. Russia's importance for global ecosystems is allied to the argument that Russia should more actively pursue the establishment of a global compensation system for the ecological services which its forests, for example, offer as a carbon sink on a global scale (Kontratev et al., 2003, pp. 12–13). Russia's negotiating position in global climate policy processes proceeds from that argument (Tynkkynen, 2010). A UNDP report indeed notes that at present Russia is a global environmental donor as the impact of its economy on the environment is much lower than the valuable input of its ecosystems for global environmental stability (UNDP, 2010). However, Russia may lose this status because of the negative impacts arising from the development of its fuel and energy complex. Finally, Russia's relatively advanced scientific and technical capabilities are also articulated as a basis for an ecological superpower position. Overall, the ecological superpower frame is in balance with the recent trend of Russian environmental policy to emphasize natural resource management rather than environmental regulation (Tynkkynen, 2005; 2010; see also below).

The current discourse of Russia as an ecological superpower, however, has not so far explicitly addressed the country's potential in the sphere of renewable energy. In the future, there may be a reason for doing this – for example,

Indra Øverland and Heidi Kjærnet (2009, p. 153) have proposed a scenario of Russia as *a renewable superpower*.

The debates and prospects related to the notions of ecological or renewable energy superpower notwithstanding, we must acknowledge that the globally frequently used term 'sustainability' (*ustoichivost'*) is only seldom used in the Russian language to refer to environmental aspects of energy. Nevertheless, on the basis of our material we identify three different environmental terms related to energy, each of which has a distinct bearing on the sustainability of Russia's energy policies. They include 'ecological safety', 'environmentally clean energy' and 'low-carbon Russia'.

In the context of energy, the Russian term 'ecological safety' (*ekologicheskaya bezopasnost'*) refers first and foremost to the environmental impacts of energy production, transport and use. The term does not extend to the adequacy of energy resources, nor to the equality aspects inherent in the international sustainable energy discourse. Ecological safety is heavily emphasized in the energy strategies of Russia (Government of the Russian Federation, 2003; 2009c). In the 2009 strategy, ecological safety is listed among the four main strategic guidelines of the long-term state energy policy alongside energy security, energy efficiency of the economy, and budget efficiency of the energy sector (Government of the Russian Federation, 2009a, p. 10). The document notes that in terms of the energy sector's ecological safety, the main interest driving the state's energy policy is to consistently limit the impact of the fuel and energy complex on the environment and climate by reducing GHG emissions and other pollutants, and by decreasing both production and consumption-originated waste (ibid., p. 19). To realize this interest the strategy emphasizes measures such as the promotion and creation of conditions to introduce environmentally clean, energy efficient and resource saving technologies; to expand electricity and heat production from renewable energy sources; to develop stricter controls for compliance with environmental requirements when implementing energy projects and operating energy facilities; and harmonization of Russian and international environmental laws (ibid., p. 19–20). The preceding energy strategy of 2003 notably failed to mention the ecological safety of energy in its list of measures (see Government of the Russian Federation, 2003, p. 22–24; see also Troitskii and Anikeev, 2009, p. 27–28).

Another term used in this context is 'environmentally clean energy' (*ekologicheski chistaia energia*). According to V.V. Bushuev and P.P. Bezrukikh, the concept appeared in the late 1980s, when the Scientific and Technological Committee of the Soviet Union introduced a programme of the same name. The initial core meaning of the term refers to the development of heat energy units (*teplovye energobloki*) in a way that enables the greatest possible reduction of detrimental emissions (Bushuev and Bezrukikh, 2006, p.

6). In the current language, however, the term lacks an exact definition. Thus, the concept is widely tapped by various energy lobbies, the gas and nuclear sectors in particular, to promote their respective businesses (ibid., p. 6). The energy strategies (Government of the Russian Federation, 2003; 2009c) do not use the concept but in some cases rely on the related term 'environmentally clean technology'.

The third Russian term referring to environmental sustainability in the context of energy originates from global climate policy, calling for a radical reduction in GHG emissions. As the energy sector is the main source of these emissions in Russia, efforts have been undertaken to make it less carbon-intensive. This target has given rise to the concept of '*nizkouglerodnaia Rossiia*', or low-carbon Russia. Igor Bashmakov, head of the Center for Energy Efficiency of Russia (CENEF), illustrates the means by which low-carbon Russia can be enforced using the formula 45: 35: 90 – energy intensity should be reduced by 45 per cent (from the level of 2007), the share of non-fossil sources of energy (*netoplivykh*) should be increased to 35 per cent by 2020, and greenhouse gas emissions should be kept below 90 per cent of the 1990 figure (Bashmakov, 2009). In other words, the emergence of low-carbon Russia entails the realization of energy saving potential, accelerated research and development of renewable energy, and reform of energy pricing and taxation mechanisms. Even if the concept is not yet widely used, it appears a fruitful conceptual basis for framing sustainable energy in Russia as it takes into account both energy efficiency and renewable energy. Yet the concept approaches sustainability only in terms of low coal intensity and CO_2 emissions, thus including the highly controversial nuclear energy and large-scale hydropower.

To complement these three terms in the Russian debates, the terms 'alternative energy resources' (*alternativnye energoresursy*) and non-carbon energy resources (*neuglevodorodnye energoresursy*) refer to all alternative energy sources to fossil fuels, including nuclear power, the environmental friendliness of which is highly controversial given the possibility of leaks, other accidents, and the storage of nuclear waste, an issue which is not yet properly resolved in Russia.

In sum, even if these terms approach the issue from (at least slightly) differing angles, they indicate the scope by which the environmental sustainability frame can evolve in Russia. Currently, the environmental sustainability frame is most actively supported by environmentalists and scientific experts, but it is likely that in the future the group of actors supporting that type of frame will grow, in particular as important aspects of it are more closely incorporated into the strategic objectives of Russian energy policies (see for example Government of the Russian Federation, 2009a; b; c).

THE POLICY ENVIRONMENT FOR SUSTAINABLE ENERGY POLICY

The Resource Geographic Dimension: Enabling Factors

The resource geographic dimension of the policy environment contains the seeds for the development of an environmental sustainability frame for Russia's energy policies. In the course of time, the exploitation of Russia's hydrocarbon reserves will become more difficult and expensive. This implies a long-term interest in considering alternative sources and more efficient use of energy. Yet admittedly for at least a few decades fossil fuel exports will form the backbone of Russia's economy. As the deposits are depleted the role of energy efficiency and savings, and renewable energy sources, will become significant for sustaining fossil fuel exports. Accordingly, the linkages between fossil fuel exports and 'greener' energy policy are mutually reinforcing (Aalto, Blakkisrud and Smith, 2008; Aalto, 2011a).

Second, as noted, Russia's economy is highly energy intensive and wasteful (World Bank, 2008). Deteriorating infrastructure built during the Soviet era, and inadequate maintenance, are the main reasons for energy inefficiency. The energy strategy up to 2030 finds considerable untapped potential in organizational and technological energy saving, amounting to 40 per cent of total domestic energy consumption (Government of the Russian Federation, 2009a, pp. 15–16). In short, the energy currently wasted could become the country's main energy source.

Third, given its geographical size and the consequent variation in climate and topography, Russia has the potential to become the type of renewable energy superpower mentioned above. According to the Guidelines for State Policy of Energy Efficiency Increase through Use of Renewables for the Period up to 2020 (Government of the Russian Federation, 2009c), the technical potential of renewable energy in Russia amounts to at least 4.6 billion tons of coal equivalent per year, thus exceeding the current energy consumption in the country more than fourfold. Some Russian experts put the economic potential of renewable energy at more than 270 million tons of coal equivalent per year, which corresponds to about 25 per cent of Russia's annual consumption (Kulagin, 2008, p. 6; OECD and IEA, 2003, p. 29; see also Øverland and Kjærnet, 2009, pp. 7–8).[3] The Energy Charter Protocol on Energy Efficiency and Related Environmental Aspects (see Box 5.1) more conservatively estimates the economic potential of renewable energy sources at some 181 million tons, or a fifth of domestic energy consumption (Energy Charter, 2007, p. 25; see Table 5.1).

Russia's Federal Law on Energy Saving (1996) defines renewable energy sources as 'solar energy, wind, earth thermo energy, natural hydro movement

Table 5.1   Potential of non-traditional renewable energy sources in Russia

Resource	Technical potential Mtoe/year	Economic potential Mtoe/year
Small hydro	88	49
Geothermal	—	80
Wind energy	1400	8
Biomass energy	37	5
Solar energy	1610	2
Low-grade heat	136	37
Total	3271	181

Source: Energy Charter Protocol on Energy Efficiency and Related Environmental Aspects PEEREA (2007), p. 25.

and nature heat production', thereby excluding conventional large-scale hydroelectricity production.[4] The energy strategy up to 2030 stresses the need to develop 'alternative' ways of generating energy, including the non-renewable energy sources of nuclear power and peat. Other alternative measures, or by-products of Russia's currently-in-use fossil fuel fields, include helium extraction from the same deposits, the exploitation of unconventional gas, and putting an end to gas flaring. In January 2009, the Russian government passed a resolution limiting the flaring of associated gas in oil fields to only 5 per cent of the entire output, set to be in force from 2012 (Kristalinskaya, 2010).

Practically all regions of the Russian Federation have at least one or two commercially exploitable sources of renewable energy. Some regions are rich in all sources of renewable energy. For example, the northern coastal regions have considerable wind energy potential; the southern regions have a great deal of sunshine per hour; the White Sea and the Sea of Okhotsk have tidal potential; the regions with numerous rivers, including small ones, provide opportunities for hydropower development, and the north-western part of Russia with its well-developed pulp and paper industry allows for large-scale use of biomass for energy production (Kulagin, 2008, p. 6; OECD and IEA, 2003, p. 11; for more, see Box 5.1).[5]

Renewable energy sources currently account for less than 1 per cent of Russia's total primary energy supply (Government of the Russian Federation, 2009c). So these sources are clearly underdeveloped and could 'contribute tremendously to the energy balance, export potential, emissions trade potential and economic development of the Russian Federation' (Øverland and Kjærnet, 2009, p. 8).

Moreover, the regional structure in Russia favours the more extensive

BOX 5.1   REGIONAL POTENTIAL OF NON-FOSSIL FUELS IN RUSSIA

Hydro

Globally Russia ranks second after Brazil in terms of the level of annual river run-off, but is currently using only about 20 per cent of its economically viable hydropower resources. The US, Canada, several countries in Western Europe and Japan are using 50 to 90 per cent of their resources. The extent of use varies from 48 per cent in the European part of Russia to 25 per cent in Siberia and 3 per cent in the Far East (Gati, 2008). Currently Russia is the world's fifth largest hydropower producer at about 167TWh a year (Karamotchev, 2011, p. 6). According to a report by the OECD and IEA (2003, p. 11), small hydro development is attractive in the North Caucasus, the Urals and in Eastern Siberia. The problem with small hydro is that it usually requires backup power supply: some hydropower stations generate much less energy in winter due to the freezing of rivers, some in summer time due to their drying up (Malik, 2005, p. 15). The state-owned RusHydro signed agreements with the French company Alstom and German Voith Hydro in 2010 to upgrade existing plants, new exploration and small facilities (Lee, 2011, p. 9). Agreements also exist with Enel of Italy (Karamotchev, 2011, p. 4).

Geothermal

In 2010, the top three countries generating geothermal electricity were the USA, the Philippines and Indonesia. Russia was ranked 13th with a fraction of electricity generating capacity installed compared to the leaders (Holm et al., 2010, p. 7). Exploration of geothermal resources started in the Soviet Union in the late 1950s on the Pauzhetsk thermal field in Kamchatka. Most of Russia's geothermal potential has been explored, and a significant number of fields have been discovered. Substantial geothermal resources are located in seismically active areas on the Kamchatka Peninsula, the Kurile Islands, in the Sakhalin and the North Caucasus (OECD and IEA, 2003, p. 37). Two functioning Mutnovsky geothermal power stations in Kamchatka have already significantly increased local electric power supply with their 62MW combined capacity, with further projects planned with Iceland (Lee, 2011, p. 9).

Wind

Alongside small-scale hydro energy, the most accelerated growth of renewable energy sources is expected in wind energy. This can be exploited in many parts of Russia, with most of the potential situated in Russia's far northern and eastern territories, coastal areas in particular, and on the steppes along the Volga River and in the North Caucasus (OECD and IEA, 2003, p.11). In many of these territories population density is less than one person per square kilometre. In these instances wind power can be used to supply small isolated consumers. The annual variation in mean wind speed is insignificant for most parts of Russia; wind speeds tend to be greater in the daytime than at night (OECD and IEA, 2003, p. 30). Russia's largest wind power facility to be grid connected, with an initial capacity of 50MW rising to 100MW, has been planned for Yeisk on the Sea of Azov adjoining the Black Sea (Lee, 2011, p. 7). Siemens has a partnership agreement with RusHydro and Rostechnologii to develop 1250MW of wind power capacity by 2015 (Karamotchev, 2011, p. 4).

Biomass

Russia's significant biomass resources include vast forests, open woodlands, and agricultural and wood waste. In 2001, Russia had 1.1 million hectares of forested land, which accounts for 64.1 per cent of the total land area. According to Intersolarcenter, Russia produces about 15 billion tons of biomass (wood, agricultural waste, wood waste from forestry and the pulp and paper industry, municipal solid waste and sewage waste) every year (Lins et al., 2005, p. 7). These resources can be used for the production of biogas, butanol ethanol, and other bio-fuel products. In addition, firewood is currently used by five million households, consuming over 50 million cubic meters of timber (see Sidorenko et al., 2001). Urban domestic waste, particularly as a source of biogas, is an important local source of fuel. Urban enterprises in the field of solid domestic waste utilization possess the necessary financial and technical infrastructure to collect the raw material, produce and use the biogas; the same, however, does not apply to biogas production in agriculture (Kulagin, 2008, p. 6). A wood pellet facility with an annual capacity of 150 000 tons was to be completed by autumn 2010 in the Archangel *oblast*; bio-fuel projects as well as projects for converting boilers from coal and diesel to biomass also existed in this region (Energo-Enviro, 2010, p. 2).

Solar
Russia's location between 41 and 82 degrees of latitude north suggests that solar radiation levels vary considerably; solar radiation depends mainly on latitude and is strongest at the equator, diminishing towards the poles. Solar energy potential is therefore greatest in Southwest Russia, near the Black Sea and the Caspian Sea, and in the Altai Republic in Southern Siberia (OECD and IEA, 2003, p. 32). Construction of the first significant solar plant, a 12MW facility, is to start in Kislovodsk in the Northern Caucasus during 2011, in a project led by Rusnano with the participation of Rostovteploelektroproekt (Karamotchev, 2011, p. 4; Lee, 2011, p. 8).

Tidal power
Tidal power has been piloted in Mezen Bay on the White Sea, Tugurskaia on the Okhotsk Sea and Kislogubskaia on the Barents Sea (Gati, 2008).

exploitation of renewable energy resources. Over 60 per cent of Russian territory (populated by about ten million people in 2003) is not connected to centralized energy supply systems. In addition, five million families have a summer cabin (*datcha*), which is not connected to an electricity grid and has unreliable and expensive power supply (OECD and IEA, 2003, p. 8). In these areas, energy supply is maintained by diesel and gasoline power stations (which in some cases are supplied by helicopter!), domestic fuel materials such as firewood, peat and coal, or other fossil fuel-powered local grids. In many of these isolated settlements, renewable energy sources can offer the most economic, and in future perhaps even the only way to provide electricity and heat. This is the case because, on the one hand, delivery of fuels, and the extension and maintenance of the electricity grid to isolated areas is expensive (Karghiev, 2004, p. 2); and, on the other hand, a significant share of the unexploited potential of renewable sources of energy, hydropower in particular, is located in regions that currently have insufficient energy infrastructure such as North Caucasus and the Far East (cf. ibid., p. 5).

On-grid areas also suffer from unstable power supply with frequent blackouts, mainly because of old and poorly maintained infrastructure. Many existing heating systems are inefficient with high heat loss and poor quality service (interview with Finnish expert on Russian energy 1, 2009). Especially in sparsely populated regions there has been a tendency to disconnect from the grid because of the unprofitability of maintaining the transmission lines for local power supply organizations (Karghiev, 2004). In these conditions, implementing renewable energy solutions may be more attractive than constructing new grid lines, and sometimes indeed the only alternative to liquid-fuel power generators.

A further infrastructural factor is Russian renewable energy technologies, which are comparable to foreign technologies in function and in their scientific and technical characteristics in almost all areas of the renewable energy sector, except wind energy. Russia had already started to systematically exploit renewable energy sources in the early twentieth century (Karghiev, 2004, p. 5; interview with Russian energy expert 1, 2009). There is also industrial potential that could result in multiple increases in the application of renewable energy solutions.

The Resource Geographic Dimension: Constraining Factors

The infrastructural and technological conditions to exploit Russia's currently abundant fossil fuel resources are favourable and better developed than more environmentally sound energy sources. This situation, sometimes associated with a 'resource curse' (cf. UNDP, 2010), may discourage interest and investments in sustainable development, and hence constrain the prospects for an environmental sustainability frame to emerge more powerfully in Russia's energy policies.

Russia's centralized energy production system with its rigid organization is clearly another constraining factor. It has determined the development path of energy infrastructure, the means of production, forms of transportation, and energy technologies, indeed, the energy sector as a whole. Here we must recall the 'lock-in' factors inherent in the complex and expensive nature of energy policy, where decisions and investments made today will have consequences lasting for decades (Scrase et al., 2009, pp. 225–6).

The development and realization of the full potential of renewable energy solutions, which would have to recognize the great regional variety in their applicability in Russia as explained above, presupposes a very different system of energy production – a system that allows for regional and local adaptation (cf. interview with Russian energy expert 1, 2009). Nevertheless the existing renewable energy infrastructure is underdeveloped in Russia. Besides, even though Russia's renewable energy technologies are comparable to foreign technologies in function and in scientific and technical characteristics, no commercial industry for efficiently capitalizing on this potential exists (Interview with Russian energy expert 2, 2009). This is due to the underdeveloped energy market, which restricts the research and development of renewable energy technology to what the OECD and IEA (2003, p. 13) have described as the stage of demonstration. In other words, actors such as energy market regulators face a big task in building market entry mechanisms, promoting the market entry of small and medium size enterprises (SMEs) in a still largely oligopolistic market, and opening up for foreign investment, issues that are part of the financial dimension of the policy environment.

The Financial Dimension: Enabling Factors

The enabling factors along the financial dimension are fairly clear as far as energy efficiency and savings are concerned. If the potential from increased energy efficiency and energy savings were fully translated into practice in Russia, it could save fossil fuels for export and help to increase revenues by some US$84–112 billion (Gromov, 2009).

The decision of the Russian government to gradually start increasing the long subsidized natural gas prices domestically will prove a major boost to energy efficiency, savings and the development of renewable energy sources. Domestic prices were first increased by 15 per cent in 2010. By 2014 netback prices are to be reached, that is, domestic gas prices are set to reach the prices of Russian gas at the country's borders minus export taxes, transportation costs, and transit tariffs paid as gas enters the major European export markets. This would abolish the domestic discount that was long seen as a market violation by the EU. This move will cause consumers to control their use of energy better and consider efficiency and savings measures. It will also make renewable energy more competitive on the market. Although we have suggested that renewables are already competitive in many of Russia's remote settlements, in larger scale production units the initial costs are often higher. The electricity sector reform of 2003–07 created some preconditions for more widespread renewable energy production. The former public vertically integrated electricity monopoly RAO UES was unbundled so as to allow competition in generation and in consumer sales, and the sector was privatized in a series of auctions open to international companies. However, to become competitive in Russia's central markets – which are likely to be regionally differentiated because of the country's vast territory and low capacity for interregional high-transmission voltages (see Øverland and Kjærnet, 2009, p. 25) – electricity produced from renewable sources needs access to centralized electricity supply systems. Although such grid access is guaranteed in Russia, its full use presupposes contacts and know-how which newcomers are unlikely to possess (ibid., p. 26; see also below).

The main renewable energy solutions are likely to be local, at least in the short to medium term. As noted, renewable energy solutions have notable economic potential in Russia's remote northern and far Eastern settlements. In many cases, where the energy is produced from fuels transported from afar, the costs of the expensive system have not been borne by the end users (OECD and IEA, 2003, p. 11). The Central Asian Republic of Tyva spends more than half of its budget on fuel (Lee, 2011). The investments for those projects are likely to come from small and medium size enterprises (SMEs) in areas where connections to the central grids are not available or would be expensive (Kulagin, 2008, p. 7). For example, in the Karelian Republic in north-western Russia, coal is transported from thousands of kilometres away to supply heating facilities, while environmentally viable wood-burning or biomass-fired facilities using local energy sources could provide an alternative solution (Aalto, Blakkisrud and Smith, 2008, p. 233; for other solutions, see box 5.1).

The potential for Russia to trade in the European renewable energy market, by contrast, may be limited. This is because the European switch to renewable energy relies largely on domestically available resources, partly for climatic reasons and partly to decrease external dependence (Aalto, 2011a). There is potential for technological and scientific exchange in fields such as solar cells and hydrogen (Øverland and Kjærnet, 2009, p. 15). In 2011, Lukoil and the Italian firm ERG Renew signed a declaration of intent on cooperation in Eastern Europe in the renewable energy segment of the market (Karamotchev, 2011, p. 4).

The Financial Dimension: Constraining Factors

The electricity market reforms mentioned have not met with universal acclaim. According to Øverland and Kjærnet (2009, p. 37), the reforms have failed to create a level playing field for non-renewable and renewable sources of energy, which would be crucial. Feed-in tariff type mechanisms, which would guarantee an adequate price level for producers to make the investments to start supplying renewable energy to the networks, and which are widely used in European markets, were introduced in Russia in December 2010. The tax regime, for its part, has made it more profitable to export bio-fuels instead of selling them domestically because of a €4.30 excise tax levied on transportable bio-fuel produced at €0.20 (June 2009 exchange rates). The adoption of the planned federal law 'About the Main Principles of Bioenergy Development in Russian Federation' which would have resolved this problem, was already delayed at the end of 2009 (see Pristupa, Mol and Oosterveer, 2010, p. 3322).

To alleviate the investment needs, and constraints, of energy efficiency and renewable energy production, the EBRD provided a 875 million rouble loan to Rosbank in 2010 to finance Russian companies' projects in these areas through its Russian Sustainable Energy Financing Facility (Rosbank, 2010). The World Bank, for its part, made US$150 million available for renewable energy investments (Barents Observer, 2010). Similar projects have also been funded on a small scale through the Northern Dimension Environmental Partnership

Fund. Alas, according to the Russian Ministry of Energy, US$80 billion needs to be invested by 2020 in energy efficiency, and US$300 billion in renewable energy; while in 2010 Russia invested only US$2 billion in the latter (Ketting, 2011). Major investments in new research and development in the field of renewable energy also suffer from a lack of adequate political signals. As Gati (2008) reported, the financial and institutional dimensions are linked:

> With an economy based on abundant reserves of oil and gas, not only is very little state budget money allocated for the development of renewables, but there are few incentives to invest in alternative sources of energy. The current focus on economic policy is on investment in 'national priority' projects, state corporations, and in major strategic sectors. Companies may be hesitant to risk millions of dollars in sectors or industries that the state appears to find less attractive and they will want to wait for more favourable political and legal environment before undertaking costly projects. The well-trodden path of innovation in the West – small start-ups with innovative ideas that then become mainstream – is not easy to transfer to any sector of the Russian economy (p. 2).

The Institutional Dimension: Enabling Factors

To analyse the institutional dimension of the policy environment properly we have to start from the informal institutions and rules of the game (see Chapters 2 and 3). In this sphere we can discern a framing of Russia as an energy superpower that gained prominence in the 2000s and which to an extent at least still underwrites the energy sector's institutional development. It continues to rely heavily on hydrocarbons, but as noted, in certain future scenarios renewable energy is proposed as an alternative basis of Russia's energy superpower status (see Øverland and Kjærnet, 2009, p. 153). In addition, the framing of Russia as 'the leader and pioneer in science' in general (Velikhov, 2003) encourages a similar development through Russia's research and educational institutions.

Recent years have witnessed a great leap forward in the recognition of energy efficiency as an important aspect of Russia's institutional regulation of energy policies. The presidential decree 'Concerning some measures for improving the energy and ecological efficiency of the Russian economy' established an energy efficiency goal of a minimum 40 per cent reduction in the energy intensity of the Russian economy (defined as energy use, or total final energy consumption, per unit of GDP), by 2020 compared to 2007. The decree identified several target areas and called for the drafts of the laws and regulations, federal targeted programmes, and other relevant legislative acts in the field to be finalised. On 27 November 2009, the decree was followed by the federal law 'On Saving Energy and Increasing Energy Efficiency, and on Amendments to Certain Legislative Acts of the Russian Federation' referred to above (Government of the Russian Federation, 2009b). This legislation aims to meet the official target of improving energy intensity by 40 per cent during

2007–20. The law establishes the basic principles for the regulation of energy consumption to increase its efficiency and to encourage energy saving. It also provides for various amendments to the existing legislation, for example, on technical regulation, housing, urban planning and taxation to enforce energy-saving measures. The law is a framework act calling for the implementation of supplementary legislation. At the same time it introduces certain economic incentives for energy saving, such as restrictions on the sale of incandescent light bulbs, requirements for labelling electrical equipment based on its energy efficiency, and reductions in budget spending on purchasing energy resources. The new law also provides a basis for the transition to long-term tariff regulation as well as the establishment of a common inter-ministerial energy efficiency information and analysis system (Russian Law Online, 2010; Novikova et al., 2009, p. 2).

Energy saving is also one of the most important strategic initiatives of the Energy Strategy of Russia for the period up to 2030. The strategy calls for the development, *inter alia*, of adequate incentives for energy saving among energy producers and consumers. In the implementation of the strategy, the priority in the first period until 2013 is on overcoming the effects of the global economic and financial crisis of 2008–09 that hit Russia and its key European gas sales particularly hard. Thereafter efficiency and savings in the energy sector and the economy as a whole are set to become a more prominent priority alongside the development of new oil and gas fields in Russia's adaptation to the new energy agenda (Gromov, 2010).

Renewable energy is part of that new agenda and has recently received growing institutional attention in Russia. Contrary to the earlier energy strategy up to 2020 (2003) which referred only implicitly to renewables, the new strategy (2009) assigns an essential role to the development of renewable energy. It states that '(i)nvolvement of renewable energy, including geothermal, solar, wind and bioenergy, etc., into the fuel and energy balance will make it possible to balance the demand for energy and reduce environmental load of energy sector facilities' (Government of the Russian Federation, 2009a, p. 61; for the options and prospects of realization, see Box 5.1).

According to the strategy, renewable energy should account for 14 per cent of the country's energy demand by 2030. A practical step towards this target is provided by the recent legislation adopted to increase the share of renewable energy in Russian electricity generation to 4.5 per cent by 2020, excluding large-scale hydro power (Government of the Russian Federation, 2009c). To achieve this goal, the aim is to 'develop a complex of measures of the state policy... providing for the system state support and harmonized with projected and actual growth rates of renewable energy development. The stated growth rates shall also be harmonized with construction of required infrastructure, enhancement of competitiveness of electricity production on the base of renewable energy, as well as with rational involvement of renewable energy into the fuel and energy balances of individual regions' (Government of the Russian Federation, 2009a, p. 111). Although many of the more precise means of implementation are still unclear, the new strategy and the guidelines document offer a promising basis for developing a meaningful state policy, together with legal and fiscal support mechanisms for renewable energy. The reform of the Russian electricity sector for its own part offers support schemes for renewable energy generation and for limiting environmental pollution (cf. Abdurafikov, 2009).

The historical strength of Russian scientific institutions in education and research on energy issues constitutes a further enabling factor within the institutional dimension of the policy environment. Some of the scientific institutions have long traditions in renewable energy, the early Soviet state having been a pioneer in this field (see Øverland and Kjærnet, 2009, pp. 41–58). Although the amount of research declined considerably with the collapse of the Soviet Union, towards the 2000s it started to grow again (cf. Ostergren and Jacques, 2002). There are also plans for government reforms of Russia's innovation policy (Øverland and Kjærnet, 2009, p. 58). Hopefully these plans will result in successful environmental innovations in the energy sector, too.

At the international level, institutions like agreements, regimes and other cooperation arrangements contribute to the development of the environmental sustainability frame in Russia's energy policy. The international climate regime as enshrined in the Kyoto treaty in force until 2012, with the accompanying policies and obligations related to energy, is perhaps the most significant institution of this nature. So far the climate policy process has brought about only minor changes on the national level in Russia,[6] but, depending on the results of future international negotiations, an effect on domestic environmental and energy policies in various forms is to be expected (see Chapter 10). In addition, international economic and energy institutions (OECD, IEA, and so on) are increasingly emphasizing environmental sustainability in energy policy. However, as Russia is not a member of these bodies, their policy recommendations have not yet been much in evidence in the development of Russia's energy sector, where the combination of developments in Russia's main markets and its own domestic processes constitute the main mechanism of change.

The Institutional Dimension: Constraining Factors

In the preceding section we suggested that in the longer run, the framing of Russia as an energy superpower might eventually evolve towards an environmental sustainability frame as well. Currently, however, the energy superpower frame portrays Russia not as a front runner in renewable energy, but as an 'energy fossil' leaning on the exploitation of hydrocarbons. Both in domestic debate and in international fora, Russia's potential for renewable energy is still relatively rarely discussed. Public debate is almost completely lacking, and there is little conception of the role renewables could play (interviews with Russian energy experts 1 and 3, 2009). Interestingly, President Medvedev opened the expanded meeting of the State Council's Presidium on improving Russia's energy efficiency in Arkhangelsk in July 2009 by noting that '... to a certain extent, we are falling behind not only because of the difficulties we faced in the 1990s and even earlier, but also because of our mindset, because we have never tried to save energy. We always believed that we were entirely self-sustaining when it came to energy' (Medvedev, 2009a).

The role of natural gas as the 'social foundation of Russian society' suggests that it cannot be expensive nor become exhausted (interview with Russian energy expert 1, 2009). This logic contradicts the idea of the need for energy savings. The belief that new deposits of oil and gas are to be found and that technologies to exploit them will be developed, in addition to optimistic estimations about the adequacy of these resources, reproduce the energy wasting frame. In addition, 'energy sovereignty' thinking underlines the need to remain independent of European energy investments and, to some extent, from know-how related to the development of renewable energy technologies (Deliagin, 2006). Such 'rules of the game' in some cases go against the financial needs of Russia and more general business logic (see above and Chapter 3).

As noted in Chapter 2, the energy power of Russia comes with a long history of energy sector development (Goldman, 2008), which creates significant lock-in factors and path dependencies. The whole centralized energy production system with giant energy production units is indicative of this. The institutional set-up of large-scale projects constrains the development of renewable energy which mostly, and inevitably, is on a small(er) scale (interview with Russian energy expert 4, 2009). The long history of energy sector development also implies that networks of energy actors and their mutual relationships are well-established, and traditional energy lobbies, such as the nuclear lobby, are extremely strong. In the contemporary Russian 'network society', where tacit rules of the game are strong and highlight the role of 'insiders', the lack of important contacts and a certain 'outsider position' may cause insurmountable problems for new actors in charge of small, mainly local and regional businesses engaged, for instance, in renewable energy development or production. Many of these informal, as well as formal, institutional arrangements result in a lack of information, which the government's document on renewable energy (Government of the Russian Federation, 2009c) regards as one of the main obstacles to developing renewable energy sources in Russia. Information gaps include potential renewable energy resources and the prospects for their exploitation. There is also uncertainty among the public about what is defined as renewable energy, or as environmentally friendly energy. Peat, which is not really renewable and is as carbon-intensive a fuel as coal, is treated as a renewable resource even in the guidelines document of 2009. Nuclear power is also marketed as renewable and environmentally friendly, especially by the nuclear lobby (Interview with Russian energy expert 4, 2009). Consumer awareness needs to be raised substantially by public information campaigns and by supporting natural scientific and technological research and training with socio-political studies and development projects (Aalto, Blakkisrud and Smith, 2008, p. 229).

Therefore, it seems clear that in the short to medium term renewables will be overshadowed by Russia's hydrocarbon resources, which, according to the energy strategy up to 2030, are to be specifically developed in Eastern Siberia, in the Far East, as well as in the country's far north and Arctic waters. Actually, one of the scenarios in the strategy sees growth of up to 26–27 per cent in hydrocarbon exports to the Asia-Pacific region (see Government of the Russian Federation, 2009a; also Chapter 8).[7] Besides, even if a more explicit environmental policy existed for the energy sector, with corresponding regulation and institutions, implementation would still be questionable. As noted in Chapter 2, Russia's formal institutions continue to be weak, especially with regard to the implementation and control of compliance. The actors in charge of the implementation of policies in this field on the federal level include the Ministry of Energy, the Ministry of Industry and Trade, the Ministry for Economic Development, the Ministry of Regional Development, the Ministry of Natural Resources, the Ministry of Agriculture, and the Rosatom and Transneft state corporations. On the regional level the relevant actors include the administrations of the Russian Federation Constituent Subjects. Construction and development projects of energy infrastructure are handled by individual industrial companies which for their part are also represented by their lobby groups (see also Tkachenko, 2007).

Even worse, the role of environmental policy proper has been marginal in the Russian political hierarchy since the 2000s. This further limits the prospects of an environmental sustainability frame emerging more forcefully in energy policy. In 2000, environmental administration as a whole was transferred to the Ministry of Natural Resources. This Ministry's principal responsibility is for natural resource management and issuing licenses to companies seeking to exploit natural resources. Tasks related to environmental protection, regulation and monitoring are not among its core activities (for example Peterson and Bielke, 2001; Kotov and Nikitina, 2001; Oldfield, 2005, pp. 82–85). As regards energy efficiency issues, duties are shared between the Ministry of Energy and the Ministry for Natural Resources; problems persist both in the allocation of responsibilities and the sharing of the existing experience and know-how (Interview with Russian energy expert 5, 2009).

The Ecological Dimension: Enabling Factors

As noted in Chapter 2, the logic of the ecological dimension of the policy environment in the formation of energy policy is quite different from those of the resource geographic, financial and institutional dimensions. Indeed, one element of this is criticism of what is going on when viewed along the other dimensions. The two areas of energy policy in focus in this chapter – energy efficiency and savings, and renewable energy resources – both resonate strongly with the different logic of the need to do everything to ensure as minimal an ecological footprint as possible. For this reason we do not find a similar set of enabling and constraining factors along this dimension when the underlying rationale is rather to 'problematize' or question, not merely to 'conduct' energy policy. The policy importance of energy efficiency and savings, and renewable energy is considerable, especially from this point of view, for example in decreasing hazardous emissions into air, water and soil. Naturally, not all renewable energy sources are equal in their environmental side-effects, but in comparison to (most) traditional energy sources, in particular fossil fuels, they tend to have a less harmful impact on the environment. This is best seen vis-à-vis emissions of carbon dioxide.[8] Accordingly, renewables help to combat climate change.

Public pressure to consider the environmental side-effects of energy is not (yet) decisive in contemporary Russia. Nevertheless, it can be assumed that this pressure will not ease in future. Rather it will increase as the international culture of 'day-to-day environmentalism' reaches Russia, perhaps as the middle class expands. There are already signs of it: for example, WWF Russia conducted a survey in which half of the respondents were ready to pay more for renewable energy (Interview with Russian energy expert 1, 2009). To the extent that international environmental policy lobbies can influence Russia and the Russians (see for example Tysiachniouk and Reisman, 2005; 2004), there will be ever growing pressure on Russian energy actors from policymakers to business actors.

The Ecological Dimension: Constraining Factors

The ecological dimension may, however, also entail factors that constrain the evolution of an environmental sustainability frame. Namely, it can lead to biased policies. The current climatic concerns in Western countries are indicative of such biases: while focusing exclusively on carbon emissions, other environmental considerations often become blurred (see also Chaturvedi, 2011). In Russia it is possible that, given the strong role of the nuclear industry, climate policy will only encourage the building of more nuclear power. Another example is large-scale hydropower, which is carbon-neutral but has other fairly severe environmental side-effects.

The ecological dimension may also constrain the development of an environmental sustainability frame in case renewable energy and energy saving become labelled as environmental blackmail or phenomena of the 'green marginal'. At the time of writing, it seems that energy efficiency and energy saving have become mainstream – which is, of course, mostly due to economic interests, but they are also labelled as ecological safety issues. Another related constraint is the way environmental rhetoric is exploited in Russian politics. For example, environmental rhetoric is inherent in the energy strategy up to 2030 in the numerous references to 'ecological safety'; however, these references often lack any more precise definition. At the same time, environmental arguments tend to be used to legitimize other purposes. Russian participation in global climate policy is indicative of this (see for example Korppoo, 2008, with the illustrative title: 'Russia and the Post-2012 Climate Regime: Foreign rather than Environmental Policy'). Some might even argue that the commitments Russia has made in the framework of global climate policy have in actual fact confounded environmental purposes. There has been little at stake for Russia, because the collapse of the Soviet economy and the ensuing economic transition fulfilled Russia's commitment to reduce GHG emissions relative to 1990 levels without any additional effort. The same trend continues in connection with the negotiations for a post-Kyoto treaty (see Chapter 10). Thus, notwithstanding the fact that emission cuts can be considered as a welcome by-product of the national modernization programme, climate mitigation issues do not drive macroeconomic or energy policies in Russia (Interview with Russian energy expert 2, 2009; Novikova et al., 2009).

CONCLUSION

In this chapter we looked at issues of environmental sustainability in the conduct of Russia's energy policies. To do this we examined both enabling and constraining factors that could influence the extent to which an environmental sustainability frame emerges to guide energy actors' perceptions of the policy environment in Russia. We also noted how their understandings of environmentally sustainable energy differ from those widely used in the West. Thus not everything is globalized in energy policy although energy chains and their environmental effects extend thousands of kilometres beyond Russia. This again reminds us of the need to study the different levels – regional, national, interregional and so on – in the conduct of energy policy in Russia and elsewhere, which is one of the goals of this book. In our discussion of sustainable energy in Russia we have only been able to hint at the differences in the applicability and rootedness of environmental frames along regional and other scales in Russia.

We conclude that, first, although energy saving and energy efficiency are currently among the most important strategic initiatives of Russian energy policies, these issues are framed in terms of economic rather than environmental sustainability. Second, as regards renewable energy, we found that a non-fossil fuel or 'non-pipeline' framing of Russian energy policies is possible at least in the longer term, but does not currently play a significant role when considering the country on the whole. Along the resource geographical dimension Russia possesses huge resources of both fossil and non-fossil fuels, making the country a potential renewable energy superpower. However, the current infrastructure does not yet support such a path very well. Along the financial dimension regionally based, limited niche projects that plug the holes in Russia's centralized energy networks are currently most profitable. The institutional dimension indicates promising changes to the rules and regulations on more environmentally sustainable energy policies but several informal rules of the game and lock-in factors gear Russian actors to marked inertia, if not path-dependence, in the use of the country's vast fossil fuel reserves. The one-time nature of fossil fuels – which becomes evident when viewed through the more critical lens of the ecological dimension – is something on which widespread awareness has yet to develop in Russia. More instrumental, profit-oriented thinking dominates in the resources sector as it does around energy efficiency and savings; expectations for 'energy rents' are huge in several different economic, social and political circles (see Chapter 4).

On the most general level our discussion permits certain conclusions about the role of time and events in the formulation of energy policies. In the tension – and simultaneous compatibility – between the (fossil fuels) energy superpower and renewable energy superpower frames in Russia much depends on our time perspective. Sustainable energy solutions range from small and regional scale solutions here and now, from Karelia to Kamchatka, to our global futures. In the latter case, however, the huge investments needed and the revision of existing institutional set-ups are motivated by events that have made, or are making us more acutely aware of megatrends such as resource scarcity and climate change. Russia has always been part of the global flow of ideas, with its long-standing drive for 'modernization', but it has only rarely been in the vanguard of change.

NOTES

1. The research for this chapter was planned jointly by Aalto and Tynkkynen. Tynkkynen bears the primary responsibility for the majority of the chapter, while Aalto is the lead author for the sub-sections on the financial dimensions of sustainable energy and also for the conclusion. For compiling material and conducting field interviews we thank Laura Salo. The research was supported by the projects on 'sustainable energy' (University Alliance Finland, 2008–09),

'Russia's Energy Policy and Its External Impacts' (Academy of Finland, 2008–11, Kivinen), 'Energy Policy in European Integration' (Academy of Finland, 2011–14, Aalto, no. 139686) and 'Knowledge management for the Baltic Sea protection' (Academy of Finland, 2010–2014, Tynkkynen, no. 131901).

2. The International Energy Agency's (IEA) 'new policies' scenario, which foresees modest energy policy reforms in response to climate change, expects oil production not to peak before 2035, while in the '450' scenario, which entails more radical policy measures globally, the peak in production would materialize by 2020. Natural gas resources are more plentiful but will be more in demand than oil and coal. The share of renewable sources may reach one third in electricity generation, 16 per cent in heat production and 8 per cent in road transport fuels (IEA, 2010b, p. 1).

3. The technical potential of renewable energy sources is defined by the technological possibility of their use, whereas their economic potential is defined by comparison to the cost of traditional energy by region (Energy Charter, 2007, pp. 25–26). Accordingly, the economic potential will increase with the rise in fossil fuel prices.

4. While stressing the need to develop renewable energy, the new Law on Energy Saving from November 2009 and the Energy Strategy of Russia for the period up to 2030, do not define what are counted as renewable energy sources.

5. For more on the technical potential of renewable energy in various Russian regions, see Energy Charter (2007, p. 26).

6. Russia's Climate Doctrine from December 2009 forms the basis for state climate policy (Government of the Russian Federation, 2009d). The implementation of climate policy instruments set by the international process, such as joint implementation projects (JI), has proven indifferent for Russia's day-to-day policymaking (see Korppoo and Spencer, 2010, p. 29–31).

7. The strategy states that by 2030 energy exports will remain a major source of revenue for the development of the national economy, although their relative share in the national economy will decrease. The intention is also to develop value-added industries around the energy sector such as petrochemicals.

8. Biomass burning emits carbon dioxide emissions, but these emissions are generally considered 'climate neutral' because the resource is renewable, as forests grow back and absorb the carbon dioxide.

PART III

The interregional level

6. Russian foreign policy and energy: the case of the Nord Stream gas pipeline

Hanna Smith

INTRODUCTION

This chapter looks at the interregional level of Russia's energy policies by examining developments within the institutional dimension of energy policy formation (see Chapter 2), in particular the linkages between the conduct of Russian foreign policy and foreign energy policies. The chapter takes as a case study the Nord Stream Gas Pipeline (NSGP) project, where we can identify a number of different interests and frames through which the Russia–EU energy relationship has been articulated and approached: security of supply and demand, security of transit, as well as the associated bargaining processes, and degree of integration and interdependence among the actors.

This chapter first discusses existing research on the NSGP project in an effort to assess how this project became a controversial 'event' in Russia–EU energy relations in the mid-2000s. In the second section the process of materializing the NSGP project is explored in more detail. The third section will attempt to tackle wider institutional questions relating to the connection between foreign policy and energy policy, with emphasis on Russian agency and choices to examine the reasons for launching the Nord Stream project. Finally, the institutional environment of the Russia–EU energy dialogue and relations are approached to assess which interests play a central role there.

The Nord Stream project shows that alongside material interests, ideational and identity-based factors such as feelings of *ressentiment* towards the former Soviet republics and former Eastern European satellite states, play a significant role in Russian foreign relations whether economic, security or policy-related. In this project security concerns trump the economic benefits, although it is clear that ultimately the project should not do any harm to Russian business interests. But at the same time the NSGP is a project driven by the global energy system, its development and future prospects. The chapter portrays the NSGP as an example of the complex interaction of different energy policy interests informed by historical aspects of foreign relations. It illustrates well the challenges of cooperation between liberalized markets and markets where the rules of the game are still blurred and only in the making, and where institutional and bilateral policymaking co-constitute the framework within which cross-border projects materialize in contemporary Eurasia.

HOW DID THE NORD STREAM PIPELINE PROJECT BECOME AN 'EVENT'?

Prior to the NSGP deal between Russian and German actors in 2005, these issues did not receive sufficient attention in the academic literature or in the mass media. In English-language literature, Jonathan Stern is one of the few authors to continuously investigate Russian energy policy and Gazprom's role in it. As early as 1999 he discerned attempts to diversify export routes as part of a Russian energy strategy (Stern, 1999). In his study of 2002 Stern looked at the security of gas supplies from a range of perspectives: reserves and reserve-to-production ratio, supply/demand balance, long-term contracts, import dependence, transit dependence, and management of energy cooperation between liberalized and more monopolistic markets. He mentions the idea of building the NSGP only in the subcontext of Russia's plans to increase gas deliveries to Europe. However he also addresses the security risk scenario regarding transit dependence: 'Each border crossed adds an additional layer of security risk with the potential for conflict within these transit countries and between the latter and the supplying country' (Stern, 2002, p. 15).

On the Russian side, in 2004 Nodari Simonia wrote that

> ... problems continue to hinder further progress [in Russian natural gas production]. For example, there has been the reoccurrence of illegal gas siphoning from Russian pipelines that travel through neighbouring CIS countries. This has forced Russia to take measures in order to ensure the uninterrupted flow of gas supplies to Europe. Gazprom and Finland's Fortum, for example, will conduct a feasibility study for the construction of a 5.7-billion-dollar North European gas pipeline that will bypass all intermediate countries on the way to Europe (Simonia, 2004, p. 116).

Simonia's contribution strongly reflects Russia's growing realization – noted by Stern in 2002 – that each transit country adds to the security risk. The issue of transit country versus gas importing country is also the central theme in a 2005 article by Christian von Hirschhausen, Berit Meinhart and Ferdinand Pavel (2005), who examine Russia–Ukraine relations and assess the feasibility of creating alternative transit capacities to weaken the dominant role of Ukraine in Russian energy transit. The paper models the options for transporting Russian gas to Western Europe. It concludes, among other things, that if Russia were to build alternative transport routes bypassing Ukraine (that is, through a Northern pipeline route), Ukraine, not Russia or Western Europe, would be the loser in the game. However, the gain comes at the price of import/export dependence.

From the beginning of 2006 most writings on European energy security that include the NSGP, take the dispute between Russia and Ukraine over natural gas prices, transit and debts in January 2006 as an example that highlights the energy security risks of dependence on a few energy suppliers (see Chapters 2, 7). That risk is also linked to politically framed accounts where Russia is increasing its grip on Europe:

> On international spot markets for oil, this issue would be handled by the price mechanism related to supply and demand, but when it comes to regional gas trade, there are risks of Russia attaching a political premium to its energy supplies in the same way as it has done before against the Eastern EU and the Commonwealth of Independent States (CIS). Russia has the ability to do this today, but the Nord Stream project will, to some extent, increase Russia's ability to tamper with gas flows and apply an arbitrary price policy without affecting the most important customers in Moscow's view, for example Germany (Larsson, 2008, p. 4).

The year 2006 was also when writings on the linkage between foreign policy and energy politics began to emerge. As commented by Dominik Smyrgala, an expert on energy issues on academic leave from the Polish Ministry of Foreign Affairs: 'If Gazprom were a normal Western company, interested in profits and building customer relations, the situation would not be so drastic, but as we have seen, Gazprom is not this kind of company; it is better understood as a tool of foreign policy for the Russian Federation' (cited in Hundley, 2010).

This change of emphasis in writings on Russia's energy politics coincided with the 2006 Ukraine–Russia gas dispute, which was the most important incident concerning gas with widespread implications for Europe.[1] The following summer Russia hosted the G8 summit in St. Petersburg, where energy security was one of the main themes. At the global level energy issues had also begun to assume a more significant place in foreign relations due to increasing demands for energy both in Asia and in the West. According to Andreas Wenger, 'The global energy system is in the midst of a major transformation and Russia's energy power is a key in the process. New consumers in Asia have joined their Western counterparts, in rapidly growing energy demand, and the producers, among them Russia, have gained considerable influence over global energy issues' (Wenger, 2009, p. 240).

From the Russian perspective the dispute with Ukraine was the best example of the high risk of being dependent on transit countries. As President Dmitry Medvedev said, 'The pipeline (NSGP) will ensure reliable fuel supplies to European consumers at affordable, reasonable prices. It will also protect us against problems that may be caused by the imperfections of the current legal framework, in particular with regard to transit' (Radio Free Europe, 2010).

The Nord Stream Gas Pipeline project from Russia to Germany along the Baltic Sea floor is now one of the best known energy projects in Europe. In the 'energy superpower' type framings of Russian energy policies (see Chapter 2), it is seen as a tool for realizing the power interests in Russian foreign policy, both punishing the transit countries that have caused Russia trouble and providing foreign policy muscle to maintain political influence in Russia's relations with the EU and its individual Member States. In formulations of the 'business frame' type, particularly in the Russian perspective, it is a project with profit interests (no transit fees involved), and in 'energy security' framings a response to increased energy demand (securing the supply and ensuring the future use of the gas fields first in the Yamal Peninsula and then later the Shtokman fields in the Barents Sea). At the same time at issue is the protection of Russia's national interests by avoiding any political leverage that transit countries may exert on Russia. However, as the NSGP is also a European project, with strong German interests involved,[2] and the governments of Finland, Sweden and Denmark officially approving the construction project, the nature of the project is more difficult to determine than might at first appear.

The remainder of this chapter addresses a number of questions: can we find a clear linkage between foreign policy and energy policy in the context of the interests and behaviour of Russian actors in the NSGP project? Whose interests are the greatest determinants and drivers of the project? To what extent do historical frames affect the project and the underlying interests? Why has the project also been identified by the European Commission as one with European interests, and why is it mentioned in the Russia–EU dialogue as a significant project to the EU planned along one of the priority axes of the Trans-European Gas Networks? What role does interdependence play, and what interests weigh heaviest: profit, energy security or power interests in the EU–Russia institutional game?

CASE STUDY: THE NORD STREAM GAS PIPELINE

The common view of the Nord Stream Gas Pipeline deal is best illustrated by a statement of the Finnish Minister of Foreign Affairs, Alexander Stubb: 'This has been an almost completely bilateral deal between Russia and Germany, when there should have been consultations with many other EU Member States. But perhaps this is proof of the fact that the European Union really needs a unified energy policy, so that these types of decisions are taken together' (Juselius, 2009). When the agreement was signed, it did indeed have the appearance of a bilateral arrangement. It is still viewed by many as a bilateral deal that put the EU's attempt to unify its energy policy severely to the test. However, the project does indeed involve several other interests, not only those of Russia and Germany. Several EU Member States had and continue to have a vested interest in the project.

The pipeline will be 1220 kilometres (758 miles) long and will consist of two parallel lines. Once completed, it will be one of the longest offshore pipelines in the world. Its route is from Portovaya Bay near Vyborg, Russia, to the coast of Germany near Greifswald, Mecklenburg, in the Northeast corner of Germany. It will cross Russian, Finnish, Swedish, Danish and German exclusive economic zones (EEZ) (see Figure 6.1). The first line, with a carrying capacity of around 27.5 billion cubic metres a year, is due for completion in 2011. The second line is due to be completed in 2012, doubling the annual capacity to around 55 billion cubic metres. This is enough to supply more than 26 million households. Gazprom has already signed long-term contracts to supply gas through Nord Stream to customers in several EU countries including Germany, Denmark, the Netherlands, Belgium, France and the United Kingdom. The gas supplies are planned to come from the Yuzhno-Russkoye oil and gas reserve, Yamal Peninsula (under development), and the Shtokman field (under planning). The financing comes partly from Nord Stream's shareholders, who are providing investments amounting to 30 per cent of the total

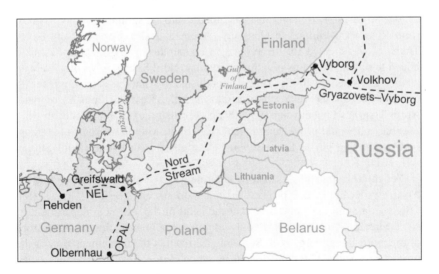

Source: Wikimedia Commons, Samuel Bailey (sam.bailus@gmail.com).

Figure 6.1 The Nord Stream natural gas pipeline

project cost pro rata into their holding in the company, with 70 per cent of the total project cost coming from external project financing from 24 banks. According to Nord Stream itself, the estimated investment budget is €7.4 billion. Doubts have been expressed regarding the accuracy of the estimated budget. The pipeline will cost €8.8 billion according to Nord Stream representative Irina Vasilieva in the newspaper *Vedomosti*. This is almost €4 billion more than the estimates from 2005 and €1.4 billion more than estimates from 2008 (Staalesen, 2010).

It is not always sufficiently accentuated how the project has its roots in the immediate aftermath of the collapse of the Soviet Union. The head of the technical department of Nord Stream AG, Sergei Serdyukov, linked the planning of a pipeline not dependent on any transit countries to the collapse of the Soviet Union and to Russia losing control over the main pipelines delivering gas to Europe (Godzimirski, 2010, p. 33). This referred particularly to Ukraine. Russia was not alone with these thoughts. As Debra Johnson has argued, 'The construction of an East–West energy bridge has been a European strategy goal since Russian gas first entered Western Europe amid great Cold War controversy over 20 years ago' (Johnson, 2005, p. 188). The Internet site of Nord Stream AG has it that planning started in 1997, when talks began with the Finnish energy company Fortum. However, some Finnish officials[3] and Gasum's[4] project leader Seppo Nurminen place the starting point some years earlier, around 1995. Seppo Nurminen stated in 2005 that over ten years earlier the Finnish oil company Neste (subsequently split into two companies, Fortum and Neste Oil) started planning a gas pipeline project similar to today's NSGP from Russia via Finland to Germany (Avomaa, 2005). The company North Transgas was created for the project in cooperation with Gazprom. Finland hoped to obtain the status of a transit country. Nord Stream AG's own website claims that the feasibility studies conducted by international engineering companies, Russian research institutes and the Russian–Finnish company North Transgas Oy between 1997–09 showed that the project was technically feasible and would prove economically efficient. Alternative routes for transporting Russian gas to Europe were investigated at that time (Nord Stream AG, 2011).

Yet in 1998 the then Gazprom chairman Rem Vyakhirev stated that the North European pipeline project was not economically feasible (Grib, 2007). This was around the same time that the head of the technical department of Nord Stream AG, Sergei Serdyukov, claimed in a presentation on the history of the Nord Stream project in September 2010 that the implementation of the project was delayed by the Russians being on close terms with Ukraine's then President Leonid Kravchuk, resulting in a political decision to abandon plans to bypass Ukraine (Godzimirski, 2010, p. 33). The project nevertheless moved forward despite doubts about its final form.

In 2000 the European Commission named the project as one of the four energy projects involving European interests. The four projects were: the North European gas pipeline (the Nord Stream pipeline), the Yamal–Europe II natural gas pipeline, a natural gas pipeline linking Denmark, Germany and Sweden (Baltic Gas Interconnector) and increasing transmission capacity on the Germany–Belgium–United Kingdom axis. Nord Stream in fact became a multilaterally approved project, enjoying the approbation of all 15 EU Member States at that time. This would not have been possible without the active support of several Member States. The EU even agreed to co-finance a feasibility study of the project in 2003 and in 2006 as part of the Trans European Natural Gas Network (TEN-E). The project's status was confirmed by the European Council and Parliament, then with 27 members. Finland seemed well placed to become a new transit country and at the beginning of 2003 the Finnish Prime Minister at the time, Paavo Lipponen, held bilateral talks with his Russian counterpart, Mikhail Kasyanov, about the gas pipeline.

In early 2004 the Finns still considered themselves to be actively participating in the planning process, through the Finnish company Fortum, of a gas pipeline that would connect the Baltic Sea countries with the rest of Northern Europe (Lehtomäki, 2004). Fortum withdrew in 2005 on its own initiative (Godzimirski, 2010, p. 33). A few months after the Hanover Trade Fair, where Gazprom, BASF Wintershall and E.On Ruhrgas signed the initial contract to start work on the Nord Stream gas pipeline, Fortum's Senior Vice President Tapio Kuula said: 'Gazprom will continue to be an important partner of Fortum. We have a mutual interest in facilitating the future use of gas-powered energy also in Stockholm and the mid-Sweden areas. We are very pleased to see this option as part of Gazprom's plans' (Fortum, 2005). This does not necessarily imply that the company changed its business plan in 2005 or that it no longer had any interests in the project in 2005. Regarding the role of Sweden, Robert Larsson wrote in 2006: 'There has been a discussion on whether a leg would be built to Sweden. According to the official website, there will be a spur to Sweden, but Sweden has not officially approved it' (Larsson, 2006b, p.16).

During the period 2000–05 interest was also expressed by the French company TotalFinaElf and London-registered Shell. In 2002 the head of Gazprom, Aleksei Miller, said that Gazprom was looking for partners for the project and was aiming at the Dutch, British and German markets (Hirvikorpi, 2003). In June 2003 a Russian–British memorandum of understanding on the project was signed. Dutch interest in the project was also high. The process up to the signing ceremony of the deal between Russia and Germany in September 2005 was not a bilateral business between Russia and Germany, and was most definitely not decided before the turn of 2004 and 2005. It seems probable that the deal became known as a bilateral project between Russia and

Germany with European Union backing as a result of the EU enlargement of 2004. The Baltic States and Poland were the loudest critics of the project. Poland clearly stated that the pipeline was an energy security risk for Poland. As Marek Sivec, vice-president of the European Parliament, put it in an interview to the Russian *Kommersant* newspaper:

> What would you say about the Nord Stream project then? I think it is a very costly solution to the problem. Gazprom could have built the pipeline through Poland and Belarus, but Russia and Germany decided to do it differently. We can recall the ecologic issues caused by the project. There is something else: unless a project bypasses other countries for political reasons, it can be accepted. Yet, if Russia is simply unwilling to sell gas to Poland, and is looking for ways to sell it directly to Western Europe, then it is a threat to Poland's energy security (Gabuev, 2008).

In Sweden some aspects of the hard security risks the pipeline might create were debated. Then Minister of Defence, Mikael Odenberg, declared in the Swedish newspaper *Dagens Nyheter* 'We get a pipeline that motivates a Russian navy presence in our exclusive economic zone and the Russians can use this for military intelligence should they want to. Of course that is a problem' (Nandorf, 2006). The loud objections and concerns raised by the Baltic States and Poland were heard in the EU. The European Parliament voted in 2008 for resolution 543/60 demanding an additional study of the potentially negative impact of the Nord Stream pipeline on the Baltic Sea (*Kommersant*, 2008). This was no surprise, since many members of the European Parliament (MEPs) had been working on this issue since the signing of the agreement. The Finnish MEP Satu Hassi of the Green Party had already submitted a written inquiry in 2006 to the Commission about the construction of the pipeline and the environmental risk analysis that should have been carried out in connection with the agreement to build it (Hassi, 2006). The vocal campaign managed to create a vibrant public debate in several countries but this did not halt progress.

On 12 February 2010, the environmental authorities of Southern Finland gave their consent. The final victory for the project came in autumn 2009, when the governments of Denmark, Sweden and Finland approved the project. Overall it took Nord Stream AG four years to obtain construction permits from the countries concerned, after spending €100 million on environmental analysis along the entire route (Mityayev, 2009). The pipeline was also rerouted several times on environmental grounds.

The Danish Energy Agency (DEA) was the first to grant permission on 27 October 2009. The Danish approval referred to the European Commission's approval of the project as part of the Trans-European Natural Gas Network (TEN-E) project and confirmation of that by the European Parliament and Council. The DEA had consulted 14 different institutions, among them three in Estonia, one more in Europe, and the Admiral of the Danish Fleet. In accordance with the Espoo Convention on transboundary impacts the Danish authorities had consulted all eight Baltic Sea states. Thirteen conditions were set for the permission, including strict guidelines on how to proceed if the pipeline became defunct. The Danish permission listed mostly environmental issues and stipulated that the permit was issued in accordance with the Continental Shelf Act, with state sovereignty over territorial waters, as well as with Executive Order No. 361 of 25 April 2006 on certain pipeline installations for the transport of hydrocarbons in territorial waters and the continental shelf (Danish Energy Agency, 2009).

Sweden and Finland both granted permission on 5 November 2009. The Swedish permit was prepared by the Ministry of Enterprise, Energy and Communication and was a governmental decision. The authorities sent the NSGP application to 65 different Swedish institutions in addition to six ministries. These included the Swedish armed forces, the Swedish coastguards, the National Defence Radio Establishment and the Swedish National Police Board. The Swedish permit also referred to international law by stating firmly that even if Article 79 of the UN Convention on the Law of the Sea gives every state the right to lay pipelines on a coastal state's continental shelf within the economic zone, the right is not unconditional. Sweden included 12 conditions in its permission, among them a stipulation similar to that made by the Danish authorities regarding the situation when the pipeline becomes defunct. The Swedish permit did not frame the project in European terms or note the role of the EU in any way (SWE document, 2009).

The permit from the Finnish government, prepared by the Ministry of Employment and the Economy, refers to 14 different laws in accordance with which the permission was granted. Among them were two international laws, one EU law, and one bilateral agreement between Finland and Estonia, the rest were Finnish national laws. The Finnish permit stressed rather strongly the European dimension of the project. Finland had consulted all the Baltic Sea states as Denmark and Sweden had done, but the permit only included responses from Estonia, Latvia, Lithuania and Sweden. The Finnish authorities asked opinions directly from 11 different institutions but also put out an open call for anyone's opinion on the matter. Among the agencies whose opinions were asked were the General Staff of the Finnish Defence Forces, the Ministry of Defence and the Border Guard. The open call was published in all major Finnish and Swedish-language newspapers with information on where the documents could be viewed and by what date any opinion regarding the matter should be delivered to the Ministry of Employment and the Economy. There were 12 such further opinions, among them four individual opinions and those of two companies. The companies were Elisa Oy (telecommunications) and Baltirail ry, paying attention to the future plans for the possible construction of a rail tunnel under the Gulf of Finland connecting Estonia and Finland. The Finnish permit laid down 11 conditions but, unlike the Danish and Swedish permits, refrained from stipulating what to do when the pipeline was no longer in use (Ministry of Trade and the Economy of Finland, 2009).

The permits granted by the Danish, Swedish and Finnish authorities for the NSGP reflect well the countries' overall attitude to the project as well as the complexity of the issue. They also rounded up the whole complex process of the project's evolution. At the beginning of the 1990s the Russian government foresaw the possibility of conflicts with the former Soviet republics. In the EU expectations were similar. Finland and Russia formed an alliance through Gazprom and Neste Oy to explore the possibility of another gas pipeline delivering gas from Russia to continental Europe. Possibly the Ukrainians obstructed the Finnish-Russian plans with the backing of some EU Member States, or rather companies with strong ties to those states. By 2000 the project had been named a project with European interests with several states expressing interests. Disagreements emerged over the materialization and route of the pipeline. With the EU enlargement of 2004, Russian attitudes clearly changed from cautiously exploring the multilateral option, with the possibility of a number of transit states, to favouring the bilateral option with Germany. This might have been the underlying aim all along but for a while other possibilities were open. In the final project four EU Member States are involved through the companies they host. The NSGP also enjoys the approval of the Baltic Sea countries, whose economic zones the pipeline crosses. How can all this be explained in the context of the linkages between foreign policy and energy policies? Why should an initially bilateral project be turned into a multilateral issue, from that retreat into a bilateral deal between two states, and then get reconverted into a multinational project with shareholders from five companies and four countries?

RUSSIAN FOREIGN POLICY, ENERGY AND THE EU

Russian Foreign Policy Interests and Energy

We know from a wealth of studies that Russian foreign policy and Russia's energy-related interests are very closely linked, but how is it in this particular case? Do foreign policy priorities and interests determine energy policy choices or do the domestic political determinants in energy policy determine foreign policy? Which is the tool of the other? Or are they equally important interests with some common ground?

As with all Russian policy areas, questions relating to choices and behaviour can be interpreted in many ways and competing explanations exist. Quite often the dominating factors in shaping perceptions of Russia's foreign policy have been individual events themselves, with the argument running that these events represent a simplistic pattern of behaviour and *ad hoc* opportunism (Orttung and Overland, 2010, p. 74). Other typical ways of explaining Russian foreign policy relate to geopolitical features (Donaldson and Nogee, 2005). Alternative explanations refer to Russian foreign and national security concepts situating Russia's foreign diplomacy in the context of bilateral relations and manifest a world view of multipolarity taking Russia as one of the leading world poles (Mankoff, 2009). Some Western studies stress the importance of multilateralism in Russian foreign policy; certainly the multilateral framework in international relations is the one that the Russian leadership often refers to (Wilson Rowe and Torjesen, 2008). To complement these institutional explanations of Russian agency and interests, identity and historical discourses represent additional explanatory factors (Hopf, 1999, 2002, 2008; Neumann, 1996; Smith, 2005; Legvold, 2007; Petro and Rubinstein, 1997). The domestic-institutional aspects and their relationship to foreign policy have also been dealt with (Checkel, 1997; McFaul, 1997; Smith, 2010 and 2011; Bukkvoll, 2003; Zimmerman, 2002; Malcolm et al., 1996).

Alongside these accounts focusing mostly on what here is termed the institutional dimension, there is a significant body of economics-related literature that looks at Russian foreign policy as determined by features of the financial dimension. These are certainly important but it can be argued with some confidence that profit interests and market considerations are often secondary in Russian foreign policy choices (Orttung and Overland, 2010; Smith, 2004). While this list of explanatory factors could be continued, it highlights how many different structural dimensions help to explain and understand Russian foreign policy, and how easy it is to miss something very important while trying to make sense of Russian foreign policy choices and behaviour.

One important factor runs across several of the foreign policy determinants mentioned above – *ressentiment*. The *Encyclopédie Philosophique Universelle* mentions *ressentiment* as 'a state of hostility maintained by the memory of an offense which it aspires to avenge' (Fitzpatrick, 2001, p. 579). The origin of *ressentiment* thinking is most strongly associated with Nietzsche, for whom at its root are memory and the inability to forget past injuries or hurts (ibid., p. 580). The politics of *ressentiment* accuse outside forces for every problem, seeking scapegoats (Prizel, 1998). It is by no means a new phenomenon in Russian history. The concept has been used as an explanatory feature in a number of historical studies (Greenfeld, 1993). However, as Ilya Prizel has shown, it is also a concept that can be used not only in the context of domestic politics but also in contemporary foreign relations. *Ressentiment* represents an ideational or identity-based feature underlying the institutional dimension, and is clearly present in geopolitics and historical discourses. It also manifests itself in Russian reactions to certain world events and casts its shadow over domestic and economic policies. *Ressentiment*-type behaviour in Russia includes the government's accusations against Russian oligarchs living abroad trying to weaken the current Russian government and create a detrimental image of it in the West, claiming that citizens' organizations, particularly those funded from abroad, are hotbeds of anti-government political activity.

A typical consequence of *ressentiment*-driven behaviour in foreign policy is a preference for bilateral relations, which allow the states to reward friends and punish or refuse to deal with countries against which it has a grievance. Given the closed nature of the Kremlin's politics, evidence for such *ressentiment* in international energy policy must be indirect. As Fredholm has argued, from the Russian perspective being dependent on transit countries makes Russia vulnerable not only to fluctuations in business conditions but, more importantly, to economic or political blackmail (Fredholm, 2005, p.14). Seeking alternative routes would make some sense in order to avoid such risk, but in the case of Nord Stream it is hard to escape the conclusion that it was the particular countries involved that inspired *ressentiment*-type behaviour. As noted above, the whole project was shelved in the late 1990s at a time when relations between Russia and Ukraine were on a positive footing. Between then and the signing of the Nord Stream agreement in 2005, not only had a series of difficulties arisen between Russia and Ukraine over gas transit, but the Orange Revolution was a humiliation for Russia and signalled Ukraine turning away from Russia in favour of the West.

As Harley Balzer put it at the time: 'Mr. Putin's preferred model of international collaboration is the deal announced at the Hanover Trade Fair in mid April 2005 to build a gas pipeline under the Baltic Sea, which will avoid Russian dependence on pipelines crossing Ukraine, Poland, Belarus and the Baltics' (Balzer, 2005, p. 220). Of these, the Baltic republics, which had led the disintegration of the Soviet Union and consistently stood up to Russia since, and Poland, which has adopted an almost unbroken hostile stance towards Russia since the sixteenth century, come not far behind Ukraine as obvious targets for Russian *ressentiment*. If cutting out the middlemen was a strong motive behind the purely bilateral deal with Germany, then this can be seen as a product of the influence of *ressentiment*.

However, the importance of realizing profit interests as a result of an efficient energy policy and secured supply of Russian energy is also very significant for the Russian state, even though it comes some way behind geopolitical interests. It is questionable whether *ressentiment* would be a sufficiently strong motive to inspire a decision which went directly against economic interests. The fact that Gazprom and the Russian government have made no comprehensive effort to provide an economic justification for the Nord Stream project reinforces the suspicion that *ressentiment* is at work. But according to one study from September 2010, although it would not necessarily lead to a major increase in the flow of gas to Europe, in the period from 2011 to 2040 Nord Stream would make additional profits of between US$500 million and US$30 billion (Chyong, Noël and Reiner, 2010). This academic study confirms the business forecasts made in technical studies in 1997–99, as mentioned above, which saw such a project as economically viable. In terms of the model presented in Chapter 2 of this volume, it would thus appear that Nord Stream is based on a strong business frame. The authors also argue that a large part of this additional profit accrues from the pipeline bypassing Ukraine, since it not only removes transit tariffs from gas travelling through Nord Stream, but the existence of Nord Stream will also force Ukraine to rethink and renegotiate the tariffs it charges on any gas still transported across Ukraine (ibid., pp.16–17).

It is clear that one aim of NSGP is to cut out transit states between Russian gas and European markets, whether for economic reasons, *ressentiment* or both. However, by shifting transit away from Ukraine and Belarus in particular, Russia will lose part of its foreign policy leverage, given that either the NSGP has to be filled with the gas that is now mostly flowing through Ukraine or from the currently undeveloped fields. Nevertheless, there is at least some reason to suppose that the Kremlin may view the pipeline as a potential foreign policy tool. Robert Larsson has identified some of the elements which appear to link energy politics with foreign policy: interruptions in supply (total or partial), threats of interruptions in supply (covert or explicit), pricing policy (prices as carrots or sticks), use of existing energy debts, creating new energy debts and hostile takeovers of companies and infrastructure (Larsson, 2006b, p.177).

Kari Liuhto has identified three different categories introducing more measures into Larsson's list. The first category Liuhto has called 'unacceptable methods' that include use of obscure agents as investors and traders on behalf of Russian energy giants, reversal of PSAs in Russia and dubious pipeline problems causing delivery cut-offs. The second category is called 'questionable methods' and refers to the recruitment of top foreign politicians to Russian-dominated energy projects, building of new terminals and overly expensive pipes to bypass natural transit countries, under-priced gas sales in Russia, and no free access for the Central Asian states to the Russian pipe system. The last category, where foreign policy and energy are linked, is labelled by Liuhto as 'acceptable methods': use of transparent middlemen as traders of Russian energy, business-driven Russian energy investment abroad (Liuhto, 2010, p. 40). Although the categorization is highly normative, the factors listed by Liuhto taken in conjunction with Larsson's features are significant in identifying political purposes behind business decisions.

In this case, the NSGP includes in its development stage several of the elements from Liuhto's list: recruitment of foreign top politicians and overly expensive pipes to bypass existing lines and to avoid transit countries, for example. Once the project is completed the use of energy as a foreign policy tool will be more limited but cannot be fully excluded. The NSGP can be a tool for supply interruptions or be used as a threat of supply interruptions, pricing policy or dubious pipeline problems causing delivery cut-offs. As long as the route through Ukraine remains viable, there is also the possibility of playing the two pipelines off against each other. But this runs the risk of severely back-firing on Russia. Energy as a policy tool in Russia's hands has a very different nature when it comes to Western European countries. The problems that the Western EU Members States (which are less energy dependent on Russia than East European countries) have encountered when dealing with Russia have been more subtle.

In response to accusations that Russia uses energy as a foreign policy tool, Russia has produced counterarguments but in general has not denied that energy might be an important part of Russian foreign relations. Energy consti-tutes an important instrument in Russia's foreign policymaking, both in protect-ing national interests and advancing them. The Russian Federation's energy strategy up to 2020, dated 28 August 2003, formally states that Russia's natural resources and the large energy sector forms a base for Russian economic well-being and a tool in its domestic and foreign policy (Government of the Russian Federation, 2003, p. 4) The Russian energy strategy up to 2030 approved on 13 November 2009 formulates the matter somewhat more mildly but implies much the same: 'The objective of the energy policy of Russia is to maximize the effective use of natural energy resources and the potential of the energy sector to sustain economic growth, improve the quality of life of the population and promote strengthening of foreign economic positions of the country' (Government of the Russian Federation, 2009a, p. 10).

The 2009 strategy determines the objectives and goals of Russian energy policy: 'In order to address these concerns [that energy policy is used as a foreign policy tool] President Medvedev proposed a "Conceptual Approach" to a New Legal Base of International Cooperation in the Energy Sector in April 2009' (Gupta, 2010). Russia has expressed a need to create a legally binding framework for energy cooperation. This would also mean some limits for Russia in its use of energy as a tool. Russia worked hard in bilateral rela-tions when pursuing the Nord Stream gas pipeline and obtained permits from Denmark, Finland and Sweden for the use of their EEZs. Likewise it reached an agreement with Turkey for use of the latter's EEZ to construct the South Stream gas pipeline (Gupta, 2010), thus underlining Russia's commitment to legal processes in energy deliveries.

Without access to the inner workings of the Kremlin, it is difficult to assess the relative weight of the different factors behind Russia's decision to engage in the Nord Stream gas pipeline project. From the fact that Russian policy has changed depending on the state of relations with Ukraine, it is clear that political factors and the politics of *ressentiment* have played a major role. Energy remains a potential tool of Russian foreign policy, but at the same time it would be uncharacteristic for the Russian government to pursue policies that directly contradict business interests, especially given the importance of energy exports to the Russian economy and state budget. During the Putin and Medvedev presidencies, there has also been a growing tendency to put international business relations on a legally sound footing, but this has never been an overriding concern, as a series of incidents starting from the Yukos affair have shown (see Chapter 3).

Russia-EU Energy Dialogue: Bilateralism and Multilateralism in Interplay

Between the Hanover spring trade fair where the companies signed the agreement to start developing NSGP and the high-level signing ceremony in September 2005, the EU and Russia stated 'The key objective of the Road Map of the Common Economic Space adopted at the EU–Russia summit of 10 May 2005, is the intensification of cooperation in the energy area, with particular emphasis on addressing issues related to the sustainability and continued reliability of the production, distribution, transportation and efficient use of energy' (EU–Russia Energy Dialogue, 2005, p. 2). This statement was not only followed by the NSGP but also the Russia–Ukraine gas disputes.

Where energy is concerned it is nothing new in the post-Soviet space for originally economic questions to escalate into disputes. Disputes relating to energy between Russia and the EU did not escalate into politically motivated hostile action although during the Russia–Ukraine gas dispute in 2006 and in 2009 EU Member States were affected during a spell of particularly cold weather in the middle of winter. This coincided with increasing concerns in the EU about internal political developments in Russia, as well as Russia's more aggressive foreign policy expressed in then President Putin's speech at the Munich security conference in 2007. All three factors – the energy dispute with Ukraine, Russian internal developments and clearly toughened foreign policy rhetoric – contributed to the fact that Russian energy policy was increasingly also linked to foreign policy uses and referred to as an energy weapon in Russian politics.

The media attention to energy issues between Russia and the EU accelerated when Schröder and Putin signed the Northern gas pipeline bilateral deal in September 2005. How the media and popular opinion in Poland and the Baltic States regarded the matter can be highlighted through the opinion of the former leader of Lithuania, Vytautas Landsbergis, as expressed in the Estonian newspaper *Postimees*: 'We, the new democracies in Eastern Europe, have learned from history that behind every diplomatic step by Russia lies imperial ambitions' (Landsbergis, 2005). The initial reactions to the deal were mostly hostile and the European dimension of the project was downplayed. This reflected the overall tone of Russia–EU relations and in particular energy politics at the time.

The relationship between Russia and the EU has never been an easy one. It has always consisted of two levels: one level involves negative images and mutual misperceptions, and the other an effective working relationship with a common history and exchange of culture. As the EU expanded in 2004 to include eight new members which, 15 years before, lay on the Soviet-dominated side of the Iron Curtain, the question was raised as to whether this process would lead to a new division of Europe or would rather bring Russia closer to the rest of Europe. The fact is that President Putin's second presidential term coincided with increased irritation between Russia and the EU after the fairly positive year of Russia–EU relations in 2003. During Putin's second presidency two events can be singled out as significant milestones in the new basis of Russia–EU cooperation.

The first milestone was the EU enlargement of 2004 that provided new opportunities and challenges for the EU in its relations with Russia. The economic relationship grew stronger and with it also Russia's part as a major energy supplier to the EU. The Russia-EU economic relationship did, however, experience increasing tensions over energy issues.

But, at the same time that enlargement opened up new opportunities for deepening and strengthening the ties between Russia and the EU, especially in the area of economics and energy, the challenges came from the new East European members' common history with Russia and the crises over the European Constitution that followed in the spring of 2005. With an even greater diversity of opinions, the EU has found it even harder to build a united front than before the enlargements of 2004 and 2007. Even if the clear wish is for diversification of the EU's energy sources, the EU's front still remains divided. In February 2011 the EU heads of government convened in Brussels in another attempt to move closer together to a united line of action. The goal remained the same as years before: 'We want to have more diversification, more routes, and more regions from which we can import gas', said Günther Oettinger, the Commissioner for Energy. 'To go to the Caspian region is not a policy against Russia. It is a policy for Europe and the Caspian region' (Chaffin, 2011). EU Member States stress the importance of acting together and with common views but at the same time, and again especially in the case of energy policy, they are not ready to transfer executive power over energy policy to the European Commission (Aalto and Westphal, 2007, pp. 2–3; Nalbantoglu, 2006).

Persistent bilateralism in the execution of energy policy leaves Russia a loophole to exploit, and lowers the credibility of the EU as a unitary actor. In addition to the NSGP, another good example can be found in the process of developing the South Stream pipeline project. Bilateral agreements are the pillar of the South Stream project and Russian leadership has worked hard for these. One more example of a bilateral agreement that received much criticism from some of the EU members was that between Gazprom and Italian Eni signed as a 50-50 agreement on South Stream in 2007. Furthermore there have also been increasing bilateral talks between Russian companies and British energy companies. One good example of these is the share swap and cooperation that BP plans to have with Rosneft, announced in January 2011, also subject to a great deal of controversy and complaint (see Chapter 10).

The second milestone was the agreement between Russia and Germany on the NSGP pipeline. From the smaller EU Member States' point of view, both the enlargement of the EU and the Russo-German pipeline agreement have given good cause to rethink their relationships with both the EU and Russia. The EU is and was supposed to be the framework that would give small countries a stronger voice and the chance to have their own views heard. Through the EU smaller states interact with states that can be categorized as great powers, with a wide international agenda. Strengthening the EU's common foreign and security policy is not only a natural goal for small Member States, but is also aspired to because of the strong emphasis the EU places on normative aspects and the role of civilian power (Möttölä, 2006). Both milestone events mentioned above have undermined this.

Enlargement should have been a strengthening factor, and indeed still can be if EU Member States find a workable united line. But if they harbour their own internal suspicions towards the other Member States and cooperation only works when the national interests of all have been taken into account, the EU will become a paralyzed organization that will not keep up with the changing world and so will not be able to provide a wider and stronger framework for its members.

CONCLUSION

The Nord Stream gas pipeline project started as a fairly small scale cooperation project between Finnish and Russian actors, then expanded into a project of European significance acquiring a multilateral dimension and eventually materialized as a bilateral deal between Russia and Germany. As of 2011 the company behind the NSGP (Nord Stream AG) is owned by Gazprom (51 per cent), BASF (15.5 per cent), E.ON Ruhrgas (15.5 per cent), Gasunie (9 per cent) and GDF SUEZ (9 per cent) (Godzimirski, 2010, p. 33). Therefore technically it is not any longer a bilaterally run company. Whatever the format it has created a new dimension to the Russia–EU relationship and kept energy as one of the main subjects in the Russia–EU dialogue. The NSGP project has reawakened questions about the EU's own energy policy and the EU's dependence on Russia for natural gas.

Responses to the NSGP pipeline among EU Member States have largely been conditioned by the respective traditional attitudes in each state towards Russia, raising the prospect of a damaging split between 'old' and 'new' Europe on major issues of foreign, security and energy policy. The three Baltic States and Poland have been most negative in their framings of the project and most open in voicing their suspicions of Russia's interests in using energy for political ends and its alleged 'energy superpower' frames. To some extent the former Eastern bloc countries have it right: '… Russia's plans to diversify its gas supplies to Europe, which would increase the energy security of the Old World, and to abolish Ukraine's gas transit monopoly are about to come true' (Mityayev, 2010). If the NSGP starts functioning by 2012 the 'new' Member States (since 2004) will be dependent, to a certain extent, on the 'old' Member States like Germany in their energy security, just as in the past the 'old' Member States have been (fully) dependent on them and other post-Soviet states further to the East.

The 'old Europe'/'new Europe' split, which is well illustrated by the Nord Stream case study, is one that in some respects reflects different approaches in Russian foreign policy: since the collapse of the Soviet Union, and especially since Putin's first presidency, Russian leaders have regarded the 'near abroad' (that is the former republics of the Soviet Union) as lying within their own sphere of influence. Hence one political advantage of excluding countries like Ukraine from the gas delivery system is that it allows Russia to pursue independent policies on energy supplies with different gas customers. Such a differentiated approach also ties in with the politics of *ressentiment* which, as seen, figures heavily in Russian domestic and foreign policy actions. But even this is to oversimplify the situation. The reality is that a number of Russian interests lie behind the decision to pursue the NSGP. Both Germany and Russia have a clear preference for pursuing bilateral relations with each other, but many other countries and businesses are involved in the NSGP. Russia's business frame also needs to be considered as a secondary, but extremely important, factor. Finally, gas will continue to be a potential foreign policy tool for Russia. The decision to pursue Nord Stream over the objections of several EU Member States has been facilitated by divisions and weaknesses within the EU.

The process of materializing the NSGP project is a very good illustration of how bilateralism and multilateralism play a role in Russian foreign policy, and of how one of the driving forces behind Russian decision-making processes is the politics of *ressentiment*. With business interests added to the picture, we can identify trends in Russian foreign policy behaviour and the preferences it prioritizes. Whatever gas field will be filling the Nord Stream pipes, and whatever the quantity of gas flowing through the pipes, is not as significant for Russians as the very fact that the process happened and the pipeline was built. Both the Danish and the Swedish permits for using their EEZs condition Nord Stream's responsibility for what to do once the pipeline is defunct. The authorities in both countries clearly envisage a relatively short lifespan for the pipeline. Long term or not, viable or not, the Nord Stream gas pipeline project can be viewed as a success for Russia both in foreign policy and in international business cooperation. In other words, the Russian state and Gazprom can work together, and with European and other international partners, and in the process strengthen their actor status. The building of a Baltic Sea pipeline will help to preserve those actor roles on the European interregional front even if the transit routes through the former Soviet territories may become obsolete.

NOTES

1. Note that there have been several oil transit conflicts with Belarus which have had impacts on Europe, in 2004, 2007 and 2008 (see Chapter 7).
2. There are several German interests involved in the NSGP deal: Germany is set to become a supplier of Russian gas to Central and Northern Europe; the German metallurgy industry also gained from the deal, because only Germany possesses the industrial process technology and skilled labour necessary for manufacturing the pipes to the exacting technical specifications required; Germany occupies first place in foreign direct investment in Russia, which eases cooperation with Russia over agreements involving a high level of interdependence of direct German interests.
3. Interviews conducted by the author in 2009.
4. Gasum is owned 31 per cent by Fortum Heat and Gas Oy, 25 per cent by Gazprom, 21 per cent by the Finnish state and 20 per cent by E.ON Ruhrgas International GmbH.

7. Russia's central and eastern European energy transit corridor: Ukraine and Belarus

Margarita M. Balmaceda

INTRODUCTION

This chapter looks at the formation of Russia's energy policies by examining the coexistence, synergy and competition between various frames guiding the behaviour of Russian actors in foreign energy relations. It takes as a case study Russia's energy relationship with its main transit partners, Ukraine and Belarus. In addition to their transit role, these two countries are both heavily dependent on Russia for energy. This is an important element that affects their interaction with Russian players. In addition, their common feature of transit specifically to European markets implies a similar role in the value-added chain of Russian energy actors.

The chapter first briefly presents the prevailing approaches to Russian energy relations with the energy-poor transit states. The second section proposes an alternative explanatory framework for understanding this relationship. The third section applies the model to shed light on important instances of Russian oil and gas policies vis-à-vis Ukraine and Belarus during the period 1994–2010.

CONVENTIONAL EXPLANATIONS AND THEIR LIMITATIONS

Our knowledge of energy relations between Russia and post-Soviet transit states such as Ukraine and Belarus has so far been rather superficial. While this has partially to do with the inherent difficulties of data-gathering in an area marked by lack of transparency, part of the problem may lie in our explanatory frameworks themselves. Conventional knowledge about Russian energy interactions with its energy-poor transit neighbours comes in two main varieties, focusing on the energy superpower and business frames (see Chapter 2).

By focusing on the energy superpower frame we highlight Russia's use of energy as a 'soft power' weapon (see Orban, 2008; Smith, 2008; Goldman, 2008; Bugajski, 2005; Lucas, 2008) and posit that Russian energy relations with its energy-dependent neighbours, including Ukraine and Belarus, have always been about politics, and, more specifically, the advancement of Russian neo-imperialist goals through economic means. Domestically, this frame emphasizes the role of companies such as Gazprom as an instrument of the Russian state. Such 'Russian energy imperialism' makes for high-impact headlines, but exhibits two crucial limitations as an analytical approach. It fails to account for agency and policy differentiation among the recipients of Russian energy, and indeed for differentiation between actors in Russia itself. On the first issue, this conventional frame has approached the states dependent on Russian energy as mostly passive recipients of Russian designs. The crucial role of domestic actors and domestic energy policy-relevant behaviour in these states is as yet unexamined. On the second issue, this frame takes for granted the role of important energy actors such as Gazprom as simply executors of Russian governmental decisions, neglecting the variety of domestic factors affecting Russian energy behaviour. Thus, this frame is not only largely uni-directional, but also largely unidimensional.

On the other hand, focusing on the business frame directs attention to economic rather than political explanations of this relationship. One such explanation remains largely at the theoretical level, urging us to look not so much at the political 'noise' around high-profile energy relationships, but at the structural economic issues inherent in any relationship between energy suppliers, transit states and consumers: monopoly supply, transit monopoly and bargaining. Another variety of this view, widely promoted by the Russian government, argues that – paradoxically as this may at first seem – the re-establishment of state control over the sector starting in 2003 and initiatives towards gas prices based on 'equal profitability' in all its markets since 2004, have meant an increase in transparency in pricing, and a turn away from a more political frame. In this view, decisions by Russian energy actors are about 'just business'. Accordingly, long-term strategic initiatives such as the development of export routes bypassing Ukraine and Belarus are seen as having to do with Gazprom's long-term business interests, and not with a desire to put pressure on these countries to adopt more pro-Russian positions.[1]

Examining business frames provides important insights into Russia's relations with its energy-poor transit neighbours such as Ukraine and Belarus, and helps us place these countries within the larger context of energy-dependent transit states worldwide. However, at both the theoretical and factual levels these frames have serious limitations functioning our main guide to under-standing Russian policies towards its energy-poor neighbours. At a more general level, we should concede that trade is seldom 'just trade', but may be highly politicized depending on the background of the trading partners (see Gowa, 1994). Particularly in the countries of the former Soviet Union (FSU), energy issues remain highly politicized as foreign policy issues. For them, energy is the most sensitive part of trade with Russia, and trade with Russia is not just trade but trade with the former hegemon. The fact that some Russian politicians have at times openly called for the use of energy as a political weapon in this context, and the track record of economic sanctions – such as import bans on specific products under the thin pretext of non-adherence to health and other standards – in response to unwelcome political actions has not helped to create a more trusting atmosphere. As a result, trade in this part of the world cannot be explained solely by considerations of profit. Even if Russian energy policies towards the FSU states were totally depoliticized, the legacies of the past would affect the way these policies are received and interpreted.

At a more factual level, the Russian track record even after 2005 displays continued politicization. This is especially clear in the area of pricing. The argument that Gazprom is simply moving to commercially based 'world market prices' in the form of netback pricing in its gas trade with all former Soviet states loses much of its explanatory power given that, for much of the mid- and late 2000s, various FSU states were paying very different prices for Gazprom gas (see Table 7.1).[2] Even keeping in mind the difficulties in comparing these prices, given varying costs of transit and other conditions, the differences remain significant.

Table 7.1   Pricing of Gazprom's gas to selected FSU states, in US dollars per thousand cubic metres, 2005–10

	Ukraine	Belarus	Lithuania	Moldova	Georgia	Armenia	Border price (July) in Germany
2005	50	55	84	80	65	54.1	220.7
2006	95	55	146	160***	110	91.7	304.4
2007	135	118	220	172[a]	235	110	280.4
2008	179.5	126.8	345	232[a]	235	110	517
2009	232.4*	151	N/A	263[a]	270	154**	244.4
2010	230 (Q2)	170	N/A	252*	280	180**	305 (July)

* Estimated; ** Effective 1 April; *** Effective 1 July; [a] average.

Sources: Armenia and Georgia prices: RFE/RL Armenian service (2010); Belarus: Stern et al. (2010, Table 1, p. 7); Lithuania (2005–07): Janeliunas (2009, p. 206); Moldova (2005–09): National Agency for Energy Regulation (ANRE) and 2010: RosBiznesKonsulting (2011); border price in Germany: Index Mundi; Ukraine prices: IEA (2006a).

AN ALTERNATIVE EXPLANATION: COEXISTING ACTORS, COEXISTING AND COMPETING RATIONALITY FRAMES, AND DISTINCT VALUE CHAINS

To counter the limitations of these conventional explanations, this chapter offers an alternative based on coexisting actors, coexisting and competing rationality frames, and distinct value chains. Within the transit countries dependent on Russian energy, it focuses on domestic actors, including the winners and losers of various ways of organizing the energy dependency and transit relationship with Russia. It also examines the role of these actors in maintaining or challenging certain patterns of energy relations with the largest supplier.

On the Russian side of the question, which is of more direct interest for this chapter, our alternative explanation focuses on how various energy actors' interactions with the state and with actors across borders affect policy-relevant behaviour, mediated by the distinct value chains prevalent in their industries. Below we discuss the two sides of this alternative explanation.

The Energy-poor Transit States as Real, Complex Actors

The main transit states in the export of Russian oil and gas to Western Europe are also some of the states most heavily dependent on Russian energy. This means that any approach used to understand Russia's policies and relationship with these transit states must also take into account these states' significant energy dependence on Russia.

Energy superpower frames have largely concentrated on the ways in which Russia has sought to use these states' energy dependency to pursue certain foreign or commercial policy goals, obscuring consideration of domestic policies and factors. Yet while Russia undeniably uses energy to pursue foreign policy goals, to look at the question solely in terms of Russia's expansion is not enough; it is no less important to look at the domestic conditions that may affect Russia's ability to use energy as a foreign policy tool in specific countries. Domestic institutions, through the way they affect interest intermediation, can affect the ability of domestic players to impose their preferences regarding the organization of energy trade with Russia, including preferences directly or indirectly affecting the continuation of energy dependency. What these preferences actually are has much to do with distributional consequences – that is, the winners and losers of various ways of organizing energy trade – and with the rents of energy dependency that may accrue.[3] Such rents may accrue through local actors on their own or, more often, shared between players on both sides of the border, often at the expense of both states. As will be discussed below, such transborder sharing of rents can have important implications for the management of energy trade and transit conflict.

Sharing the rents of energy dependency constitutes one – but by no means the only – way in which the interests of local actors in the energy-dependent transit states may be linked to those of energy actors in Russia. More generally, the links created by distinct value-added chains provide a crucial connection between the interests of energy actors in Russia and the energy-poor states. We are concerned here with *distinct* value-added chains. They differ significantly between different energy sectors (oil versus gas, for example) and between different sub-sectors and companies.[4] These value-added chains are significant in terms of their length and direction, and in terms of the various sets of local actors they involve. Understanding value-added chains also helps to elucidate the possible interest of various Russian energy actors in cooperating with specific actors in the energy-poor states to access important infrastructure – oil refineries, gas storage facilities, and so on. Such interest may relate to the completion of particular value chains, of which transit relationships are only one example. Value-added chains also connect rent-seeking schemata on both sides of the border. Different Russian energy actors, such as oil and gas companies, have distinct market and value-added chains. This affects the way they will involve actors on the energy-dependent transit country side of the border both in terms of their interactions with their main supplier and of the resulting domestic rent-seeking relationships.

Thus, while not all value-added chains involve corruption, the larger point is that to fully understand the relationship between the energy-poor transit states and Russia, we cannot focus on Russia simply as an external actor. Nor, as will be discussed below, is it productive to focus on Russia as a unitary actor.

A View of the Russian Side as an Interaction of Complex Actors and Actors within Actors

In order to understand de facto Russian policies towards the energy-poor transit states, it makes sense to focus on issues such as coexisting parallel rationalities, coexisting actors, and distinct value chains. Nowhere are these issues seen more clearly than in the case of Gazprom. The hypothesis central to the 'just business' frame of Gazprom as acting mainly on the basis of corporate economic profit is challenged on the one hand by the intermingling of political and business frames in its relationship with the state, discussed below, and, on the other, by the existence of significant private interests within the corporation, especially in the early 2000s, but also today. Yet these very elements also seriously undermine any explanation based on the energy superpower and imperialism frames. Below we take a brief look at how the interaction between these elements played out in practice.

Intermingling of Political and Economic Frames in Gazprom's Relationship with the State

As in the case of the energy-dependent states, domestic institutional issues are crucial for understanding Russia's external energy behaviour, as they affect the ability of domestic actors to indulge their preferences regarding the organization of external energy relations. Nowhere has this issue called for more attention than in the case of relations between the state and Russia's largest energy company, Gazprom.

The question of Russian state influence over Gazprom or Gazprom's influence over state policy is complex and longstanding, and by no means unidirectional. Continuing tensions between Gazprom's dual roles – fulfilling both important domestic and external, economic and political roles – has been an important driving force in Russian energy behaviour. While on the one hand the Russian state has relied on Gazprom the economic player as an important source of foreign revenue and other budget contributions, it has also relied on the company to accomplish a number of broader political and social tasks. These include both domestic (providing social services, helping maintain social stability through low energy prices) and foreign-oriented tasks (helping to manage the relationship with Russia's energy-poor neighbours, among others). These two goals have often been at odds.

One example of this conflict has to do with differing understandings of Gazprom's desirable role in domestic energy supply. Crucial to Gazprom's domestic role has been its large-scale supply of gas to residential consumers at subsidized prices, as well as to electricity generating plants. This has helped to keep electricity prices low. Here we encounter the issue of how much gas Gazprom should supply at home at subsidized prices and, thus, how much it has available for export.

We also encounter the diversity of interests concerning Gazprom's role and the impact of this diversity on relations with the energy-poor transit states. There has also been a large gap between energy prices in Russia's domestic and international markets. This has affected the relationship with Russia's energy-poor neighbours by helping to shape the incentives for selling domestically or exporting (see Table 7.2).

In November 2006, the Russian government announced that domestic gas prices would gradually increase so as to reach European 'netback levels' by 2011 (see note 2). According to the plan, between 2007–11 gas prices for industrial and household users would increase 40 per cent.[5] By 2011 domestic gas prices for industry would be on a level guaranteeing equal profitability *(ravnaia dokhodnost)* of foreign and domestic sales.[6] Yet it soon became clear that, in order to realize this goal, the actual increases would need to be much more significant than 40 per cent, as European gas and oil prices continued to

Table 7.2   Average gas sale prices by Gazprom to domestic, CIS/Baltic and European markets (excluding export taxes and customs duties), 2003–06, in US dollars per thousand cubic metres

	2003	2004	2005	2006
Average (industrial and household) Russian domestic gas tariffs (prices)	22	28	33	40
Average selling price for CIS/Baltic	34.40	36.33	50.02	76.37
Average selling price for Europe	95.72	101.61	140.09	192.59

Note: Average selling prices for CIS/Baltic do not include taxes and customes duties.

Sources: CIS/Baltic and Europe from Stern (2009, Table 12.1, p. 396); domestic gas prices from IEA (2006b, p. 42).

soar. After much debate on the possible economic and social consequences of increases in domestic prices larger than originally planned, in March 2010 the target price parity date was postponed to 2014.

The issue of domestic versus export prices also affected the relationship between Russia and the energy-poor states through its effects on these states' understanding of the relationship and the frames through which it was viewed. This connection became especially clear in the case of Belarus, which for most of the period 1994–2010 claimed a right to domestic Russian gas prices stemming from its special relationship with Russia and where Russia's differentiated pricing practices played an important role. Without a difference between domestic and export prices there would simply be no reason for Belarus to insist on paying 'domestic Russian prices'.[7]

Coexisting and Competing Rationality Frames: 'Convertible Points', Gazprom-state Relations and Energy Relations with the Energy-poor Transit States

The issue of prices is illustrative of a larger issue: that Gazprom's interests as a corporation and those of state have not always been compatible. Indeed, it is fair to ask why Gazprom would choose to forego the large profits implied in exports to Western markets in favour of domestic sales, especially when export revenue is crucial to Gazprom as a means to compensate for low domestic gas prices and preferential price deliveries to former Soviet republics (see also Chapter 10). One possible explanation is that the company has simply been forced to do so by the state. A better way to look at this, however, is through the prism of the tension and complementarity between Gazprom's various roles, as the company, while losing revenue from the opportunity cost of not exporting to higher-paying Western European markets, also benefited from its subsidization of domestic consumers. From Gazprom's corporate perspective, the goal of profit maximization through exports to Western Europe coexisted – and at times collided with – the goal of fostering good relations with the state through the provision of various services. It is exactly the provision of such services that largely explains the state's support for Gazprom's monopoly role.

The concept of 'convertible points' provides a useful tool for understanding both the relationship between Gazprom and the Russian state and between the more political and business frames in Gazprom's behaviour. Although the Russian state may not be able to dictate to Gazprom what corporate policies to pursue, the company may find it useful to follow state and/or presidential preferences anyway, as services provided can help the company to accumulate 'points' with the Russian state. In addition to the domestic-level services discussed earlier, beyond-the-border services have included helping to manage the relationship with Russia's neighbouring states by supplying gas to energy-poor neighbours at preferential prices, or tolerating repeated non-payment on their part.

So although Gazprom (and other companies) lost potential profits by selling gas to Belarus or Ukraine at preferential prices, they accumulated informal 'points' with the Russian state, 'points' which could be later 'converted' into advantages in other areas. How these virtual points were transferred from the foreign policy realm to the domestic arena and eventually converted into monetary benefits varied from sector to sector and case to case. In the gas sector, the conversion often took place informally through access to credits, the setting of gas prices, and the granting of privileges in privatization contracts and other investment opportunities.

One of the most important benefits derived by Gazprom in exchange for services provided was a not directly monetary one, rather support for its continued monopoly role despite pressure from international corporations to break up the company.[8] This monopoly role has constituted, in turn, the central feature of Russia's gas-related political economy, and has been crucial to the relationship with its energy-poor neighbours. Since the late 2000s, Gazprom has controlled more than two-thirds of Russia's gas reserves and over 80 per cent of Russia's gas production. As the owner of the unified system of gas supplies Gazprom has been able to dictate terms to independent gas producers and control all gas exports. Moreover, in addition to its export monopoly role inherited from the Soviet Ministry of Gas Industry (and enshrined in the Law on Gas Exports in 2006),[9] the company has also deliberately blocked new players from entering the domestic market, in particular independent gas

producers. Only in spring 2011 did the Russian government start procedures
for opening pipeline access to these companies.

With Gazprom a gas export monopolist, the energy-dependent states found
themselves at a great disadvantage, not being able to play different producers
off against each other. In addition, Gazprom's active role in obstructing the
operations of other gas producers has prevented them not only from becoming
alternative suppliers, but also alternative voices to be reckoned with in the
Russian energy policy-making process. Gazprom's gas export monopoly has
also increased the Russian state's potential ability to use these exports for
political ends. However, as will be discussed below, Gazprom's monopoly has
also had more complex effects, especially on energy trade schemes and transborder rent-seeking alliances.

The relationship between Gazprom and the state is hence two-sided. On the
one hand, 2001's easing out of Rem Viakhirev as Chairman of Gazprom's
board and his replacement by Aleksei Miller strengthened the state's formal
role in the company. These gains were consolidated after October 2004, when
the state gained control over 50 per cent of Gazprom's shares, as well as a
majority of the seats on its board of directors, ensuring it a direct say in the
company's most important decisions. At the same time, the company has
successfully repelled repeated attempts to make it accept its full tax liability,
which shows its power vis-à-vis parts of the state apparatus.

Personal Interests within Gazprom

When describing the relationship between Gazprom and the state in the
section above, the picture presented was one based on a simplified view of the
company pursuing corporate interests, and the state pursuing state interests.
Yet looking at the company as an amalgam of three different sets of interests:
state, corporate and personal yields a more realistic picture of the institutional
dimension of Russia's transit politics. While most obvious in the case of
Gazprom, this coexistence of interests can also be expected in other Russian
energy companies with important state participation, such as Rosneft (see also
Chapter 2; cf. Chapter 9). Most prominently at issue have been personal interests within the corporation, which have frequently been pursued separately
from the company's corporate interests. Some of the ways in which these
personal interests have manifested themselves have been through the misuse
of corporate property for the pursuit of private profit with individuals
allegedly helping set up murky intermediary companies.

Role of Intermediary Companies

Intermediary companies were originally developed as a means to facilitate the barter of Turkmenistan gas for Russian products at a time of severe liquidity constraints in the mid-1990s. Their growth was facilitated by the intermingling of state, corporate and personal interests in Gazprom, as well as by the company's dominant role in Central Asian gas markets. Good relations with Gazprom allowed intermediary companies such as Itera to produce or buy gas at especially low prices; in particular, Gazprom sold gas to Itera at below market 'internal transfer' prices (thus minimizing taxes), gas which was subsequently exported at a higher price. Itera was able to do this because, in contrast to Gazprom, it operated outside formal state-to-state agreements, was not subject to price ceilings, and could sell gas to countries such as Ukraine for prices higher than those charged by Gazprom. With the acquiescence of important players in each of the countries involved, Itera and related companies were able to divert significant profits from both Gazprom and the importing countries by charging high prices for services such as 'arranging transit' – this benefited not only Itera itself but, it has been argued, members of Gazprom's top management as well (see Guillet, 2002; Hermitage Capital Management, 2005, p. 4 cited in Global Witness, 2006, p. 35). The best-known incidents of asset-stripping to the detriment of Gazprom but to the benefit of intermediary companies probably concern Itera, but the case is hardly unique. Numerous similar examples exist of situations where formally state-owned companies have been used by some of their top managers for the pursuit of personal interests.[10]

The important role played by intermediary companies has had significant effects on Russian gas relations with the CIS, especially Ukraine. Seen from the perspective of the energy-poor states, intermediary companies especially active in the trade in gas with Central Asia offered the promise of paving the way to geographical and contractual diversification. However, the excessive fees and conditions they imposed – perks the companies possibly received due to the improper use of their political influence – in reality weakened state companies and the budget, for the benefit of their own enrichment.

The misuse of corporate property for the pursuit of private profit through companies such as Itera also impacted on the energy-poor states' policy environment by affecting the pressures and rent-seeking opportunities experienced by domestic actors, giving some of them new incentives to engage in corruption.[11] The fact that intermediary companies provided actors in both Russia and the energy-poor states with important rent-seeking opportunities is proof that they cannot be seen as benefiting the Russian side alone. Their multifaceted role in the energy-poor states, is, significantly, directly related to Gazprom's internal organization and domestic role. Paradoxical as this may at first seem, it was Gazprom's de facto monopolization of the post-Soviet gas trade which gave Gazprom – or, more likely, influential players within it – the leverage to sway local actors into accepting such intermediary companies.

With privileged access to proprietary information on gas flows, as the sole regulator of the export pipeline, and with a 'relatively costless and effortless way of hiding its profits' (Weinthal and Loung, 2006, p. 235), Gazprom's managers were able to effectively present their preferred schemes as alternatives to the company's monopoly.[12] In other words, these monopoly and gatekeeping powers held by Gazprom as a corporation gave individual actors within it the perfect conditions to create artificial scarcities that could then be turned into rent-seeking opportunities.[13]

At the same time, the issue of personal interests within the corporation cannot be wholly separated from Gazprom's relationship with the state or political elites close to the Kremlin, which often benefited from the murkiness inherent in Gazprom's amalgamation of interests. Thus the maintenance of Gazprom's monopoly privileges is best understood as being related not only to its provision of important domestic services, but also to the lack of transparency in the company which enabled its economic resources to be transformed into a little-regulated source of revenue. This revenue could later be used by the Russian leadership with little independent control. The connection between Gazprom's monopoly role and lack of transparency in the company also helps to make sense of the apparent contradiction discussed in Chapter 1 of this book, namely that implied in the coexistence of '[T]erms portraying Russia as an "energy superpower", "energy giant", "petro-state" (…) and, on the other end of the spectrum, a possible "Dutch disease" or "resource curse" in Russia' (see Chapter 1).

The coexistence of state, corporate and personal interests within Gazprom had other important effects on the energy-poor states. First, the coexistence of these multiple interests added a variety of unofficial but real actors in negotiations between Russia and each of these states. Second, Gazprom's own lack of transparency, lack of clear corporate governance, and merging of personal, corporate and state interests in its management impaired the company's ability to act coherently with the energy-poor states.

Constraints on Russian Actors' use of Energy for Foreign Policy Goals

The coexistence of state, corporate and personal interests within the corporation in companies such as Gazprom also shows that a multitude of pressures and influences affect foreign energy policy relevant behaviour by Russian energy actors. This implies an important limitation to how the energy superpower frames can explain Russia's behaviour in the FSU. If, indeed, energy can be used as a political weapon, it can also be used for other purposes, with these various ways of using energy often in competition with each other.

Energy actors in Russia with control over energy resources – producers, regulators, and transit monopolists such as Transneft – are constantly making choices about where to use or direct these energy resources. These choices occur along several dimensions (see Chapter 2). Along the resource geographic, financial and institutional dimensions, the main choices revolve around whether these resources will be used domestically (see also Chapter 4) or externally. When introducing the financial dimension into the picture, energy can be used or traded in a spectrum ranging from sale in open markets to trade under various special deals, to political use in domestic and foreign directions. And as noted, as a scarce commodity with great potential for arbitrage gains, of course, energy resources can also be used as a means of personal economic gain.

Within this framework, the use of energy to exert direct external economic pressure on Russia's post-Soviet neighbours is only one among several options. While in practice the dividing lines between these choices are more blurred than they appear on paper, each of these ways of using energy implies different incentive structures for the players involved. These decisions, in turn, are not made in a vacuum, but in the context of the interplay of factors such as the desire for profit maximization (at state, company or personal level) given certain value-added chains, maintenance of markets or political influence in an area, and relationships with the Russian state and actors within it. As discussed in Chapter 2 of this book, the frames used by energy players may change quickly as a result of specific events or changes in political relationships, but value-added chains based on technological processes, many of them inherited from the Soviet Union, change more slowly.[14]

COMPLEX ACTORS, RENTS AND INTERESTS INTERACTING ACROSS BORDERS: EXAMPLES FROM UKRAINE AND BELARUS

The next question to be addressed in this chapter is: how have the mechanisms and interests discussed above manifested themselves specifically in the case of relations with the transit states Ukraine and Belarus?

Gas: Ukraine 1994–2004

When looking at energy, and especially gas relations between Ukraine and Russia between 1994 and 2004, we can see the predominance of politically loaded frames, plus an important role of private interests within the corporations on both sides.

On the Russian side, a broad political–institutional frame was predominant. This was related, at the state level, not only to the desire to affect concrete Ukrainian actions – such as in the 1993 and 1995 attempts to gain significant

control over the Black Sea Fleet – but also to the Russian elite's general desire
to exert continuing influence in the post-Soviet area, including over Ukraine.
This desire for continuing influence contributed to the maintenance of barter
and other murky multiple-pricing schemes. This softened the impact of the
worsening terms of energy trade on Russia's resource-poor neighbours, but
conflicted with a business frame. At the same time, this coincided with the
increased importance of Ukraine's transit and storage facilities in Gazprom's
corporate level value-added chain for growing exports to Western Europe.

These frames dovetailed nicely with the priorities observable on the
Ukrainian side. During this period, Ukrainian leaders sought to buffer the
shock of deteriorating external energy conditions through both political
arrangements and specific ways of organizing the gas trade. This laid the country open to a particular combination of political-institutional frames accompanied by private interests within the corporations on both sides. How did this
combination manifest itself?

In terms of political arrangements, what was most important during this
period was the 1997 Black Sea Fleet agreement giving Russia control of most
of the fleet in exchange for writing off gas-related debt.[15] Further, despite
frequent friction between the sides – especially concerning suspected
Ukrainian stealing of Russian gas from the export pipeline and related doubts
about Ukraine's reliability as a transit state – trade terms relatively beneficial
to Ukraine in the short term were applied. In particular, the Russian side
agreed to keep gas prices unchanged despite pressure from increasing
European prices, as a means of showing support for President Kuchma and his
candidate Viktor Yanukovich in the run-up to the 2004 election. These low
prices, however, were compensated for by extremely low (by international
comparison) transit and storage fees which Ukraine charged Russia (see Pavel
and Chukhai, 2006; IEA, 2006a, p. 213; Energy Charter Secretariat, 2006, pp.
63–4).

Whether intentionally or not, some of the trade mechanisms supposed to
protect Ukrainian end-users against high prices also served to foster the role
of corruption and private interests within the corporation.[16] In particular, the
organization of energy (especially gas) imports from Russia on a barter basis
during this period was conducive to a lack of transparency and accountability
in the relationship.[17] In addition, the important role of intermediary companies
in Ukraine's energy imports from other suppliers was one manifestation of the
growing role of personal interests. Although technically not directly related to
Russia – as such intermediary companies were originally developed as a
means to facilitate the barter of Turkmen gas for Ukrainian goods – their
growth, as discussed above, was facilitated by the merging of state, corporate,
and personal interests in Gazprom, as well as by the company's dominant role
in Central Asian gas markets. With the acquiescence of important players in

each of the countries involved, companies such as Itera, EuralTransGas and RosUkrEnergo were able to divert significant profits from both Gazprom and Ukraine by charging high prices – from 37.5 (RosUkrEnergo) to 41 per cent (Itera) of the gas supplied from Turkmenistan – for services such as '"arranging transit" that could have been easily provided by Ukraine's NAK Naftohaz itself, leading to significant loss of revenue for both NAK Naftohaz and Gazprom' (Balmaceda, 2010, p. 92).

Gas: the January 2006 Ukrainian–Russian Agreements

Ukrainian–Russian gas relations changed radically in January 2006 with the move to cash payments instead of barter, and Ukraine stopping direct purchases from Gazprom, as all gas purchases came to be managed by the intermediary company RosUkrEnergo. However, the coexistence of political, business and private interests within the corporation continued. Poor state-to-state relations following Viktor Yuschenko's accession to power facilitated this by opening the space – in a similar way as Gazprom's monopoly had before – for intermediary companies involving the participation of Gazprom, as well as private interests within the corporation in NAK Naftohaz Ukraine, to emerge as last-minute 'saviours'.

The agreements of 4 January 2006 gave RosUkrEnergo an even larger role than before as intermediary in the import of Turkmenistan gas.[18] This serves as a prime example of how, as also seen in other aspects of the Ukrainian–Russian relationship, conflict between the sides often came to be resolved through the transborder sharing of rents between elites, using new types of informal institutions such as intermediary companies rather than through the use of formal governance mechanisms.[19] If such practices may be compatible with a business frame, then it is only in a very unusual sense of the term, as the profit interests involved would be those of personal players within the corporation, and not those of the corporation as such.

Through its own perverse value-added chain, the misuse of corporate property, ties, and insider knowledge for the pursuit of private gain through intermediary companies such as RosUkrEnergo, affected the Ukrainian policy-making environment by expanding the rent-seeking opportunities available to local actors. A caveat must be noted, however. The examples discussed above indicate that in order to fully understand post-Soviet energy relations it is crucial to have an understanding of the role of personal interests within the corporation – including corruption – in both business and energy superpower approaches. Note therefore that other interpretations are possible concerning the interrelationship between these two frames. For example, it has been argued that intermediary companies and the associated corruption opportunities could be part of a Russian political strategy to undermine Ukrainian resolve to deal with its dependency on Russia (see Balmaceda, 2006a; D'Anieri, 2006).

Gas: the April 2010 Ukrainian–Russian Agreements

The April 2010 agreements – providing for a 30 per cent gas price reduction in exchange for a 25-year extension on the lease of the Sevastopol Black Sea Fleet naval base to Russia – clearly show the limits of business frames in explaining the dynamics of Russian–Ukrainian energy relations. The agreements seemed to reflect a temporary coincidence between political interests in the case of Russia, and domestic economic interests in the case of Ukraine. The latter manifest themselves at three levels: short-term survival of the Ukrainian economy, survival of NAK Naftohaz, and the economic interests of specific influential groups within Ukraine, first and foremost those of energy-intensive metallurgical producers who emerge as winners given the export advantages created by reduced energy prices. The interests of the Firtash group associated with Dmytro Firtash, the main Ukrainian owner of gas trader RosUkrEnergo, are also likely to be strengthened by the agreements, although this link remains much less clear.[20] Despite losing its central role in Ukrainian gas trade policy in 2009, this group gained control of crucial positions in the Yanukovich cabinet.

The actual details of the April 2010 agreement are important. They prove that, seen from the Russian side, despite the largely political motivation for the agreements, very important elements of the business frame are still present. Thus, for example, although the agreements provide for a significant price discount for gas, the underlying trend towards netback pricing continues, remaining the base price used in calculations (that is, before discount). However, the 2010 agreements re-emphasize the positive political aspects rather than the highly onerous January 2009 agreements, signed by then Prime Minister Tymoshenko, which moved the relationship to a commercial basis.

In addition, despite the largely political motivation of the April 2010 agreements, the main contours of most Russian actors' energy strategy in Europe as a whole imposes serious limitations on how far politically-motivated concessions to Ukraine can go and what forms they could take. For example, despite the political commitment represented by the agreements, Gazprom's export diversification projects and strategy of building new pipelines that would side-step the transit countries altogether – the result, among other factors, of repeated transit disputes with Ukraine and Belarus in the early and mid-2000s – is set to continue. Of these new pipelines, Nord Stream is already well advanced, with its second branch set to be completed in 2012. This delimits the level of commitment Gazprom can make on new investments in Ukraine's gas transit system.[21] This lack of motivation for significant investment in

Ukraine's transit system coincides, however, with a continued interest in Ukraine as a large and solvent (or potentially solvent) market.[22]

Oil and gas: Russian–Belarusian Gas and Oil Rent Sharing, 2000–06

In the case of post-Soviet Russian energy relations with Belarus, both politically loaded and business frames have also been present, although in a somewhat different combination. The general nature of Russian energy policy towards Belarus has been related, not only to Russia's general interest in maintaining a presence in the post-Soviet area, but to the fact that, since 1995, Belarus and Russia have been in the process, at least officially, of building a single state.[23] In particular, this affected gas policy where, starting in 2002, Belarus was offered gas at domestic prices.[24] Yet economic issues, especially value-added considerations involving Gazprom as a corporate player, were also part of this process, and indeed crucial to its unravelling. With transit through Belarus crucial to Gazprom's exports and value-added process, the expectation of Belarus' full collaboration, both in supporting the swift completion of the Yamal pipeline and in allowing Gazprom a degree of ownership control over the state gas transit company Beltransgas, was an indispensable condition for this arrangement. When Belarus's foot-dragging on both issues became clear in 2004, the agreement was cancelled (see Balmaceda, 2006b).

Russian policies on oil during this period (much less directly controlled by the Russian state than it would be after 2004) were based on a combination of political concessions and an important role for private actors. This became clear through the absolutely unique system of sharing oil rents between both countries during the period 1999–2006 (and, in a milder form, 2007–09). During this period, Belarus received Russian oil at lower than market prices, and refined it at large profits. This was because the export of oil products was conducted at world market prices, which were constantly on the increase, while the increase in prices charged to Belarus was much more gradual. The International Monetary Fund (IMF) estimated this additional yearly benefit as being to the order of 2–3 per cent of GDP in the mid-2000s (IMF, 2005, p. 9). At the same time, the value-added-chain interests of individual Russian oil sector actors played an important role. The abolition of customs barriers made it possible for Russian companies to embark on advantageous schemes refining oil in Belarus to avoid taxes and export duties levied by Russia, making Belarus an important part of these companies' value-added chain.

At the same time, the importance of the more political frame in this area was seen clearly, not only through the actual concessions provided, but also through the high politicization and low level of de facto institutionalization of the agreements. Thus, for example, between 1995 and the early 2007 oil trade crisis all export duties on refined oil went to Belarus. This seemed to be in clear violation of agreements signed by both countries, in particular the 1995 Agreement on a Customs Union, stating that both states would impose the same customs duties on third countries and that the proceeds from export duties would be divided on a 85–15 basis, with the lion's share going to Russia (see Balmaceda, 2010, p. 27).

Oil and Gas: the End of Preferential Treatment for Belarus, 2007–10?

The next issue to assess is how the coexistence of political and business frames manifested itself after the December 2006–January 2007 gas and oil crisis involving both countries. Note here that in late 2006, in the negotiation of prices for 2007, Gazprom started to propose prices as high as US$200 per thousand cubic metres, an almost four-fold increase. This was accompanied by an even more dire confrontation in the oil trade, where, effective 1 January 2007, Russia decided to eliminate the oil export tax preferences in place since 1995. This confrontation led to the brief suspension of Russian oil supplies to several EU countries.

Although the main justification on the Russian side for tightened conditions in oil and gas reflected a business framing of the relationship, actual developments over the following three years reveal the de facto primacy of the political frame. After the confrontation, a gradual transition to a new system of shared oil re-export rents was arranged.[25] Regarding gas, Russia softened the blow by offering a gradual transition to world prices. Belarus became the first post-Soviet state to be offered a gradual transition to European gas prices. According to the December 2006 agreement, gas prices paid by Belarus would be equivalent to 67 per cent of European prices in 2008 (that is, prices to Poland, not counting additional transit costs); in 2009 they would be 80 per cent, and in 2010 they would be 90 per cent, before moving to full European prices in 2011 (IPM, 2007, p. 2). In reality, however, prices charged to Belarus throughout October 2008 remained well below this price formula, for example, reaching US$127.9 per thousand cubic metres in the second quarter of 2008, when European (Polish) prices had reached US$340 (a 67 per cent share would amount to US$220).[26]

In 2010, however, relations deteriorated again, with a new crisis in June 2010 sparked by allegations of unpaid Belarusian debts. Gazprom threatened to suspend supplies should the accumulated debt not be paid in full. After a warning 30 per cent reduction in supplies and Belarus's payment in full of the amount owed, full supplies were restored and the crisis narrowly averted. This latest confrontation came in the wake of President Alexander Lukashenko's refusal to recognize the independence of Abkhazia and North Ossetia, and was followed by an unprecedented cooling of relations, including a virulent Russian PR campaign against Lukashenko.[27]

These examples make clear the main point of Belarusian–Russian energy relations during this period: that both the actual softening of the agreed price increases in 2009 and the sharpening of conditions in 2010 were the result of largely political rather than business considerations. That 2010 saw a hardening of gas trade conditions with Belarus at the same time as a softening of positions towards Ukraine is also evidence of the importance of political elements in framing these relationships.

CONCLUSION

Were political or business frames more relevant in Russia's energy policies towards the energy-poor transit states? The evidence presented in this chapter illustrates the need to move beyond a view of Russian energy policies based primarily on either political energy superpower ('energy as a weapon') or business type frames. What we see in reality is a complex interrelationship between the two. Most importantly, our cases have shown that in addition to the frames held by decision-makers, it is also crucial to consider the relationship between the actors. This entails examining the relationship between Gazprom and the Russian state at the domestic or national level, while simultaneously looking at interregional relations across borders, and at the interest, influence and value-added chains creating tensions and competition – but also synergies and at times collusion – in their relationship. Thus, rather than focusing narrowly on Russian energy policy, it may make more sense to think in terms of a variety of Russian energy actors' policy-relevant actions and their relationships with actors across borders.

NOTES

1. Among these initiatives, the most important have been, in oil, the Baltic Pipeline System (BPS-1, commissioned in 2001, and BPS-2, due for completion by 2012) developing Russia's capacity to ship oil from Russian Baltic Sea ports, thus saving unnecessary transshipment through Butinge (Lithuania) or Ventspils (Latvia). In gas, the main initiatives have been the Yamal Pipeline through Belarus and Poland (inaugurated in 2004), the Nord Stream pipeline connecting Russian gas fields with Germany (completion scheduled for 2010–11) and the South Stream pipeline (completion scheduled for 2015).
2. Netback pricing refers to the replacement value of gas (based on the price of competing fuels, in particular fuel oil) at the delivery point. The basic rationale behind netback pricing is the desire to achieve a level of pricing that ensures equal levels of financial return on export operations to different markets or countries.
3. The concept of 'rents' of energy dependency refers to the significant profits that under some circumstances can be wrung from a situation of energy dependency by economic groups within a country. Large energy-related rents may seem obvious in the case of energy-rich countries such as Russia, but counter-intuitive in a situation of energy dependency. Yet, energy can be a very lucrative business for local actors in the dependent country itself – from

profits made by intermediaries to mark-ups imposed on monopolized markets to outright stealing from the state, especially in situations where corruption is widespread.

4. 'On oil and gas' distinct market and value chains and their effects on local actors, see Balmaceda (2010, pp. 43–5).

5. It must be noted, however, that this initiative was not so much about a deregulation of gas prices, but about a 'regulated transition to higher prices'; see Mitrova (2009, p. 36).

6. On the significant methodological difficulties of calculating 'equal profitability' gas prices, see Stern (2009, pp. 73–4).

7. This issue came to affect the Russian–Belarusian relationship most immediately after 2007. According to the gas agreements of 31 December 2006, by 2011 Belarus should pay 100 per cent of the Polish price minus the difference in transportation costs. This was interpreted on the Belarusian side as valid as long as Belarus and Russia were moving simultaneously to netback prices by 2011. But when Russia announced a delayed timeline, Belarus considered this sufficient reason for new negotiations on the issue and for delaying the applicable price increases.

8. As stated by the International Energy Agency, 'it is the system of subsidized prices to Russian gas consumers principally that maintains Gazprom's dominant position' (IEA, 2002b, p. 145).

9. While Gazprom has enjoyed a de facto monopoly on exports since the Soviet period, its monopoly was given legal status in 2006 when a law was passed giving Gazprom's arm Gazprom Export a legal monopoly on exports. Article 3 of the law confers this monopoly on the owner of the UGSS transit network, that is, as of 2008 Gazprom and Gazprom Export (see Stern, 2009c, p. 91).

10. The relationship between Itera and the formal Gazprom management has changed throughout the years, with a significant decline after 2003. While direct evidence of this link has not been brought to light, indirect evidence has been presented, among others by Guillet (2002) and Global Witness (2006).

11. It has been argued that intermediary companies and the associated corruption opportunities were part of a Russian strategy to undermine Ukrainian resolve to deal with its energy dependency on Russia (see Balmaceda, 2006a; D'Anieri, 2006).

12. As most likely happened during the January 2006 negotiations involving Ukraine's Naftohaz, Gazprom, and the intermediary company RosUkrEnergo (see Chalii, 2009).

13. On the intentional creation of artificial scarcities as a means of rent-seeking, see Buchanan (1980).

14. This does not mean, however, that they cannot change at all, as seen in the example of changes expected as a result of the lower relative price and widespread use of LNG technology.

15. As part of the 1997 Black Sea Fleet agreements on the division of the fleet on an equal basis, Ukraine received, in exchange for a 20-year contract leasing Black Sea Fleet bases in the Crimea to Russia at a reduced rate, a US$526 million relief on its debt to Gazprom, plus a further US$200 million debt relief in connection with the 1992 transfer of nuclear weapons to Russia; a subsequent agreement gave Russia an additional share in the fleet in exchange for additional energy debt relief, bringing the Russian total to 81.5 per cent of the Black Sea Fleet (see Balies et al., 2003, p. 39; Molchanov, 2002, pp. 232–3).

16. Whether the main purpose of such measures was to protect Ukrainian end users against high prices, or to create opportunities for rent-seeking is a separate issue; see Balmaceda (2010).

17. For most of the period between 1994 and 2005 much of the gas imported from Russia was, although nominally priced in US dollars, paid for mainly through the barter of transit services.

18. If in the previous period intermediary companies had been responsible only for the transit of Central Asian gas to Ukraine, as a result of the January 2006 agreements they (RosUkrEnergo) came to control the organization of Ukraine's gas imports as a whole.

19. For a discussion of the transborder sharing of corrupt rents through intermediary trader RosUkrEnergo as a means to resolve the 2006 Russian–Ukrainian gas confrontation, see Balmaceda (2010).

20. Although it is not immediately clear how the interests of the Firtash group will be affected

by the April 2010 agreements, there is at least one instance where its close connections with the Yanukovich government are assumed to have led to significant benefits for the groups: the June 2010 ruling by the Stockholm Arbitrage Court ordering the Ukrainian government to return to RosUkrEnergo some US$5.4 billion for gas illegally taken from the company. In this instance, many Ukrainian commentators suspect that the new leadership of NAK Naftohaz consciously decided to take a passive position in the trial, making it impossible for a decision against RosUkrEnergo to be taken.

21. Although Gazprom has repeatedly claimed that the volumes to be transited through Nord Stream constitute new volumes, the point is that there is little reason to believe that any additional volumes would be coming through the Ukrainian transit system. On the contrary, should this pipeline project materialize by 2012, even without a reduction in transit through Ukraine, the country's share of Russian gas exports could decline from 73.22 per cent in 2008 to 65.64 per cent in 2012; see *UkraineAnalysen* 50/09 (27 January, 2009) Graph 3; Table 1 (source: Forschungstelle Osteuropa, University of Bremen). These figures refer to Ukraine's share of gas export pipelines, volume *capacity*, not in terms of *actual transit*, which may be different. Completion of the proposed South Stream pipeline, whose capacity, according to the South Stream Consortium's CEO, is expected to grow from some 10–15 bcm by 2016 up to 60 bcm by 2019–20 (Kramer, 2011) would further reduce Ukraine's role in Russia's gas exports.

22. If this statement seems counter-intuitive at first, given Ukraine's chronic problems in paying for gas imports since 2005, it is worth keeping in mind that some sub-sectors of this market, such as domestic distribution for sales to industrial users, may be especially profitable; direct access to payment-able domestic gas consumers has been a priority in Gazprom's strategy in Europe since the mid-1990s.

23. While much in these agreements was only 'virtual integration', they still had important symbolic value, and created the basis for closer cooperation in military and strategic areas. This proceeded much more successfully, and gave the parties – especially Belarus – special expectations in their energy relationship. On the early contradictions in the integration process, see Balmaceda (1999).

24. Prices equal to those paid by a comparatively located area of Russia (Smolensk) were offered for a preset volume of yearly supplies.

25. After originally insisting on accruing 100 per cent of the oil export duties, on 10 January, Russia agreed to a gradual transition regarding the way export duties for Russian oil refined in Belarus would be shared: in 2007, 70 per cent for Russia and 30 per cent for Belarus, in 2008, 80 per cent and 20 per cent, in 2009, 85 and 15 per cent, and 100 per cent to Russia starting in 2010.

26. The Belarusian economist Leonid Zlotnikov confirmed that in 2008 the price formula was not applied and estimated the agreement-based price would have been some US$200–220 per thousand cubic metres (Zlotnikov, 2007).

27. The real motivation for the June 2010 confrontation remains unclear. However, as was later revealed, Gazprom owed more to Beltransgas for transit services than Beltransgas to Gazprom.

8. Russia's energy policy in the Far East and East Siberia

Shinichiro Tabata and Xu Liu[1]

INTRODUCTION

Russian oil and gas development policies have attached great importance to oil and natural gas development in the Russian Far East and East Siberia.[2] The Russian initiatives seem to have three objectives: along the resource geographic dimension of energy policy formation, exploitation of oil and gas fields replacing those in West Siberia; along the financial dimension, diversification of Russia's oil and gas exports or increase in exports to the East Asian market (for a definition of the dimensions, see Chapter 2); and the wider objective of economic growth in the Far East and East Siberia. These initiatives represent an eastward shift in Russian oil and gas development. This chapter examines the formation of concrete policies adopted to achieve these aims, the results of these policies so far, and problems expected in the future implementation of these policies.

RUSSIA'S AIMS FOR THE EASTWARD SHIFT

Exploitation of Oil and Gas Fields Replacing West Siberian Fields

One of the most serious challenges for Russian oil and gas production is to develop new oil and gas fields, because production in the West Siberian fields, the centre of Russian oil and gas exploitation, has been projected to stagnate in the near future. A possible alternative is the oil and gas fields in the East Siberian and Far Eastern regions.

In Russia, the centre of oil production since the mid-1970s has been West Siberia (Tyumen' *oblast*). Since the mid-1980s the share of Tyumen' in Russia's oil output has been 65–70 per cent (see Table 8.1). According to the 'Energy Strategy of Russia in the Period until 2030', which was approved by the Russian government in November 2009 (Government of the Russian Federation, 2009a), oil production in Tyumen' will soon reach its peak and the

Table 8.1 Crude oil production in East Siberia and the Far East, 1970–2030

	1970	1980	1985	1990	1995	2000	2005	2006	2007	2008	2009	2010	2013–2015	2020–2022	2030
in million tons															
Russia, total	284.8	546.7	542.3	516.2	306.8	323.5	470.2	480.5	490.9	488.0	494.3	504.9	486–495	505–525	530–535
Tyumen' *oblast*	28.5	307.9	361.1	365.3	201.6	213.5	320.2	325.5	323.8	319.0	311.0	307.0	282–297	275–300	291–292
East Siberia	0.0	0.0	0.0	0.0	0.1	0.1	0.2	0.3	0.4	0.6	5.2	16.1	21–33	41–52	65–69
Krasnoiarsk *krai*	0.0	0.0	0.0	0.0	0.1	0.1	0.1	0.1	0.1	0.1	3.6	12.9	...	...	...
Irkutsk *oblast*	0.0	0.0	0.0	0.0	0.0	0.0	0.2	0.2	0.2	0.5	1.6	3.2	...	...	...
Far East	2.5	2.5	2.6	2.0	1.9	3.8	4.4	6.6	15.2	13.6	17.4	18.3	23–25	30–31	32–33
Sakha Republic	0.0	0.0	0.0	0.1	0.2	0.4	0.4	0.4	0.4	0.8	2.0	3.5	...	...	...
Sakhalin *oblast*	2.5	2.5	2.6	1.9	1.7	3.4	4.0	6.2	14.8	12.9	15.4	14.8	...	...	...
Other regions	253.8	236.3	178.6	148.8	103.2	106.2	145.3	148.2	151.5	154.8	160.7	163.5	140–160	142–159	141–142
in per cent of total															
Russia, total	100.0	100.0	100.0	100.0	100.0	100.0	100.0	100.0	100.0	100.0	100.0	100.0	100	100	100
Tyumen' *oblast*	10.0	56.3	66.6	70.8	65.7	66.0	68.1	67.7	66.0	65.4	62.9	60.8	58–60	54–57	55
East Siberia	0.0	0.0	0.0	0.0	0.0	0.0	0.1	0.1	0.1	0.1	1.1	3.2	4–7	8–10	12–13
Krasnoiarsk *krai*	0.0	0.0	0.0	0.0	0.0	0.0	0.0	0.0	0.0	0.0	0.7	2.6	...	...	...
Irkutsk *oblast*	0.0	0.0	0.0	0.0	0.0	0.0	0.0	0.0	0.0	0.1	0.3	0.6	...	...	...
Far East	0.9	0.5	0.5	0.4	0.6	1.2	0.9	1.4	3.1	2.8	3.5	3.6	5	6	6
Sakha Republic	0.0	0.0	0.0	0.0	0.1	0.1	0.1	0.1	0.1	0.2	0.4	0.7	...	...	...
Sakhalin *oblast*	0.9	0.5	0.5	0.4	0.6	1.0	0.9	1.3	3.0	2.6	3.1	2.9	...	...	...
Other regions	89.1	43.2	32.9	28.8	33.6	32.8	30.9	30.8	30.9	31.7	32.5	32.4	28–32	27–31	26–27

Sources: Compiled by the authors from *RSE*; *SEP*, various years; Government of the Russian Federation (2009a); for Krasnoiarsk and Sakha in 2008–09, and Irkutsk in 2008, websites of regional statistical offices.

Table 8.2 Natural gas production in East Siberia and the Far East, 1970–2030

	1970	1980	1985	1990	1995	2000	2005	2006	2007	2008	2009	2013–2015	2020–2022	2030
							in billion cubic metres							
Russia, total	83.3	254.0	462.0	640.6	595.5	583.9	640.8	656.3	653.0	666.0	584.0	685–745	803–837	885–940
Tyumen' *oblast*	9.5	160.0	380.7	574.2	544.6	530.4	585.3	600.9	590.4	601.0	514.0	580–592	584–586	608–637
East Siberia	0.2	0.0	0.1	0.0	0.0	0.4	0.8	1.1	1.3	1.5	2.4	9–13	26–55	45–65
Krasnoiarsk *krai*	0.2	0.0	0.1	0.0	0.0	0.4	0.8	1.0	1.2	1.4	2.1	...	...	...
Irkutsk *oblast*	0.0	0.0	0.0	0.0	0.0	0.1	0.1	0.1	0.1	0.1	0.4	...	...	...
Far East	1.2	1.6	1.8	3.2	3.3	3.6	3.5	3.9	8.4	9.8	19.5	34–40	65–67	85–87
Sakha Republic	0.2	0.7	1.0	1.4	1.7	1.6	1.6	1.6	1.6	1.8	2.0	...	...	...
Sakhalin *oblast*	1.0	0.8	0.8	1.8	1.6	1.9	2.0	2.2	6.8	7.9	17.5	31–36	36–37	50–51
Other regions	72.4	92.4	79.4	63.2	47.5	49.6	51.1	50.5	52.8	53.7	48.1	62–100	128–129	147–151
							in per cent of total							
Russia, total	100.0	100.0	100.0	100.0	100.0	100.0	100.0	100.0	100.0	100.0	100.0	100	100	100
Tyumen' *oblast*	11.4	63.0	82.4	89.6	91.5	90.8	91.3	91.6	90.4	90.2	88.0	79–85	70–73	68–69
East Siberia	0.2	0.0	0.0	0.0	0.0	0.1	0.1	0.1	0.2	0.2	0.4	1–2	3–7	5–7
Krasnoiarsk *krai*	0.2	0.0	0.0	0.0	0.0	0.1	0.1	0.1	0.2	0.2	0.4	...	...	...
Irkutsk *oblast*	0.0	0.0	0.0	0.0	0.0	0.0	0.0	0.0	0.0	0.0	0.1	...	...	...
Far East	1.5	0.6	0.4	0.5	0.6	0.6	0.6	0.6	1.3	1.5	3.3	5	8	9–10
Sakha Republic	0.2	0.3	0.2	0.2	0.3	0.3	0.2	0.2	0.2	0.3	0.3	...	...	...
Sakhalin *oblast*	1.3	0.3	0.2	0.3	0.3	0.3	0.3	0.3	1.0	1.2	3.0	5	4	5–6
Other regions	86.9	36.4	17.2	9.9	8.0	8.5	8.0	7.7	8.1	8.1	8.2	9–13	15–16	16–17

Sources: Compiled by the authors from Government of the Russian Federation (2009a); *Promyshlennost'*; *RSE*; *Regiony*; *SEP*, various years; for Krasnoiarsk in 2008–09, website of the regional statistical office; for Irkutsk in 2008–09, *Neft' i kapital* (various issues) and website of the company.

projected increase in Russia's oil output will be realized mainly in East Siberia, the Far East and the North Caucasus. Among these regions, the biggest increase is expected in East Siberia, with its share projected to grow from 0.1 per cent in 2008 to 12–13 per cent (65–69 million tons) in 2030. Accordingly, the share of the East Siberian and Far Eastern regions will increase from 2.9 per cent (14.2 million tons) in 2008 to 18–19 per cent (97–99 million tons) in 2030.

With respect to natural gas, while the share of Tyumen' *oblast* is projected to drop from 90 per cent in 2008 to 68–69 per cent by 2030, the share of East Siberia and the Far East of Russia will rise (see Table 8.2). The share of East Siberia and the Far East is to increase from 1.7 per cent (11.3 billion cubic metres) in 2008 to 15 per cent (132–52 billion cubic metres) in 2030.

Diversification of Oil and Gas Exports

Exports of oil and gas are of crucial importance for the growth of the Russian economy and its financing (Gaddy and Ickes, 2010). For example, state budget revenues of mineral extraction taxes (severance taxes) and export duties on oil and gas alone amounted to US$180.1 billion in 2008.[3] This was 58 per cent of the export values of oil and gas and accounted for 28 per cent of state budget revenues.[4] Because of this importance, approximately half of the crude oil produced in Russia has been exported in recent years, excluding exports of refined petroleum.[5]

It should be noted here that oil and gas export revenues have increased not only due to recent price increases, but also due to increases in export quantities. Exports of oil increased by 79 per cent from 2000 to 2007: the annual growth rate was 8.7 per cent on average (FCS; *Belarus'*, various years; Belstat, 2010). According to statistics of the IEA, during this period 60.8 per cent of the increase in world oil exports was accounted for by Russia alone. The corresponding figure for 2000–08 is 55.3 per cent (IEA, 2005a; 2010a).

This seems to suggest that a steady increase in oil export quantities is necessary for a boom in the Russian economy. Most exports of Russian oil and gas were bound for the European market. About 70 per cent of oil was exported to Europe and another 15 per cent to countries of the CIS (FCS; *Belarus'*, various years; Belstat, 2010). As for gas, until 2008 natural gas was exported only to Europe, including Turkey and CIS countries, in the absence of LNG exports from Russia – which forced all exports of natural gas to rely on pipeline deliveries.

One of the problems for Russia's oil and gas exports in the future is stagnating demand in the European market. This tendency was already apparent in the 2000s. From 2000 to 2008, while 35 per cent of the increases in world oil consumption were brought about by China and another 8.6 per cent by India, consumption in Germany decreased as well as in the USA and Japan. With respect to natural gas, China's contribution to the increase in world total consumption amounted to 12 per cent, while Germany and Italy recorded only modest increases (see IEA, 2005b; 2010b).

In these circumstances, it is natural and rational for Russian actors to target the East Asian market for oil and gas in the future. In 2009, East Asia (China, Japan and the Korean Republic) accounted for 16.9 per cent of world oil consumption and 21.6 per cent of imports. According to the Energy Research Institute under the National Development and Reform Commission of China, China's demand for oil will reach 490–520 million tons in 2015 and 560–600 million tons in 2020. Its demand for gas is projected to grow to 200 billion cubic metres in 2015 and 300 billion in 2020 (Xinhuanet, 2010). China's oil imports have grown tremendously since the beginning of the 1990s, as China became a net importer of oil (see Table 8.3). Heavy dependence on oil imports from the Middle East and Africa (around 80 per cent) is regarded as one of the main problems in its energy security.

For Japan, by contrast, no increase in the consumption of oil is expected, but supplies need to be diversified. The Middle East's share of Japan's petroleum imports was around 90 per cent in the 2000s (see Table 8.4). As for natural gas, Japan is one of the world's largest importers, and the Japanese government intends to shift to natural gas in energy consumption due to ecological considerations. Japan might therefore increase its imports of both oil and gas from Russia. The same is true of South Korea, which ranked fifth in the world in terms of crude oil imports in 2008 (see IEA, 2010c). The Middle East's share of South Korea's imports of crude oil has been around 85 per cent (see Table 8.5). South Korea also seeks to diversify its oil supply.

As the demand for Russian oil and gas is expected to increase in East Asia, one of the most rational strategies for oil and gas development for Russia is to combine exploration of oil and gas fields in the East Siberian and Far Eastern regions with exports to the East Asian market. According to Russia's Energy Strategy (Government of the Russian Federation, 2009a), while the share of eastward exports of crude and petroleum products was about 8 per cent in 2008, it is expected to reach 22–25 per cent in 2030. As for natural gas, the share of exports to Asia-Pacific Ocean countries in Russia's total gas exports is to grow from almost zero in 2008 to 19–20 per cent in 2030.

Economic Growth in the Far East and East Siberia

The fundamental change in the strategy of regional development which took place after the collapse of the Soviet Union has significant consequences for the institutional dimension of energy policy formation in Russia (see Chapter 2). This was especially true of the Russian Far East and East Siberia. In the

Table 8.3 China's imports of crude oil, in million tons

	1990	1995	2000	2001	2002	2003	2004	2005	2006	2007	2008	2009
Total	2.9	17.1	70.3	60.3	69.4	91.1	122.8	127.1	145.2	163.2	178.9	203.8
Middle East	1.2	7.8	37.6	33.9	34.4	46.4	55.8	60.0	65.6	72.8	89.6	97.5
Africa	...	1.8	16.9	13.5	15.8	22.2	35.3	38.5	45.8	53.0	54.0	61.4
Russia	...	...	1.5	1.8	3.0	5.3	10.8	12.8	16.0	14.5	11.6	15.3
by rail	...	...	...	...	...	...	6.1	8.0	10.3	9.0	8.9	9.0
by tanker	...	...	...	...	...	...	4.7	4.8	5.7	5.5	1.7	4.8
by pipeline	...	...	...	...	...	...	0.0	0.0	0.0	0.0	1.0	1.5

Source: Compiled by the authors from China Customs statistics (n.d.), available at http://www.customs.gov.cn, accessed 1 March 2011 (in Chinese).

Table 8.4 Japan's imports of crude oil

	2002	2003	2004	2005	2006	2007	2008	2009	2010
	in thousand kL								
Total	235 649	248 496	243 395	245 186	243 139	238 822	243 207	211 863	215 350
Middle East	202 565	216 382	216 278	221 257	216 776	207 040	211 398	190 210	186 260
Russia, total	880	1 629	1 643	1 736	1 797	8 387	8 170	9 396	15 297
Vityaz	545	821	1 476	1 736	1 150	1 268	520	1 081	2 892
Russia-B	335	808	166	0	0	159	0	160	595
Sokol	0	0	0	0	560	5 565	4 905	5 418	3 893
SRFO	0	0	0	0	87	1 222	2 601	2 578	2 729
Espo-B	0	0	0	0	0	0	0	0	5 132
Other	0	0	0	0	0	173	143	159	56
	in per cent of Japan's total imports								
Total	100.0	100.0	100.0	100.0	100.0	100.0	100.0	100.0	100.0
Middle East	86.0	87.1	88.9	90.2	89.2	86.7	86.9	89.8	86.5
Russia, total	0.4	0.7	0.7	0.7	0.7	3.5	3.4	4.4	7.1
	in per cent of total imports from Russia								
Russia, total	100.0	100.0	100.0	100.0	100.0	100.0	100.0	100.0	100.0
Vityaz	61.9	50.4	89.9	100.0	64.0	15.1	6.4	11.5	18.9
Russia-B	38.1	49.6	10.1	0.0	0.0	1.9	0.0	1.7	3.9
Sokol	0.0	0.0	0.0	0.0	31.1	66.4	60.0	57.7	25.4
SRFO	0.0	0.0	0.0	0.0	4.9	14.6	31.8	27.4	17.8
Espo-B	0.0	0.0	0.0	0.0	0.0	0.0	0.0	0.0	33.6
Other	0.0	0.0	0.0	0.0	0.0	2.1	1.8	1.7	0.4

Notes: Vityaz is from Sakhlin-2; Russia-B implies Russian Export Blend; Sokol is from Sakhalin-1; SRFO means Russian Straight Run Fuel Oil; Espo-B is from ESPO pipeline.

Source: Compiled by the authors from ANRE (n.d.) 'Resource and energy statistics'.

Table 8.5 Korea's imports of crude oil, in million tons

	2004	2005	2006	2007	2008	2009	2010
Total	111.8	114.0	120.2	117.9	116.7	113.8	118.6
Middle East	89.3	94.5	100.5	97.4	101.9	97.4	97.9
Africa	4.8	3.7	4.6	3.1	0.5	0.7	0.2
Russia	1.1	1.0	1.7	4.9	3.1	3.7	6.7
Other	16.6	14.8	13.4	12.5	11.2	12.0	13.8

Source: Compiled by the authors from KITA (n.d.).

Soviet era the development of these regions was financed by subsidies from central government because of their military importance and potential for energy production. The subsidies were provided regardless of the efficiency of their use. After 1991, due to the growing economic efficiency considerations in public finance and to the relative decrease in the military significance of these regions, in addition to political and economic turmoil in the country, subsidies were drastically reduced and the responsibility for economic development was left to the regions themselves.

However, it became clear by the end of the 1990s that Far Eastern and East Siberian regions were not able to develop their economies by themselves. From the end of 1991 to the end of 1999, while Russia's population as a whole decreased by 0.9 per cent (1.38 million), the population of the Far East shrank by 14.3 per cent (1.15 million); the population of the island of Sakhalin decreased by 20.4 per cent (0.15 million). In this context, the Russian government adopted the specific federal programme 'Economic and Social Development of the Far East and Zabaikal until 2013' under Government Resolution No. 801 of 21 November 2007.[6] One of the salient features of this programme was the commitment by the federal government to finance a substantial part of this programme from the federal budget, including the preparation of the Asia-Pacific Economic Cooperation (APEC) summit meeting to be held in Vladivostok in 2012.

The so-called Eastern gas programme for energy development was adopted in 2007. Its formal title was the 'Programme of Creating a Single System of Gas Extraction, Transportation and Supply in East Siberia and the Far East, Taking into Account Possible Gas Exports to China and Other Countries of the Asia-Pacific Region'. It was approved by Order of the Ministry of Industry and Energy No. 340 of 3 September 2007.[7] The programme was drawn up under the direction of Government Order No. 975 of 16 July 2002, which put Gazprom in charge of coordinating its implementation. The characterization of this programme suggests from the very start that 'Increasing the speed of socio-economic development in East Siberia and the Far East requires the creation of a corresponding energy base in the region'. Thus, the oil and gas industries are regarded as the driving force of economic advancement in these regions.

In order to achieve these goals, the Russian government embarked on major policies in the 1990s and 2000s in the following three spheres: oil and gas development in Sakhalin, the construction of the East Siberia–Pacific Ocean (ESPO) pipeline and the exploitation of oil fields in East Siberia.

MAJOR POLICIES

Sakhalin's Oil and Gas Development

Oil and gas development in Sakhalin has a specific feature: foreign countries or companies were and are permitted by the Soviet and Russian governments to participate in its development. Only in Sakhalin were foreign companies allowed to join in the exploration and exploitation of oil and gas resources in the Soviet era – for example, the concession given to Japan in the 1920s and 1930s, and joint exploration works with Japan in the 1970s. In the post-Soviet period, a production sharing agreement (PSA) was drawn up and introduced for the first time in the Sakhalin-1 and Sakhalin-2 projects. The special status of Sakhalin is probably due to its remoteness from the centre of Russia and to the intention by the Soviet and Russian governments to ensure possible consumers for this oil and gas.

The first PSA was signed in June 1994 for Sakhalin-2 between the Sakhalin Energy Investment Company (a joint company with Royal Dutch Shell, Mitsui and Mitsubishi),[8] the Russian government and Sakhalin *oblast* administration. The second one was signed in June 1995 for Sakhalin-1 between the Russian side and Exxon, SODECO (Sakhalin Oil and Gas Company, a consortium of Japanese companies), ONGC (Oil and Natural Gas Corporation Limited, an Indian national oil company) and Rosneft. It should be noted that initially no Russian companies were involved in Sakhalin-2. The PSA legislation in Russia was finally approved in December 1995 after the signature of these two PSAs.

As the initial PSA legislation was criticized in Russia for being too generous to foreign investors, it was amended in 1999 and again in 2003. While the 1999 amendments were seen as harmonizing the PSA law with existing Russian legislation (Oda, 1999), those of 2003 were regarded as making the PSA law unattractive to foreign investors (Sakaguchi, 2003).[9] In fact, PSAs function in only three oil and gas fields, including the two in Sakhalin. The third is in Khar'iaga in the Timan-Pechora basin. It was signed between the

Russian side and Total, Norsk Hydro and Nenets Oil Company in 1995 before the adoption of the law on PSA and was put into effect in 1999 (Krysiek, 2007).

With respect to Sakhalin-2, the big news was the entry of Gazprom into the consortium in 2006. One of the aims of Gazprom's approach was the acquisition of LNG production techniques (Motomura, 2005, p. 151). Although Gazprom's entry was criticized in Western mass media as an act of resource nationalism, it was welcomed by foreign investors, including Japanese companies, as collateral for the stability of the project.

Construction of the ESPO Pipeline

The construction of the ESPO pipeline consisted of two phases. The first phase from Taishet in Irkutsk *oblast* to Skovorodino in Amur *oblast* was started in April 2006 and completed in October 2009. Until the completion of the second phase in 2014 from Skovorodino to Kozmino in Primorskii *krai*, oil will be transported by train from Skovorodino. From 2011 oil will also be piped from Skovorodino to Daqing in China (see Figure 8.1).

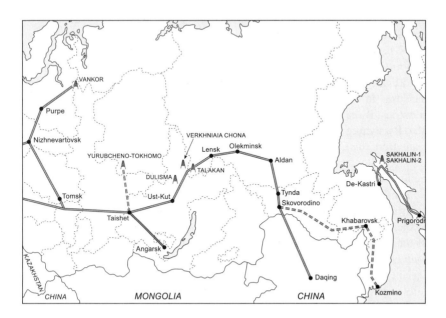

Note: Broken lines show planned routes.

Figure 8.1   Crude oil pipelines in the Eastern regions of Russia

A few important features of this construction project can be mentioned here.[10] First, the decision to construct this pipeline was conditioned by highly political frames of Russia's decision-makers who were the main actors driving the project forward. In Russia, where territory is vast and oil and gas fields are located inland far from consuming regions, oil and gas need to be transported through long-distance pipelines. Here, a chicken and egg question arises between oil and gas development and pipeline construction. On the one hand, pipelines are necessary for the development of oil and gas fields; on the other hand, in order to construct a pipeline, the existence of oil and gas fields with substantial reserves is essential. In the case of the ESPO pipeline, although no big oil fields have been discovered yet in East Siberia, the oil supply from the Western Siberian oil fields is regarded as a substitute, because there is already a trunk pipeline from Western Siberia to Angarsk in Irkutsk *oblast*. In this sense, the decision to construct the ESPO pipeline was politically motivated in order to discover new oil fields in East Siberia that will replace the stagnant Western Siberian fields. Until then all Russian oil trunk pipelines delivered oil westwards, including those reaching the former East European and Baltic countries and those connecting to export terminals at the Black or Baltic Sea. The ESPO pipeline is an epoch-defining project in that it exports oil eastward from Siberian oil fields.

Second, the decision on the pipeline route was economically motivated to avoid so-called hold-up problems or a monopoly of demand. Therefore, the ESPO pipeline is destined to transport oil both to China (from Skovorodino to Daqing) and to Japan and other Pacific countries (from Kozmino, where an oil export sea terminal is being constructed). Although immediate substantial increases in oil demand are expected only in China among the East Asian countries, Russia expects competition among them in terms of price in particular. By signing agreements in February 2009, Rosneft and Transneft received loans from the China Development Bank to the amount of US$15 billion and US$10 billion respectively, by promising to deliver nine million tons and six million tons of oil respectively, per year for 20 years from 2011.

Third, the concrete route of the pipeline was determined taking account of environmental factors. Putin changed the route just two days before the start of the pipeline construction at a public hearing on the environmental aspects of the project. Even after the beginning of the construction, numerous environmental claims and problems were raised (Liu, 2010). This may be the first case in Russia where considerations linked to the ecological dimension forcefully impacted the processes of decision-making on pipeline construction.

Exploitation of Oil Fields in East Siberia

In order to develop oil fields in East Siberia, the Russian government has adopted special measures: exemptions or reduction of extraction taxes and export duties on oil produced in these regions, including the Sakha Republic. These tax reductions and exemptions were applied to these areas for the first time in Russia since the introduction of these taxes. This gives us a good opportunity to consider the tax burden on oil companies in Russia.

The tax rate of oil extraction fees is determined by the formula $T = (P - 15) \times 0.22$, where T and P are the tax rate and oil prices (Urals oil prices at the Mediterranean Sea and Rotterdam), expressed in US dollars per barrel respectively.[11] This means that 22 per cent of the increase in revenues is levied by the government when oil prices increase.

Exemptions from oil extraction taxes have been introduced since the beginning of 2007 by Federal Law No. 151 of 27 July 2006. This law stipulated that this tax relief would be applied to oil fields located entirely or partly in the Sakha Republic, Irkutsk *oblast* or Krasnoiarsk *krai* and producing less than 25 million tons of oil since the beginning of their exploitation.

Interestingly, the same kind of tax relief has been granted to oil fields in other regions since 1 January 2009, including the Arctic Circle, the Azov Sea, the Caspian Sea, Nenets AO and the Yamal Peninsula, by Federal Law No. 158 of 22 July 2008.

Export duties on crude oil, when oil prices are higher than US$25 per barrel, have been calculated by the formula (Federal Law No. 33 of 7 May 2004): $T = 4 + (P - 25) \times 0.65$. Exemptions of export duties on oil were introduced from the beginning of December 2009 by Government Resolution No. 954 of 26 November 2009. It set the tariff of export duties of the commodity of code '27.09.009001' at zero. Commodity code '27.09.009001' was introduced by Government Resolution No. 574 of 16 July 2009 for crude oil of specific quality. This resolution specified in its footnote 8 that this code would be applied to 13 oil fields in East Siberia and the Sakha Republic.

The application of this tax relief was expanded to another nine fields in this region. Decision of the Commission of Customs Union No. 155 of 19 December 2009 replaced code '27.09.009001' with a new code '27.09.009002', from 19 January 2010. The definition of the quality of crude oil was broadened in order to include all crude oil produced from Vankor oil field (Motomura, 2010, p. 22), and another nine oil fields in East Siberia were added to the list of oil fields to which this new code would be applied.[12]

This tax relief continued for only seven months. At the beginning of July 2010, it was replaced by tax reductions, as a compromise between the Ministry of Finance and oil companies – indicating the intermingling of private and public actors within the institutional dimension of energy policy formation in Russia. Government Resolution No. 472 of 26 June 2010 set the tariff of export duties of the commodities of code '27.09.009002' at 69.9 roubles per ton, while the rate for regular crude oil (code '27.09') was 248.8 roubles per ton. Since then tax rates for the item '27.09.009002' have been changed every month together with other export duty rates of oil and petroleum products.[13] The calculation formula for this tax reduction was announced identically by both an official of the Ministry of Finance and a representative of Rosneft:[14] $T = (P - 50) \times 0.45$. When the oil price is US\$75 per barrel, oil producers in East Siberia pay 30.8 per cent of the taxes levied in other regions, that is, they enjoy a tax reduction of almost 70 per cent. According to Sergei Shatalov, this privilege of export duties is in fact granted to only four oil fields, namely Vankor, Talakan, Verkhniaia Chona and Dulisma, because other oil fields are neither producing nor exporting. He added that as the profitability of these oil fields improves, Vankor will be excluded from the list of privileged fields in 2011; Verkhiyaia Chona and Dulisma in 2012; and Talakan in 2013 (Shatalov, 2010).

In addition, Krasnoiarsk *krai* reduced profit tax rates from 18 per cent to 13.5 per cent for oil producers for five years from 1 January 2009 to 31 December 2013 by Law of the *krai* No. 7-2619 of 18 December 2008. Note that profit tax revenues are paid to both federal and regional budgets and the tax rate of 13.5 per cent is the minimum rate of profit taxes that are paid to the regional budget, as designated by the tax code. In order to qualify for this privilege, oil companies have to produce more than three million tons in the first year of the application of these reduced tax rates; 15 million tons in the first two years; 34 million tons in three years; 52 million tons in four years; and 70 million tons in five years. This privileged rate was also to be applied to producers of petroleum products satisfying specified minimum production criteria. By Law of the *krai* No. 7-2622, adopted on the same day, Krasnoiarsk *krai* also reduced property tax rates from 2.2 per cent to 1.1 per cent for producing companies of oil and petroleum products that satisfy the same production conditions, as specified in the case of profit tax privileges. This reduced rate was introduced from the beginning of 2009 without indicating the expiry date of this privilege. The high minimum production criteria for these privileges suggest that only Vankorneft, a producer in Vankor oil field and a subsidiary of Rosneft, enjoy them.

The Sakha Republic followed Krasnoiarsk by reducing profit tax rates to 13.5 per cent for oil producers for two years from 1 January 2009 to 31 December 2010 by Law of No. 285 of 17 June 2009.[15] The Republic attached no production conditions for receiving this privileged rate. On the whole, it is interesting to note here that export duty revenues have gone exclusively to the federal budget. As for oil extraction taxes, while previously a part of their revenues was paid to the regional budget, by a recent revision they are now paid only to the federal budget.[16]

RESULTS OF THE POLICIES

Russia's determined formulation of policies and their implementation in East Siberia and the Far East have had an impact on East Asia in terms of the resource geographic dimension and the financial dimension owing to the emergence of Russian actors in this regional market. The opening up of the Eastern front has provided more options for the Russian state and several of its energy companies (see also Chapters 4 and 10).

Oil and Gas Production in the Far East and East Siberia

There was a steady increase in oil production in Sakhalin from 2000 (see Table 8.1), due to the beginning of production in Sakhalin-2 in 1999. Its further increase from 2007 was brought about by the start of production in Sakhalin-1 in September 2005. In 2008, year-round production started in Sakhalin-2. The share of the Far East in Russia's oil production has been around 3 per cent since 2007 (see Table 8.1). Since 2009, a rapid increase in oil production has been observed in Krasnoiarsk, Irkutsk and Sakha (see Table 8.1). Production in the Vankor oil field expanded most impressively. The Talakan and Verkhniaia Chona fields greatly contributed to the oil production growth in these regions as well.

With respect to natural gas, due to the increase in production in Sakhalin, the share of the Far East amounted to 3.3 per cent in 2009 (see Table 8.2). Its production has increased since 2007 due to the Sakhalin-1 project. In 2009, production of LNG was started by the Sakhalin-2 project in Prigorodnoe, located at the south end of Sakhalin Island.

Oil and Gas Exports to the East Asian Market

The share of East Asian countries in Russia's oil exports began to increase at the beginning of the 2000s owing to Chinese demand.[17] Since the middle of the 2000s, exports to South Korea and Japan have increased as well. In particular, since 2007, the share of East Asia has been around 9 per cent, due to the beginning of crude oil exports in October 2006 from De-Kastri, an export terminal of Sakhalin-1 in Khabarovsk *krai*. Its export capacity is 10 million tons per year. In December 2008, crude exports from Prigorodnoe, an export terminal of Sakhalin-2, started. With the opening of this terminal, year-round oil production at the Sakhalin-2 project became possible. Its export capacity was 5 million tons as of 2010, but was projected to be 7.5 million tons in the near future (Motomura, 2010, pp. 26–7).

Concerning Japan's imports of oil from Russia, detailed data reveals that up to 2006, crude oil from Sakhalin-2 (Vityaz oil) constituted the largest share in

Japan's imports from Russia. Imports of Sokol oil from Sakhalin-1 began in 2006, and they were the largest among oil imports from Russia in 2007–09 (see Table 8.4).[18]

Oil exports began from Russia's Kozmino in December 2009. They amounted to 15.3 million tons by the end of 2010, of which 30 per cent were exported to Japan; 29 per cent to South Korea; 16 per cent to the USA; 11 per cent to Taiwan; and 8 per cent to China (*Prime-TASS Financial News*, 2010).

In 2010, Japan imported 5.13 million kL (about 4.4 million tons) from Kozmino. Crude oil from Kozmino amounted to 33.6 per cent of Japan's imports from Russia, the largest share among Russian sources in 2010. Crude oil imports from Russia accounted for 7.1 per cent of Japan's total oil imports in 2010 – the largest ever recorded share, jumping from 4.4 per cent in 2009 (see Table 8.4). Motomura (2010, p. 27) anticipated that if Japan receives half of Russia's exports from Sakhalin and Kozmino, Russia's share will reach 8 per cent and the share of the Middle East will be under 85 per cent.

South Korea's imports of oil from Russia have increased since 2007, with most of the increase probably coming from Sakhalin-1 (see Table 8.5). Russia's share reached 4.2 per cent in 2007. Owing to imports from Kozmino, this share increased to 5.6 per cent in 2010.

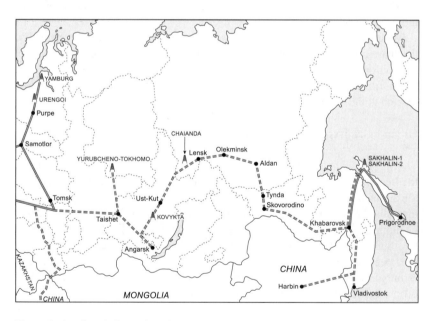

Note: Broken lines indicate planned routes.

Figure 8.2   Natural gas pipelines in the Eastern regions of Russia

Similar increases have failed to materialize in China's imports of crude oil from Russia during the same period. Russia's share in China's total imports of crude oil, having grown from 2.1 per cent in 2000 to more than 10 per cent in 2005 and 2006, decreased to 7.5 per cent in 2009 (15.3 million tons; see Table 8.3). As explained above, the volume is expected to expand significantly after imports of 15 million tons of oil by pipeline via Skovorodino begin in 2011.[19]

Natural gas exports to the East Asian market began in 2009 with LNG exports from Prigorodnoe (Sakhalin-2) (see Figure 8.2). Its export capacity is 9.6 million tons per year (13.2 billion cubic metres). According to Russia's customs statistics, Japan imported 2.14 million tons of natural gas and accounted for 1.6 per cent of Russia's natural gas exports.[20] Together with exports to China, South Korea and Taiwan, the share of the East Asian market amounted to 2.1 per cent.

Table 8.6   Japan's imports of LNG by country

	2000	2008	2009	2010
		in million tons		
Total	53.7	69.3	64.6	70.0
Malaysia	11.0	13.1	12.6	14.0
Australia	7.3	12.0	11.9	13.0
Indonesia	18.0	14.1	13.0	12.8
Qatar	5.8	8.2	7.7	7.6
Russia	0.0	0.0	2.8	6.0
Brunei	5.7	6.2	6.1	5.8
UAE	4.7	5.6	5.1	5.2
Oman	0.1	3.2	2.6	2.9
Other	1.2	6.9	2.7	2.7
		in per cent of total		
Total	100.0	100.0	100.0	100.0
Malaysia	20.4	19.0	19.6	20.0
Australia	13.5	17.3	18.5	18.6
Indonesia	33.5	20.4	20.1	18.3
Qatar	10.9	11.8	12.0	10.9
Russia	0.0	0.0	4.3	8.6
Brunei	10.6	8.9	9.4	8.3
UAE	8.7	8.0	8.0	7.4
Oman	0.1	4.6	4.0	4.1
Other	2.3	9.9	4.2	3.9

Sources: Compiled by the authors from Ministry of Finance, Japan (n.d.).

Table 8.7   Korea's imports of LNG by country, in million tonnes

	2000	2008	2009	2010
Total	15.2	27.3	25.8	32.6
Qatar	3.3	8.7	7.0	7.4
Indonesia	6.6	3.1	3.1	5.5
Malaysia	2.5	6.2	5.9	4.7
Oman	1.6	4.5	4.6	4.6
Russia	0.0	0.0	1.0	2.9
Equatorial Guinea	0.0	1.0	1.1	1.2
Australia	0.1	0.4	1.3	1.0
Other	1.1	3.4	1.8	5.3

Source: Compiled by the authors from KITA (n.d.).

According to Japan's customs statistics, Japan imported 2.8 million tons of LNG from Russia in 2009. Russia's share of this amounted to 4.3 per cent (see Table 8.6). In 2010, Russia was the fifth largest LNG supplier to Japan and its share reached 8.6 per cent. South Korea imported 1.0 million tons of LNG in 2009 from Russia (see Table 8.7). In 2010, its volume increased to 2.9 million tons and Russia's share reached 8.9 per cent.

Interestingly, increases in oil and gas imports from Russia have contributed to a significant increase in Japan's total imports from Russia since 2007 (see Figure 8.3). The share of oil and gas exceeded 40 per cent of Japan's total imports from Russia in 2007 and amounted to 67.0 per cent in 2010.[21]

Economic Growth in the Far East and East Siberia

The impact of oil and gas development has also reached outside the energy sector proper and been positive on the economic performance in these regions. First of all, a tremendous increase in investments related to the development of oil and gas fields in these regions, the construction of ESPO and other pipelines, and the start of oil and gas production in new oil and gas fields, contributed to the economic growth in these regions. For example, the economic development of the Sakhalin *oblast* was outstanding by several indicators. The GRP of Sakhalin grew considerably faster than the Russian average in most of the 2000s (see Table 8.8). From 2000 to 2007, while Russia's GDP grew by 1.57 times, GRP of Sakhalin increased by 2.61 times. Increases in fixed capital investments were impressive, and apparently,

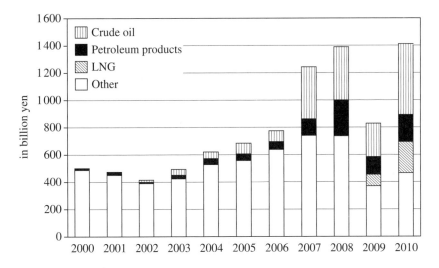

Source: Compiled by the authors from Ministry of Finance, Japan (n.d.).

Figure 8.3   Japan's imports from Russia

growth in industrial production, prompted by oil and gas extraction, contributed to GRP growth in Sakhalin. It should be noted that Sakhalin ranked second after Moscow city in terms of inflow of foreign direct investments in the period from 2000 to 2008, receiving US$21.2 billion or 19.2 per cent of the total, with Moscow accounting for 35.7 per cent.[22]

Other projects described in the federal programme 'Development of the Far East and Zabaikal until 2013', including the preparation of the APEC summit in Vladivostok in 2012, also contributed to the development of these regions. Economic relations with East Asian countries, at least partly activated by the increase in fuel trades, promoted this development as well. China became the largest exporter to Russia in 2008 and Japan ranked third in 2008 due to its huge car exports. In 2008, China, Japan and South Korea accounted for 23.9 per cent of Russia's total imports.[23]

The decrease of population in Russia's Far East, however, continued at higher rates than in Russia as a whole. From the beginning of 2000 to the beginning of 2010, Russia's population decreased by 3.4 per cent (4.98 million) but in the Far East and Sakhalin the decrease was 6.8 per cent (0.47 million), and 10.3 per cent (58 000) respectively.

Table 8.8 Economic development of the Russian Far East and Sakhalin, as a percentage of the previous year

		2000	2001	2002	2003	2004	2005	2006	2007	2008	2009
GDP/GRP	Russia	110.0	105.1	104.7	107.3	107.2	106.4	108.2	108.5	105.2	92.2
	Far East	103.1	105.9	103.7	105.9	106.6	104.6	105.3	109.4	103.4	...
	Sakhalin	84.7	116.6	106.3	116.4	117.3	108.8	112.2	126.3	95.7	...
Industrial production	Russia	108.7	102.9	103.1	108.9	108.0	105.1	106.3	106.3	100.6	90.7
	Far East	112.4	102.8	102.1	104.4	107.5	102.6	104.2	122.6	99.1	103.9
	Sakhalin	141.9	112.1	88.3	102.5	109.3	112.7	131.1	210.0	87.0	123.8
Fixed capital investment	Russia	117.4	110.0	102.8	112.5	113.7	110.9	116.7	122.7	109.9	83.8
	Far East	98.4	147.9	115.3	106.7	140.3	107.4	102.3	118.9	111.7	129.9
	Sakhalin	36.0	190.5	141.7	139.3	280.0	101.7	100.3	81.9	94.5	67.9
Retail trade turnover	Russia	109.0	111.0	109.3	108.8	113.3	112.8	114.1	116.1	113.5	95.1
	Far East	104.3	110.2	110.7	111.2	110.3	112.5	112.9	111.2	110.6	100.7
	Sakhalin	116.5	127.8	118.3	110.7	114.9	114.6	122.1	107.9	120.0	102.5
Real average wages	Russia	120.9	119.9	116.2	110.9	110.6	112.6	113.3	117.2	111.5	96.5
	Far East	...	115.2	119.8	111.1	108.3	111.2	107.8	112.6	110.3	98.8
	Sakhalin	106.9	112.2	119.6	116.4	113.8	113.8	110.3	112.7	113.8	95.9

Sources: Compiled by the authors from RSE; Regiony; NSR, various years.

PROSPECTS

Our analysis of Russia's energy policy on this Eastern interregional front and its impacts so far allow us to make some concluding observations on the role of Russian actors in the energy political processes of East Asia in the future. Overall, an impressive eastward shift in oil and gas development in Russia is underway. This is particularly true of Sakhalin after decades of exploration. However, many problems remain to be resolved (Bradshaw, 2010a, pp. 343–7). This means that we can point out some serious constraints on Russian actors in this region as well.

Heavy Tax Burden

One particularly important but often overlooked issue affecting the formulation and implementation of energy policies through the institutional dimension is taxation. To illustrate the point let us here concentrate on the development of oil and gas fields in East Siberia, including the Sakha Republic. The first point to note is that oil production in East Siberia should be increased further in order to increase the oil supply to the ESPO pipeline. Otherwise Russian oil companies will have to deliver more West Siberian oil to the East Asian market after the second phase of the ESPO pipeline is completed (expected in 2014).

The tax burden is generally regarded as heavy for oil companies in Russia, reflecting the interests in economic development, and other sociopolitical and political interests the sector conveys for the Russian state. As explained above, in extraction taxes and export duties alone, oil companies pay 87 per cent of increases in oil prices. At an oil price of US$75 per barrel, the tax rates of these two taxes amount to 66.3 per cent. This heavy taxation has been caused by the creation of the stabilization fund and its successor funds. In Russia, the government has been able to collect relatively large revenues from its oil producers (Alexeev and Conrad, 2009, pp. 98, 109).[24] In such circumstances, for the first time in Russia, oil producers in East Siberia received a tax exemption from these two taxes: for extraction taxes from January 2007 and for export duties from December 2009.

As noted above, a tax exemption was replaced by a tax reduction of export duties in July 2010. In addition, a tax exemption from oil extraction taxes has been applied to other regions since the beginning of 2009. For major oil companies, such as Rosneft, TNK-BP and Surgutneftegas, the incentives for developing new oil fields in East Siberia might have been undermined.

It is generally argued that increases in oil prices enable oil companies to develop new oil fields in remote areas with harsh geological and climatic conditions. In the Russian case, however, because 87 per cent of increases in oil prices are transferred to the state budget, such incentives may be relatively weak. It is a fundamental question whether to maintain stabilization-like funds for a rainy day or to give priority to developing new oil fields. To make the matter more complex, the Russian stabilization fund and its successor funds have played an important role in keeping inflation rates low by sterilizing increased money supply resulting from strong interventions in foreign exchange markets by the Central Bank of Russia (Tabata, 2007; 2009a). Strong interventions in exchange markets, in turn, were necessitated by the growing influx of oil dollars. This problem is beyond the scope of the present article.

High Transportation Fees

Another constraint on the development of oil fields in East Siberia is the growth in transportation fees. As the ESPO pipeline is being constructed by Transneft, a state-owned monopoly of the transportation of oil and petroleum products in Russia, it has to increase its transportation fees, in order to offset the increasing cost of construction. Basic tariffs are applied to all crude oil transported through the trunk pipelines of Transneft. They have been raised considerably, especially since 2008. Their level as of 2010 (23.5 roubles per 100 ton kilometres) is 2.4 times higher than three years earlier. Average tariffs, which include basic tariff (dispatch tariff), service charge for usage of pipelines controlled by different affiliated companies and service charge for pumping oil into the pipeline, reloading and unloading, have rapidly increased since 2008 as well (see Table 8.9).[25] The increases have exceeded the corresponding figures for producer prices in industry since 2008.

The ESPO tariff, which is a network tariff applied regardless of the distance of transportation, was introduced at the beginning of 2009. It includes the charge for the use of railroad transportation and for the transportation terminal and special seaport for oil exports at Kozmino.[26] It was set at 1598 roubles per ton and increased to 1651 roubles per ton at the beginning of August 2010, and was to be raised to 1815 roubles per ton from December 2010.[27] Thus the planned increases during 2010 were 13.6 per cent. Although the distance and means of transportation are different, this tariff is to be applied to the transportation of oil through the ESPO pipeline and the pipeline reaching the Chinese border for exports to China.

The ESPO tariff at the beginning of August 2010, 1651 roubles per ton, was converted to US$7.5 per barrel by the exchange rate of that time. In addition, if oil is supplied from the West Siberian fields, oil companies have to pay transportation fees from West Siberia to Taishet (see Figure 8.1). Transportation cost is a considerable burden. Transneft, however, may be compelled to raise transportation fees in the years to come as well due to the continuation of pipeline construction in the territory of Russia.

Table 8.9   Oil pipeline tariff of Transneft, in roubles per 100 tkm

	2006	2007	2008	2009	2010
Average tariff in Dec.	167.3	180.4	23.85	29.31	33.96
Increase rate (%)	9.9	7.8	32.2	22.9	15.9
Basic tariff	from Jan. 1	from Jan. 1	from Jan. 1	from Jan. 1	from Jan. 1
	8.6228	9.6778	12.8927	17.8338	22.3249
	from Oct. 1		from Aug. 5	from July 1	from Aug. 1
	8.9691		15.4103	19.1795	23.5059
					from Dec. 1
					25.3830
Increase rate (%)	5.6	7.9	59.2	24.5	32.3
Increase rate in producer prices in industry (%)	10.4	25.1	–7.0	13.9	16.7

Notes: Average tariffs are from Federal Tariff Service, including its plan for 2010; see 'Srednii tariff na transportirovku rossiiskoi nefti po sisteme OAO AK Transneft', 1 June, available at http://www.fstrf.ru/tariffs/analit_info/oil/0 (accessed 3 March 2011). Basic tariffs are determined by FTS orders. Increase rates are from December to December.

Sources: Compiled by the authors from FTS Order No. 612 of 13 Dec. 2005; No. 196 of 15 Sept. 2006; No. 320 of 1 Dec. 2006; No. 461 of 13 Dec. 2007; No. 132 of 5 Aug. 2008; No. 421 of 24 Dec. 2008; No. 143 of 30 June 2009; No. 526 of 24 Dec. 2009; No. 167 of 29 July 2010; *RSE* 2010; *SEP* 2010, No. 12.

Shortage of Natural Gas Demand

There are also constraints on natural gas development in East Siberia and the Far East along the financial dimension. One of the underlying problems is the overall decrease in demand for Russia's natural gas due to the prolonged recession in developed countries and increased production of shale gas in the USA. This will inevitably cause a decrease in the prices of natural gas supplied by Russia, and in turn may delay investments in the exploration of new gas fields and for the construction of gas pipelines in Russia.

While China's demand for gas is projected to grow considerably, negotiations are still continuing between Gazprom and the Chinese side concerning supply routes, quantities and prices. Japan, for its part, is one of the largest natural gas importers in the world. Its natural gas imports have been in the LNG format so far and will be so in the future as well. Therefore, Japan will import from Russia only LNG produced in Sakhalin-2. Russia has a plan to construct an LNG facility near Vladivostok. However, Japanese specialists doubt its competitiveness because in this plan natural gas, transported a long way through pipelines from Sakhalin or East Siberia, is liquefied in Vladivostok (Motomura, 2010, p. 30).

Under these circumstances, there could be difficulties in finding sufficient foreign demand for natural gas produced in Sakhalin and East Siberia. Construction of the Sakhalin–Khabarovsk–Vladivostok (SKV) gas pipeline started in September 2009 and phase I will be completed by the third quarter of 2011. The transportation capacity will be only 6 billion cubic metres per year (Gazprom, 2011). After the completion of phase II capacity will expand to 30 billion cubic metres (Motomura, 2010, p. 28), and production in Sakhalin will be increased substantially. Gas production in Sakhalin is expected to reach 31–36 billion cubic metres by 2013–15 and 36–37 by 2020–2022, according to the Energy Strategy of Russia (see Table 8.2).

In addition, the Yakutiia–Khabarovsk–Vladivostok (YKV) pipeline will be constructed by 2016, when the start of gas production in Chaianda gas fields in the Sakha Republic is expected (see also Chapter 4). The sum of the transportation capacity of these two pipelines will be 47.2 billion cubic metres by 2016 (Motomura, 2010, p. 28). According to the Energy Strategy, gas production in East Siberia and the Far East will amount to 43–53 billion cubic metres by 2013–15 and 91–122 by 2020–22 (see Table 8.2).[28] The main sources of gas will be Sakhalin-3 and Chaianda. Gazprom purchased the production licences of these two fields in June 2009 and in September 2008 respectively (Motomura, 2010, pp. 28, 32).

According to Russia's Eastern Gas Programme, gas supply to the domestic market in Eastern regions will be 18 billion cubic metres in 2015 and 27 billion in 2020.[29] This means that there will be ample capacity for exports through the SKV and YKV pipelines. According to the Eastern Gas Programme, natural gas exports to China and South Korea through these pipelines may reach 25–50 billion cubic metres from 2020. Although the success of the Eastern Gas Programme depends heavily on exports to these two countries, as recent negotiations between Gazprom and the Chinese side suggest, there is a possibility that Russia might put a higher priority on exporting West Siberian natural gas to China over other projects, as has been the case in crude oil (*RBK daily*, 2010).

CONCLUDING REMARKS

We would like to emphasize that as a result of the eastward shift, Russian oil and gas companies could export their oil and gas produced in the Western Siberian fields to the East Asian market. This strategy has already decreased Russia's dependence on the European market for oil and gas and it will continue to do so. This merit should be evaluated against the background of stagnated demand for conventional natural gas in the USA and Europe since 2009. For East Asian countries, such as China, Japan and South Korea, imports of oil and gas from Russia improve their energy security in the sense that they can avoid excessive dependence on the Middle East and North Africa.

Thus we can conclude that in adopting the strategy of the eastward shift, Russian oil and gas companies are acting basically in a business frame. However, due to the overwhelming importance of oil and gas export revenues for the Russian economy, the Russian government (simultaneously the owner of Gazprom and Rosneft) initiated this strategy by constructing the ESPO pipeline and introducing a preferential tax regime in the region. In this sense, we might argue that the state, too, has acted in a business frame.

NOTES

1. This research was supported by the Environment Research and Technology Development Fund (E-0901) of the Ministry of the Environment, Japan, and the fund of the Ministry of Education and Science, Japan, for the joint project, 'The Establishment of the Network of Environmental Studies in the Pan-Okhotsk Region' (2007–11). We thank Alexander Kramskoy and Tomoko Tabata for helping us to collect some statistical data.
2. In this article, we define East Siberia as including only Krasnoiarsk *krai* and Irkutsk *oblast*, because in other regions that are usually included in 'East Siberia' such as the Buriatiia, Tyva and Khakasiia republics and Zabaikal *krai*, oil and gas production potential is limited.
3. Data derived from Federal Treasury (n.d.) converted into the US dollar by the official exchange rate, reported at the Central Bank of Russia (CBR, n.d.). In addition to these two taxes, oil and gas companies pay profit taxes, property taxes, value-added taxes and so on; see Tabata (2006) and Alexeev and Conrad (2009) for the Russian taxation system on oil and gas.
4. Oil and gas export values are reported at CBR (n.d.).
5. About half of the crude oil was refined, and half of that was exported in these years.
6. In fact, it fundamentally revised the original programme adopted by Government Resolution No. 480 of 15 April 1996.
7. The preamble to the programme notes that this order was issued in accordance with Protocol No. 1 of the meeting of the Government Commission on the Fuel and Energy Complex and Regeneration of the Mineral and Raw Materials Base on 15 June 2007. This government commission was set up by Government Resolution No. 794 of 21 December 2005 and its present Chairman is Igor Sechin.
8. At that time, McDermott and Marathon were members of Sakhalin Energy, but they sold their holding and left the project in the second half of the 1990s.
9. Because of the grandfather clause (that is an exception that allows current businesses to continue operating under the previous laws), these amendments are not applied to existing PSAs.
10. A brief prehistory of the construction of the ESPO pipeline is summarized in Motomura (2008, pp. 75–8).
11. This is the formula applied from the beginning of 2009, introduced by Federal Law No. 158 of 22 July 2008. Previously, since the beginning of 2005 the following formula had been applied (Federal Law No. 102 of 18 August 2004): $T = (P − 9) \times 0.22$.
12. Government Resolution No. 32 of 28 January 2010 set the tariff of export duties of the commodities of code '27.09.009002' at zero from the beginning of February 2010. Government Resolution No. 115 of 3 March 2010 stipulated that this Resolution No. 32 was effective from 19 January 2010.

13. In December 2010, two oil fields in the Caspian Sea were added to the list of oil fields to which reduced tax rates would be applied, by replacing code '27.09.009002' with a new code '27.09.009003' (Decision of the Commission of Customs Union No. 436 of 14 October 2010).
14. S.D. Shatalov, Deputy Minister of Finance, talked about this formula in an interview with the mass media on 8 June 2010 (Shatalov, 2010); for his part Igor Sechin, Deputy Prime Minister and Chairman of the Board of Directors of Rosneft, proposed this formula at the cabinet meeting on 16 June 2010 (Sechin, 2010).
15. This law was retroactively applied.
16. Distribution of extraction tax revenues is prescribed by Article 50 of the budget code. While 5 per cent of their revenues had been paid to the regional budget until the revision, Federal Law No. 218 of 22 September 2009 revised this. The application of this revision was, however, stopped until 1 January 2010 by Federal Law No. 229 of 3 October 2009.
17. In Russia's customs statistics, not all of China's oil imports are recorded. If we compare Russia's exports to China and China's imports from Russia, it is suggested that Russia's statistics fully report Russia's exports of oil to China by rail, but cover only a part of Russia's exports by tanker. Most of Russia's exports to China by tanker may have been included in exports to transit countries, such as the Netherlands.
18. The data released by the Agency of Natural Resources and Energy (ANRE) under the Ministry of Economy, Trade and Industry, Japan, were based on reports by all oil importers in Japan. The data include not only crude oil, but also straight run fuel oil. Therefore, the import quantity of the ANRE data exceeds the data reported in customs statistics of Japan.
19. In Table 8.3, imports from Russia by pipeline arrive from the West Siberian fields through Kazakhstan.
20. These imports were not included in the code '27.11.210000' (natural gas in the gaseous state), but in code '27.11' (petroleum gases and other gaseous hydrocarbons) of Russia's customs statistics (FCS, 2009, p. 62). Therefore, these figures were expressed in tons. Note that total exports under the code '27.11' reported in Russia's customs statistics do not include those to Belarus. According to Russia's customs statistics, seven countries were listed as importers of Russia's natural gas in 2009 that have not imported natural gas in the gaseous state and that were not listed as such in 2008. Therefore, these seven countries are regarded as importers of LNG. They are Japan, Kuwait, India, South Korea, China, Taiwan and Malta in order of import volumes. Total imports by these countries amounted to 3.76 million tons and Japan accounted for 57.1 per cent of them.
21. Although the share of petroleum products has been large, especially since 2007 (see Figure 8.3), we should approach these figures cautiously. On the one hand, in Japan's customs statistics, imports of Russia's straight run fuel oil are classified as imports of petroleum products, and on the other, they were regarded by Japanese oil importers as imports of crude oil owing to their low quality. Therefore, in the ANRE data, they are included in crude oil imports (see Table 8.4).
22. Calculated from *Investitsii* (2007; 2009).
23. Calculated from FCS (2009, pp. 7–10).
24. If we compare Russia with Saudi Arabia, state budget revenues from oil and gas (in Saudi Arabia they are simply called 'oil revenues') were significantly larger in Saudi Arabia in 2002–07 both in terms of their volumes in dollars and of their ratios against oil and gas exports (Tabata, 2009b, pp. 85–6).
25. The methodology for setting the tariff of oil transportation by Transneft was determined by Federal Tariff Service (FTS) Order No. 380 of 17 August 2005.
26. This transportation through the ESPO pipeline is defined and called 'complex oil transportation' by Government Resolution No. 1022 of 16 December 2009, which amended Government Resolution No. 980 of 29 December 2007, named 'State Regulation of Tariffs for the Service by Natural Monopoly Subjects in Oil and Petroleum Products Transportation'.
27. FTS Order No. 525 of 24 December 2009 and No. 167 of 29 July 2010.
28. In the Eastern Gas Programme, production of natural gas is to reach 50 bcm in East Siberia and 35 bcm in the Far East by 2015. Apparently, these figures are too ambitious.

29. Motomura (2010, p. 30) indicated that domestic demand in the area of Khabarovsk and Vladivostok would be 6 billion cubic metres and Bradshaw (2010a, p. 332) cited Gazprom's estimates for demand in these regions: 3 billion cubic metres in Khabarovsk *krai*, 4.5–5 bcm in Sakhalin *oblast*, and 5 bcm in Primorskii *krai*. Compared with these figures, the forecast of the Eastern Gas Programme again seems too ambitious.

PART IV

The global level: Russian energy in a wider
perspective

9. 'They went East, they went West...': the global expansion of Russian oil companies

Nina Poussenkova

INTRODUCTION

In any state, governmental and big business actors are inextricably linked, particularly when it comes to the management of strategic resources such as oil and gas. In the case of Russian energy policy, the two actors are so close as to be at times indistinguishable. This symbiotic relationship is particularly strong in the global expansion of Russian oil companies guided by an intricate network of business and political power interests. In other words, to successfully pursue their global expansion, Russian energy companies not only have to pay close attention to features of resource geography – the type of natural resources available beyond Russian territory and the related infrastructure needed to exploit those resources – they also need to carefully assess the features that characterize the financial and institutional dimensions of the policy environment (or structure) in which they find themselves (see Chapter 2).

In this chapter I focus on the global expansion of Russian oil companies, which has been much less often examined than, for example, the power of Russian actors in gas markets and operations throughout the world. I will argue that the relative importance of the three dimensions – resource geographic, financial and institutional – has varied throughout the history of Russia's oil sector. I will first briefly reflect on the situation under socialism, and then analyse the 1990s and the 2000s in greater detail (for pre-Soviet history, see Goldman, 2008).

Throughout the 2000s actors regulating the institutional dimension strengthened their role, with the result that the oil and gas sector came increasingly within the sphere of influence of the state. At the same time the problems of the maturing resource base in Russia's oil industry gained prominence. As the growth rate in oil production decelerated, the constraints imposed by the availability of resources for the pursuit of global expansion became an issue for oil companies. While the policy environment was unidimensional under socialism (institutional dimension), and became two-dimensional during the 1990s (with the financial dimension assuming greater importance), it finally became much more complicated in the 2000s, when the resource geographic dimension occupied the companies' horizons. Now companies try to negotiate these three dimensions and their interrelationships in what has become the complex and controversial context of their global expansion. In some situations the resource geographic and financial dimensions enable them to act coherently. However, they often encounter institutional obstacles to their globalization endeavours. Given Russia's desire to re-establish itself as a global power, it is to be expected that the institutional dimension will to a great extent condition the oilmen's globalization aims.

EXPANSION IN THE SOVIET ERA

Under socialism, Soviet oil resources seemed limitless, and neither the government nor Communist Party officials paid sufficient attention to their efficient use. Consequently the Soviet leadership did not regard other countries with abundant hydrocarbon reserves and lower production costs as potential business opportunities. Similarly, no one at that time was concerned about market mechanisms, profitability or other financial aspects of oil production. The concerns made themselves felt through the two oil crises of 1977–78 and 1982 (see Gustafson, 1989), causing experts to predict serious troubles for the oil sector.

At that time, interests extending beyond the Soviet Union were formulated by actors of the institutional dimension. In the Cold War context the main driver of energy expansion abroad came to be geopolitical considerations and the desire to form strategic alliances against imperialist forces with ideologically and politically compatible countries. The state company Zarubezhneft founded in 1967 under the Ministry of the Oil Industry of the Soviet Union implemented this expansion. It helped to establish oil industries in countries loyal to the Soviet Union, thus earning political advantages for the Soviet Union. The geography of Zarubezhneft's activities speaks for itself: it operated in Angola, Cuba, Iraq, Iran, Libya, Syria and Vietnam. In 1972 it commissioned the first Iraqi oil field, North Rumaila, and later developed the South Rumaila and West Kurna-1 fields. Its most successful overseas project was the joint venture VietSovPetro established in 1981 in Vietnam with the state-owned PetroVietnam.

The Soviet oil production associations were not only forced to leave overseas expansion to Zarubezhneft, but also had to refrain from exporting any of their crude oil. This is because the monopoly Soyuznefteexport established in 1931[1] dealt with oil exports. Mashinoimport was in charge of procuring foreign oilfield equipment since the domestic machine builders were unable to manufacture modern high-quality machinery. Therefore, Soviet oilmen operating behind the Iron Curtain had no experience of cooperating with international partners and in fact, no knowledge of how to operate on global markets governed by universally accepted rules of doing business.

Oil exports became a vital source of hard currency for the Soviet Union, which used the proceeds to enhance its military might, procure oilfield equipment, support the living standards of the population and expand its global influence by assisting friendly foreign regimes. The 6000-kilometre oil export pipeline Druzhba (Friendship) was built in 1960–64. Its northern branch went to Germany through Poland and its southern branch through Ukraine to Czechoslovakia and Hungary. Five years later it became clear that Druzhba-1 was not large enough to support the development of the oil industry in Western Siberia. During the period 1969–74 the second branch was built doubling its export potential.

GOING GLOBAL: THE 1990s

Since the 1991 collapse of the Soviet Union, Russia has been adjusting economically and cognitively to the loss of its superpower status. During the 1990s market transformations were begun and Russian oil companies were partially or totally privatized. Becoming masters of their own destiny, they took their first cautious steps abroad, driven by an uneasy combination of their desire to make profits and awareness of foreign policy considerations.

It is noteworthy how quickly Russia's oil companies learned to manoeuvre in their new environment as far as the financial dimension was concerned. Resolutely relinquishing their former dependence on the state in all strategic matters, the most successful corporations exhibited a true entrepreneurial spirit, even becoming global trendsetters in certain corporate activities, such as hostile takeovers. They hired high-flying foreign managers, used the services of international consulting firms, underwent financial and resource audits by top global accounting and engineering companies, and trained their key employees at the best business schools. They entered global capital markets, made foreign investments, developed export and import operations, acquired assets abroad and in the process learned the international rules of the game.

Lukoil was the biggest Russian oil company in the 1990s and also the first to embrace a globalization policy. Though Lukoil has always preferred to be identified as more of a Western style oil corporation driven by profit interests rather than the pursuit of political influence, in practice it has often acted as a petroleum ambassador for Russia, particularly in the Caspian region – an area for two centuries regarded as Russia's backyard. Owing to this dual role, Lukoil has accepted that both the institutional and financial dimensions condition its operations and complement each other naturally in its overseas expansion.

Lukoil's impressive progress abroad would not have been possible without the political support enjoyed by its CEO, Vagit Alekperov, the former first deputy minister of the oil and gas industry. The company had a powerful advocate in Victor Chernomyrdin, the Russian Prime Minister for most of the 1990s. The then Minister of Fuel and Energy, Yuri Shafrannik, said at the meeting of the company's shareholders in April 1995 that 'projects of Lukoil always had been, are and will be supported by the state' (Savushkin and Kukolev, 1995).

To further its business interests Lukoil needed a source of low cost production and access to solvent customers. In the Russia of the 1990s, the non-payment crisis raged, undermining the profitability of the oil industry. Given the hyperinflation of this period, companies tried to delay payments for goods and services as much as possible. Petrol stations, which received payment from their customers in cash, were relatively well off, while oil producing companies, particularly those obliged to supply the bankrupt agricultural sector or defence enterprises, faced serious financial difficulties. Lukoil decided to internationalize, and quite naturally headed for countries within Russia's traditional sphere of interest. Russia wanted to maintain its political and economic dominance of the Caspian region and initiated an energy dialogue with the former Soviet republics. Lukoil was heavily involved and largely determined Russia's foreign policy in the region. This policy was implemented by maximizing Russian involvement in Caspian petroleum projects and controlling export routes out of the landlocked region.

There were sound profit interests for Lukoil to invest in the Caspian region. A typical new well in Western Siberia cost US$1 million to drill and yielded 150 barrels of oil per day. By contrast, a well in the Caspian region cost US$200,000 to put into operation and was likely to produce 1500–5000 barrels per day (see Gorst and Poussenkova, 1998).

Azerbaijan hosted the bulk of Lukoil's Caspian operations. Psychologically, it was understandable since President Vagit Alekperov himself is half Azeri. Politically this made sense because Lukoil provided a Russian counterweight to the numerous foreign companies involved in the area. However, ultimately some of these operations disappointed Lukoil, and a number of unsuccessful projects, such as Karabakh in Azerbaijan, were closed.

Hydrocarbon-rich Kazakhstan served as another important base for Lukoil's Caspian expansion. In 1995, Lukoil acquired a 50 per cent stake in the Kumkol field. In November 1997, Lukoil bought a 15 per cent share in the

PSA to develop the Karachaganak field, one of the world's biggest. In 1997, Lukoil purchased a 2.7 per cent share in the giant Tengiz field with 4.4 billion barrels of proven oil reserves. This was possible through its joint venture Lukarco with the American ARCO, which had a 5 per cent holding.[2] Through Lukarco, Lukoil joined the Caspian Pipeline Consortium (CPC) with a 12.5 per cent holding, fully understanding the importance of export pipelines. The 1500-kilometre CPC pipeline was to connect the oil fields of Western Kazakhstan with the Russian terminal in Novorossiysk on the Black Sea. Determined to emerge as the leading company throughout the Caspian Sea, in 1996 Lukoil persuaded Moscow to make it a coordinator of Russian projects in the area.

Lukoil also moved much further abroad. In 1995, it bought a 24 per cent share in the Meleya block in Egypt with 16.3 million barrels of proven oil reserves. Most importantly, in 1997, Lukoil acquired a 68.5 per cent holding in the giant West Kurna-2 field in Iraq. Even though Lukoil and its partners signed a PSA with the Iraqi government, they failed to start operations on time because of the sanctions imposed on Iraq by the UN. Thus in 2002 the Iraqi leader Saddam Hussein terminated the contract.

What clearly indicated the long-term vision of Lukoil's leadership was its move to the European downstream. During the late 1990s, the company bought controlling interests in the Romanian Petrotel refinery, petrochemical complex Neftokhim Burgas in Bulgaria, and in the Odessa refinery in Ukraine. Presumably this breakthrough into European downstream in 1990 was possible because, on the one hand, Lukoil dealt with countries that were relatively loyal to Russia, and, on the other hand, Russia in its weakened state at that time lacked superpower status; consequently the Europeans did not consider that it compromised their energy security interests. Therefore at that time the institutional and financial dimensions did not present conflicting logics to Lukoil.

Yukos was also setting its sights abroad. In 1995, its subsidiary Yuganskneftegas acquired an exploration licence in Peru. Although this experience was not an unqualified success, it failed to deter Yukos. Afterwards it started to investigate opportunities in Africa and the Middle East. In the late 1990s, it began to view China as a potential export market.

During the 1990s, the weak and corrupt Russian government lacked coherent, long-term energy policies. More often than not it hindered rather than helped the Russian oilmen's attempts at international expansion. Russia's failure to regulate the institutional dimension of the policy environment and to link it up with the financial logic guiding the interests of strong and visionary companies such as Lukoil are best demonstrated by the fiasco of the Leuna-2000 project. At issue was the construction of a refinery in Germany by Elf Aquitaine where the state-owned Rosneft together with Surgutneftegas and

Table 9.1 Lukoil involvement in foreign upstream projects during the 1990s

Project/country	Project timeframe	LUKOIL's share	Other participants
Azeri–Chirag–Guneshli (Azerbaijan)	1994–2024	10%[1]	BP (34.1%) Chevron (10.3%) SOCAR (10%) Statoil (8.5%) ExxonMobil (8%) TPAO (6.8%) Devon Energy (5.6%) Itochu (3.9%) Amerada Hess (2.7%)
Shah–Deniz (Azerbaijan)	1996–2036	10%	BP (25.5%) Statoil (25.5%) Total (10%) NICO (10%) SOCAR (10%) TPAO (9%)
Yalama (Azerbaijan)	1998–2035	65% (operator)[2]	SOCAR (20%) GDF Suez (15%)
Kumkol (Kazakhstan)	1995–2021	50%	CNPC (50%)
Karachaganak (Kazakhstan)	1997–2038	15%	BG Group (32.5%) ENI Group (32.5%) Chevron (20%)
Tengiz (Kazakhstan)	1997–2032	2.7% through Lukarco (5%)	Chevron (50%) ExxonMobil (25%) KazMunaiGaz (20%)
Meleya (Egypt)	1995–2024	24%	EGPC (56%) IFC (20%)
West-Kurna 2 (Iraq)	1997–2020	68.5%	SOMO (25%) Zarubezhneft (3.25%) Mashinoimport (3.25%)

Notes:
1. Lukoil sold its 10 per cent share to INPEX in 2003.
2. Lukoil exited this project in 2009.

Source: Lukoil Key Facts (2009).

Megionneftegas were to supply crude oil as the refinery's shareholders. However, the Russian authorities, presumably protecting the interests of other companies, delayed the preparation of the documents that Surgutneftegas, Rosneft and Megionneftegas needed to be involved in Leuna-2000 for so long that they became obsolete. The export benefits provided by the state to companies to help them supply oil to the refinery were negligible. Negotiations between Elf and the Russians came to a total impasse (see Azarova, 1997). Now, Leuna-2000 is refining oil – but without Russian oilmen.

GOING GLOBAL: THE 2000s

In the 1990s, the Russian oil industry was fighting for survival in the face of severe difficulties ensuing from developments on the financial dimension. These included chronic lack of capital, coupled with low world oil prices not conducive to the implementation of complex and expensive new projects, and Russia's own economic meltdown in 1998. Russian companies also tried to cope with resource use challenges as production was in a state of drastic decline. In this type of operating environment international expansion was not the top priority.

However, the situation changed radically in the new century. With rising oil prices and production, Russian oil companies matured and endeavoured to become global players. Rejecting the most inefficient and counterproductive socialist business practices, they benefited from the privatization of the 1990s, corporate restructuring, use of foreign advanced technologies and managerial experience now introduced into the formerly closed Soviet oil sector by international companies. Yukos and Sibneft were leaders of low-cost oil production growth owing to the application of modern technologies and competent personnel.

Russian companies were steadily growing larger and more powerful. In 2005, only three companies (Gazprom, Lukoil and RAO UES) were included in the global Fortune-500 list, while in 2010, there were six Russian members in this select club, namely Gazprom (ranked 50th), Lukoil (93rd), Rosneft (211th), Sberbank (256th), TNK-BP (318th), and Sistema (460th) (Fortune, 2010). Apart from accessing capital and know-how on how to optimize the use of resources, Russian companies had a wider frame of action whereby 'going global', in particular doing downstream business in Europe, helped to gain credibility and a good reputation. At the same time the oil oligarchs wanted to legitimize their fortunes made amidst the political and economic instability of the 1990s.

Supporting the globalization ambitions of the key oil companies, the strengthened Government of the Russian Federation began to re-establish the country's former might and to reassert its global influence, though now with an emphasis on becoming an energy power rather than the nuclear power of the Soviet era. Significantly, the 'Energy Strategy of Russia until 2020' adopted in 2003 stated that 'Russia possesses substantial energy reserves and a powerful fuel and energy complex that forms the basis of its economic development and is a tool for implementing its domestic and foreign policy. The role of the country in the global energy markets largely determines its geopolitical influence' (Government of the Russian Federation, 2003).

Later the government tried to distance itself from this blunt statement and insist on pure business interests for global expansion. The new energy strategy until 2030, adopted in 2009, moderates this idea: 'The goal of Russia's energy policy is to ensure the most efficient use of natural energy resources and potential of the energy sector to support sustainable growth of economy, improvement of living standards of the population and strengthening of its global economic positions' (Government of the Russian Federation, 2009a). Thus institutional actors operated with an interest in gaining more political power, and achieved this through increasing involvement of the state in the oil sector and the gradual replacement of private corporations by state-owned ones. Moreover, state companies enjoyed preferential treatment from the federal authorities helping them to build substantial competitive advantages over their private rivals. Thus, the state-owned Rosneft and Gazprom became the sole actors on the continental shelf of Russia; Rosneft successfully lobbied tax breaks for its East Siberian fields and twice obtained credits from China, as well as exclusive access to the ESPO oil pipeline branch leading to China (see Moe and Kryukov, 2010; also see below and Chapter 8).

One of the reasons given by the ruling elite for expanding the state's role in the economy is that Russia needs powerful corporations capable of competing successfully in world markets, or 'national champions' (see Chapter 2). The authorities also consider it a matter of national prestige to create gigantic companies in order to confirm Russia's claim to a global energy power status. Rosneft fits this role well (see below).

The mentioned resource geographic drivers of Russian companies' global expansion in the 2000s are related to the end of the era of cheap and easily produced hydrocarbons in Russia. It was simply easier to produce oil and gas abroad than, for example, to develop the extreme North of Russia. Russian actors increasingly linked the considerations on the resource geographic and financial dimensions together in promoting global expansion. More favourable taxation regimes abroad also represented further important financial drivers for the international expansion of oil companies (Lukoil, 2003).

In general, such a globalization policy of successful national oil companies (NOCs) from oil producing countries has been gaining momentum with the high prices of the 2000s. Such dynamic NOCs as the Brazilian Petrobras, the

Malaysian Petronas, the Algerian Sonatrach, the Kuwait Petroleum Company, the Norwegian Statoil and others are quickly expanding their global presence both in upstream and downstream sectors of other oil producing and oil consuming countries. Researchers have even coined a term 'i-NOC' to emphasize their growing similarity to international oil companies (IOCs) (Brogan, 2008) and their competition for leadership. Acknowledging the growing parallels between NOCs/national champions and private energy companies/IOCs (see Chapter 2), I will next discuss the Russian setting by moving from more private-like companies towards the national champions end of the spectrum.

Private Companies

Lukoil

Throughout the 2000s Lukoil led the global expansion of Russian oil companies although Rosneft took its place as the flagship of the Russian oil industry towards the end of the decade. Among Russian oil companies, Lukoil best exemplifies the criteria of an international oil company. About 25 per cent of its activities are conducted abroad. It operates in 35 countries in both upstream and downstream sectors.

Starting with the upstream, by the late 2000s Lukoil was operating in Columbia, Venezuela, the Ivory Coast, Ghana, Egypt, Saudi Arabia, Kazakhstan, Uzbekistan and Azerbaijan. In 2007 alone, Lukoil joined three new projects. It reached an agreement with Vanco Energy on buying 56.6 per cent holdings in three exploration projects in Guinea Bay. With the Indonesian Pertamina it closed a two-year agreement on joint geological exploration in Indonesia. With Qatar Petroleum it signed a memorandum of understanding on joint activities in Qatar.

In 2009, Lukoil made an important acquisition by purchasing BP's share in the CPC and TengizChevrOil for US$1.6 billion.[3] Lukoil bought 46 per cent of Lukarco B.V. to complete its full ownership of this company. The key assets of Lukarco are its 12.5 per cent stake in CPC and 5 per cent stake in TengizChevrOil which develops Tengiz and Korolevskoye fields in Kazakhstan.

In December 2009 Lukoil won a contract for the Iraqi oilfield West Kurna-2 (85 per cent) with the Norwegian Statoil (15 per cent). The partners proposed to the Iraqi government a fee of US$1.15 per barrel and a peak production of 1.8 million barrels a day. Lukoil and Statoil plan to invest up to US$5 billion in the field's development, with drilling to begin in 2011, oil production in late 2012, and the planned peak production capacity scheduled for 2017 (Tutushkin and Vasiliev, 2009).

West Kurna-2 is an important milestone for Lukoil. However, Lukoil's victory should not be exaggerated, since it received only a service contract with relatively modest profit prospects. It is estimated that Lukoil will earn some US$450 million per year operating in a country where the institutional dimension of oil production is still underdeveloped with very serious security risks. On the other hand, Iraq is an extremely oil-rich low-cost producer.[4] Having gained a foothold there, and helping the country to revive its oil industry devastated by war, Lukoil probably expects improvements in the investment climate in the future, and access to other lucrative contracts. Besides, since Iraq's ambitions are to become the second biggest oil producer in the world and, therefore, a serious competitor for Russia, Lukoil may also be proceeding from the logic of 'If you can't beat them, join them'. All in all, though Lukoil may not be as close to the government as it was during the 1990s, it may still help the government of the Russian Federation to pursue interests of political power, making the institutional dimension also present in its advances to Iraq.

As for Lukoil's expansion into the European downstream, its track record is not as impressive as it is in upstream projects abroad. After initial breakthroughs in the 1990s, in the 2000s Lukoil failed to buy the Gdansk refinery in Poland, the Lithuanian Mazeikiu Nafta, Hellenic Petroleum in Greece and the Europoort refinery in Rotterdam.

Of these failures, the case of Hellenic Petroleum exemplifies the wider structural constraints. In 2002–03, together with the Greek Latsis Group, Lukoil wanted to acquire Hellenic Petroleum. The Government of the Russian Federation supported this wholeheartedly. In December 2001, when Vladimir Putin visited Greece, much attention was devoted to the development of petroleum dialogue between the countries. Vagit Alekperov was a prominent member of the Russian delegation. Lukoil's chances of success seemed very good as its consortium with the Latsis Group was the only contender for Hellenic Petroleum. However, in early 2003 the Greek authorities decided against selling, calling the offer 'unacceptable in terms of the national interests of Greece' (Gaiduk and Lukin, 2006).

The intrigue in Lukoil's negotiations at the end of 2008 regarding the acquisition of a 29.9 per cent holding in the Spanish Repsol further confirms the structural problems. The Prime Minister of Spain accentuated how, in contrast to Gazprom, which was also reportedly interested in Repsol, Lukoil was a private company (Malkova and Khripunov, 2008). In other words, though not exactly highly desirable, it was still a more acceptable contender. In general, Europeans are wary of state companies as a vehicle of Russia's political interests. Yet judging by the large-scale campaign in the Spanish press, to the Spaniards Lukoil seemed no less frightening than Gazprom. Here the Europeans operated with double standards: on the one hand, they tended to forget that there were European fully or partly state-owned companies; on the other hand, they did not seem to object to the presence of the Venezuelan

PDVSA in the European downstream,[5] a powerful tool of Hugo Chavez' authoritarian, market sceptical regime.

What we can gather from this is that while state support for Russian oil companies' expansion into Europe is necessary, it sometimes backfires. Paradoxically, Russian involvement in Europe's downstream realizes European business interests by offering relatively cheap Russian crude permitting lower costs for petroleum products; however, at the same time, through their acquisition of European refineries, in some eyes Russian companies endanger European political interests by strengthening their global competitiveness and influence in Europe.

Only in 2008 did Lukoil claim its first successes of the 2000s, with its acquisition from the Italian ERG in Sicily of 49 per cent of the ISAB oil refinery with 320 000 barrels per day capacity. Then in 2009, Lukoil bought 45 per cent of the 150 000 barrels per day Vlissingen refinery in the Netherlands from Total for US$600 million, thereby gaining its first foothold in Northwest Europe. This latter deal concomitantly realizes the business interests of Total as in that way it might have been repaying the advance it received when it was invited to the Shtokman gas condensate field project in the Barents Sea together with Statoil. Total has followed the asset swaps model of German companies in doing successful business in Russia – exchanging 'our downstream for your upstream' (see Westphal, 2007). In addition to bringing in a powerful Russian player with ample crude supplies, Total's decision to sell to Lukoil rather than to the US refining giant Valero may have furnished the political goodwill for a subsequent deal with the Russian independent gas producer Novatek.[6] Both transactions have political undertones. The Lukoil deal coincided with a visit to the Netherlands by Russian President Dmitry Medvedev, while the Novatek agreement followed a meeting between Total's CEO Christophe de Margerie and Russian Prime Minister Vladimir Putin (Petroleum Intelligence Weekly, 2009).

By 2009, the retail network of Lukoil consisted of 6 700 fuel stations in 25 countries, including Russia, the CIS, Europe and the US. Lukoil is the only Russian oil company to gain a foothold in the US. In 2000, the company bought a controlling interest in Getty Petroleum with 1 300 fuel stations. In 2004, it acquired another 779 fuel stations from its partner and shareholder ConocoPhillips. However, since Lukoil does not have a refinery in the US, fuel stations with Lukoil's logo must be taken as part of a wider 'going global' frame rather than as a manifestation of pure profit-making interests.

Lukoil has long planned to buy or build a refinery in the US to accommodate its rising oil output in Russia's north. Lukoil intended, together with its partner ConocoPhillips, to invest in a new refinery on the eastern coast of the US that would focus on processing Russian crude blends (Reuters, 2009). However, in spring 2010 ConocoPhillips decided to sell half of its 20 per cent stake in Lukoil. CEO James Mulva explained the decision by the unfavourable investment climate in Russia. The Russian government allocates major oil and gas fields to the state-owned Gazprom and Rosneft and does not permit private companies to develop as quickly as they initially planned (Lenta.ru, 2010a). Then the American company decided to divest itself of the whole stake in its Russian partner by the end of 2010 (Gavshina, 2010b).

We thus find that the domestic energy policy of the Russian government can affect Lukoil's chances of strengthening its foothold in the US because of a cooling in relations with its key foreign partner. In other words, Lukoil finds developments within the institutional dimension conflicting with its profit interests.

Yukos
Yukos also continued its advance beyond Russia's borders, mainly driven by profit-making interests along the financial dimension. In the downstream, it opted for Eastern Europe. In 2002, Yukos acquired a blocking interest in the Lithuanian refining complex Mazeikiu Nafta. In 2001, it bought 49 per cent of the shares and managing rights over the Slovak oil transportation company Transpetrol. Its pipelines located in the centre of Europe facilitated oil deliveries to refineries in Slovakia, the Czech Republic and Germany. Yukos lobbied for the Adria pipeline's reversal and upgrading that would help transport Russian oil to the Mediterranean Sea. The company invited the Hungarian MOL to work on the Zapadno-Malobalyksk field in West Siberia, and this alliance helped Yukos to secure a niche on the Hungarian retail market.

Yukos considered the US a promising export market, anticipating deliveries of up to 35 million tonnes a year. Trial shipments began on 3 July 2002, when the supertanker *Astro Lupus* brought 1.7 million barrels to Texas (Oil and Energy Trends, 2002). Yukos also lobbied for the initiative that would have improved the profitability of exports to the US through a new oil pipeline from Western Siberia to Murmansk with a capacity of 80 million tonnes per year. But neither the government nor Transneft were willing to give up their monopoly on trunk pipelines that served as an important tool for regulating the oil sector (see also Tkachenko, 2007, p. 180).

Developing major fields in Russia's east, Yukos was one of the first Russian oil companies to understand the benefits of exporting crude from these regions to China. Yukos has cooperated with China since 1999, when the first trial cargo of 12 000 tons of oil was delivered. In May 2003, Yukos and CNPC signed a three-year contract to supply 6 million tonnes of oil from Russia to China by rail.

In 1999, Yukos, Transneft and CNPC signed an agreement on a pre-feasibility study for the construction of a Russia–China pipeline, and in September 2001, a general agreement on a feasibility study proper. In May

2003, the heads of Yukos and CNPC signed a long-term contract to pump 20 million tonnes for the first five years, and 30 million tonnes through the planned pipeline starting from 2010. Yukos proposed a pipeline from Angarsk to Daquing, which for a while competed with the Angarsk–Nakhodka pipeline promoted by Transneft. Yukos's version was a shorter, cheaper and profitable pipeline with smaller volumes of crude to be pumped through it. As for Transneft's option, it was unclear whether the eastern Siberian oil reserves would suffice to fill it. However, the delivery of crude to Nakhodka, a major seaport, would diversify export markets for Russian crude compared to the Angarsk–Daqing option, which would have made Russia dependent on a single buyer, namely China. At that time it was clear that political interests would determine the choice, but later both routes were vetoed by the authorities because of environmental considerations (see also Chapter 8).

When the Yukos court case started, the company was bankrupt and sold off (mainly to Rosneft and Gazprom) and gradually its foreign assets found other owners (see also Chapter 3; and Tkachenko, 2007). In March 2009, the Government of Slovakia acquired Transpetrol. A month later, the Polish PKN Orlen purchased Mazeikiu Nafta, and state-owned Rosneft, which bought most of Yukos's oil assets, continued its eastern expansion.

Other actors
Other private companies in Russia have achieved much less in terms of global expansion. For example, Tatneft operates the largely depleted fields in Tatarstan. Therefore increasing its resource base through global expansion is a matter of survival for the company. However, this resource geographic challenge has only prompted it to work in Libya and Syria under service contracts.

TNK-BP bought the Lisichansk refinery in Ukraine in 2000 and has moved to Venezuela. However, it is noteworthy that for TNK-BP, in contrast to Lukoil, the presence of a foreign partner hindered rather than helped its foreign activities. The global expansion of TNK-BP was one of the bones of contention for its joint Russian and British shareholders in their much publicized corporate conflict of 2008. One of the Russian oligarchs behind TNK-BP, Mikhail Friedman, complained in 2008 that since the creation of TNK-BP in 2003, BP blocked more than 20 international projects. Robert Dudley, the then CEO of TNK-BP, retorted 'to my mind, the company should focus on exploration and development of fields and refining primarily in Russia' (Malkova, 2009). For example, TNK-BP wanted to develop Iraq's Kurdistan subsurface. However, the British shareholders objected. Friedman said 'We discussed with BP this opportunity [buying assets in Kurdistan] for a long time, and ultimately their key argument was not that it was an inefficient field, [but that] investments in Iraqi Kurdistan are not very well perceived by the US state department' (Malkova, 2009). Again we have a case of a Russian business actor finding financial and institutional dimensions at odds with each other.

However, following BP's Gulf of Mexico oil spill of spring 2010, the situation may change, as BP was expected to divest itself of assets worth up to US$30 billion in order to finance the clearing up of the environmental damage. Lukoil could be interested in BP's refineries and fuel stations in the US and Rosneft in its European refineries. BP is ready to sell assets in Venezuela, Pakistan and Vietnam, among others. TNK-BP is seeking to expand its presence in Venezuela by buying shares in BP's projects. In October 2010, during the Venezuelan President Hugo Chavez's ninth visit to Moscow, a memorandum was signed to support TNK-BP's acquisition of BP's assets in Venezuela. In August 2010, TNK-BP and PetroVietnam signed a memorandum envisaging the creation of two joint ventures to explore and produce hydrocarbons in Russia. The plans for Vietnam could involve expanding the capacity of the Dung Quat refinery (Gavshina, 2010c). Presumably TNK-BP was considering cooperation with PetroVietnam in the context of its possible purchase of BP's Vietnamese assets. Additionally, TNK-BP was viewing the Algerian assets of BP, and Prime Minister Vladimir Putin was ready to help the company in its negotiations with the Algerian authorities (Nikolskiy, 2010).

In 2009, Surgutneftegas, a privately-owned company that is very close to the Kremlin also made its debut in Europe: it bought 20.2 per cent of the Hungarian MOL for €1.4 billion from the Austrian OMV. This step was quite unusual for the cash-rich Surgutneftegas, which never acquires assets just for the sake of acquisition – and it does not even have any production links with MOL. The key assets of MOL are several refineries and 5000 km of gas distribution networks. It is quite possible that Surgutneftegas's CEO Vladimir Bogdanov was required to help Gazprom, which has been trying to gain control over distribution assets in Europe.

However, there are serious problems with this acquisition. MOL's leadership considered it a hostile takeover and made amendments to the company's charter that significantly expanded the authority of its board of directors. Surgutneftegas is not admitted to the meeting of shareholders, as, allegedly, the Russian company failed to provide the documents needed for its registration as MOL's shareholder. The Hungarian energy regulating authority presumably requires Surgutneftegas to disclose its own shareholders (Malkova, 2010). However, the real owners of Surgut are among the best-kept secrets in the Russian business community. Again we find the institutional dimension hindering the promotion of business interests.

State-owned Companies

Rosneft

While during the 1990s the state-owned Rosneft was mainly fighting for survival, in the new century, amidst increasing state involvement in the oil sector, it turned into a powerful and aggressive player and began expanding its activities abroad. After purchasing most of Yukos's oil assets Rosneft became the undisputed leader of the domestic oil industry. It had even aspired to equality with ExxonMobil and BP by 2010. Russia's leadership wants to have a national oil company matching the international oil companies, also in terms of global influence. Rosneft could be such a company and enjoys state support for its ambitions (see Poussenkova, 2007).

Rosneft's position in Russia was significantly strengthened by the Deputy Prime Minister Igor Sechin's chairmanship of its board of directors from 2004, until his resignation in spring 2011 as part of President Medvedev's reforms to decouple some state–business relationships (see Chapter 2). Yet it is fair to say that actors operating within the institutional dimension are driving Rosneft's globalization efforts. Rosneft is active in the CIS, where it is helping to re-establish Russian influence over the post-Soviet space. Since 2001, Rosneft has been developing the Adaisk zone in Western Kazakhstan together with the Chinese Sinopec on a 50-50 basis. Rosneft is working on the Kurmangazy structure in the Caspian Sea with a 25 per cent stake with Kazmunaigaz, which holds 50 per cent. The owner of the remaining 25 per cent is not determined yet, but Rosneft is financing this share as well during the exploration phase. In this way it is playing the role that foreign companies usually have in Russia: to bear the financial burden of exploration efforts.

Rosneft's successes on the more global scene are less spectacular. In 2001, together with Petrotesting Columbia S.A. and Holsan Chemicals Ltd it won a tender for the development of the Columbian field Suroriente, but soon exited the project. Yet Rosneft is active in Algeria. In 2001, together with Stroitransgas, it signed a contract with Sonatrach for exploration and production in the block 245-South. According to Rosneft's management the company's interest is purely business-related. But was it mere coincidence that the company arrived in Northern Africa when the Russian-Algerian political dialogue began to revive?

Rosneft is now planning to invest some US$630 million in the development of a relatively minor gas field in the United Arab Emirates (UEA) by joining forces with Crescent Petroleum from the UAE. In May 2010, it acquired 40 per cent of the project, with Crescent retaining 60 per cent. Experts believe that Crescent can serve as a conduit for Rosneft's overseas expansion since it is implementing projects in Egypt, Pakistan, Yemen, Tunisia and Iraq (Gavshina and Noviy, 2010). Given the geography of Crescent's activities, both political and business interests could be involved.

The expansion of Russian oil and gas companies to Venezuela – which is becoming an important strategic ally of Russia – shows how Rosneft is replacing Lukoil as the envoy of the Russian government abroad. Until recently, Russian–Venezuelan cooperation was mainly focused on the arms trade. In 2008, Vladimir Putin regretted the small number of joint investment projects between the two countries, and recommended that Gazprom, Lukoil and Russian Railways expand partner relations with Venezuela (Mazneva, 2008). In 2005, Lukoil acquired the Junin-3 block in the Orinoco belt and together with PDVSA certified its reserves. In 2008, Lukoil extended the Junin-3 agreement. Simultaneously, TNK-BP and Gazprom acquired the Ayacucho-2 and Ayacucho-3 blocks respectively. In October 2008, at the suggestion of Igor Sechin, Rosneft, Lukoil, TNK-BP, Surgutneftegas and Gazprom established the National Oil Consortium for joint activities in Venezuela. In February 2010 they signed an agreement establishing a joint venture between the consortium (40 per cent) and PDVSA (60 per cent).

Investments in the Junin-6 block with 53 billion barrels of oil resources alone are estimated at US$20 billion over 40 years. The Russian companies expect to gain valuable experience of producing and upgrading extra-heavy oil. However, this money could also have been invested in the Russian oil sector, for example in research and development, exploration and prospecting, refining or transportation infrastructure. Realizing business interests in Venezuela may also be difficult owing to frequent changes in the tax regime, political instability and the risk of nationalization of foreign assets. Moreover, PDVSA is inviting NOCs from oil and gas producing countries instead of IOCs to work in the Orinoco belt being guided as much by Caracas' political agenda as by the promise of upstream expertise or financing. In short, the business risks connected with the largely financially insolvent and technologically unsophisticated Venezuelan company seem fairly high. It seems that in Venezuela, Russia's geopolitical considerations dominate.

However, upstream involvement in Venezuela may help to realize some business interests. Rosneft has been striving to access the European downstream without any particular success, probably because of the reputational losses following its acquisition of Yukos[7]. In 2010, during Hugo Chavez's visit to Moscow, an agreement was signed on the acquisition by Rosneft of PDVSA's 50 per cent stake in Ruhr Oel GmbH which itself owns stakes in four German refineries. With these refineries Rosneft will reduce its imbalance between oil production and refining, and also realize its globalization ambitions. Therefore, this acquisition of Rosneft was driven both by institutional and financial logics.

However, the political interests underwriting the foreign expansion of Rosneft sometimes do it a disservice. In 2003, it wanted to buy a 25 per cent plus one share of the Croatian state oil company INA, competing with the

Hungarian MOL and Austrian OMV. Of particular importance for Rosneft was INA's 38 per cent ownership of the pipeline company Janaf, which controls a section of the pipeline between the Croatian deepwater Omishal port – where crude is loaded onto tankers for delivery to the US – and the Druzhba pipeline. Rosneft hoped to obtain a guarantee from the Croatian government permitting it to increase its stake in INA to 51 per cent. For Croatian officials this demand was unacceptable. Hence while in the 1990s the weak Russian government could not help Russian companies to access European downstream assets, in the 2000s the help of the strong Russian government sometimes actually impedes the advances of Russian oilmen. Both strong and weak Russian governments seem to be less than optimal for Russian oil companies.

In addition to inheriting Yukos's oil assets, Rosneft inherited Yukos's Chinese vision.[8] China became a new key energy partner for Russia. According to Russia's energy strategy to 2030, the share of Asia-Pacific markets in the exports of Russian oil will increase from the current 6 per cent to 20–25 per cent in 2030, and that of gas from nil to 20 per cent (Government of the Russian Federation, 2009a). In 2006, during the official visit of President Putin to Beijing, Rosneft and CNPC signed an agreement on cooperation both in Russia and in China. In mid-2006, a joint venture Vostok Energy was established between Rosneft (51 per cent) and CNPC (49 per cent) to explore and produce hydrocarbons in Russia. In August 2007, Vostok Energy was granted a licence for two small fields in the Irkutsk region located close to the route of the ESPO oil pipeline (see Chapter 8). Another joint venture, the Russian-Chinese Petrochemical Company, was established in October 2008 in China between Rosneft (49 per cent) and PetroChina (51 per cent), a subsidiary of CNPC, to build a refinery and a network of 300–400 fuel stations. Finally, in 2009 the Chinese Development Bank provided credits of US$15 billion to Rosneft and US$10 billion to Transneft to be repaid by deliveries of 300 million tonnes of oil over 20 years. Igor Sechin actively and personally helped to achieve the deal, which is unprecedented in size in Russian history. According to him, the terms under which Russia will for 20 years deliver 15 million tonnes annually to China are acceptable to both parties (Mazneva, 2009). Here we could well ask if Rosneft is the tail that wags the dog in Russia's current rapprochement with China.

However, Rosneft is facing certain problems in its attempts to establish a niche in China's downstream markets. The company expected in autumn 2009 to sign an agreement on the construction of a refinery in Tianjin with a capacity of 15 million tonnes a year to refine oil pumped through the ESPO pipeline. By autumn 2010, the feasibility study was completed, all documents from the Russian side were ready, but there was no Chinese state expert assessment. In addition to project financing, Russia and China disagreed on a number of issues. In February 2010, China demanded that Russia should double the volume of oil deliveries through ESPO raising them from 15 to 30 million tonnes per year. It now seems that the increase in deliveries represents a *sine qua non* for the commencement of the Russian–Chinese refinery construction in 2010 (Lenta.ru, 2010b). China also seems disappointed with the two small fields that the Vostok Energy joint venture has in the Irkutsk region. Furthermore, the Chinese party seems to have sufficient refining capacity either already operating or under construction. But they would be eager to invite international majors such as ExxonMobil to help them build new modern refineries with their state-of-the-art technologies and skills. In contrast to them, Rosneft can only offer crude oil.

It was only in September 2010 that the construction of the 13 million ton refinery in Tianjin began, to be completed in 2015. Sechin was present at the official ceremony to launch construction. There are also plans to create a network of 500 fuel stations in the North of China (Mazneva, 2010). This breakthrough to the Chinese market could become a serious challenge to Rosneft. China is the world's second biggest consumer of petroleum products after the US, and therefore a very promising opportunity. However, only Sinopec and PetroChina, subsidiary of CNPC, hold licenses to import and export petroleum products. Moreover, the competition in the refining sector will be extremely tough, since actors like ExxonMobil and Saudi Aramco are present there. In addition, China exercises price control over petroleum products with rules that change fairly frequently. Therefore, given all these business risks, it appears that both financial and institutional constraints are at play in Rosneft's advance to the Chinese downstream.

In the ESPO pipeline project, Rosneft gained a substantial competitive advantage over its private rivals by becoming an exclusive supplier of crude to China. In December 2009, the first stage of the pipeline from Taishet in East Siberia to Kozmino Bay on the Pacific Ocean was launched. Vladimir Putin called this a 'geopolitical' project. Indeed, the commissioning of ESPO will open the door to the East, particularly to China – which is Russia's close military and political partner in the making. By starting to build ESPO in 2006 Russia wanted to put pressure on Europe and show that it has other attractive export markets. However, in this project geopolitical goals outweigh business considerations, that is, we find actors mainly looking at the institutional dimension, at the expense of the financial dimension. The deadlines of the project have been postponed several times. The construction costs of the first stage grew from US$6.6 to 14.5 billion. With the pumping tariff established by the state, Transneft's crude deliveries to China will be loss-making for the pipeline monopoly. In addition, crude will be pumped to China from oil fields that could be used to supply other export destinations. For example, oil from Rosneft's Vankor field could be delivered by pipelines to Europe or by tankers to the US (see also Chapter 8).

In January 2011, it seemed that a new stage in Rosneft's globalization efforts might begin after an agreement was reached between the Russian company and BP on joint activities in the Arctic and on a share swap (see also Chapter 10). However, this important deal failed because of the resistance of TNK-BP Russian shareholders, and now Rosneft is searching for other foreign partners.

Other players

Other state-owned oil companies have also been intensifying their overseas activities both in upstream and downstream sectors. In January 2010, Gazpromneft – the former Sibneft and new oil subsidiary of Gazprom – signed a contract as operator for the development of the Badra field in Iraq, with a 30 per cent stake in a consortium with the Korean Kogas (22.5 per cent), Petronas (15 per cent) and the Turkish TPAO (7.5 per cent).

In November 2009, Gazpromneft and the National Iranian Oil Company signed a memorandum of understanding to develop the Azar and Shangule oil fields in Iran. In addition, as Gazpromneft will represent Gazprom in the Elephant Project of ENI in Libya, Gazpromneft will take advantage of international links established by its parent company. Gazpromneft is involved in Angola through the Serbian NIS, which has shares in several projects on four blocks in the country. Gazpromneft also reached an understanding on joining an exploratory project under PSA terms in Cuba. It is also going to develop the continental shelf of Equatorial Guinea with an 80 per cent stake together with the national company GEPetrol (20 per cent). In mid-2010, the potential partners and the Ministry of Energy of Equatorial Guinea signed a PSA on two oil blocks. The Russian side will initially cover all expenses. According to Gazpromneft's deputy director of exploration and production Boris Zilbermints, the company's long-term strategy is to produce some 10–15 per cent of its total crude output abroad by 2020 (Gazpromneft, 2010). In the implementation of this strategy we find Gazpromneft following the same model as other Russian state-owned companies or the NOCs of oil and gas producing countries; that is, establishing alliances with their counterparts, probably in order to compete more successfully with international majors.

Moving on to developments in the downstream sector, Gazpromneft bought 51 per cent of the Serbian NIS in 2008 when Russia and Serbia signed a 30-year intergovernmental agreement on cooperation in the oil and gas business. Serbia will be one of the transit countries for Gazprom's planned South Stream gas pipeline to EU markets. In this case actors found features of the financial and institutional dimensions supporting joint action. Elsewhere in Europe, in 2009 Gazpromneft acquired Chevron's oil and lubricants plant in Italy. In the CIS, Gazpromneft closed a deal with the Kazakh company ARNA Petroleum in mid-2010 to buy a network of 20 fuel stations and land plots to build new stations. By 2011, the Russian company intends to open a further 20 stations in Alma-Ata and Astana. It already has 96 stations in Kirgizia and 21 in Tajikistan.

The state-owned Zarubezhneft has re-established relations with countries where it worked before the collapse of the Soviet Union. Under intergovern-mental agreements signed in 2003–04, it resumed cooperation with India and Syria. It is working in Turkmenistan and Kazakhstan. Cuba invited the company to develop the Varadero field. In 2006, during Vladimir Putin's visit to Vietnam, Zarubezhneft and PetroVietnam established a joint venture to work in Vietnam and other countries. Vietnam offered Zarubezhneft the chance to replace BP in the development of two blocks of Vietnamese gas fields. BP decided to exit these projects in March 2009, presumably for polit-ical reasons. Zarubezhneft also opened a motor oil plant in Serbia, and plans to commission the second phase of the Bosanski Brod refinery and expand its network of fuel stations

CONCLUSION

In this chapter I have described the institutional, financial, and resource geographic dimensions most significant for Russian energy companies' glob-alization efforts. Sometimes the dimensions present complementary and some-times contradictory environments for the companies. Another major finding is that during the 2000s, with the growing nationalization of the energy sector and attempts by the Russian leadership to re-establish the former global might of the country through control over energy resources, political interests have been gaining in importance in the globalization processes. In the Russian case, the state is keenly involved in globalization.

However, the support provided by the Russian government for the global expansion of energy companies has sometimes backfired, since even pure business initiatives have been perceived by the target and partner actors as being controlled by the Kremlin. After two gas conflicts with Ukraine, the Europeans in particular believe their energy security interests to be threatened (see Chapter 7). Gazprom's actions have not only impeded its own overseas expansion, but indirectly impacted on Russian oil companies. As a result, their upstream cooperation with energy producers has been generally more success-ful than their attempts to acquire downstream assets of energy consumers wary of the growing international power of Russia. Moreover, after years of a seller's market, when Russian energy companies could dictate their terms to consumers, the global economic crisis since 2008 revealed that developed countries did not after all need Russian energy quite as much as was thought in Moscow. This new economic situation will probably make Russian companies rethink their corporate interests and frames of action on the global level. The government will also have to revise its energy-based means of realizing foreign policy interests and trying to exercise political influence by resorting to subtler political manoeuvres and becoming more aware of how other actors view business interests and developments in the financial dimension overall.

NOTES

1. It became Nafta-Moskva in 1992.
2. In 1996, ARCO bought 8 per cent of Lukoil for US$300 million, and in 1997 they established the Lukarco joint venture. In 2000, BP became shareholder of Lukarco when it acquired ARCO.
3. BP decided to exit the CPC project because of its dispute with the CPC partners. They wanted to increase the pipeline capacity from 33 to 67 million tonnes per year, while BP was against the proposed financing scheme. In 2008, CPC shareholders agreed that BP would sell its share in 2009, and Lukoil began negotiations with it; see British Petroleum (2009).
4. According to BP, Iraq had 15.5 billion tons of proven reserves in 2009, or 8.6 per cent of the world's reserves. It was fourth in the world in terms of proved reserves, and had a reserves-to-production ratio enabling production for more than 100 years.
5. PDVSA has a 50 per cent stake in AB Nynas, a Swedish operator of five refineries, as well as a 50 per cent stake in Ruhr Oel in partnership with BP. Ruhr Oel owns from 24 to 100 per cent of Gelsenkirchen, Bayern-oil, MiRO and Schwedt refineries with a total capacity of some 50 million tonnes a year; see http://www.mergers.ru/review/comments/comments_2788.html.
6. In mid-2009, Total and Novatek reached an agreement on establishing a joint venture (49 and 51 per cent respectively), to develop the Termokarstovoye gas condensate field in the Yamalo-Nenetsk Autonomous District. This decision was personally approved by Prime Minister Putin.
7. In 2007, Rosneft was interested in the Miro refinery, in which Ruhr Oel holds 24 per cent. Rosneft negotiated with Shell, another shareholder of the refinery, a swap of its stake in Miro (32.5 per cent) for the right to participate in the development of Russian oil fields. However, the negotiations failed at that time.
8. It is noteworthy that the acquisition of Yuganskneftegas, the key oil producing subsidiary of Yukos, was partly financed by a US$6 billion loan from the Chinese banks.

10. Russian energy dilemmas: energy security, globalization and climate change

Michael Bradshaw[1]

INTRODUCTION

> The World's energy system is at a crossroads. Current global trends in energy supply and consumption are patently unstable – environmentally, economically and socially. But that can-and must-be altered; there's still time to change the road we're on. (IEA, 2008, p. 3)

This chapter is somewhat different from the detailed case studies presented so far in this book. Although the same theoretical model is used, the focus here is on the big issues that will shape the context for Russian energy policy-making over the next 20 years or so. In doing so, the chapter taps the structural dimensions of Russia's energy policy formulation – resource geographic, financial, institutional and ecological (see Chapter 2) – and marries them to the wider conceptual framework of 'energy dilemmas' relating to energy security, economic globalization and climate change policy that I have developed elsewhere (Bradshaw, 2010b, 2012).

Russia's post-socialist economic transformation has taken place during a phase of accelerated economic globalization. Russia, and before it the Soviet Union, was incorporated into the global economy mainly as a purveyor of natural resources. In the Soviet era, exports of natural resources were used to earn convertible currency that was used to purchase food (principally wheat) and Western technology. Thus, the central planning system marshalled the rents generated by natural resource exports to address structural weaknesses in the domestic economy. This also represented a massive transfer of rent from Siberia to the European regions of the country (Bradshaw, 2006). When global resource prices fell, the costs to the national economy of Siberian development continued to increase (Hill and Gaddy, 2003). As the resource rents dried up, those weaknesses were exposed and the economic system fell into decline and eventual collapse (Travin and Marganiya, 2010).

The Soviet Union's centralized resource rent distribution system was replaced by a far more complex, contested and murky set of actors and processes (see Gel'man, 2010 and Jones Luong and Weinthal, 2010, pp. 121–80). During the 1990s competition for control over Russia's resources industries was intense and much of the rent generated fell into the hands of a few businessmen who later became known as 'oligarchs', in no small part due to the 'loans for shares' deal orchestrated by President Yeltsin in 1995–96 (Treisman, 2010; see also Chapter 3). When Vladimir Putin became President in 2000, Russia's resource wealth was marshalled to the service of the Russian state. Against a backdrop of rapidly rising resource prices, there was more than enough rent to share out to satisfy different interests. Russia's impressive rates of economic growth fed hyperbole about Russia being an 'energy superpower' (see Chapters 1, 2, 3).

However, resource dependent economies are subject to 'boom and bust cycles' owing to the price volatility of natural resources. Moscow rode the boom to its peak in July 2008 when the oil price hit US$147 a barrel; it then felt the full force of the bust when the global financial crisis of autumn 2008 triggered a collapse in the oil price to US$42 dollars a barrel by the year's end. The structural weaknesses of Russia's economy were once again revealed. Through the global economic crisis Russia fared the worst of the G20 economies and was one of the 15 most affected states, according to the IMF. This hard landing reinforced a new mantra among politicians and policy-makers, that of diversification and modernization. In his 'Go Russia' essay, President Medvedev demanded that Russia rid itself of its 'primitive economy based on raw materials' by overcoming corruption and backwardness, diversi-fying its economy and developing a new modern knowledge-based economy (Medvedev, 2009b, p. 1). In true Kremlin-style, this modernization programme is to be driven by the state. Students of the Soviet economy will hear the echoes of the scientific-technical-revolution of the Brezhnev period and Gorbachev's policy of *uskorenie* (acceleration), both of which failed. The literature on resource abundant economies suggests economic diversification is the right antidote, but the real problem in Russia is a failure to correctly diagnose and address the pathologies that have caused Russia's resource addiction. Gaddy and Ickes (2005, p. 559) explain the centrality of the resource sector to Russia's political economy when they state:

> Throughout its modern history, the country's political economy has centred on the transfer of value created in the resource sector to other parts of the county. During the Soviet era, resource abundance made it possible to impose a costly economic structure on society. Today, the bounty from Russia's resources continues to fuel its economy and its polity.

The literature on the 'resource curse' does not suggest a deterministic rela-tionship between a heavy reliance on natural resource rents and poor economic performance, conflict or authoritarianism. Resource wealth has formed the bedrock of sustained economic development and democracy for example in Australia and Canada (as in the Scandinavian countries). Rather it is the lack of appropriate institutions and political structures to support what Auty (2001) called the 'developmental state' that leads instead to what he called the 'staple trap'. In short, resource wealth *per se* is not a curse, but its presence often undermines the creation of the right state structures necessary, on the one hand, to develop the state with the wealth generated by resource exports, and on the other, to deal with the dangers associated with price volatility and so-called 'Dutch disease' (for more, see Ellman, 2006).

Gaddy and Ickes (2010) in fact see the availability of large amounts of rent from Russia's (energy) resource sector as an essential feature of its contemporary political economy. The sustained export of oil and gas to a very large degree defines Russia's current role in the global economy: in 2009 Russia was the second largest exporter of crude oil in the world (241 million tons or 12.4 per cent of total world exports) and the largest exporter of natural gas (160 billion cubic metres or 21.7 per cent of total world exports) (IEA, 2010d, pp. 11, 13). This status also exposes Russia to the volatility of the global economic system where energy demand and oil and gas prices play a key role. Put another way, the rhythms of the Russian economy are syncopated to those of the price of oil. This also means that Russia's energy policymaking is not just about producing sufficient energy to satisfy domestic demand, it is also about ensuring the maintenance of an 'exportable surplus' sufficient to generate the revenues required by the Russian state.

Thus, in all sorts of ways, energy strategy is central to Russia's economic well-being. Any state driven strategy of modernization in Russia is dependent on the availability of large and sustainable amounts of rent from the resource sector that can be redeployed to diversify the natural economy. Consequently, Russia finds itself in a catch-22 situation: in order to diversify its economy away from resource dependence, it needs to ensure the continued development of the resource sector to deliver the rents to finance diversification and modernization. As Pavel Baev (2010, p. 893) notes:

> The central paradox of this strategy for overcoming the 'resource-curse' is that the necessary volume of revenue in the energy sector can only be generated by massive new investment in the upstream [oil and gas production] and power generation, so priority in resource allocation effectively cannot be changed.

In fact, the current level of taxation on oil exports in Russia is so high that it returns insufficient rent to the oil companies to develop new fields and thus maintain the current level of exports (with reference to East Siberia, see Chapter 8). Russia's predicament would be challenging enough if it were sure of future security of demand for its oil and gas exports. But, as the next section explains, there is good reason to doubt that hydrocarbon exports would ensure a sustainable future for Russia. This reinforces the logic of diversification, but also strengthens the paradox identified by Baev above.

THE GLOBAL ENERGY DILEMMA

...the future of human prosperity depends on how successfully we tackle two central energy challenges facing us to day: securing reliable and affordable energy; and effecting a rapid transformation to a low-carbon, efficient and environmentally benign system of energy supply. (IEA, 2008, p. 37)

It is clear that Russia's resources are part of a global energy dilemma, which put simply is: can we have secure and affordable energy services that are also environmentally sustainable? Our current system of energy supply, dominated by fossil fuels, is increasingly unsustainable. There are two major reasons for this: first, the doubts about the ability of future fossil fuel supplies to meet growing demand (energy security); and second, even if sufficient fossil fuels could be supplied climate change science tells us that their combustion would generate sufficient increases in greenhouse gases (GHG) to bring about cata-strophic climate change. This chapter considers in more detail the current global concerns about energy security and climate change before turning to their implications for Russian energy policymaking.

Global Energy Security

It is unfortunate that much of the current discussion about energy security has focused on threats to security of supply, polarized around issues such as peak oil and resource nationalism, and has largely failed to consider the position of energy exporting states and the issue of security of demand that is most rele-vant to Russia. While the geopolitics of energy security is a wide literature (see Bradshaw, 2009b; also Chapter 1), here I wish to focus on the causes of current concerns about what I will call fossil fuel scarcity. In doing so, I will discuss the structural dimensions of the environment of energy policy formulation (see Chapter 2) one by one in light of the simple framework on scarcity developed by resource geographer Judith Rees (1991, p. 6).

First, physical scarcity pertains to the resource geographic dimension of structure and relates to the exhaustion of non-renewable energy supplies, such as fossil fuels, which results in the inability of energy supplies to meet demand. The largely geological peak oil argument proposes that we will soon reach the physical limit to the maximum rate of oil production and that there-after we might see a rapid reduction in levels of production. With growing demand, the result will be a substantial increase in the price of oil and increased competition and conflict over securing access to dwindling oil supplies. The more extreme proponents of 'peak everything' suggest also a shortage of coal and gas, as well as uranium for nuclear power generation (Heinberg, 2007). The critiques of peak oil refer to the large unexplored areas of the globe, such as the Arctic, that may hold significant reserves of oil and gas; and to how new technologies will improve rates of recovery and provide access to hitherto untapped reserves. Large reserves of unconventional oil (oil sands) and natural gas (shale gas, coal bed methane and so on), if exploited, can increase oil and gas production.

The compromise position is that we are now witnessing the 'end of easy oil' (and gas for that matter) as the easy-to-exploit and lower cost reserves are depleted and new sources of production are harder and more costly to exploit. The expansion of deep-water offshore production is part of this story. The notion of the 'end of easy oil' has resonance with the energy situation in Russia as the more accessible fields of the Volga-Urals and the West Siberian plateau are now in decline and new fields need to be developed in the high Arctic and East Siberia and the offshore areas of the Barents and Kara Seas and the Sea of Okhotsk. This suggests that the cost of sustaining, let alone substantially increasing, global (and Russian) oil and gas production is going to be higher in the future. For energy importing states, the possibility of high cost fossil fuels in the future provides an added incentive to diversify their energy mix in favour of nuclear and renewable energy. This in turn may lead energy exporting states to wonder about increased price volatility and future security of demand and the wisdom of investing ever-increasing sums in developing oil and gas production for which there might not be sufficient demand. In assessing the problems of price volatility and possible demand destruction, UNDP Russia (2010, p. 18) reached the following conclusion:

> This threat is not only short-term (causing such temporary difficulties as were seen in 2008–09), but also long-term, in case of the development and large-scale application of alternative technologies by importing countries. We doubt that such technological breakthroughs are likely in the next 10–15 years, but changeover of this kind is more probable by 2030.

Second, geopolitical scarcity pertains to the institutional dimension – or to the lack of institutionalization balancing supply and demand. This relates to the use of energy exports as a political weapon, the most obvious case being the OPEC embargo in the early 1970s. More recently, Russia has been accused of using control over oil and gas exports to further its foreign policy by punishing those that oppose its policies (see Perovic et al., 2009; Liuhto, 2010; see Chapter 1). It also results from low-cost energy sources shifting to locations perceived by energy importing states to be hostile or unstable. A similar outcome can result from resource nationalism: resource-holding states adopting a more aggressive and nationalist approach to control over and access to their energy reserves (Bremmer and Johnson, 2009). In combination with a decline in indigenous production in the OECD states, the changing geography of oil and gas production is increasingly dominated by non-OECD states and states that favour their own national oil companies (NOCs) over international oil companies (IOCs). Although Russia is not a member of OPEC, it has throughout the 2000s increased state control of its oil and gas sector and restricts access by foreign companies (Bradshaw, 2009b). The rise of China, and to a lesser extent India, is now complicating the geopolitical landscape. China is supporting its NOCs to access oil and gas production by striking bilateral agreements with energy exporting states as part of its so-called 'going out' policy. In some instances China's NOCs are operating in countries such as Sudan, which the host governments of the IOCs find unacceptable to invest in; in other cases they are simply outbidding the IOCs in tenders or tying access to oil and gas fields to generous foreign aid packages. Russia's private and state oil and gas companies are also part of this increasingly competitive process around securing access to future reserves of oil and gas (see Chapter 9; Mitchell, 2010).

A more obvious way in which Russian actors have contributed to geopolitical scarcity relates to conflicts with transit states in Europe (see Chapters 6, 7), which now sit between Russian territory and its lucrative oil and gas markets in the EU. The transit conflicts have resulted in gas flows to Europe being disrupted. This has changed the attitudes of European policymakers on the reliability of Russia as an energy supplier. Despite 30 years of uninterrupted supply from Russia (and the Soviet Union), many European politicians, because of a combination of historical animosity towards Moscow, growing state control over its energy sector, and its transit disputes with its neighbours, now see Russia as a hostile and unstable source of energy supply. As a result, official EU policy now includes putting in place policies to reduce reliance upon Russian energy supplies, through the creation of single European energy market, diversifications of sources of supply and a reduction of reliance on imported oil and gas. For Germany, a more pragmatic response has been to build a pipeline that circumvents the transit risk, but this does nothing to reduce the country risk represented by Russia, nor does it promote solidarity among EU member states (see also Chapter 6).

The current geopolitical friction between the EU and Russia is clearly counterproductive for both sides. As domestic gas production declines in Europe, so demand for imports will increase, unless, as the policymakers hope, the absolute level of gas demand falls in the face of increased energy efficiency and competition from nuclear power and renewables. This should create a market opportunity for Russia. However, the more geopolitical framings of energy policy in Europe make it difficult to sanction substantial increases in reliance on Russian gas in the future. Instead the EU is looking to alternative sources of supply such as LNG, the Nabucco pipeline and the so-called southern corridor. Longer term, there is hope that the shale gas revolution currently being experienced in North America will be transferred to Europe, increasing domestic gas production (Stevens, 2010; Gény, 2010; Wood et al., 2011). This may turn out to be a forlorn hope, but it certainly complicates investment decisions over future gas supply. The current uncertainty threatens Russia's security of gas demand in Europe, that in turn questions the logic of investing in expensive new gas fields in the Yamal Peninsula and the Kara and Barents Seas to deliver gas to markets in Europe. At the same time, it strengthens the case for diversifying markets and developing exports to Northeast Asia (Bradshaw, 2010a and Chapter 8).

Third, economic scarcity pertains to the financial dimension. This is the situation where demand at current prices exceeds the quantity supplied and therefore leads to shortages. Such a situation results in higher prices, which means only the wealthier countries and individuals can afford to purchase increasingly costly energy supplies (Barnett, 2008). In the textbooks, high prices and shortages stimulate new investment that results in new supply, which brings down the cost. In reality, the problem in the oil and gas industry is that the investment cycle that delivers new supplies is invariably out of sync with the business cycle that drives demand. As a result, new capacity often comes on stream just at the time when demand is falling, which further depresses the price, which has the effect of reducing new investment in additional capacity. Thus, when demand picks up there is inadequate supply and prices spike. This pattern helps to explain the gas glut since 2008–09 caused by the perfect storm of a surge in new LNG capacity, the growth of unconventional gas production in the US and falling demand due to the global economic downturn. At the same time, there are also fears of a near-term oil price crunch as the global recession of 2008–09 substantially reduced investments in new production. The net result would be insufficient supply when global demand recovers, resulting in economic scarcity. That said, this chapter was completed in the wake of the devastating earthquake and tsunami in Japan and already energy specialists are speculating that the problems encountered by Japan's nuclear power industry would increase demand for LNG and oil, which could lead to higher prices. A countervailing analysis is that the impact of these events on Japan's economy would slow global economic growth and this would depress demand for energy. Whatever the outcome, these tragic events demonstrate the fragility and volatility of the global energy system.

All of this contributes to the additional risks of price volatility. New upstream oil and gas projects are capital intensive; involving tens of billions of dollars, which have to be paid off over a long period and across a number of business cycles. In the Russian context, such financial calculations were inconsequential in the Soviet era when many of the currently-producing fields were first developed. But they are of great significance now as Russia's oil and gas companies seek to finance costly greenfield developments in East Siberia and the Arctic offshore (see also Chapters 4 and 8). A case in point is the Shtokman offshore gas project in the Barents Sea which has been constantly delayed by concerns over future gas demand.

Most conventional definitions of energy security refer to the affordability of energy supplies. The European Commission (2010, p. 1) frames it in terms of 'the availability of energy products and services on the market, at a price which is affordable to all consumers (private and industrial)'. One way for an individual state to insulate its population against the negative impacts of economic scarcity is to subsidize domestic energy prices to the consumer. This is a commonplace policy in the developing world and in many energy-rich states. It is not an option in the EU as such subsidies would fall foul of competition law and undermine the logic of a fully functioning market.

The G20 attempts to reduce the level of energy subsidies. The IEA (2010d, p. 569) has estimated that the total value of fossil fuel consumption subsidies worldwide in 2009 was US$319 billion, the majority of them provided in non-OECD countries. Removal of such subsidies could result in a 5 per cent fall in global primary energy demand by 2020 and reduce carbon emissions by 5.8 per cent. Subsidized prices are seen as offering little incentive for consumers to be more energy efficient or invest in alternative sources of energy supply, such as renewables. However, many emerging and developing economies maintain that without such subsidies their industries and households would not have access to the energy services necessary to improve living standards and to promote economic development. Such an approach results in a more energy and carbon intensive path to development, which the planet can no longer afford.

This debate is of direct relevance to Russia. While oil and coal prices are market driven, gas and electricity prices are regulated and under-priced, representing an explicit subsidy to the consumer. The IEA (2010c, p. 601) calculates that in 2009 the total cost of natural gas and electricity consumption subsidies in Russia was US$34 billion, that is US$238 per person or 2.7 per cent of GDP. These figures represent progress; it was only in 2009 that domestic gas prices were high enough for Gazprom to achieve its first domestic profit. These low domestic energy prices have been a sticking point in Russia's accession to the World Trade Organization (WTO) as it is argued that they present an unfair advantage to energy intensive industries, such as forest products and aluminium smelting. Low energy prices have also failed to provide an incentive to improve energy efficiency. The Russian economy is one of 'the least efficient in the world in terms of GDP per unit of energy consumed' (IEA,

2010d, p. 599). However, gas prices are supposed to converge with export prices by 2014 and the wholesale liberalization of the electricity market is scheduled for completion by the end of 2011. The Russian government has also embarked on a campaign to rapidly improve the energy efficiency of the economy and has set a target of a 20 per cent improvement by 2020. The problem is that Russian industry and the Russian consumer are currently ill-equipped to improve energy efficiency or absorb substantial increases in energy costs. The benefit in improving energy efficiency and reducing the energy intensity of the Russian economy would be a reduction in domestic demand for oil and gas that could then free-up production for export. For example, Belyi (2010, p. 2) suggests that efficiency savings could make available up to 240 billion cubic metres of gas, more than enough to satisfy the European export market. It is also worth noting that more than 50 billion cubic metres of gas is flared annually in Russia and reducing this waste is now a key element of Russia's energy strategy (see Chapter 5)

Fourth, environmental scarcity pertains to the ecological dimension or the environmental footprint of the current fossil fuel-based energy system. The production and transportation of fossil fuels has a potentially negative impact on the environment that if not properly managed results in pollution and threatens biodiversity through habitat destruction. The disaster at BP's Macondo field in the Gulf of Mexico in 2010 is an extreme case of the negative environmental impacts of oil and gas production, but there are numerous other examples across the globe and many in Russia itself. However, no moratoriums constraining the development of oil and gas reserves have been declared in Russia, or in the Soviet Union before it.

A further environmental constraint is the negative consequence of energy consumption in the form of air pollution. Before the global warming debate there was a concern about smog and its impact on human health, and about acid rain and its impact on the environment. In OECD countries, both of these problems resulted in measures to reduce pollution from coal burning and promoted the expansion of oil, gas and nuclear power. However, they remain a major concern in China's coal-based economy. Today, our concerns are global in scale and relate to the impact of fossil fuel combustion on the global climate system and the need to decarbonize our energy services. In the future, energy security discussions may not any more be about gaining sufficient access to fossil fuels at a price that we can afford; we may not wish to consume these fuels even if they are available, either because of carbon tax making them prohibitively expensive or because of carbon quota limitations, either as a household, company or national economy. This may seem wishful thinking, but drastic measures are required to address global climate change. The EU and other industrial countries are seeking to reduce their carbon emissions by 80–95 per cent by 2050 (European Commission, 2010, p. 3). This is bound to have significant implications for energy and carbon intensive economies such as Russia that rely on exports of hydrocarbons as a major source of income.

This discussion of energy security has highlighted that its global framing is changing from a simple focus on secure and affordable supplies of fossil fuels, to a wider and more complex set of issues. One of these is the future impact of climate change policy that will have serious implications for Russian energy policymaking.

Climate Change Policy

The collapse of the Soviet Union and the emergence of an independent Russian state paralleled a global awakening to the dangers of anthropogenic climate change. The UN Conference on Environment and Development (Earth Summit) in Rio de Janeiro in June 1992 placed the issue of sustainable development on the global policy agenda. Even before that the UN had tasked the Intergovernmental Panel on Climate Change (IPCC) to produce a comprehensive review of knowledge about climate change. Its first assessment report was published in 1990. Since then there have been a further three reports published and work is now underway on the fifth. By the time the fourth report was published in 2007 it was widely accepted, though some remain sceptical, that human actions were causing climate change and that drastic actions were required to stop the growth in the levels of GHG being emitted into the atmosphere. The Kyoto Protocol, which was adopted on 11 December 1997 and finally ratified on 16 February 2005, is central to this process and aims to reduce GHG by an average of 5 per cent against 1990 levels over the five-year period 2008–12.

In fact, Russia's ratification of the protocol in November 2004 enabled its implementation. This policy agenda is relevant to Russia's energy policymaking for the simple reason that globally the energy sector is the single largest emitter of GHG (principally carbon dioxide or CO_2). As a result, climate change policy is driving a transition away from carbon intensive forms of energy supply such as coal, oil and gas, in favour of lower carbon nuclear power and renewable sources of energy. Such a transition to a low carbon energy system is not a straightforward matter. It may take many years before climate change policy has a significant impact on global demand for fossil fuels. According to the IEA's (2010c, p. 80) latest 450 scenario – that is limiting the concentration of greenhouse gases in the atmosphere to 450 parts per million of CO_2-equivalent and global temperature increases to two degrees Celsius – primary energy demand will increase by 35 per cent between 2008 and 2035. In 2035 fossil fuels will still satisfy 62.3 per cent of total primary energy demand, compared to 81 per cent in 2008. The vast majority of new energy demand between now and 2035 will come from non-OECD countries, with China leading the way. This is because a combination of sluggish economic growth, stable or declining populations and the impact of climate change policy in OECD states will reduce the growth of energy demand and the demand for fossil fuels. In fact, some suggest that OECD oil demand peaked in 2005 (HIS-CERA, 2009). The changing geography of growth in the demand for fossil fuels is significant for Russia because at present Europe is the largest market for its oil and gas exports. Thus, it is tied to a slow-growth market seeking to reduce substantially its reliance on fossil fuels (see also Chapters 1 and 6).

The climate change policy agenda clearly has worrying long-term implications for Russia's status as one of the world's leading exporters of hydrocarbons; but, for the time being other factors are far more significant such as the EU's energy security concerns and the gas glut since 2008–09 (see above; also Chapters 1, 6, 7). However, Russian policymakers and energy companies cannot afford to turn a blind eye to the implications of climate change. As the extreme weather of the summer of 2010 demonstrated, Russia is vulnerable to the impacts of climate change. At the same time, as a major emitter (now third largest in the world) with an energy and carbon intensive economy, Russia has an important role to play in reducing GHG emissions. On the positive side, its forests provide a major ecosystem service as a huge carbon sink, but there are also fears that the melting of its permafrost will release large amounts of GHG. All this means that the framing of Russia's energy policy over the next 20 years or so will have to be markedly different from that of the past 20 years.

THE RUSSIAN ENERGY NEXUS

In this section global concerns are combined with the domestic policy agenda in what I will call the Russian energy nexus: energy security, economic globalization and climate change policy. Russia's current political economy is heavily reliant upon access to rents from the production and export of hydrocarbons, yet, as the current economic crisis has revealed, there are both internal and external threats to the sustainability of this resource-based model of economic development. However, in the short- to medium-term, to be able to diversify its economy Russia has to rely on its resource abundance. An added complication is that for a combination of reasons, again both external and internal, Russia's energy industry may not be able to deliver sufficient income to finance diversification. Furthermore, Russia's current diversification strategy has many critics and there is no guarantee of success (see Table 10.1).

Table 10.1   The Russian energy nexus

Dimension	External global/regional	Internal national/local
Energy security	Security of demand Security of transit	Resource nationalism Sustainability of oil and gas production and exports
Economic globalization	Russia's role in the global economy	Diversification Modernization Innovation
Climate change policy	Energy efficiency Low carbon transition Climate change policy	Energy intensity Carbon intensity Climate change impacts

Russia's Energy Security Concerns

One of Russia's consistent complaints in the sphere of global energy security is that it favours the security of supplies interests of the developed energy importing economies (namely the members of the IEA/OECD) and fails to consider security of demand (see also Chapter 2). At the same time, Russia does not wish to be part of OPEC and is suspicious of the EU-promoted Energy Charter Treaty, which originated in the early 1990s with the intention of strengthening the rule of law on energy issues, and has refused to ratify it. Instead, it has proposed its own alternative to the charter and is a leading force in the Gas Exporting Countries Forum. Thus, in many ways, despite its high share of global oil and gas exports, Russia is an outsider and consequently a price taker when it comes to energy markets. This situation is exacerbated by the fact that Russia cannot directly control its partners' interests in security of demand and security of transit. In fact, trust and cooperation is needed to build a relationship with Russia's major market – the EU – and its transit states. The counterproductive consequences of conflict have been well demonstrated since 2005–06 (see Chapters 6, 7).

Russia's internal energy-related policies are also a concern for the EU and other consumers of Russian energy. Starting with the Yukos affair (see Chapter 3), the state regained control over the domestic oil and gas industry; and, as demonstrated by the conflict over Sakhalin-2, has rewritten the terms for foreign involvement in the upstream sector (Goldman, 2008). It is now clear to all that major investments and transactions in Russia's oil and gas industry require the sanction of the Kremlin. While the IOCs may actually see the current situation as more stable and workable, it is an affront to the principles of the EU and others who believe that equal access and treatment should be afforded to their IOCs that seek to invest in Russia. It has also resulted in a hostile attitude to Russian companies when they seek to invest in downstream assets in the EU.

The net result of Russia's resource nationalism was a reduced level of foreign investment in its oil and gas sector just at the time when more investment was needed to develop new fields to sustain production. Undoubtedly, the global financial crisis has been a sobering experience for the Kremlin and it is instructive that in September 2009 Prime Minister Putin invited senior representatives of the IOCs to a meeting in Salekhard, in West Siberia, to discuss cooperation. He got a lukewarm reception. There is now even the possibility of rehabilitating PSAs to attract the IOCs to invest in the Arctic and offshore. Unfortunately, the story of Sakhalin, where PSAs have been successful, is one of the IOCs taking the risks and making the investments only to be forced into a minority share just as the project was nearing completion (Sakhalin-2) or being denied access to the export market needed to deliver a return on their investments (Sakhalin-1) (see Chapters 4, 8). The net result of all of this activity is that the Russian state has created two national champions – Gazprom and Rosneft – and has given them favoured access to new fields in Siberia and the Far East and offshore that need to be developed to sustain future oil and gas production (see also Chapters 2, 3). But there are now major concerns about their technical and financial ability to develop these new regions. Although the IOCs understand that these companies are the partners of necessity, they have been understandably hesitant about making the large-scale, long-term commitments needed to open up Russia's new oil and gas frontier.

However, in late 2010 Shell signed a protocol with Gazprom on strategic cooperation that included an intention to 'further development of bilateral cooperation in exploration and production of hydrocarbons in western Siberia and the far east of Russia' (Shell, 2010). More significantly, in January 2011, BP and Rosneft announced their intent to form a Global and Arctic Strategic Alliance involving an equity swap through which BP acquires a further 9.5 per cent stake in Rosneft (it already owns 1.3 per cent). In return, Rosneft would be issued new BP shares giving it a 5 per cent stake (BP, 2010). The initial focus of their activities was to be to create a joint operating company with 66.67 per cent Rosneft and 33.33 per cent BP participation to explore three licence areas in the Kara Sea (Bradshaw, 2011). The logic of the agreement is clear when viewed along the resource geographic dimension. BP gains access to new potential hydrocarbon production and Rosneft gains access to BP's offshore technology and also has the opportunity to partner with BP on projects outside Russia. Although many saw this agreement as a reaction to BP's problems in the Gulf of Mexico, this alliance has been 12 years in the making. BP and Rosneft are already working together on the Sakhalin-5

project through the Elvary Neftegas joint venture. Unfortunately, the alliance
never came into fruition as the Russian partners in the TNK-BP joint venture
protested that they were the sole entry vehicle for BP to invest in Russia and
that it should be TNK-BP, rather than BP who should partner with Rosneft.
However, it is BP and not TNK who have the access to finance and the technology needed to open up the arctic offshore. The case ended up in the Court
of International Arbitration in Stockholm, which sided with TNK-BP. As a
result, at the end of August 2011 Rosneft reached a very similar agreement
with Exxon Mobil to develop the Kara Sea and prospects in the Black Sea.

Elsewhere, much of the new production in East Siberia is being delivered by
non-state companies – BP-TNK and Slavneft, while private gas producer
Novatek is involved in a new gas project in Yamal Peninsula (see Chapter 2).
Soon after the BP-Rosneft agreement, Novatek and Total announced that they
were entering into a strategic partnership, with Total taking an initial 12.08 per
cent sharing holding in Novatek (with the intent to increase it to 19.4 per cent
within three years) and with Total becoming the main international partner in
the Yamal LNG project, with a 20 per cent share. Novatek will hold a 51 per
cent interest in the project (Total, 2011). However, Gazprom and Rosneft
remain the major new reserve holders. Although IOCs such as BP and Shell are
positioning themselves to become major players in the development of Russia's
Arctic shelf (as are Total and Statoil through the Shtokman project), it may be
that China's NOCs will prove to be the wildcard when it comes to opening up
the oil and gas reserves of Siberia and the Far East. Already a US$25 billion
deal has been struck with Transneft (10 billion) and Rosneft (15 billion) to
complete the ESPO pipeline and open up new fields in East Siberia in return for
infrastructure provision and 15 million tons of crude oil a year between 2011
and 2031 (Blank, 2009; see also Chapter 8). A similar 'gas for cash' agreement
with Gazprom could finance the development of new fields in Yamal, Kovytka
(which Gazprom has recently acquired after TNK-BP forced Rusia Petroleum
into bankruptcy), East Siberia and in Sakha-Yakutia in the Russian Far East. But
relations between Moscow and Beijing are complex and a gas deal has proved
elusive for 30 years (Paik, 2011). In addition, becoming a resource appendage
to China does not sit well with the Kremlin's plans for modernization and
Russia's global economic standing, but it may be a case of needs must.

Russia and Economic Globalization

Russia's role in the global economy and its energy sector are closely linked to
the current debate about diversification and modernization (see also Hanson,
2009b). Russia's post-Soviet economic performance can be divided into two
phases, with the economy now at the beginnings of a third phase (see Figure
10.1). Russia's deep and prolonged 'transitional recession' brought with it a

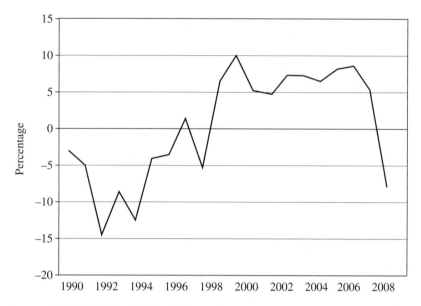

Sources: OECD (2011), *OECD.StatExtracts*, http://stats.oecd.org (accessed 6 April 2011); World Bank (2010), *World Development Indicators 2010*, Washington, DC: World Bank, p. 237.

Figure 10.1   Russia's annual GDP growth 1996–2009, per cent

deindustrialization of the economy as much of the heavy industry simply lost its rationale for existence. At the same time, the payments system failed and a virtual economy emerged, dependent on non-market exchange (Gaddy and Ickes, 2002). The resource sector remained relatively resilient. Although there was a substantial decline in oil production, gas production and export remained relatively stable. Similarly, export-oriented sectors such as mining, forestry and metals production remained active. The net result was a primitivization of the Russian economy as the relative weight of the resource sector increased. Much of the resource sector was privatized and ended up in the hands of the oligarchs, with the 'loans for share' deals playing a major role in the privatization process (see Chapter 3).

In 1998 the Russian financial crisis brought an abrupt end to this phase. The devaluation of the rouble prompted resource-substituting recoveries in the food and light manufacturing industries, and the service economy started to expand. Rising resource prices resulted in the growth of income from exports. Between 1998 and 2008, in what Hanson (2009c) calls the 'inter-crisis period' before the financial crisis of 2008, the Russian economy boomed. Between 1998 and 2007 the economy grew on average at 7 per cent per year and this promoted Russia from 72nd in the world in terms of wealth to 53rd in 2007.

At the same time, wages increased and average disposable incomes increased by 26 per cent in nominal terms (McKinsey Global Institute, 2009, p. 10).

There is considerable debate as to the sources of Russia's economic growth during the inter-crisis boom. Hanson (2009c, p. 12) suggests that: 'What was going on was much more than a mere pressing into service of under-utilised capital and labour to feed growing demand financed by petro-dollars'. In its analysis of Russia's economic performance, the McKinsey Global Institute (2009, p. 10) concludes that: 'Improved productivity and positive demographic factors were responsible for Russia's economic growth over the past decade'; however, it warned that: 'The source of Russia's economic prosperity were close to being depleted even before the onset of the current crisis'. The World Bank (Ahrend, 2005) highlighted that official statistics tend to underestimate the role of industry and overestimate the role of the service sector in the Russian economy. Its analysis led it to conclude that: 'Natural resource sectors directly accounted for roughly 70 per cent of the growth of industrial production in 2001–04, with the oil sector alone accounting for just under 45 per cent' (ibid. 2005, p. 11).

As for the second half of the decade, Sutela (2009, p. 3) observes: 'The shift of resources (money, labour and skills) from inefficient heavy industries that made things most people did not want into more productive manufacturing and modern services has been the true source of Russian growth in recent years'. The sound macroeconomic policies of the Russian government, such as the establishment of a stabilization fund and the elimination of state debt, also played a role in the growth story. Bogetic et al. (2010, p. 27) propose that: 'Arguably, sound fiscal policy has been a key policy contributor to the strong growth performance of the Russian economy up to the global crisis of 2008'. Thus, we can conclude that during the inter-crisis boom positive things were happening to restructure the economy and increase labour productivity. This contributed to Russia's economic performance, but this does not mean that Russia reduced its dependence on oil and gas rents.

Russia continued as a resource exporter in the global economy. In 2008, exports of mineral resources accounted for nearly 70 per cent of total exports and when adding the other resource sectors – chemical, forestry and metals – the total is 91.9 per cent! Of equal concern is the very low share of machinery and equipment in Russian exports. This weakness is further demonstrated by the fact that Russia's imports are predominantly food products, consumer goods and machinery and equipment (the latter includes automobiles) (see Rosstat, 2010, p. 726). It is also noteworthy that during the boom Russian enterprises accessed international capital markets to finance investment and growth. Thus while the foreign debt of the Russian state was paid off, the private sector took on substantial foreign debt, much of it short term.

While the negative consequences of this oil addiction are known (see above), one positive factor is how the rapid increase in oil and gas prices enabled the value of exports to grow much more rapidly than the volume of exports; in fact, between 2005 and 2008 some of the volumes actually fell. Of course, the situation changed dramatically in 2008–09 when oil and gas prices fell very rapidly. Between 2008 and 2009 the value of oil exports fell by 37.6 per cent and gas by 39.3 per cent (see Rosstat, 2010, p. 730); yet their share of total exports only fell by modest amounts as overall exports contracted (see ibid., p. 726).

Just as Russia's boom period is not explainable by increasing oil and gas rents alone, so the impact of the global economic crisis is more than just a consequence of falling oil and gas prices (Sutela, 2010, p. 5). The sudden loss of a substantial amount of oil and gas revenue was a major contributing factor, but so was capital flight, the general weakness of the domestic banking system and the level of debt being carried by the private sector (see also Gaddy and Ickes, 2010, p. 289). Most of the fundamental structural and systemic impediments to sustainable economic growth remain even after the crisis. Therefore the current recovery in energy prices is unlikely to return Russia to pre-crisis levels of economic growth. For that to happen major economic reforms are required.

The current economic rhetoric in Moscow, at least on the part of President Medvedev, is dominated by terms such as diversification, modernization and innovation which may also mean substantial new investment in the energy sector. For many commentators, diversification is read as a reduction in the relative importance of the energy sector in the Russian economy. But this can be achieved by the non-energy sector growing at a faster rate and making a greater contribution to total GDP than in the past. However, Russia's new energy strategy does not foresee a substantial increase in the volume of production in the oil and gas sectors, rather its objective is:

> ...to set up [an] innovative and efficient energy sector in Russia meeting the energy needs of a growing economy, as well as the foreign economic interests of the country and ensuring the necessary contribution to the country's social-oriented and innovative development. (Government of the Russian Federation, 2009a, p. 15)

Clearly, the need to modernize and innovate is just as relevant to the energy sector as the rest of the economy. UNDP Russia (2010, p. 21) maintains that by deploying already existing technologies Russia could reduce its energy consumption by 45 per cent of current levels. Equally, many of the technologies needed to develop frontier oil and gas resources already exist in the international oil industry (that does not mean that Russian industry should not develop innovative capacities to open up frontier oil and gas). Thus, the current emphasis placed on innovation is probably misplaced, especially when one considers the poor state of Russia's research and development capacity and the long-standing barriers to the innovation process (Cooper, 2006; 2010); rather, perhaps the emphasis should be on imitation and the deployment of widely available technologies (Sutela, 2009, p. 5).

After all, the Russian economy has now experienced 20 years of underinvestment and its infrastructure is badly in need of renewal. To do so requires Russia to open itself up to foreign investment and technology transfers, rather than rely on state-centred top down programmes to promote innovation and high-tech business. However, the problem with this is that the current investment environment is simply not internationally competitive. The Heritage Foundation's (2011, pp. 343–4) *Index of Economic Freedom* ranks Russia 143rd out of 188 countries and concludes that: 'Economic freedom is severely challenged in Russia'. Transparency International's (2010) *Corruption Perception Index 2010*, ranks Russia 154th out 178 countries and gives it a score of 2.1 (10 means very clean and 0 means very corrupt). The World Bank/IFC (2010) *Ease of Doing Business* analysis ranks Russia 123rd out of 183 economies. Finally, the World Economic Forum's (2010, pp. 286–7) *Global Competitiveness Report*, ranks Russia 63rd out of 139 countries and identifies corruption as the most problematic factor in doing business. The message is clear and consistent, and one that is not denied by Russia's leadership. The investment environment in Russia requires substantial improvement if the country is to modernize and become globally competitive beyond its resource sector. According to Sutela (2010, p. 4):

> Russia must face two key issues: ensuring that its workers are employed in a diverse range of globally-competitive jobs and maintaining export capacity through greater domestic energy efficiency, as oil and gas production volumes will not grow much in the future.

Russia and Climate Change Policy

This section examines how future climate change may affect the energy sector in Russia.[2] Russia does not have a clearly elaborated climate change policy, though it does have a Climate Change Doctrine (Korppoo, 2009).

As a lasting legacy of the Soviet Union the Russian economy is still one of the most energy and carbon intensive in the world. The structural reasons for this include the Soviet economy's bias towards heavy industry and the fact that energy services were never adequately priced in the Soviet system, leading to no incentives to conserve energy or promote efficiency. This situation is aggravated by the thermal inefficiency of the Soviet era buildings and the absence of thermostats and metering to enable consumers to control their consumption. As a result of all of this, Russia still needs 2.3 times more energy to produce one unit of GDP than the world average (Kulagin, 2008, p. 2). Because of climatic conditions and its geographic size, one might expect Russia to have a higher than average level of energy intensity, but the current inefficiencies are staggering even after the economy has experienced significant amounts of deindustrialization and economic restructuring, which usually drive reductions in energy intensity. If we compare Russia with Canada, whose geography and natural resource endowment is similar, we find that the carbon intensity of the Canadian economy is 0.6 kg CO_2 per US dollar produced, compared to 1.18 kg CO_2 per US dollar produced for Russia (IEA, 2006c, p. 53). As a result, Russia is still the third largest emitter of CO_2 in the world, after China and the USA. However, the dynamics of energy intensity, that is the amount of energy used per unit of output, and GHG emissions are quite different.

The level of Russia's energy intensity (see Figure 10.2), which is measured as tons of oil equivalent energy consumed per thousand US dollars of GDP produced (2005 at purchasing power parity), demonstrates the impact of the primitivization process; as discussed above, in the early 1990s Russia's economy shrank and much of Russia's heavy industry went into decline, but the resilience of the resource sector made the Russian economy more dependent on it. As a consequence, the energy intensity of GDP increased. However, because the absolute level of industrial production declined significantly, so the level of GHG emissions fell dramatically (see Figure 10.2).

The situation changed fundamentally after 1998. In the 'inter-crisis' period the Russian economy experienced a period of restructuring as the service and light-manufacturing sector grew rapidly. These sectors are far less energy intensive and thus as the economy grew, so the overall level of energy intensity began to fall. The level of decline in GHG emissions also levelled off in 1998 and then started to increase, though it is estimated the recent economic crisis resulted in a 7–8 per cent decline in Russia's emissions in 2008–09 (Safonov and Lugovoy, 2010, p. 15). Over this period we find a dramatic fall in stationary source air pollution and a significant increase in mobile source air pollution (Oldfield, 2005). This reflects the decline of smokestack industry and the growth of automobile ownership and road transportation. However, as the economy grew, old inefficient and polluting power stations had to be brought back into operation to meet growing demand. This also contributed to the emission growth (Korppoo et al., 2009, p. 93). Nonetheless, consumption processes now drive air pollution as much as, if not more than production processes. Despite these changes, the Russian economy still remains highly energy intensive. In 2008, Russia's energy intensity was 0.324 tons of oil equivalent per thousand US dollars (2005 by PPP), compared to 0.122 for the EU 27, 0.275 for Canada, 0.126 for Japan, 0.175 for the USA and 0.274 for China (UNDP, 2010, p. 159; see Figure 10.2). This means that Russia remains a profligate consumer of energy and emitter of GHGs; but it also means that there is a huge amount of potential to improve energy efficiency and further reduce GHG emissions.

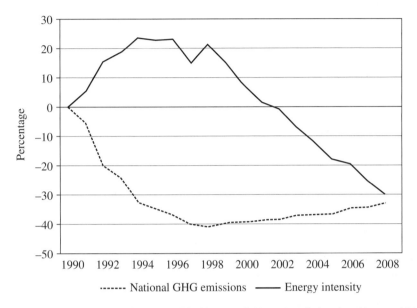

Sources: GHG emissions: CAIT-UNFCC (2011), available at: http://cait.wri.org/ (accessed 21 January 2011); Energy intensity: UNDP Russia (2010), *National Human Development Report on the Russian Federation 2009: Energy Sector and Sustainable Development*, Moscow: UNDP Russia, p. 159.

Figure 10.2   Trends in Russia's greenhouse gas emissions and energy intensity 1990–2008

According to estimates from the World Bank, working with the Russian Center for Energy Efficiency, Russia can save up to 45 per cent of its total primary energy consumption if it implemented economy-wide efficiency measures (World Bank/IFC, 2008). Russia's energy strategy for the period up to 2030 calls for the economy's energy intensity to fall significantly, to match the likes of Canada and the Scandinavian countries, because the low-energy intensive sectors will grow at a much faster rate than the energy-intensive sectors, and because of substantial improvements in energy efficiency. The strategy suggests that through organizational and technological energy savings the total volume of domestic energy consumption could fall by 40 per cent (MERF, 2010, p. 31). This target is enshrined in new Russian legislation on energy efficiency introduced in 2009 (Kononenko, 2010, p. 4; see also Chapter 5).

As noted above, such improvements would make it possible to maintain, or even expand, the exportable surplus of oil and gas without having to increase the overall volume of production. However, this requires the liberalization of energy prices and substantial investment in the energy infrastructures of both producers and consumers. Clearly, such investment would sit well with the modernization campaign, thus creating a virtuous circle of improved efficiency and economic growth, with falling energy intensity and GHG emissions. However, it will also come at considerable cost; according to UNDP Russia (2010, p. 92), to improve Russia's energy efficiency by 45 per cent compared to 2005 would cost US$324–57 billion. But they also point out that by exporting all the gas and oil products saved in this way, Russia could obtain an additional US$80–90 billion a year and could keep GHG emissions well below 1990 levels, even allowing for strong economic growth (UNDP, Russia, 2010, p. 93; UNFCCC, 2010, pp. 18, 20; see also Figure 10.2). Russia hence has an enormous opportunity, but to seize it Russian actors have to maintain high levels of oil and gas production and ensure sufficient markets for their exports.

Given that Russia has seen a substantial decline in its level of GHG emissions since 1990, it is surprising that it has not played a more positive role in international climate policy negotiations. Under the terms of the Kyoto Protocol, Russia has pledged to stabilize emissions at 1990 levels with its total GHG emissions not surpassing this level during 2008–12 (see Figure 10.2). Assuming that GHG emissions in Russia fell by a further 7 per cent between 2005–09, then the overall level of reduction over 2004–09 is 34 per cent. Russia's ratification of the Kyoto Protocol in 2004 had more to do with the politics of WTO membership than a sudden greening of Russia's leadership (Henry and Sundstrom, 2007). In fact, at the time Russian politicians and their advisers were deeply suspicious of the intentions of the protocol. The Russian economy was growing rapidly, emissions were increasing and having to constrain emissions might have compromised economic growth.

Now Russia's own assessments identify the potential impact of climate change as overall harmful. The potential synergy between modernization and emissions reduction discussed above, mean that pledging to reduce emissions should not mean reduced economic growth rates. In 2009 President Medvedev stated that: '…climate change is real, that global warming threatens Russia's future, that Russia has a responsibility to address it both domestically and in international forums, that doing so can be economically beneficial' (quoted in Charap, 2010, p. 11). That said; Russia remains bullish on the prospects for a post-Kyoto agreement. In the run up to the Copenhagen Summit, in June 2009, Medvedev stated that Russia's post-Kyoto target would be 10–15 per cent below 1990 levels, which would actually be an effective 30–35 per cent increase over 2007 levels (ibid., p. 13). However, in December 2009 Medvedev increased Russia's target to a 20–25 per cent reduction. By comparison, the EU aims for a 20 per cent reduction by 2020 and would increase this to 30 per cent if a post-Kyoto agreement were reached. Russia did sign the Copenhagen Accord and agreed to pay into the Green Climate Fund.

Despite Medvedev's earlier pledge, at the Cancun Summit in December 2010 Russia announced that it would not sign up to a post-Kyoto agreement that would tie it to a specific emissions target. This is because Russia has a number of outstanding issues it wants to see resolved, specifically the issue of the carry-over of its emissions surplus from the 1990–2012 period and the role of its forest sink; it is also true that Russia has not benefitted that much from selling its surplus emissions nor from Joint Implementation and Join Initiative programmes that aim to assist transition economies in reducing their emissions. Though there are still many climate sceptics in positions of influence, Russia's official position may reflect a lack of faith in the Kyoto Process rather than a dismissal of the need to reduce emissions. This is a position it shares with many other countries, such as Canada and Japan. Now is not the place to delve into the details of climate change negotiations (see Korppoo, 2010b), but it is fair to conclude that while Russia is showing greater willingness to participate, its current pledge of up to a 25 per cent reduction on 1990 levels seems unambitious when it is likely that its business-as-usual levels will be 30–35 per cent lower in 2020 than in 1990. If Russia were to achieve even half of its potential energy savings then a much more ambitious cut would allow it to claim international leadership and would help to drive the efficiency campaign at home.

There is now widespread acceptance that anthropogenic climate change is real and that it is already happening. What does this mean for Russia? It is clear that the impact of climate change is greater in the more northerly latitudes, particularly in the Arctic, and as a northerly country Russia is particularly vulnerable to its impacts. Yet one initial reaction, shared by then President Putin, was that a warming climate would be good for Russia as winters would be shorter and its agricultural potential would be improved.

There is truth in both views. Roshydromet (2005) estimates that by 2015 the winter heating season will be 3–4 days shorter on average and in some regions the growing season will be extended; there are also negatives as an increased probability of droughts and extreme weather events (such as experienced in the summer of 2010) will result in reduced and more variable productivity levels. But, as expected, it is in the Arctic where the impacts of global warming are already being felt (for a review, see ZumBrunnen, 2009). The permafrost is already melting. This is creating problems with subsidence, making transportation and construction activity even more difficult, and threatening indigenous lifestyles and biodiversity (WWF-Russia, 2008b).

At the same time, while it is true that retreating sea ice is opening up the Northern Sea Route, ice conditions are actually much more difficult to predict, the iceberg hazard is increasing and storm wave heights are increasing. Given that much of Russia's current and future oil and gas production comes from these Arctic regions there are obvious consequences. A recent assessment

(NIC, 2009, p. 21) concludes: 'Critical new upstream development areas, such as the Yamal Peninsula [and one could add the Kara Sea], will be more complicated to reach by land and harder to develop in the face of thawing permafrost and shorter winter seasons'. The existing infrastructure will also be threatened as increased run-off in northern rivers will threaten the integrity of buried oil and gas pipelines. Roshydromet (2005, pp. 13–14) reports that the oil and gas pipeline networks that were built in the 1980s cross numerous rivers and that this infrastructure is close to the end of its serviceable life.

Thus, substantial new investment is required to protect the existing energy infrastructure against the impact of climate change. New development will be even more costly and challenging. Contrary to the virtuous circle of improved energy efficiency and reduced GHG emissions discussed above, there is a negative feedback here. As one of the world's leading producers and exporters of fossil fuels, Russia is dependent upon the continued consumption of hydrocarbons, yet that continued consumption will drive climate change, making it increasingly difficult and costly to maintain Russia's oil and gas production. This situation leads one to conclude that Russia should promote modernization and diversification so that it can achieve significant energy efficiency savings because it will be unable to sustain current levels of oil and gas production, let alone increase them.

CONCLUSION: FRAMING RUSSIA'S ENERGY DILEMMAS

If we return to the social structurationist model of energy policy formation presented in Figure 2.1 (see Chapter 2), we can see that structural dimensions of the policy environment identified there – resource geographic, financial, institutional and ecological – all have direct bearing on the analysis presented above. This chapter has focused on how global issues relating to energy security, economic globalization and climate change are shaping Russia's political economy and impacting energy policy formation; however, the analysis has not delved in detail into identifying the institutions and actors, though all of the actors identified in Figure 2.1 (see Chapter 2) have also been mentioned in this chapter.

In many ways, the analysis offered here provides a global context for the different 'framings' of energy policy presented in that model. A key feature of the current situation is the high level of volatility and uncertainly in the global energy and financial systems, which when coupled with Russia's desire to modernize and diversify its economy and growing concerns about climate change all mean that the future direction of Russia's energy economy is far from clear. While the analyses presented in this volume can shed new light on events in Russia over the past 10–20 years, it may be the case that our framing of the recent past is not the basis upon which to forecast what might happen in the future.

To return to the opening quotation from the IEA, it is increasingly clear that the current energy system is unsustainable and that we may well be at the crossroads in terms of the relationship between energy, economy and environment. However, Russia remains in the paradoxical situation of having to continue to invest in its fossil fuel energy economy to generate the income needed to finance programmes to reduce its reliance on the energy sector and make it more resilient to price volatility and the possibility of future demand destruction. The first half of the last decade may now be seen as a missed opportunity when energy revenues could have been used to renovate Russia's infrastructure and create the macroeconomic conditions and business environment to promote diversification. At the same time, as of early 2011 it would seem that Russia has weathered the storm of the global financial crisis. If the oil price remains high, there is once again the opportunity to implement reforms needed to promote a more diversified, efficient and sustainable model of economic development. But, there is also the danger that with the return to times of relative plenty, Russia will once again squander the opportunity. The analysis presented above suggests that if that is the case, then Russia is fast running out of opportunities, as storm clouds are gathering that threaten the viability of Russia's current political economy.

NOTES

1. This chapter is partially supported by the Russian and Caspian Energy Developments Project (RUSSCAP), funded by the Norwegian Research Council and by a Major Research Fellowship funded by the Leverhulme Trust (UK).
2. For a detailed assessment of the potential impact of climate change on Russia, see Roshydromet (2005); and CCRM (2008); Russia's attitudes toward international climate change policy, see Korppoo et al. (2006); and Korppoo et al. (2009, 2010).

11. Conclusion: learning about Russian energy policies

Pami Aalto

INTRODUCTION

In the introduction to this book we suggested that the processes by which Russian energy policies are formulated are characterized by complexity on multiple levels, ranging from national, regional and federal, to interregional and global, owing to the length of energy chains from Russia towards nearby and more distant markets. We also presented a new structurationist analytical model designed to tackle the complexity and multiple levels which Russian energy policy actors have to tackle when navigating through their policy environment.

In this book we have mainly looked at these processes from the Russian perspective(s). Yet the model we have used is also applicable to the examination of Russia's partners and competitors using the same concepts and then comparing the results. We started our examination by speaking of Russian energy poli*cies* in the plural, and by now that choice has become vindicated. Although lengthy energy strategy documents have been formulated in Russia in the 2000s, representing the concrete policy outcomes of the structuration processes or interaction between actors and structures that our model elucidates, in reality there are several concurrent energy policies in contemporary Russia. This situation is likely to continue in the 2010s.

In addition to the complex and multilevel nature of energy policy, this book directs attention to the diversity of actors in energy policy.[1] To better understand these our model highlights the cognitive frames through which they attempt to make sense of their policy environment – including what we have termed its resource geographic, financial, institutional and ecological dimensions. In addition, events such as the building of new pipelines and cut-offs, and other problems in energy deliveries, may play a crucial role in how actors perceive each other and develop the corresponding policy frames to better grasp their changing environments, the actors therein and their mutual relationships or the nature of the 'game'.

In the contributions to this book the insights and limitations of the model in studying the formation of Russian energy policies have been highlighted from several angles. In some contributions the model has served as an explicit basis for approaching a particular problem, project or subject in Russian energy policies. In others the model has served less as an in-built tool, and rather as an external 'yardstick', offering some points of reference with which to set the empirical findings into a more general context enabling comparisons across cases and instances. We are now in a position to draw some more general conclusions about the frames Russian actors use in formulating energy policies, the characteristics of the policy environments they face when implementing concrete energy projects in the country and beyond its borders, and other lessons emerging from our analyses.

In this conclusion I will discuss some of these lessons learned in light of our model, without, however, attempting to summarize individual chapters or going into great empirical detail (for chapter summaries, see Chapter 1; and for a discussion setting Russian energy policies in a more general context, see Chapter 10). This discussion will also lay the basis for assessing to what extent we have been able to shed light on the six hypotheses on Russian public and business actors proposed in Kivinen's chapter (see Chapter 3). Finally, as our aim in this book has been to rethink Russian energy policies, and lay some foundations for further such efforts, at the end of this conclusion I will also briefly reflect on what directions further research efforts might take as part of their agenda.

LESSONS LEARNED

Taken together, the contributions to this book prove that Russia's energy policies are likely to be sub-optimal. This is so regardless of the many, not only fossil fuel-based resources, the vastly improved finances in the 2000s that seem to have weathered the financial and economic storm of 2008–09, and the strengthened institutions – which admittedly are viewed by experts with mixed feelings. Both the Russian state and company actors repeatedly come up against the constraints imposed by the resource geographic, financial, institutional and ecological dimensions from which they also derive enormous benefit. Russia's energy policies are also likely to remain plural and vary from one region, energy type, and individual project to another even if general principles are formulated in energy strategies. Our case studies show that each instance and energy political process and its outcome may be a different combination of actors, levels, causes and dimensions. Therefore different accounts of Russia's energy policies will continue to appear. What we want to show here is that they are best assessed in a level-headed manner when related to a more general model or framework. In our model the frames held by actors, the policy environments they face and the events impacting their perceptions of those environments have a central role.

The Frames held by Actors may not only Conflict but also Co-exist

It seems clear that Russian energy policy actors map their policy environments with relative flexibility by employing different frames depending on the time, geographical context and individual project. This makes sense given the complex character of the subject. In Chapter 3 Kivinen argued that historically the predominant frames have varied from what was termed the Soviet interdependence frame to the at times uneasy co-existence of the business frame and the more ambiguous energy superpower frame in the 2000s. Chapter 6 by Smith found power political interests, usually associated with an energy superpower frame of sorts, to be most pronounced in the project of building the Nord Stream gas pipeline on Russia's northern European front in the Baltic Sea. At the same time Smith noted the co-presence of business and energy security frames guiding some actors in the conduct of the project, alongside historically coloured identity-based factors that Smith discussed in terms of *ressentiment*, thereby extending our model in a more socio-cultural direction. In Chapter 7, Balmaceda argued that in the intricate cases of Russian–Ukrainian and Russian–Belarusian pipeline politics, we find actors holding onto a complex pattern of different varieties of business frames and power political frames. In the case of Russia's emerging northeast Asian market, in Chapter 8 Tabata and Liu found profit interests and business frames to be predominant in informing both the activities of Russian energy companies and the Russian state.

In Tynkkynen and Aalto's analysis in Chapter 5, the environmental frame was found to be at best emergent in the conduct of Russia's energy policies. Nevertheless it gained strength in the energy strategy of 2009 and related policy measures. In instances in which the environmental frame partially defines the perceptions of Russian governmental and business actors about their policy environment, it does so mostly in an instrumental manner (see Chapter 5). In short, environmental considerations enter the conduct of Russian energy policy when they help to improve or secure business. The capacity to create new business through ecological thinking has not yet been fully embraced. On this score Russia is of course not alone as the same situation concerns, for example, several EU Member States as well.

Alongside the co-existence of different frames guiding the processes by which Russian energy policies are formulated, when looking at Russia's energy customers in Europe and Asia in particular, we find energy security frames stressing the security of energy supplies. Domestic energy supply and gasification in particular are an important task for the Russian governmental, regional and municipal actors as well, but reconciling the Russian conceptions with the energy security frames of Russia's energy customers requires skilful energy diplomacy on the part of institutional actors.

The Policy Environment is Increasingly Multi-dimensional

We argued in Chapter 2 that assessments of the features of the resource geographic dimension should constitute the backbone for any energy policy frames developed and held by the actors. Failing to properly understand the material characteristics of the resources, and the technology and infrastructure needed to exploit them, together with the necessary distribution network, will result in failing energy policies not serving the interests of energy companies, host states or end consumers. But such are the requirements along the financial dimension of using Russia's resources, especially in the emerging and new fields in the country's northwest, the Arctic Sea Shelf, Eastern Siberia and the Far East that many Russian business actors examine their options for accessing and producing energy resources beyond Russia – in the CIS, northern Africa, the Middle East and Latin America as shown by Poussenkova in Chapter 9. This shows how the resource geographic and financial dimensions are closely linked in the actors' considerations.

Indeed, practically all contributions to this book highlight the huge financial needs of the large development projects of Russian energy policy actors. In practice this translates into a need for cooperation and building of international consortia among Russian and other companies, and bi- and multi-lateralism to support the business ties on the political plane, in place of the often dreaded image of a Russian energy predator(s) or the Russian bear at the gas pipe. While the governance of global finance has proved elusive since the economic crises of 2008–09 in particular, also severely affecting Russian energy actors, it is clear that international financial institutions and Russian and other energy companies are capable of identifying joint interests and pooling their resources to facilitate promising energy projects. Otherwise many of the emerging energy projects in the Sakhalin and elsewhere in Russia's new energy provinces would simply not exist, or would not produce at the current volumes. Access to finance has become indispensable in international political economy (Strange, 1994), even for Russia, which has built relative wealth from energy proceeds since the 1990s, and especially in the 2000s, a substantial part of it stored in the country's reserve and national wealth funds. On this point, in Chapter 10 Bradshaw implies that Russia should improve the transparency and investment environment within the country and reconsider the level of state involvement that increased considerably in the 2000s.

In Chapter 4 Dusseault discusses how Russian actors face big problems along the institutional dimension. Put simply, the question is how the Russian institutions, federal and regional, are to hold all keys at the same time when resource geographic, financial, ecological, and wider socio-economic pressures indicate conflicting directions for state policies. The functioning of Russian energy political institutions and decision-making could improve – as

Russia's energy policies

was well demonstrated by how ineffective or even counterproductive the political support of the Russian state in many cases was to the global market conquest attempts of Russian companies, as shown by Poussenkova in Chapter 9. Nevertheless the bigger problem is that institutions are not easily altered due to their ingrained informal rules of the game, which at bottom define their characteristics (Meulen, 2009; see also Chapters 2 and 3). Notable shifts in how the energy sector is governed usually take years. When large-scale reforms are initiated – as they were for example in the centralization of Russia's (fossil fuel) energy policies in the early 2000s, and in the marketization and unbundling of Russia's electricity sector in the late 2000s – a degree of inertia may be found on resource geographic and infrastructural grounds, for example, which are not easily malleable unless new technologies are forthcoming. Major policy changes are also made more complex by the stiff competition among Russian governmental and business actors over choosing the right institutional models of taxation, regulation, state involvement and so on (see Chapters 3, 4 and 7).

The ecological dimension, for its part, highlights the need for a generous time perspective when assessing Russia's energy policies. Ecological considerations are clearly not as important in the Russia of the 2010s as they have been since the 1990s within Russia's main energy markets in the EU – where they constitute the third pillar of energy policies alongside markets and competition, and security of supplies (Aalto, 2009; Aalto and Westphal, 2007). At the same time the ecological dimension also poses a question of level of analysis: whether we look at national, European or global level pressures and tendencies. On each level the relative weight of this dimension in the calculations of actors varies. But as Bradshaw shows in Chapter 10, climate change challenges pose currently imperfectly understood, serious questions for the long-term viability of Russia's current models of energy extraction and production, and ultimately, the economic and environmental sustainability of the whole state. Concomitantly, steady income from the apparently recovering energy markets of the 2010s can help Russia to make the necessary policy moves in favour of economic diversification, greater energy efficiency, lower greenhouse gas emissions and so on, without abandoning its natural (fossil fuel-based) strengths. Such priorities have also been stressed by President Medvedev, but the proceeds from the fossil fuels trade can also persuade Russian actors to stick with the old habits and models.

The Dangers of Focusing on Individual Energy Political 'Events'

The chapter by Smith highlights the prevalence of political interests in the building of the Nord Stream gas pipeline – itself a hotly contested event involving shifting coalitions and impacting significantly on regional energy policies (Aalto and Korkmaz Temel, 2011; Whist, 2008). Looking at the almost equally eventful history of the ESPO pipeline from Russia's East Siberia to China and Russia's Pacific Coast, in Chapter 9 Poussenkova finds geopolitical or power political interests to have outweighed business considerations in the overall design of the project. Tabata and Liu identify the power political interests predominant in the initial decision to construct the pipeline; however, according to them the pipeline's format was decided mainly with business interests in mind as through its two trunk lines it opens both Chinese and other markets to Russian supplies, while its more precise route was determined on the basis of ecological considerations, as also noted by Poussenkova.

What we can glean from this is that we need to be attentive to what questions we ask; that we cannot automatically generalize actors' interests and policy frames from a single energy project or given phase of its realization; and that in each individual case we must remain open to specific and complex patterns of structuration and causation.

In the end, energy political events can have profound repercussions for the relations among actors and their mutual perceptions, but events cannot prompt such kick-starting effects unless actors choose to make them important. Also, events rarely manifest a new permanent end state on their own, and consequently we gain most by scrutinizing the transformatory potentials they may help to release.

Hypotheses on Public and Business Actors

In Chapter 3 Kivinen presented six hypotheses concerning public and business actors in Russia's energy policies and tentatively assessed them on the basis of insights drawn from expert interviews and the existing literature. Revisiting these hypotheses now will help us to discern where we stand in the study of Russian energy policies, and in which directions research efforts may yield the best return in the future.

As for the first hypothesis 'Gazprom is not a coherent entity but a conglomerate of interests', Balmaceda's detailed analysis, based on several years' work and numerous field visits, supported this in the case of the murky transit politics between Russia, Ukraine and Belarus where Gazprom appears in several guises and where its degree of involvement sometimes remains unclear. Similar studies on other geographical fronts of Russian external energy policies would be most useful.

As for the second hypothesis 'major state-owned firms lobby within the state apparatus to define the rules of the game to suit their own interests', we clearly need more research to establish the precise patterns in each instance and at each moment in time. Poussenkova elucidates the closely interlinked interests of the Russian state and the main energy companies of Russia.

Although she implies that Rosneft may be behind the recent decision to extend the ESPO pipeline to China, she also casts some doubts over the extent to which the Russian state finally serves the companies' interests. In the cases of East Siberian energy projects, Dusseault and Bradshaw note the successes of the 'national champions' Gazprom and Rosneft in accessing new production assets on a preferential basis, while Poussenkova records what in relative terms is a deteriorated position of the private company Lukoil and, before it, the dramatic fall of Yukos.

As for Kivinen's third hypothesis, 'domestic pricing causes a major conflict of interests between energy companies and the state', Tynkkynen and Aalto put it in another context by noting how necessary the price increase for gas sold in Russia's domestic markets would be for a more environmentally sustainable energy policy to emerge in Russia. It would make economic sense for the state and companies to help combat the waste of energy and to reserve more resources for more profitable export markets. Nonetheless the social cost to consumers is considerable and there is a serious legitimacy question for the state in the short run. The role of energy in Russia's modernization strategies and the potential domestic conflicts ahead are subjects definitely deserving more analyses (see also Chapter 10).

The fourth hypothesis, 'more effective private and foreign companies are trying to strike a balance between high profits and high uncertainty concerning the political risk', is part of Dusseault's analysis. He shows how in the case of the Kovytka gas field in Eastern Siberia such a balance has not yet been found, while similar trends form part of the energy politics among the Russian, Chinese, Japanese and other international energy companies in northeast Asia (see Chapter 4; also Chapters 8 and 10). Yet from here it is possible to extend the argument to the global expansion of Russian companies which through their new foreign acquisitions and agreements are after cheaper production costs, lower taxes and higher profits beyond Russia, as described by Poussenkova.

The fifth hypothesis of how 'strategic frames of action are defined by a complex combination of formal and informal rules of the game' is something on which more research is definitely needed (for examples, see Dixon, 2008; also Meulen, 2009). Our case studies provide some loose starting points for such endeavours, most notably in Balmaceda's analysis on the role of insiders and use of shady intermediary companies in gas transit and trade. This is a very promising avenue of research but necessitates extensive field research to gain the necessary access and insight.

As for the final hypothesis that 'foreign policy discourses are neither identical to nor simply dominating the business interests', we have indeed found some supporting evidence. The two are linked but not in a monocausal or deterministic manner (see Chapters 6 and 9). A large body of albeit divided literature on energy diplomacy and energy geopolitics deals with these questions (see Chapter 1). However, the dangers of focusing solely on the institutional dimension of the policy environment – where foreign policy issues fall in our model at the expense of others – are evident and can lead to skewed analyses. Well-balanced studies in this respect usually find a changing balance between foreign policy and energy business, depending on the geographic context, type of energy and so on (see also Stulberg, 2007).

Overall, the issues raised by Kivinen show that we are working with a moving target and that therefore there is a constant need for up-to-date research. Naturally we believe that our model, geared to analysing the interaction between actors and structures in the conduct of Russia's energy policies, yields long-lasting guidance on the likeliest patterns and limits of the possible. Nevertheless we must concur with Bradshaw's caution on how the volatility and uncertainty that is part and parcel of global energy politics and trade – on which Russia as a large energy exporter is heavily dependent – makes any firm predictions well-nigh impossible. Although our structurationist model of energy policy formation does not address global energy politics as such, or interactions among major players (but rather can best deal with individual cases one by one), it shares this assumption of the multi-causal and ultimately undetermined nature of global energy politics. Concomitantly our model points at the underlying features and helps to outline the causes and mechanisms relating to each actor.

THE TASKS AHEAD

The relatively complex model which we have used to give direction to our analyses in this book also requires complex research designs and ambitious field research programmes in order to fully exploit its potential, and to transfer the analytical benefits to studies of practical relevance. Although energy policy represents a formidable, and so far, inadequately confronted challenge for theorists, we reiterate our thesis of the need for a well-working theory-policy interface (see Chapter 2), and argue that energy policy is too important to be left to theorists alone (for promising starts, see also Güllner, 2008; Henriksen, 2010; Prontera, 2009). For the study of Russian energy policies to advance we will need a well-balanced marriage of theory and practice.

While several threads for further research were already identified above in the evaluation of the lessons learned, what is of paramount concern is the dearth of inside-out, fieldwork-based analyses of Russian energy policies or of energy policies elsewhere. By such a claim we do not wish to dismiss entirely top-down analyses – as archetypal studies in energy geopolitics, for example, tend to be – or documentary or statistical analyses, for example. We need several approaches to be used in parallel and at best in synch; or several sets of actors, levels and dimensions incorporated into the same framework as we have suggested here, in order to obtain a more comprehensive picture. By extension, noting the complexity of energy policy, and hence accepting the need for comprehensive approaches, and ultimately developing systematic research programmes, suggests a need for better interdisciplinary cooperation in future energy research (for such options, see Aalto, 2011b; also Aalto and Korkmaz Temel, 2011). In the study of Russian energy policies, an excessively deep divide currently separates natural scientific and social scientific studies in the area, which belies the distinction between material and social reality.

Future analyses of energy policies also need to be sensitive to the extent to which the chains of actions we observe actually constitute purposively intended energy 'policies' (see Aalto and Westphal, 2007: 6–7). Russia's eastern strategy is a case in point. No one in the 1990s knew how things exactly would or could actually develop – for example, what pipelines were to be built and where, by whom, and at what cost. Now we find a somewhat better structured eastern strategy for Russia, albeit one where the inconsistencies and numerous changes in routings and deliveries have at times belied the meaning of the word 'policy'. Even if the study of structuration – that is the interaction between actors and structures – cannot predict the future events in detail, it will reveal something about the limits of the possible and the likeliest developments, provided that all features of the policy environment are carefully considered and weighed against each other, and that the frame-formation processes of the actors are well enough understood.

In this book we have found national, or regional and federal level policies, in addition to policies designed to deal with Russia's relations with its customers and transit states on the interregional level, and more global level policies, all part of the complex sphere of energy policy formation in Russia. The way in which Russian actors map the policy environment on each level influences the shape of the respective policies. This is so for the Russian parties themselves, and the same requirements pertain for their partners, whom the Russian actors will continue to need in order to benefit from the country's resources in a long-term and sustainable manner.

NOTE

1. It has been argued that the ultimate success of energy policies, especially vis-à-vis environmental and climatic challenges, is likewise dependent on the extent to which different actors or stakeholders, and drivers and barriers on different levels, are made part of the policy process. Such broad inclusion of actors and levels fosters equity, spread of information and adaptability, among other things (see Sovacol, 2011).

References

Aalto, Pami (2007), 'The EU–Russia energy dialogue and the future of European integration: from economic to politico-normative narratives', in Pami Aalto (ed.), *The EU–Russia Energy Dialogue: Europe's Future Energy Security*, Aldershot: Ashgate, pp. 23–41.

Aalto, Pami (2009), 'European perspectives for managing dependence', in Jeronim Perovic, Robert W. Orttung and Andreas Wenger (eds), *Russian Energy Power and Foreign Relations: Implications for Conflict and Cooperation*, London and New York: Routledge, pp. 157–80.

Aalto, P. (2011a), 'The emerging new energy agenda and Russia: implications for Russia's role as a major supplier to the EU', *Acta Slavica Iaponica*, **30**, 1–20.

Aalto, Pami (2011b), 'Organizing interdisciplinary international studies: from puzzlement to research programmes', in Pami Aalto, Vilho Harle and Sami Moisio (eds), *International Studies: Interdisciplinary Approaches*, Basingstoke: Palgrave, 66–91.

Aalto, Pami and Nina Tynkkynen (2007), 'The Nordic countries: engaging Russia, trading in energy or taming environmental threats?', in Pami Aalto (ed.), *The EU–Russia Energy Dialogue: Europe's Future Energy Security*, Aldershot: Ashgate, pp. 119–43.

Aalto, Pami and Kirsten Westphal (2007), 'Introduction', in Pami Aalto (ed.), *The EU–Russian Energy Dialogue: Europe's Future Energy Security*, Aldershot: Ashgate, pp. 1–20.

Aalto, Pami, Helge Blakkisrud and Hanna Smith (2008), 'Policy recommendations for northern cooperation', in P. Aalto, H. Blakkisrud and H. Smith (eds), *The New Northern Dimension of the European Neighbourhood*, Brussels: Centre for European Policy Studies, pp. 222–36.

Aalto, Pami and Dicle Korkmaz Temel (2011), 'European/Eurasian energy security: from vulnerability to viability and sustainability', in Pami Aalto, Vilho Harle and Sami Moisio (eds), *Global and Regional Problems: Towards an Interdisciplinary Study*, Aldershot: Ashgate.

Aalto, P., D. Dusseault, M. Kennedy and M. Kivinen (forthcoming), 'Is Russia becoming an energy superpower? The social structuration of Russia's energy sector', article manuscript.

Abdurafikov, Rinat (2009), 'Russian electricity market: current state and perspectives', Technical Research Centre of Finland working papers 121, accessed 23 November 2010 at www.vtt.fi/inf/pdf/workingpapers/2009/W121.pdf.

Agency of Natural Resources and Energy (ANRE) (n.d.), 'Resource and energy statistics', accessed 15 July 2010 at www.meti-go-jp/statistics/tyo/seidou/result/ichiron/07_shigen.html.

Ahrend, Rudiger (2005), 'Sustaining growth in a resource-based economy: the main issues and the specific case of Russia', United Nations Economic Commission for Europe discussion paper series no. 3, Geneva.

Aksenova, Olga (2006), 'Sotsial'no-ekologicheskie posledstviia politicheskogo reformirovaniia: Ot Tsentralizatsii k lokalizatsii ekologicheskoi politiki Rossii', in N.M. Drobizhev (ed.), *Rossiia reformiruiushchaiasia: Ezhegodnik–2005*, Moscow: Institut Sotsiologii RAN, pp. 296–317.

Alexeev, M. and R. Conrad (2009), 'The Russian oil tax regime: a comparative perspective', *Eurasian Geography and Economics*, **50** (1), 93–114.

Al-Kasim, Farouk (2006), *Managing Petroleum Resources: The 'Norwegian Model' in a Broad Perspective*, Oxford: Oxford Institute for Energy Studies.

Ascher, William, T. Steelman and R. Healy (2010), *Knowledge and Environmental Policy: Re-Imagining the Boundaries of Science and Politics*, Cambridge, MA: MIT Press.

Auty, Richard (ed.) (2001), *Resource Abundance and Economic Development*, Oxford: Oxford University Press.

Avomaa, Pentti (2005), 'Hyötyykö Suomi jättiläisprojektista?', *Gasetti,* April, pp. 3–5.

Azarova, S. (1997), 'Alternative est!', *Neft i kapital*, **7–8**, 42–5.

Baev, P.K. (2010), 'Russia abandons the energy super-power idea but lacks energy for "modernisation"', *Strategic Analysis*, **34** (6), 885–96.

Baev, Pavel K. (2008), *Russian Energy Policy and Military Power: Putin's Quest for Greatness*, Abingdon: Routledge.

Bailes, Alyson J.K., Oleksyi Melnik and Ian Anthony (2003), 'Relics of Cold War: Europe's challenge, Ukraine's experience', Stockholm International Peace Research Institute policy paper, **6** (39), accessed 5 May 2006 at http://editors.sipri.se/pubs/RAPPORT_RELICSOFCOLDWAR.pdf.

Balmaceda, M.M. (1999), 'Myth and reality in the Belarusian–Russian relationship: what the West should know', *Problems of Post-Communism*, **46** (May/June), 3–14.

Balmaceda, Margarita M. (2006a), 'Energy business and foreign policies in Belarus and Ukraine', presentation at the conference Economic Interests and Foreign Policy Choices: The Case of Slavic Triangle, 26–27 January, University of Toronto.

Balmaceda, Margarita M. (2006b), *Belarus: Oil, Gas, Transit Pipelines and Russian Foreign Energy Policy*, London: GMB Publishing.

Balmaceda, Margarita M. (2008), *Energy Dependency, Politics and Corruption in the Former Soviet Union: Russia's Power, Oligarchs' Profits and Ukraine's Missing Energy Policy, 1995–2006*, Abingdon: Routledge.

Balmaceda, Margarita M. (2010), 'The politics of energy dependency: Ukraine, Belarus and Lithuania between domestic oligarchs and Russian pressure, 1992–2010', unpublished manuscript.

Balzer, H. (2005), 'The Putin thesis and Russian energy policy', *Post-Soviet Affairs*, **21** (3), 210–25.

Baran, Zeyno (2007), 'EU energy security: time to end Russian leverage', *The Washington Quarterly*, **30** (4), 131–44.

Barnett, J. (2008), 'The worst of friends: OPEC and G-77 in the climate regime', *Global Environmental Politics*, **8** (4), 1–8.

Bashmakov, I.A. (2009), 'Nizkouglerodnaia Rossiia', *Energetisheskaia Politika*, **9**, 11–19.

Beckman, Karel (2011), 'It is the market that will decide whether South Stream will be built', interview with Marcel Kramer, CEO South Stream', *European Energy Review*, 14 February, accessed 7 May 2011 at www. europeanenergyreview.eu/site/pagina.php?id=2746.

Belarus' i Rossiia, Moscow: Belstat and Rosstat, various years.

Belyi, A. (2003), 'New dimensions of energy security of the enlarging EU and their impact on relations with Russia', *European Integration*, **25** (4), 351–69.

Belyi, Andrei (2010), 'Latest trends in Russia's energy policy', London: Chatham House, REP Roundtable Summary.

Blank, S. (2009), 'Loans for oil, the Russo–Chinese deal and it's implications', *North East Asian Energy Focus*, **6** (2), 19–21.

Bogetic, Zeljiko, Karlis Smits, Nina Budina, and Sweder van Wijinbergen (2010), 'Long-term fiscal risks and sustainability in an oil-rich country: the case of Russia', World Bank policy research working paper 5240, Washington, DC.

BP (2010), 'Rosneft and BP form global and Arctic strategic alliance,' press release, 14 January 2011, accessed 17 January 2011 at www.bp.com/ genericarticle.do?categoryId=2012968&contentId=7066710.

Bradshaw, M. (2006a), 'Sakhalin-2 in the firing line: state control, environmental impacts and the future of foreign investment in Russia's oil and gas industry', *Russian Analytical Digest*, **8**, 6–12.

Bradshaw, M. (2006b), 'Observations on the geographical dimensions of Russia's resource abundance', *Eurasian Geography and Economics*, **47** (6), 724–47.

Bradshaw, M. (2008), 'The geography of Russia's new political economy', *New Political Economy*, **13** (2), 193–201.

Bradshaw, M. (2009a), 'The Kremlin, national champions and the international oil companies: the political economy of the Russian oil and gas industry', *Geopolitics of Energy*, **31** (5), 1–14.

Bradshaw, M. (2009b), 'The geopolitics of global energy security', *Geography Compass*, **3** (5), 1920–37.

Bradshaw, M. (2010a), 'A new energy age in Pacific Russia: lessons from the Sakhalin oil and gas projects', *Eurasian Geography and Economics*, **51** (3), 330–59.

Bradshaw, M. (2010b), 'Global energy dilemmas: a geographical perspective', *The Geographical Journal*, **176** (4), 275–90.

Bradshaw, M. (2012), *Global Energy Dilemmas: Energy Security, Globalization and Climate Change*, Cambridge: Polity Press.

Bremmer, I. and R. Johnson (2009), 'The rise and fall of resource nationalism', *Survival*, **5** (2), 149–58.

British Petroleum (2009), 'BP sells LUKARCO stake to LUKOIL', accessed 3 March 2011 at www.bp.com/genericarticle.do?categoryId=2012968&contentId=7058432.

Brogan, A. (2008), 'National oil companies – a new type of international oil companies?', accessed 30 March 2010 at http://www.ey.com/Publication/vwLUAssets/WPC_rus/$FILE/WPC _rus.pdf.

Buccellato, T. and T. Mickiewicz (2009), 'Oil and gas: a blessing for the few, hydrocarbons and inequality within regions in Russia', *Europe-Asia Studies*, **61** (3), 385–407.

Buchanan, James M. (1980), 'Rent-seeking and profit-seeking', in J.M. Buchanan, R.D. Tollison and G. Tullock (eds), *Toward A General Theory of the Rent-Seeking Society*, College Station, TX: Texas A&M University Press, pp. 3–15.

Bugajski, Janusz (2005), *Cold Peace: Russia's New Imperialism,* Westport, CT: Praeger.

Bukkvoll, T. (2003), 'Putin's strategic partnership with the West: the domestic politics of Russian foreign policy', *Comparative Strategy,* **22** (3), 223–42.

Bushuev, V.V. and P.P. Bezrukikh (2006), 'Puti i problemy perekhoda k ekologicheski chistoi energetike budushchego', *Energetisheskaia Politika*, **6**, 3–15.

Bushyev, V.V. and A.A. Troitskii (2007), *Energetika – 2050*, Moscow: OOO IATS Energiia.

Buzan, Barry (2004), *From International to World Society? English School Theory and the Social Structure of Globalisation*, Cambridge: Cambridge University Press.

Carbon Disclosure Project (2009), 'Russia 50', accessed 16 August 2010 at www.cdproject.net/CDPResults/CDP%202009%20-%20Russia%20Report%20-%20ENG.pdf.

Central Bank of Russia (n.d.), 'Statistika vneshnego sektora', accessed 24 February 2011 at http://www.cbr.ru/statistics/?Prtid=svs.

Chaffin, Joshua (2011), 'EU out to break energy dependence on Russia', *Financial Times*, 2 February 2011, accessed 20 March 2011 at www.ft.com/cms/s/0/ca9c73e2-2ef5-11e0-88ec00144feabdc0.html# axzz1H90PjEOI.

Chalii, Oleksander (2009), Radio Free Europe programme for Ukraine, *Vichirna Svoboda*, 8 January, broadcast 8 January 2009 on www.radio svaboda.org.

Charap, S. (2010), 'Russia's lacklustre record on climate change', *Russian Analytical Digest*, **79** (May), 11–15.

Chaturvedi, Sanjay (2011), 'Circumpolar Arctic in "global" climate change: (de)securitizing the ice', in Pami Aalto, Vilho Harle and Sami Moisio (eds), *Global and Regional Problems: Towards Interdisciplinary Study*, Farnham: Ashgate.

Checkel, Jeffrey (1997), *Ideas and International Political Change: Soviet/Russian Behaviour and the End of the Cold War*, New Haven, CT: Yale University Press.

Chyong, Chi Kong, Pierre Noël, and David M. Reiner (2010), 'The economics of the Nord Stream pipeline system', EPRG working paper 1026, Cambridge working paper in economics 1051, September, accessed 12 April 2011 at www.econ.cam.ac.uk/dae/repec/cam/pdf/cwpe1051.pdf.

CIS Oil & Gas (2010), 'Russia lines up gas purchases for 2010', 1 February, accessed 6 August 2010 at www.cisoilgas.com/editors-blog/russia-2010-gas-purchases/.

Climate Change Risk Management Ltd. (CCRM) (2008), *Climate Change in Russia: Research and Impacts*, Penryn: CCRM.

Closson, Stacy (2009), 'Russia's key customer: Europe', in Jeronim Perovic, Robert Orttung and Andreas Wenger (eds), *Russian Energy Power and Foreign Relations: Implications for Conflict and Cooperation*, London: Routledge, pp. 89–108.

Cooper, J.M. (2006), 'Of BRICs and brains: comparing Russia with China, India and other populous emerging economies', *Eurasian Geography and Economics*, **47** (3), 255–84.

Cooper, J.M. (2010), 'The innovative potential of the Russian economy', *Russian Analytical Digest*, **88**, 8–10.

D'Anieri, Paul (2006), 'Ukrainian–Russian relations: beyond the gas', presentation at the conference The Ukrainian–Russian Gas Crisis and its Fallout: Domestic and International Implications, 5–6 February, Harvard University, accessed 15 June 2006 at www.huri.harvard.edu/na/na_gas_conf_2006.html.

Danish Energy Agency (2009), 'Permit to section of the Nord Stream natural gas pipelines in Danish sea area', 27 October, File no. 1110/8609-0002,

1110/8609-0003 and 1110/8609-0004, accessed 12 April 2011 at www.ymparisto.fi/download.asp?contentid=111267&lan=sv.

Deliagin, Mikhail (2006), 'Assessing Russia's energy doctrine', *Russia in Global Affairs*, **4** (October–December), accessed 20 November 2010 at http://eng.globalaffairs.ru/printver/1072.html.

Dixon, Sarah (2008), *Organisational Transformation in the Russian Oil Industry*, Cheltenham, UK and Northampton, MA, USA: Edward Elgar.

Donaldson, Robert H. and Joseph L. Nogee (2005), *The Foreign Policy of Russia: Changing Systems, Enduring Interests*, New York: M.E. Sharpe.

Dusseault, D. (2010a), 'Europe's triple by-pass: the prognosis for Nord Stream, South Stream and Nabucco', *Europe-Asia Studies*, **8** (3), 379–98.

Dusseault, David (2010b), 'Elite bargaining and the evolution of centre-periphery relations in post Soviet Russia: a comparative analysis', doctoral thesis, University of Helsinki Faculty of Social Sciences.

Dusseault, David (2010c), 'Where has all the oil gone? Contradictions among Russia's socio-economic development, political legitimacy and corporate profits', in Akira Uegaki and Shinichiro Tabata (eds), *The Elusive Balance: Regional Powers and the Search for Sustainable Development*, Sapporo, Japan: Slavic Research Center, pp. 145–72.

Dynkin, A. and A. Sokolov (2002), 'Integrirovannye biznes-gruppy v rossi-iskom ekonomike', *Voprosy Ekonomiki*, Aprel 4/2002, 78–95.

Energy Information Administration (EIA) (2010), *International Energy Outlook 2010*, Washington, DC: EIA.

Ekspert On-line (2006), '"Gazprom" meshaet Iakutii', 27 September, accessed 17 October 2008 at www.expert.ru/newsmakers/2006/09/27/shtyrov.

Ekspert On-line (2007), 'Neftogazovoi bum', **39** (580), 22 October.

Ekspert On-line (2008), 'Gazifikatsiia bez gaza', 16 June, accessed 2 May 2011 at www.expert.ru/siberia/2008/24/gazifikaciya_yakutii/.

Ekspert On-line (2010a), 'Vse blizhe i blizhe', 18 February, accessed 2 May 2011 at www.expert.ru/2010/02/18/vse_blihze/.

Ekspert On-line (2010b), '"Gazprom" gruppiruetsia', 15 March, accessed 2 May 2011 at www.expert.ru/2010/03/15/gazyakut/.

Ekspert On-line (2010c), 'Gaz – tormoz, neft'– vpered', 30 August, accessed 2 May 2011 at www.expert.ru/siberia/2010/32/neftyanoy_kompleks/.

Ekspert On-line (2010d), 'Na Neftegazorgh drozhzhah', **37** (721), 20 September, accessed 1 August 2011 at http://expert.ru/expert/2010/37/na_retfegazovoh_drozhzhah.

Ekspert On-line (2011), 'Splotit'sia v komandu', Ekspert Sibir **7–8** (289), accessed 2 May 2011 at http://expert.ru/siberia/2011/08/splotitsya-v-komandu/.

Ellman, Michael (ed.) (2006), *Russia's Oil and Natural Gas: Bonanza or Curse?*, London: Anthem Press.

Emerson, Michael and Elena Gnedina (2009), 'The case for a gas transit consortium in Ukraine: a cost-benefit analysis', CEPS policy briefs, 180, January.

Energeticheskaia politika (2008a), themed issue 'Vozobnovliaemye istochniki energii', March.

Energeticheskaia politika (2008b), themed issue 'Energoeffektivnoe obshchestvo', May.

Energeticheskaia politika (2009), themed issue 'Energetika i okruzhaiushchia sreda', January.

Energo-Enviro (2010), 'Russia's renewable energy calls for additional regulations', accessed 23 April 2011 at www.energy-enviro.fi/index.php?PAGE= 2andNODE_ID=4andID=2985.

Energy Charter Protocol on Energy Efficiency and Related Environmental Aspects PEEREA (2007), 'Regular review of energy efficiency policies of the Russian Federation', accessed 1 December 2010 at www. encharter.org/fileadmin/user_upload/document/EE_rr_Russia_2007_ENG. pdf.

Energy Charter Secretariat (2006), 'Gas transit tariffs in selected Energy Charter countries', accessed 24 February 2009 at www.encharter.org/index. php?id=127.

European Bank for Reconstruction and Development (EBRD) (2005), 'Executive summary of the phase 2 environmental and social impact assessment process: Sakhalin-2 phase 2 project', accessed 2 May 2011 at www.ebrd.com/pages/project/eia/5897.pdf.

EBRD (2007), 'EBRD no longer considers current financing package for Sakhalin-2', accessed 2 May 2011 at www.foejapan.org/en/aid/jbic02/ sakhalin/070112.html.

European Commission (2010), 'Energy 2020: a strategy for competitive, sustainable and secure energy', COM (2010) 639 final, Brussels.

EU–Russia Energy Dialogue (2005), sixth progress report, Moscow/Brussels, October, accessed 29 March 2011 at http://ec.europa.eu/energy/russia/ joint_progress/doc/progress6_en.pdf.

Federal Customs Service (FCS) (various years), *Tamozhennaia statistika vneshnei torgovli Rossiiskoi Federatsii,* Moscow: FCS.

Federal Tariff Service (FTS) (2010), 'Srednii tariff na transportirovku rossiiskoi nefti po sisteme OAO AK Transneft',' 1 June, accessed 3 March 2011 at http://www.fstrf.ru/tariffs/analit_info/oil/0.

Federal Treasury (n.d.), 'Otchetnost' ob ispolnenii konsolidirovannogo biudzheta RF,' accessed 24 February 2011 at www.roskazna.ru/reports/cb. html.

Fetisov, G. (2007), 'The "Dutch disease" in Russia: macroeconomic and structural aspects', *Problems of Economic Transition,* **50** (1), 53–73.

Finon, D. and C. Locatelli (2008), 'Russian and European gas interdependence: can market forces balance our geopolitics?', *Energy Policy*, **36** (1), 423–42.

Fiss, P.C. and P. Hirsch (2005), 'The discourse of globalization: framing and sensemaking of an emerging concept', *American Sociological Review*, **70**, 29–52.

Fitzpatrick, S. (2001), 'Vengeance and ressentiment in the Russian revolution', *French Historical Studies*, **24** (4), 579–88.

Foley, Gerard and Måns Lönnroth (1981), 'The European transition from oil: mapping the landscape', in Gordon T. Goodman, Lars A. Kristoferson and Jack M. Hollander (eds), *The European Transition from Oil: Societal Impacts and Constraints on Energy Policy*, London: Academic Press, pp. 3–26.

Fortum (2005), 'Fortum sells its stake in North Transgas to Gazprom', press release, 18 May, accessed 8 March 2011 at www.fortum.com/news_section_item.asp?path=14022;14024;14026;25730;551;29371.

Fortune (2010), Global 500 list, accessed 17 September at http://money.cnn.com/magazines/fortune/global500/2010/countries/Russia.html.

Fredholm, Michael (2005), 'The Russian energy strategy and energy policy: pipeline diplomacy or mutual dependence?', Russian series 05/41, Conflict Studies Research Centre.

Gabuev, Alexander (2008), 'EU simply wants timely gas supplies without any political games', *Kommersant*, 17 April, accessed 28 March 2011 at www.kommersant.com/p883267/r_1/EU_official_speas_on_relations_with_Russia,_energy_and_security/.

Gaddy, Clifford and B. Ickes (2002), *Russia's Virtual Economy*, Washington, DC: Brookings Institution Press.

Gaddy, C.G. and B.W Ickes (2005), 'Resource rents and the Russian economy', *Eurasian Geography and Economics*, **46** (8), 559–83.

Gaddy, C.G. and B.W. Ickes (2010), 'Russia after the global financial crisis', *Eurasian Geography and Economy*, **51** (3), 281–311.

Gaiduk, I. and O. Lukin (2006), 'LUKOIL moving into Europe', accessed 18 June 2010 at www.wtexecutive.com/cms/content.jsp?id=com.tms.cms.article.Article_rpi_insight_LUKOILEurope.

Gati, Toby T. (2008), 'Renewable energy in Russia's future', *Russia in Global Affairs*, **3** (July–September), accessed 1 December 2010 at http://eng.globalaffairs.ru/printver/1219.html.

Gavshina, O. (2010a), 'V Rossiyu za sdelkami', *Vedomosti*, 1 July.

Gavshina, O. (2010b), 'Patrioty iz LUKOIL', *Vedomosti*, 2 August.

Gavshina , O. (2010c), 'Pokhod TNK–BP za tri morya', *Vedomosti*, 20 August.

Gavshina, O. (2010d), 'Vareniye ot Chaveza', *Vedomosti*, 18 October.

Gavshina, O. and V. Noviy (2010), 'Arabskiy partner', *Vedomosti*, 23 August.

Gazprom (2011), 'Gazprom's Eastern gas programme', accessed 2 May 2011 at www.gazprom.com/production/projects/east-program/.

Gazpromneft (2010), 'Interview s zamestitelem directora po E&P Gazprom nefti B.Zilbermanom', accessed 12 May 2010 at www.gazprom-neft.ru/press-center/lib/?id=1563.

Gel'man, Vladimir (2010), 'The logic of crony capitalism: big oil, big politics, and big business in Russia', in Vladimir Gel'man and Otar Marganiya (eds), *Resource Curse and Post-Soviet Asia: Oil Gas and Modernization*, Lanham, MD: Lexington Books, pp. 97–122.

Gény, Florence (2010) 'Can unconventional gas be a game changer in European gas markets?', Oxford Institute for Energy Studies, Oxford, working paper NG 46.

Giannopoulos, Ilias and Georgia Angelopouluou (2006), 'TNK–BP', CERE Energy Series No. 3, working paper of the Center for Russia and Eurasia, ETH Zurich (Swiss Federal Institute of Technology).

Giddens, Anthony (1984), *The Constitution of Society: Outline of the Theory of Structuration*, Cambridge: Polity Press.

Global Witness (2006), 'It's a gas – funny business in Turkmen–Ukraine gas trade', April, accessed 15 October 2008 at www.globalwitness.org/reports/show.php/en.00088.html.

Godzimirski, Jakub M. (2010), 'Strategic decision-making in Russian energy sector: the case of Nord Stream', NUPI working paper, 2010–007.

Goffmann, Erving (1974), *Frame Analysis: An Essay on the Organization of Experience*, New York: Harper & Row.

Goldman, Marshal I. (2008), *Petrostate: Putin, Power and the New Russia*, Oxford: Oxford University Press.

Goldthau, Andreas (2008), 'Resurgent Russia? Rethinking Energy Inc.', *Policy Review*, **147** (March).

Gorst, Isabelle (2004), 'Russian pipeline strategies: business versus politics', The James Baker III Institute for Public Policy of Rice University.

Gorst, Isabelle and Nina Poussenkova (1998), *Petroleum Ambassadors of Russia*, Houston, TX: Rice University Publications.

Government of the Russian Federation (2003), 'Energy strategy of Russia for the period up to 2020', no. 1234-p, Moscow, 28 August, accessed 17 April 2011 at www.energystrategy.ru/projects/ES-28_08_2003.pdf.

Government of the Russian Federation (2008), 'Concerning some measures for improving the energy and ecological efficiency of the Russian economy', decree of the Government of the Russian Federation no. 889-r, Moscow, 4 June.

Government of the Russian Federation (2009a), 'Energeticheskaia strategia Rossii na period do 2030 goda', adopted by Government Order No. 1715 of 13 November, accessed 17 April 2011 at www.energystrategy.ru/projects/docs/ES-2030_(Eng).pdf.

Government of the Russian Federation (2009b), 'Federal'nyi zakon Rossiiskoi Federatsii ot 23 noiabria 2009 g. N 261-FZ "Ob energosberezhenii i o povyshenii energeticheskoi effektivnosti i o vnesenii izmenenii v otdel'nye zakonodatel'nye akty Rossiiskoi Federatsii"'.

Government of the Russian Federation (2009c), 'Guidelines for state policy of energy efficiency increase through use of renewables for the period up to 2020', no. 1-r, Moscow, 8 January.

Government of the Russian Federation (2009d), 'Klimaticheskaia doktrina Rossiiskoi Federatsii, utverzdeno rasporiazheniem Prezidenta RF ot 17 dekabria 2009 g. N 861-rp'.

Government of Sweden/Ministry of Enterprise, Energy and Communications (2009), 'Regeringsbeslut 15 N2008/147/FIN', 5 November, accessed 12 April 2011 at http://www.ymparisto.fi/download.asp?contentid= 111268&lan=sv.

Gowa, Joanne (1994), *Allies, Adversaries, and International Trade*, Princeton, NJ: Princeton University Press.

Grace, John (2005), *Russian Oil Supply: Prospects and Problems*, Oxford: Oxford University Press.

Greenfeld, Liah (1993), *Nationalism: Five Roads to Modernity*, Cambridge, MA: Harvard University Press.

Grib, Natalya (2007), 'Plus gasification of entire Europe', *Kommersant*, 12 July, accessed 23 March 2011 at www.kommersant.com/p776130/r_I/ Gazprom_moves_towards_becoming_a_world_energy_giant/.

Gromov, A.I. (2009), 'Energy strategy of Russia for the year 2030: approaches, priorities and reference points', presentation at conference Energeetika XXI: Economy, Policy, Ecology, 15–16 October, St. Petersburg, Russia.

Gromov, A.I. (2010), 'Russian energy strategy up to period 2030: questions, troubles, risks', presentation at the 10th Annual Aleksanteri Conference, 27 October, Helsinki.

Gromov, Alexey (2011), 'Osnovy energeticheskoj politiki Rossii v neftega-zovom komplekse', presentation, RGU nefti i gaza im. I.M. Gubkina, 22 March, Moscow.

Guillet, Jerome (2002), 'Gazprom's got West Europeans over a barrel', *The Wall Street Journal*, 8 November, accessed 7 May 2011 at http://online. wsj.com/article/SB103671049532308148.html.

Guillet, Jerome (2007), 'Gazprom as a predictable partner: another reading of the Russian–Ukrainian and Russian–Belarussian energy crises', Institut Francais des Relations Internationales, Russia/NIS Center.

Güllner, L. (2008), 'Threat or risk? The debate about energy security and Russia: five steps for a scientific research programme', *Journal of Contemporary European Research*, **4** (2), 149–53.

Gupta, Arvind (2010), 'Renaissance of Russia's foreign policy in 2009', Institute for Defence Studies and Analysis (IDSA) comment, 11 February, accessed 17 April 2011 at www.idsa.in/idsacomments/Renaissanceof RussiasForeignPolicyin2009_agupta_110210.

Gustafson, Thane (1989), *Crisis amid Plenty: The Politics of Soviet Energy under Brezhnev and Gorbachev*, Princeton, NJ: Princeton University Press.

Hanson, P. (2009a), 'Oil and economic crisis in Russia', *Russian Analytical Digest*, **54** (3 February), 2–4.

Hanson, P. (2009b), 'The sustainability of Russia's energy power: implications for the Russian economy', in Jeronim Perovic, Robert W. Orttung, and Andreas Wenger (eds), *Russian Energy Power and Foreign Relations: Implications for Conflict and Cooperation*, Abingdon: Routledge, pp. 23–50.

Hanson, P. (2009c), 'Russia to 2020', Finmeccanica occasional paper, Rome.

Hassi, Satu (2006), 'Kirjallinen kysymys Komissiolle P-0353/06 – Aihe: Itämeren maakaasuputken ympäristövaikutukset', accessed 29 March 2011 at www.satuhassi.net/index.php?option=com_content&view=article&id=177:itaemeren-maakaasuputken-ympaeristoevaikutukset&catid=20: kysymykset-komissiolle&Itemid=29.

Heinberg, Richard (2007), *Peak Everything: Waking up to the Century of Decline in Earth's Resources*, Forest Row: Clairview.

Heinrich, Andreas (2006), 'Gazprom – a reliable partner for Europe's energy supply?', *Russian Analytical Digest*, 2–12.

Helm, Dieter (ed.) (2007), *The New Energy Paradigm*, Oxford: Oxford University Press.

Henderson, James (2010), *Non-Gazprom Gas Producers in Russia*, Oxford: Oxford Institute for Energy Studies.

Henriksen, Jan Terje (2010), *Planning, Action and Outcome – Evaluation of the Norwegian Petroleum System: A Structuration Approach to Ripple Effect Studies*, Bodø, Norway: Handelshøgskolen i Bodø.

Henry, L.A. and L. McIntosh (2007), 'Russia and the Kyoto Protocol: seeking an alignment of interests and image', *Global Environmental Politics*, **7** (4), 47–69.

Hermitage Capital Management (2005), 'How should Gazprom be managed in Russia's national interests and the interests of its shareholders?', June.

Hirvikorpi, Helinä (2003), 'Venäjän energia Lipposen kiikarissa', *Talouselämä*, 10 January, accessed 29 March 2011 at www.talouselama.fi/ uutiset/article156719.ece.

Holm, A., L. Blodgett, D. Jennejohn and K. Gawell (2010), 'Geothermal energy: international market update', accessed 21 April 2011 at www.geo-energy.org/pdf/reports/GEA_International_Market_Report_Final_May_20 10.pdf.

Hoogeveen, F. and W. Perlot (2007), 'The EU's policies of security of energy supply towards the Middle East and Caspian region: major power politics?', *Perspectives in Global Development and Technology*, **6**, 485–507.

Hopf, Ted (ed.) (1999), *Understandings of Russian Foreign Policy*, University Park, PA: The Pennsylvania State University Press.

Hopf, Ted (2002), *Social Construction of International Politics: Identities & Foreign Policies, Moscow, 1995 & 1999*, Ithaca, NY: Cornell University Press.

Hopf, Ted (ed.) (2008), *Russia's European Choice*, Basingstoke: Palgrave Macmillan.

Hundley, Tom (2010), *Global Post*, 3 January, accessed 29 March 2011 at www.globalpost.com/dispatch/poland/091221/poland-russia-nord-stream.

International Energy Agency (IEA) (1996), *Energy Policies of Ukraine*, 1996 Survey, Paris: OECD/IEA.

IEA (2002a), 'Environment, health and safety', accessed 18 November 2010 at www.iea.org/papers/2002/environnement.pdf.

IEA (2002b), *Energeticheskaya Politika Rossii*, Paris: IEA.

IEA (2005a), *Oil Information*, Paris: IEA.

IEA (2005b), *Natural Gas Information*, Paris: IEA.

IEA (2006a), *Ukraine Energy Policy Review*, Paris: IEA.

IEA (2006b), *Optimising Russian Natural Gas: Reform and Climate Policy*, Paris: OECD.

IEA (2008), *World Energy Outlook 2008*, Paris: OECD.

IEA (2010a), *Oil Information*, Paris: IEA.

IEA (2010b), *Natural Gas Information*, Paris: IEA.

IEA (2010c), *World Energy Outlook 2010*, Paris: OECD.

IEA (2010d), *2010 Key World Energy Statistics*, Paris: OECD.

IHS-CERA (2009), *The Future of Global Oil Supply: Understanding the Building Blocks*, Cambridge, MA: IHS-CERA.

Independent Institute of Social Politics (2006), 'Tipy regionov po yrovniu sotsial'no-ekonomicheskogo razvitiia (kursovom dany perekhodnye regiony)', accessed 2 May 2011 at www.socpol.ru/atlas/typology/table_types.shtml.

Index Mundi (2011), accessed 7 May 2011 at www.indexmundi.com/commodities/?commodity=russian-natural-gas&months=240.

International Atomic Energy Agency (IAEA), United Nations Department of Economic and Social Affairs (DESA), International Energy Agency (IEA), Eurostat and European Environment Agency (EEA) (2005), 'Energy indicators for sustainable development: guidelines and methodologies', accessed 22 November 2010 at www.iea.org/textbase/nppdf/free/2005/Energy_Indicators_Web.pdf.

International Monetary Fund (IMF) (2005), 'Rapid growth in Belarus: puzzle or not?', in IMF country report no. 05/217, June, accessed 7 May 2011 at www.imf.org/external/pubs/ft/scr/2005/cr05217.pdf.

Investitsii (2009), Tablitsa 8, accessed 2 May 2011 at www.socpol.ru/atlas/ overviews/econ_condition/index.shtml.

Investitsii (various years), Moscow: Rosstat.

IPM (2007), *Ezhemesiachnii obzor ekonomiki Belarusi*, 1 (52), January, accessed 7 May 2011 at http://research.by/rus/bmer/.

Jacobs, J.A. and S. Frickel (2009), 'Interdisciplinarity: a critical assessment', *Annual Review of Sociology*, 35, 43–65.

Jaffe, Amy Myers and Martha Brill Olcott (2009), 'The future of the Russian oil industry', energy forum of the James A. Baker III Institute for Public Policy, accessed 29 July 2010 at www.bakerinstitute.org/publications/EF-pub-JaffeOlcottRussOilFuture-050609.pdf.

Janeliunas, Tomas (2009), 'Lithuania's energy strategy and its implications on regional cooperation', in Andris Spruds and Rostoks Toms (eds), *Energy: Pulling the Baltic Region Together or Apart?,* Riga: Zinatne.

Johnson, Debra (2005), 'EU–Russia energy links', in Debra Johnson and Paul Robinson (eds), *Perspectives on EU–Russia Relations*, London: Routledge, pp. 175–93.

Jones-Luong, Pauline and Erika Weinthal (2010), *Oil Is Not a Curse: Ownership Structure and Institutions in Soviet Successor States*, Cambridge: Cambridge University Press.

Juselius, Jarkko (2009), 'Stubb arvostelee Itämeren kaasuputken valmistelua', *YLE, uutiset, kotimaa*, 3 September, accessed 23 March 2011 at http://yle.mobi/w/uutiset/kotimaa/ns-yduu-3-970574.

Karamotchev, P. (2011), 'Renewable energy in Russia – a giant to be reawakened', accessed 23 April 2011 at www.merar.com /weblog/2011 /03/28/ renewable-energy-russia-giant-yet-be-awakened/.

Karghiev, Vladimir (2004), 'Renewable energy in Russia – what is needed to make it feasible?' in *Renewable Energy Bulletin October 2004: Current State of Renewable Energy Development in Russia*, Moscow: EU–Russia Energy Dialogue Technology Centre, pp. 1–4.

Kennedy, Michael D. (2008), 'From transition to hegemony: extending the cultural politics of military alliances and energy security', in Mitchell A. Orenstein, Stephen Bloom and Nicole Lindstrom (eds), *Transnational Actors in Central and East European Transitions*, Pittsburgh, PA: University of Pittsburgh Press, pp. 188–212.

Ketting, J. (2011), 'Sustainable energy in Russia: a pipe dream or an opportunity?', in *How to Invest in Russia*, Moscow: Association of European Businesses in the Russian Federation, pp. 76–7.

Kivinen, Markku (2002), *Progress and Chaos: Russia as a Challenge for Sociological Imagination*, Helsinki: Kikimora Publications.

Kivinen, Markku (2007), 'Frames of Russian energy policy in transition', in David Dusseault (ed.), *The Dynamics of Energy in the Eurasian Context*, Aleksanteri Series 3, Helsinki: Kikimora, pp. 7–29.

Kjarstad, J. and F. Johnsson (2009), 'Resources and future supply of oil', *Energy Policy*, **37** (2), 441–64.

Kliuev, N.N. (2002), 'Rossiia na ekologicheskoi karte mira', *Izvestiya Akademii Nauk*, Seriya Geograficheskaya, **6**, 5–16.

Kommersant (2008), 'European Parliament voted against Nord Stream', 10 July, accessed 23 March 2011 at www.kommersant.com/p910880/ Nord_Stream_environmental/.

Kononenko, Vadim (2010), 'Russia–EU cooperation on energy efficiency', Finnish Institute of International Affairs, briefing paper 68.

Kontratev, K., K. Losev, M. Ananicheva and I. Chesnokova (2003), 'Tsena ekologicheskikh uslug Rossii', *Vestnik Rossiiskoi Adademii Nauk*, **73** (1), 3–11.

Korean International Trade Association (KITA) (n.d.), trade statistics, accessed 1 March 2011 at http://global.kita.net.

Korppoo, Anna (2008), 'Russia and the post-2012 climate regime: foreign rather than environmental policy', UPI briefing paper 23, November, accessed 20 November 2010 at www.fiia.fi/fi/publication/61/russia_and_the_post-2012_climate_regime.

Korppoo, Anna (2009), 'The Russian debate on climate doctrine', Finnish Institute of International Affairs Report 33.

Korppoo, Anna (2010), 'Implications of the Russian participation for the future climate regime', in Anna Korppoo, George Sakonov and Oleg Lugovoy (eds), *Climate Regimes: Emission Trends, Commitments and Bargains*, Copenhagen: Nordic Council of Ministers, TemaNord: 584.

Korppoo, Anna, Jacqueline Karas and Gary Grubb (2006), *Russia and the Kyoto Protocol – Opportunities and Constraints*, London: Chatham House, Brookings Institution.

Korppoo, Anna, Linda Jakobson, Johannes Urpelainen, Antto Vihma and Alex Luta (2009), 'Towards a new climate regime? Views of China, India, Japan and Russia and the United States on the road to Copenhagen', Finnish Institute of International Affairs report 19.

Korppoo, Anna, George Sakonov and Oleg Lugovoy (eds) (2010), *Russia and the Post 2012 Climate Regime*, Copenhagen: TemaNord 2010:584, pp. 47–81.

Korppoo, Anna and Thomas Spencer (2010), 'Russian climate policy: home and away', in Arielle Kramer (ed), *Greenhouse Gas Market Report 2010. Post Copenhagen and Climate Policy: Where Global Emissions Trading Goes from Here*, Geneva: International Emissions Trading Association (IETA), pp. 29–31.

Kotkin, Stephen (2005), 'The energy dimension in Russian global strategy', The James Baker III Institute for Public Policy of Rice University.

Kotov, Vladimir and Elena Nikitina (2001), 'Reorganisation of environmental policy in Russia: the decade of success and failures in implementation and perspective quests', paper presented in the first workshop of Carbon Flows between Eastern and Western Europe (CFEWE), Fondazione Eni Enrico Mattei, Milan, 5–6 July.

Kramer, Andrew E. (2007), 'Moscow presses BP to sell a big gas field to Gazprom', The New York Times, 23 June, accessed 21 March 2011 at www.nytimes.com/2007/06/23/business/worldbusiness/23gazprom.html.

Kristalinskaya, S. (2010), 'Russia tackles associated gas flaring', *Oil and Gas Eurasia*, March, accessed 23 April 2011 at www.oilandgaseurasia.com/articles/p/115/article/1143.

Krysiek, T.F. (2007), 'Agreements from another era: production sharing agreements in Putin's Russia, 2000–2007', Oxford Institute for Energy Studies working paper 34.

Kulagin, V. (2008), 'Energy efficiency and development of renewables: Russia's approach', *Russian Analytical Digest*, **46** (25 September), 2–8.

Kuusi, Osmo, Hanna Smith and Paula Tiihonen (eds) (2007), *Venäjä 2017*, Helsinki: Eduskunta, Tulevaisuusvaliokunta.

Landsbergis, Vytautas (2005), 'Impeeriumi gaasijuhe', *Postimees*, 13 December, accessed 29 March 2011 at www.postimees.ee/131205/esileht/arvamus/185984.php.

Larsson, Robert L. (2006a), *Russia's Energy Policy: Security Dimensions and Russia's Reliability as an Energy Superpower*, Stockholm: Swedish Defence Research Agency (FOI).

Larsson, Robert L. (2006b), *Sweden and the NEGP: A Pilot Study of the North European Gas Pipeline and Sweden's Dependence on Russian Energy*, Stockholm: Swedish Defence Research Agency.

Larsson, Robert L. (2008), 'Security implications of the Nord Stream Project', 12 February, FOI Memo 2336, Swedish Defence Research Agency, Stockholm.

Laudan, Larry (1977), *Progress and Its Problems: Towards a Theory of Scientific Growth*, Berkeley, CA: University of California Press.

Ledenova, Alena (2007), *How Russia Really Works: The Informal Practices that Shaped Post-Soviet Politics and Business,* Ithaca, NY: Cornell University Press.

Ledenova, Alena and Stanislav Shekshnia (2011), 'Corporate corruption in Russian regions', *Russian Analytical Digest* (February), **92**, 2–5.

Lee, Andrew (2011), 'Country profile: Russia', *Renewable Energy World Magazine*, 21 March, accessed 23 April 2011 at www.renewableenergyworld.com/rea/news/article/2011/03/country-profile-russia.

254 *Russia's energy policies*

Legvold, Robert (2007), *Russian Foreign Policy in the Twenty-First Century and the Shadow of the Past*, New York: Columbia University Press.

Lehtomäki, Paula (2004), speech at the Baltic Sea Institute, 8 January.

Lenta.ru (2010a), 'Gendirector ConocoPhillips nazval prichiny prodazhi aktsiy LUKOILa', accessed 18 July 2010 at www.lenta.ru/news/2010/03/29/reasons/.

Lenta.ru (2010b), 'Kitai potreboval ot Rossii vdvoye bolshe nefti', accessed 17 May 2010 at http://lenta.ru/news/2010/02/16/oil/.

Lesage, Dries, Thijs van de Graaf and Kirsten Westphal (2010), *Global Energy Governance in a Multipolar World*, Farnham: Ashgate.

Liberalno-demokraticheskaia partia Rossii, 'Energetika – vazhnejshee napravlenie ekonomiki Rossii', 21 March, accessed 17 April 2011 at www.ldpr.ru/events/Energy_the_most_important_direction_of_Russian_economy.

Lins, Christine, Jean-Marc Jossart and Giuliano Grassi (2005), 'Bioenergy and its potential in Russia', *Renewable Energy Bulletin October 2005*, Moscow: EU-Russia Energy Dialogue Technology Centre, pp. 7–11.

Liu, Xu (2010), 'Construction of the East Siberia–Pacific Ocean Oil Pipeline and development of oil resources: examination of its performances and problems', PhD thesis, Hokkaido University (in Japanese).

Liuhto, Kari (ed.) (2009), 'The EU–Russia gas connection: pipes, politics and problems', Pan-European Institute, accessed 30 July 2010 at www.tse.fi/FI/yksikot/erillislaitokset/pei/Documents/Julkaisut/Liuhto%200809%20web.pdf.

Liuhto, Kari (2010), 'Energy in Russia's foreign policy', Pan-European Institute, accessed 27 January 2011 at www.tse.fi/FI/yksikot/erillislaitokset/pei/Documents/Julkaisut/Liuhto_final.pdf.

Long, David (2011), 'Interdisciplinarity and the study of international relations', in Pami Aalto, Vilho Harle and Sami Moisio (eds), *International Studies: Interdisciplinary Approaches*, Basingstoke: Palgrave, pp. 31–65.

Lucas, Edward (2008), *A New Cold War: Putin's Russia and the Threat to the West*, London and New York: Palgrave Macmillan.

Lukoil (2003), 'Rossiiskiye neft i gaz: deloviye vozmozhnosti. videniye LUKOILa', accessed 10 March 2010 at www.Lukoil.com/materials/doc/presentations/2003/Russian_Oil_and_Gas.pdf.

Lukoil (2009), 'Key facts', accessed 15 May 2010 at www.Lukoil.ru/materials/doc/Books/2009/Facts2009/part3.pdf.

Malcolm, Neil, Alex Pravda, Roy Allison and Margot Light (1996), *Internal Factors in Russian Foreign Policy*, Oxford: Oxford University Press.

Malik, L. (2005), 'Kyoto Protocol and perspectives of small hydro power development in Russia', *Renewable Energy Bulletin October 2005*, Moscow: EU–Russia Energy Dialogue Technology Centre, pp. 15–16.

Malkova, I. (2009), 'Podgotovka k ekspansii', *Vedomosti*, 13 October.

Malkova, I. (2010), 'Ostalis za zakrytoi dveriyu', *Vedomosti*, 23 April.

Malkova, I. and K. Khripunov (2008), 'LUKOIL interesuetsya Repsol', *Vedomosti*, 21 November.

Mankoff, Jeffrey (2009), *Russian Foreign Policy – The Return of Great Power Politics*, Lanham, MD: Rowman & Littlefield.

Mareeva, S. Iu (2006), *Pravovoi Rezhim Ocvoeniia Mestorozhdenii Nefti i Gaza, Peresekaemiykh Raznymi Vidami Granits*, Moscow: Nestar Academic Publishers.

Mazneva, E. (2008), 'Podelili Orinoco', *Vedomosti*, 23 July.

Mazneva, E. (2009), 'Neft na 20 let vpered', *Vedomosti*, 18 February.

Mazneva, E. (2010), 'Kitaiskiy NPZ Rosnefti', *Vedomosti*, 22 September.

McFaul, M. (1997), 'A precarious peace: domestic politics in the making of Russian foreign policy', *International Security*, **22** (3), 5–35.

McKinsey Global Institute (2009), *Lean Russia: Sustaining Growth Through Improved Productivity*, New York: McKinsey Global Institute.

Medvedev, Dmitri (2009a), Opening remarks at expanded state council presidium meeting on improving energy efficiency of the Russian Federation, accessed 17 November 2010 at http://archive.kremlin.ru/eng/speeches/2009/07/02/1857_type82913 _218971.shtml.

Medvedev, Dmitri (2009b), 'Go Russia!', accessed 13 November 2009 at http://eng.kremlin.ru/text/speeches/2009/09/10/1534_type104017_221527.shtml.

Medvedev, Dmitry (2010), speech at St Petersburg International Economic Forum plenary session, 18 June, accessed 30 July 2010 at http://eng.kremlin.ru/transcripts/456.

Meulen, E.F. van der (2009), 'Gas supply and EU–Russia relations', *Europe-Asia Studies*, **61** (5), 833–56.

Ministry of Finance of the Russian Federation (2011a), 'Aggregate amount of the reserve fund', accessed 25 April 2011 at www1.minfin.ru/en/reservefund/statistics/amount/index.php?id4=5817.

Ministry of Finance of the Russian Federation (2011b), 'Aggregate amount of the national wealth fund', accessed 25 April 2011 at www1.minfin.ru/en/nationalwealthfund/statistics/amount/index.php?id4=5830.

Ministry of Finance, Japan (n.d.), trade statistics of Japan, accessed 1 March 2011 at www.customs.go.jp/toukei/info/index_e.htm.

Ministry of Trade and the Economy of Finland (2009), 'Suostumus Suomen Talousvyöhykkeen taloudelliseen hyödyntämiseen', 5 November, 678/601/2009, accessed at www.tem.fi/files/25239/307_VN_NordStreak_suostumus_051109ghdistetty.pdf.

Mitchell, John (2010), *More for Asia: Rebalancing World Oil and Gas*, London: Chatham House.

Mitrova, Tatiana (2009), 'Natural gas in transition: systemic reform issues', in S. Pirani (ed.), *Russian and CIS Gas Markets and Their Impact on Europe*, Oxford and New York: Oxford University Press for the Oxford Energy Institute, pp. 13–53.

Mityayev, Oleg (2009), 'Northern Europe greenlights Nord Stream', RIA-Novasti, Features & Opinions, 6 November, accessed 23 March 2011 at http://en.rian.ru/analysis/20091106/156738096.html.

Moe, A. and V. Kryukov (2010), 'Oil exploration in Russia: prospects for reforming a crucial sector', *Eurasian Geography and Economics*, **51** (3), 312–29.

Molchanov, Mikhail A. (2002), *Political Culture and National Identity in Russian–Ukrainian Relations*, College Station, TX: Texas A&M University Press.

Monaghan, Andrew (2007), 'Russia and the security of Europe's energy supplies: security in diversity', Conflict Studies Research Centre working paper special series 2007/1.

Motomura, M. (2005), *Revival of Russia as an Oil Power*, Tokyo: Institute of Developing Economies, Japan External Trade Organization (in Japanese).

Motomura, M. (2008), 'The Russian energy outlook and its influence on East Asia', *Acta Slavica Iaponica*, **25**, 67–87.

Motomura, M. (2010), 'Pipelines from Russia to the Far East are put into operation', *Oil and Natural Gas Review* (JOGMEC), **44** (4), 17–36 (in Japanese).

Möttölä, Kari (2006), 'Suomi suurvaltojen maailmassa', speech at the Finnish Institute of International Affairs, 2 March.

Nalbantoglu, Minna (2006), 'EU-maat haluavat puhua yhdellä äänellä energiatuottajien kanssa', *Helsingin Sanomat*, 15 March.

Nandorf, Tove (2006), 'Rysk gasledning säkerhetspolitisk problem', *Dagens Nyheter*, 14 November, accessed 29 March 2011 at www.dn.se/nyheter/sverige/rysk-gasledning-sakerhetspolitiskt-problem.

National Agency for Energy Regulation (ANRE) (2010), 'Resource and energy statistics', accessed 15 July 2010 at www.meti-go-jp/statistics/tyo/seidou/result/ichican/07_.

National Intelligence Council (NIC) (2009), 'Russia: the impact of climate change to 2030', NIC Special Report NIC 2009-04D, Washington, DC.

National Statistical Committee of the Republic of Belarus (Belstat) (2010), *Foreign Trade of the Republic of Belarus*, Minsk: Belstat.

Natorski, M. and A. Herranz Surralles (2008), 'Securitizing moves to nowhere? The framing of the European Union's energy policy', *Journal of Contemporary European Research*, **4** (2), 71–89.

Natsional'nye scheta Rossii (NSR) (various years), Moscow: Rosstat.

Nefteprovod Druzhba (2010), 'Information bulletin', accessed 17 July 2010 at www.rian.ru/spravka/20070109/58705713.html.

Neumann, Iver (1996), *Russia and the idea of Europe: A Study in Identity and International Relations*, London: Routledge.

Nies, Susanne (2008), *Oil and Gas Delivery to Europe: An Overview of Existing and Planned Infrastructures*, Brussels: Institut Francais des Relations Internationales.

Nikolskiy, A. (2010), 'Vizit v Polzu Alfa', *Vedomosti*, 7 October.

Nord Stream AG (2011), 'Project milestones', accessed 8 March 2011 at www.nord-stream.com/en/the-pipeline/milestones.html.

Novikova, Alexandra, Anna Korppoo, and Maria Sharmina (2009), 'Russian pledge vs. business-as-usual: implementing energy efficiency policies can curb carbon emissions', UPI-FIIA working paper 61/2009.

Oda, H. (1999), 'Amendments of law on production sharing and related legislation of Russia', *Oil and Natural Gas Review* (JOGMEC), **32** (3), 64–72 (in Japanese).

Oil and Energy Trends (2002), 'Russia plays energy security card to boost oil exports', accessed 19 May 2010 at http://www.oilandenergytrends.com/ger/articles/2002_12.htm.

Olcott, Martha (2004), 'The energy dimension in Russian global strategy: Vladimir Putin and the geopolitics of oil', The James Baker III Institute for Public Policy of Rice University.

Oldfield, Jon (2005), *Russian Nature: Exploring the Environmental Consequences of Society-Nature Interactions*, Farnham: Ashgate.

Oldfield, J. and D. Shaw (2002), 'Revisiting sustainable development: Russian cultural and scientific traditions and the concept of sustainable development', *Area*, **34** (4), 391–400.

Oldfield, J., A. Kouzmina and D.J. Shaw (2003), 'Russia's involvement in the international environmental process: a research report', *Eurasian Geography and Economics*, **44** (2), 157–68.

Orban, Anita (2008), *Power, Energy and the New Russian Imperialism*, Westport, CT: Praeger.

Organisation for Economic Co-operation and Development (OECD) and International Energy Agency (IEA) (2003), 'Renewables in Russia: from opportunity to reality', accessed 25 November 2010 at www.iea.org/textbase/nppdf/free/2000/renewrus_2003.pdf.

Orttung, Robert W. (2009), 'Energy and state–society relations: socio-political aspects of Russia's energy wealth', in Jeronim Perovic, Robert W. Orttung and Andreas Wenger (eds), *Russian Energy Power and Foreign Relations: Implications to Conflict and Cooperation*, London and New York: Routledge, pp. 51–70.

Orttung, Robert W. and I. Øverland (2011), 'A limited toolbox: explaining the constraints on Russia's foreign energy policy', *Journal of Eurasian Studies*, **2** (1), 74–85.

Ostergren, D. and P. Jacques (2002), 'A political economy of Russian nature conservation policy: why scientists have taken a back seat', *Global Environmental Politics*, **2** (4), 102–24.

Øverland, Indra and Heidi Kjærnet (2009), *Russian Renewable Energy: The Potential for International Cooperation*, Farnham: Ashgate.

Paik, K-W. (2011), *Sino-Russian Oil and Gas Cooperation*, Oxford: Oxford Institute for Energy Studies/Oxford University Press.

Palonkorpi, Mikko (2009), 'Matter over mind? Securitizing energy interdependencies', paper presented at the International Studies Association annual conference, 14–18 February, New York.

Pannier, Bruce (2010), 'New Turkmen–China pipeline breaks Russia's hold over Central Asian gas', Radio Free Europe/Radio Liberty, 14 December, accessed 16 August 2010 at www.rferl.org/content/Turkmenistan China_Gas_Pipeline_To_Open/1903108.html.

Pavel, Ferdinand and Anna Chukhai (2006), 'Gas storage tariffs along the route to EU Market', Kiev, Ukraine: IER, accessed 24 February 2009 at www.ier.kiev.ua.

Perovic, Jeronim (2009), 'Introduction: Russian energy power, domestic and international dimensions', in Jeronim Perovic, Robert W. Orttung and Andreas Wenger (eds), *Russian Energy Power and Foreign Relations: Implications for Conflict and Cooperation*, London: Routledge, pp. 1–20.

Perovic, Jeronim and Robert Orttung (2007), 'Russia's energy policy: should Europe worry?', *Russian Analytical Digest*, **18**, 2–7.

Perovic, Jeronim, Robert W. Orttung and Andreas Wenger (eds) (2009), *Russian Energy Power and Foreign Relations: Implications for Conflict and Cooperation*, Abingdon: Routledge.

Peterson, D.J. and E.K. Bielke (2001), 'The reorganization of Russia's environmental bureaucracy: implications and prospects', *Post-Soviet Geography and Economics*, **42** (1), 65–76.

Petro, Nicolai N. and Alvin Z. Rubinstein (1997), *Russian Foreign Policy: From Empire to Nation-State*, Harlow: Longman.

Petroleum Intelligence Weekly (2009), 'Lukoil beats Valero to Total refinery stake', 29 June.

Pirani, Simon (2009), 'The impact of the economic crisis on Russian and CIS gas markets', Oxford Institute for Energy Studies natural gas working papers 36, November.

Poussenkova, Nina (2007), 'Lord of the rigs: Rosneft as a mirror of Russia's evolution', in *The Changing Role of National Oil Companies in International Energy Markets*, Houston, TX: James Baker III Institute for

Public Policy Publications, accessed 27 June 2011 at http://www.rice.edu/ energy/publications/docs.html.

Poussenkova, Nina (2009), 'Russia's future customers: Asia and beyond', in Jeronim Perovic, Robert W. Orttung and Andreas Wenger (eds), *Russian Energy Power and Foreign Relations: Implications for Conflict and Cooperation*, London and New York: Routledge, pp. 132–54.

'Prezentatsiia osnovnykh polozhenii proekta Strategii' (Irkutskaia Oblast') (2007), accessed 2 May 2011 at www.csr-nw.ru/content/data/article/file/ st44_1903.pdf.

Prime-Tass Financial News (2011), 'Iaponia stala samyn krupnym importerom nefti s Dal'nogo Vostoka Rossi', 28 December

Pristupa, A.O., A.P. Mol and P. Oosterveer (2010), 'Stagnating liquid biofuel developments in Russia: present status and future perspectives', *Energy Policy*, **38** (7), 3320–8.

Prizel, Ilya (1998), *National Identity and Foreign Policy: Nationalism and Leadership in Poland, Ukraine and Russia*, Cambridge: Cambridge University Press.

'Proekt Plana Realizatsii Strategii Cotsial'no-ekonomicheskogo Razvitija Dal'nogo Vostoka i Baikal'skogo Regiona na period do 2025 goda (Minregion Rossii ot 25.11.2009)' (2009), accessed 28 January 2010 at http://sakhagov.ykt.ru/main.asp?c=14197.

Promyshlennost' Rossii (various years), Moscow: Rosstat.

Prontera, A. (2009), 'Energy policy: concepts, actors, instruments and recent developments', *World Political Science Review*, **5** (1), 1–30.

Pynnöniemi, Katri (2008), *New Road, New Life, New Russia: International Transport Corridors at the Conjunction of Geography and Politics in Russia*, Tampere, Finland: Tampere University Press.

Radio Free Europe (2010), 'Medvedev launches Nord Stream pipeline construction', 9 April, accessed 29 March 2011 at www.rferl.org/content/ Dignitaries_Gather_For_Symbolic_Start_Of_Nord_Stream/2007492.html.

Radio Free Europe/Radio Liberty Armenian service (2910), 'Russian gas price to Armenia to rise further', accessed 7 May at www.azatutyun.am/ content/article/2005637.html.

RBK Daily (2010), 'Rossiisko-kitaiskaia gasovaia epopeia', 30 September.

RBK Daily (2011), 'Kovytka dostalas' "Gazpromu"', 2 March, accessed 2 May 2011 at www.rbcdaily.ru/2011/03/02/tek/562949979787558.

Rees, Judith (1991), 'Resources and environment: scarcity and sustainability', in Robert J. Bennett and Robert C. Estall (eds), *Global Challenge and Change: Geography for the 1990s*, London: Routledge, pp. 5–26.

Regiony Rossii (various years), Moscow: Rosstat.

Remes, Seppo (2007), *Venäjän tulevaisuuden varmuuksia ja epävarmuuksia*, presentation in a seminar of the Future Committee of the Finnish Parliament, 25 January, Helsinki.

Reuters (2009), 'Russia's LUKOIL to invest in new US refinery', accessed 27 July 2011 at www.reuters.com/article/2009/07/06/odama-russia-lukoil-idUSL629203720090706.

Roland, G. (2006), 'The Russian economy in the year 2005', *Post-Soviet Affairs*, **22** (1), 90–98.

Romanova, Tatiana (2007), 'Energy dialogue from strategic partnership to the regional level of the Northern Dimension', in Pami Aalto (ed.), *The EU–Russian Energy Dialogue: Europe's Future Energy Security*, Aldershot: Ashgate, pp. 63–92.

Rosbank (2010), 'Rosbank becomes a partner in EBRD's Russian sustainable energy and carbon finance facility programme', accessed 23 April 2011 at www.rosbank.ru/en/news/detail/news/rosbank_becomes_a_partner_in_ebrd_s_russian_sustainable/.

RosBiznesKonsulting (2011), 'Rossia nachala postavki gaza v Moldaviui po evropeiskim tsenami', 1 January, accessed 7 May 2011 at http://top.rbc.ru/economics/01/01/2011/523960.shtml.

Roshydromet (Federal Service for Hydrometeorology and Environmental Monitoring) (2005), *Strategic Prediction for the Period of up to 2010–2015 of Climate Change Expected in Russia and Its Impact on Sectors of the Russian National Economy*, Moscow: Roshydromet.

Rossiiskii statisticheskii ezhegodnik (various years), Moscow: Rosstat.

Rossiyskiy statisticheskiy ezhegodnik (2010), Moscow: Rosstat.

Rutland, P. (2008), 'Russia as an energy superpower', *New Political Economy*, **13** (2), 203–210.

Rutledge, I. (2004), 'The Sakhalin II PSA – a production non-sharing agreement analysis of revenue distribution', accessed 2 May 2011 at www.foe.co.uk/resource/reports/sakhalin_psa.pdf.

Rytövuori-Apunen, Helena and Terhi Takkinen (2000), 'Interfaces in environmental thinking: sustainable development challenged by ecological safety', in Helena Rytövuori-Apunen (ed.), *Russian–European Interfaces in the Northern Dimension of the EU*, Tampere, Finland: University of Tampere, Department of Political Science and International Relations, pp. 447–97.

Sachs, Wolfgang (1999), *Planet Dialectics: Explorations in Environment and Development*, London: Zed Books.

Safonov, George and Oleg Lugovoy (2010), 'Economic development and emission projections in Russia', in Anna Korppoo, George Sakonov and Oleg Lugovoy (eds), *Russia and the Post 2012 Climate Regime*, Copenhagen: Nordic Council of Ministers, TemaNord 2010:584, pp. 16–43.

Sakaguchi, I. (2003), 'Trend of PSA (Production Sharing Agreement) in Russia', *Monthly Bulletin on Trade with Russia & East Europe* (ROTOBO), 48 (8–9), 19–29 (in Japanese).

Sakhalin Energy (2006), 'Sakhalin Energy at a Glance', accessed 2 May 2011 at http://www.sakhalinenergy.com/en/ataglance.asp?p=aag_main&s=14.

Sakwa, Richard (2004), *Putin: Russia's Choice,* London and New York: Routledge.

Savushkin, S. and S. Kukolev (1995), 'Na fondovyi rynok za investitsiyami', *Neft i Capital,* **5,** 16–19.

Scrase, Ivan and Gordon McKerron (eds) (2009), *Energy for the Future: A New Agenda,* Basingstoke: Palgrave.

Scrase, Ivan, Dierk Bauknecht, Florian Kern, Markku Lehtonen, Gordon MacKerron, Mari Martiskainen, Francis McGowan, David Ockwell, Raphael Sauter, Adrian Smith, Steve Sorrel, Tao Wang and Jim Watson (2009), 'Conclusions: transitions, governance, appraisal', in Ivan Scrase and Gordon MacKerron (eds), *Energy for the Future: A New Agenda,* Basingstoke: Palgrave, pp. 223–39.

Sechin, I.I. (2010), speech at the meeting of the Presidium of the Russian government 16 June, accessed 25 February 2011 at www.government.ru/docs/11026/.

SEP (Sotsial'no-ekonomicheskoe polozhenie Rossii) (monthly), Moscow: Rosstat.

Sewell, William H., Jr. (2005), *Logics of History: Social Theory and Social Transformation,* Chicago, IL: University of Chicago Press.

Shackley, S. (2001), 'The respectable politics of climate change: the epistemic communities and NGOs', *International Affairs,* **77** (2), 329–45.

Shatalov, S.D. (2010), interview 8 June, accessed 25 February 2011 at www1.minfin.ru/ru/press/speech/index.php?pg4=5&id4= 9991.

Shell (2010), 'Gazprom and Shell agree to pursue broader cooperation', news and media release, 30 November, accessed 17 January 2011 at www.shell.com/home/content/media/news_and_media_releases/2010/gazprom_shell_cooperation_30112010.html.

Sidorenko, G., G. Borisov, A. Titov and P. Bezrukikh (2001), 'Challenges for the use of bioenergy in Northwest Russia', in Paavo Pelkonen, Pentti Hakkila, Timo Karjalainen and Bernhard Schlamadinger (eds), *Woody Biomass as an Energy Source – Challenges in Europe,* European Forest Institute proceedings no. 39, 45–62.

Simonia, N. (2004), 'The West's energy security and the role of Russia', *Russia in Global Affairs,* **2** (3), 101–17.

'Skhema kompleksnogo razvitiia proizvoditel'nykh sil, transporta i energetiki Respublika Sakha (Yakutia) 2010' (2006), accessed 2 May 2011 at http://sakha.gov.ru/sites/default/files/story/files/2010_10/114/shema2020.pdf.

Smith, Hanna (2004), 'Tshetshenia on kantona EU:n ja Venäjän suhteissa', *Helsingin Sanomat,* 17 September.

Smith, H. (2005), 'Det förflutnas inflytande på rysk utrikespolitik', *Nordisk Østforum*, **19** (3), 287–306.

Smith, Hanna (2010), 'The nexus of great power thinking: Russian domestic and foreign policy', in Bertil Nygren, Bo Huldt, Patrik Ahlgren, Pekka Sivonen and Susanna Huldt (eds), *Strategic Yearbook 2008–2009, Russia on Our Minds,* Stockholm: National Defence College, pp. 177–96.

Smith, Hanna (forthcoming), 'Two faces of Russian foreign policy: domestic and international institutionalism', in Roger E. Kanet and Maria Raquel Freire (eds), *Russia and Its Neighbours*, Basingstoke: Palgrave Macmillan.

Smith, Keith C. (2006), 'Security Implications of Russian Energy Policies', Centre for European Policy Studies policy brief no 90/January.

Smith, Keith (2008), *Russia and European Energy Security: Divide and Dominate*, Washington, DC: Centre for Strategic and International Studies.

Solanko, Laura (2011), 'How to succeed with a thousand TWH reform: restructuring the Russian power sector', The Finnish Institute of International Affairs working paper 68/2011.

Solanko, L. and P. Sutela (2009), 'Too much or too little gas to Europe?', *Eurasian Geography and Economics,* **50** (1), 58–74.

Sovacol, B.K. (2011), 'An international comparison of four polycentric approaches to climate and energy governance', *Energy Policy*, **39**, 3832–44.

Staalesen, Atle (2010), 'Nord Stream more expensive', *Barents Observer*, 17 March, accessed 8 March 2011 at www.barentsobserver.com/nord-stream-more-expensive.4760460-116321.html.

Stern, Jonathan P. (1999), 'Soviet and Russian gas: the origins and evolution of Gazprom's export strategy', in Robert Mabro and Ian Wybrew-Bond (eds), *Gas to Europe: The Strategies of Four Major Suppliers*, Oxford: Oxford University Press, pp. 135–200.

Stern, Jonathan P. (2002), *Security of European Natural Gas Supplies*, London: The Royal Institute of International Affairs.

Stern, Jonathan (2009a), 'Future gas production in Russia: is the concern about lack of investment justified?', Oxford Institute for Energy Studies natural gas working papers 35, October.

Stern, Jonathan (2009b), 'Continental European long-term gas contracts: is a transition away from oil product-linked pricing inevitable and imminent?', Oxford Institute for Energy Studies natural gas working papers 34, September.

Stern, Jonathan P. (2009c), 'The Russian gas balance to 2015: difficult years ahead', in S. Pirani (ed.), *Russian and CIS Gas Markets and their Impact on Europe*, Oxford and New York: Oxford University Press for the Oxford Institute of Energy Studies, pp. 54–92

Stern, Jonathan, Simon Pirani, and Katja Yafimava (2010), 'The April 2010 Russo–Ukrainian gas agreement and its implications for Europe', Oxford

Institute for Energy Studies Natural gas working paper series no 42, accessed 1 July 2010 at www.oxfordenergy.org/pdfs/NG42.pdf.

Stevens, Paul (2010), *The 'Shale Gas Revolution': Hype or Reality*, London: Chatham House.

Strange, Susan (1994), *States and Markets*, London: Pinter.

'Strategiia sotsial'no-ekonomicheskogo razvitiia Irkutskoi Oblasti na dolgos-rochnuiu perspektivu' (2007), accessed 2 May 2011 at www.csr-nw.ru/content/data/article/file/st44_1838.pdf.

Struchkov A.A. (2009), 'Skhema kompleksnogo razvitija proizvoditelnykh sil, tranzporta i energetiki Respublika Sakha (Yakutia) i Energiticheskij Strategii Respubliki Sakha (Yakutia) do 2030', presentation by Minister of Economic Development, 22 November.

Stulberg, Adam N. (2007), *Well-Oiled Diplomacy: Strategic Manipulation and Russia's Energy Statecraft in Eurasia*, Albany, NY: SUNY Press.

Suhomlinova, O.O. (2007), 'Property rules: state fragmentation, industry heterogeneity and property rights in Russian oil industry 1992–2006', *Human Relations*, **60**, 1443–66.

Sutela, Pekka (2009), 'How strong is Russia's economic foundation?', Centre for European Reform policy brief, London.

Sutela, P. (2010), 'Forecasting the Russian economy for 2010–2012', *Russian Analytical Digest*, **88**, 2–5.

Sztompka, Piotr (1991), *Society in Action: The Theory of Social Becoming*, Chicago, IL: University of Chicago Press.

Tabata, S. (2006), 'Price differences, taxes, and the stabilization fund', in Michael Ellman (ed.), *Russia's Oil and Natural Gas: Bonanza or Curse?*, London: Anthem, pp. 35–53.

Tabata, S. (2007), 'The Russian Stabilization Fund and its successor: implications for inflation', *Eurasian Geography and Economics*, **48** (6), 699–712.

Tabata, S. (2009a), 'The impact of global financial crisis on the mechanism of economic growth in Russia', *Eurasian Geography and Economics*, **50** (6), 682–98.

Tabata, S. (2009b), 'The influence of high oil prices on the Russian economy: a comparison with Saudi Arabia', *Eurasian Geography and Economics*, **50** (1), 75–92.

Tester, Jefferson W., Elisabeth M. Drake, Michael J. Driscoll, Michael W. Golay and William A. Peters (2005), *Sustainable Energy: Choosing among Options*, Cambridge, MA: MIT Press.

The Heritage Foundation (2011), *2011 Index of Economic Freedom*, Washington, DC: The Heritage Foundation.

Tkachenko, Stanislav (2007), 'Actors in Russia's energy policy towards the EU', in Pami Aalto (ed.), *The EU–Russia Energy Dialogue: Europe's Future Energy Supplies?*, Aldershot: Ashgate, pp. 163–91.

Total (2011), 'Total enters into a strategic partnership with the independent gas company Novatek', news release, 2 March, accessed 15 March 2011 at www.total.com/en/about-total/news/news-940500.html&idActu=2534.

Transparency International (2010), *Corruption Perception Index 2010,* accessed 23 January 2011 at www.transparency.org/policy_research/surveys_indices/cpi/2010.

Travin, Dmitry and Otar Marganiya (2010), 'Resource curse: rethinking the Soviet experience', in Vladimir Gel'man and Otar Marganiya (eds), *Resource Curse and Post-Soviet Asia: Oil Gas and Modernization,* Lanham, MD: Lexington Books, pp. 23–48.

Triesman, D. (2010), '"Loans for shares" revisited', *Post-Soviet Affairs,* **26** (3), 207–27.

Tutushkin, A. and I. Vasiliev (2009), 'Obeshannogo 12 let zhdut', *Vedomosti,* 14 January.

Tynkkynen, Nina (2005), 'Russia, a great ecological power? On Russian attitudes to environmental politics at home and abroad', in Sari Autio-Sarasmo and Arja Rosenholm (eds), *Understanding Russian Nature: Representations, Values and Concepts,* Helsinki: Kikimora Publications, pp. 277–96.

Tynkkynen, Nina (2008), *Constructing the Environmental Regime between Russia and Europe: Conditions for Social Learning,* Tampere, Finland: University of Tampere Press.

Tynkkynen, N. (2010), 'Russia, a great ecological power in global climate policy? Framing climate change as a policy problem in Russian public discussion', *Environmental Politics,* **19** (2), 179–95.

Tysiachniouk, Maria and Jonathan Reisman (2004), 'Co-managing the taiga: Russian forests and the challenge of international environmentalism', in Ari Lehtinen and Jacob Donner-Amnell (eds), *Politics of Forests,* Aldershot: Ashgate, 157–75.

Tysiachniouk, Maria and Jonathan Reisman (2005), 'Market of values across the border: forest practices on certified territories in Northwestern Russia', in Sari Autio-Sarasmo and Arja Rosenholm (eds), *Understanding Russian Nature: Representations, Values and Concepts,* Helsinki: Kikimora Publications, pp. 147–76.

UkraineAnalysen (2009), 50/09, 27 January.

United Nations Development Programme (UNDP) (2010), *National Human Development Report in the Russian Federation: Energy Sector and Sustainable Development,* Moscow: UNDP, accessed 23 November 2010 at www.undp.ru/documents/180-eng2-01-04.pdf.

United Nations Framework Convention on Climate Change (UNFCCC) (2010), 'Greenhouse gas databank. Greenhouse gas inventory data detailed by party', accessed 25 November 2010 at http://unfccc.int/di/DetailedByParty.do.

Vedomosti (2008a), 'Rosnedra predostavjat Gazpromu lisenziju na Chajadinskoje mestorozhdenije', 16 April, accessed 15 November 2010 at http://www.vedomosti.ru/newshie/print/2008/04/16579520.

Velikhov, Evgeni (2003), 'Energy without borders: the "Russian Nobel Prize" awaits winners', *Russia in Global Affairs,* **2** (2), accessed 3 December 2010 at http://eng.globalaffairs.ru/number/n_624.

Von Hirschhausen, C., B. Meinhart and F. Pavel (2005), 'Transporting Russian gas to Western Europe – a simulation analysis', *The Energy Journal,* **26** (2), 49–68.

Weinthal, Erika and Pauline Jones Loung (2006), 'The paradox of energy sector reform', in Timothy Colton and Stephen Hanson (eds), *The State after Communism: Governance in the New Russia,* Lanham, MD: Rowman & Littlefield, pp. 225–60.

Wendt, Alexander (1999), *Social Theory of International Politics,* Cambridge: Cambridge University Press.

Wenger, Andreas (2006), 'Russian business power as a source of transnational conflict and cooperation', in Andreas Wenger, Jeronim Perovic and Robert W. Orttung (eds), *Russian Business Power: The Role of Russian Business in Foreign and Security Relations,* London: Routledge, pp. 3–21.

Wenger, Andreas (2009), 'Russia's energy power: implications for Europe and for transatlantic cooperation', in Jeronim Perovic, Robert W. Orttung and Andreas Wenger (eds), *Russian Energy Power and Foreign Relations,* London and New York: Routledge, pp. 225–44.

Wenger, Andreas, Jeronim Perovic and Robert W. Orttung (eds) (2006), *Russian Business Power: The Role of Russian Business in Foreign and Security Relations,* London and New York: Routledge.

Westphal, Kirsten (2007), 'Germany and the EU–Russia energy dialogue', in Pami Aalto (ed.), *The EU–Russia Energy Dialogue: Europe's Future Energy Security,* Aldershot: Ashgate, pp. 93–118.

Whist, Bendik Solum (2008), 'Nord Stream: not just a pipeline: an analysis of the political debates in the Baltic Sea region regarding the planned gas pipeline from Russia to Germany', Fridtjof Nansen Institute report 15/2008.

Wilson Rowe, Elana and Stina Torjesen (2008), *The Multilateral Dimension in Russian Foreign Policy,* London and New York: Routledge.

Wood, Ruth, Paul Gilbert, Maria Sharmina, Kevin Anderson, Anthony Footlitt, Steven Glynn and Fiona Nicholls (2011), 'Shale gas: a provisional assessment of climate change and environmental impacts', Manchester: University of Manchester, Tyndall Centre for Climate Change Research.

World Bank (2008), *Energy Efficiency in Russia: Untapped Reserves,* Moscow: World Bank.

World Bank (2010), *Russian Federation: Making a Difference for Entrepreneurs*, Washington, DC: World Bank.

World Commission on Environment and Development (WCED) (1987), *Our Common Future*, Oxford: Oxford University Press.

World Economic Forum (2010), *The Global Competitiveness Report 2010–2011*, Geneva: World Economic Forum.

WWF Rossia (2008a), *Pozitsiia ekologicheskikh NPO po sotsial'nym i ekologicheskim proizvodstva i peredachi energii*, Moscow: WWF Rossiia.

WWF Russia (2008b), *The Impact of Climate Change on the Russian Arctic: Analysis and Paths to Solving the Problem*, Moscow: WWF Russia.

Xinhuanet (2010), 'China's gas consumption will grow fast', 27 March, accessed 24 February 2001 at http://news.xinhuanet.com/fortune/2010-03/27/content_13256606.htm, in Chinese.

Zimmerman, William (2002), *The Russian People and Foreign Policy: Russian Elite and Mass Perspectives 1993–2000*, Princeton, NJ: Princeton University Press.

Zlotnikov, Leonid (2007), Deutsche Welle programme for Belarus, *Belaruskaya Khronika*, 17 December, broadcast 17 December 2010 on www.dw-world.de.

Zumbrunnen, Craig (2009), 'Climate change in the Russian North: threats real and potential', in Elana Wilson Rowe (ed.), *Russia and the North*, Ottawa: Ottawa University Press, pp. 53–86.

Index

Africa 4, 49, 160–61, 163, 179, 189,
    199, 233
Alekperov, Vagit 188, 194
Alfa Group 24, 59
Algeria 193, 198–9
Americas 4, 18
Angarsk 166, 197
Angola 186, 203
Arctic 110, 167, 203, 210, 213, 218, 227,
    233
Asia 3–5, 9, 18, 28, 59–60, 119, 232
    Central Asia 3, 12, 22, 129, 145, 148
    East Asia 9, 156, 160, 166, 169, 171,
        173, 175, 178
    Northeast Asia 4, 9, 74, 80–83, 85,
        212, 232, 236
    Asia Pacific region 110, 160, 163, 201
Australia 171, 208
Azerbaijan 188, 190, 193

Baev, Pavel 208–9
Baltic Sea 9, 120, 123, 166, 232
Baltic Sea States 125–6, 128
Baltic States 124, 131, 133, 142, 166
Barents Sea 7–9, 17, 27, 102, 120, 195,
    210, 212–13
BASF 123, 133
Belarus 4, 9, 17, 124, 128–9, 136–8,
    142–3, 147, 150–53, 232, 235
Belgium 121, 123
Black Sea 9, 101, 102, 166, 189
Biomass 10, 99, 101, 105
BP 24, 56, 133, 190, 193, 197–9, 203–4,
    214, 218–19
Brazil 3, 100, 192
BRIC 3, 4
business studies 10, 31

Canada 56, 100, 208, 224–5, 227
Caspian region 8, 18, 132, 187–8
Caspian Sea 102, 167, 189, 199

Caucasus 3, 18, 100–102, 159
Chaiadinskoe 16, 63, 80, 83
Chaianda 79, 83–5, 88–9, 178
Chavez, Hugo 195, 198, 200
Chevron 190, 203
China 3–4, 17, 22, 59–60, 62, 80, 88,
    159–61, 163, 165–6, 170–71, 173,
    176–8, 189, 192, 196, 201–2, 211,
    214, 216, 219, 223–4, 235–6
China Development Bank 166, 201
climate change 4, 6, 16, 18, 27, 39, 41,
    64, 92–3, 111, 113, 206, 209,
    214–17, 223, 226–8, 234
    see also greenhouse gas; Kyoto
        protocol (treaty)
CNPC 84, 190, 196–7, 201–202
Commonwealth of Independent States
    (CIS) 5, 8, 22–4, 27, 59, 118–19,
    142, 145, 159, 195, 199, 203, 233
Conoco-Phillips 24, 195
corruption 13, 55, 58, 140, 145, 148–9,
    207, 223
Cuba 186, 203–4

Daqing 165–6, 197
Denmark 120–26, 130, 135
Dixon, Sarah 55, 57
Dutch disease 3, 10–11, 146, 208
    see also resource curse
Dynkin, A. 58–9

East Siberian Pacific Ocean (ESPO)
    pipeline 9, 77, 164–6, 175–6, 179,
    201–2, 219, 235–6
Eastern gas programme 9, 163, 178
economics 6, 10, 14, 31, 33, 60, 127, 132
E.On Ruhrgas 123, 133
Egypt 189, 193, 199
electricity 6, 24, 26–7, 48, 52, 67, 71,
    94, 96, 100, 102, 104–5, 107–8,
    141, 213–14, 234

Elf 189, 191
energy diplomacy 11–13, 22, 61, 232,
    237
energy efficiency 4, 6, 16, 18, 64, 70,
    92–4, 96–8, 104–7, 109–13, 211,
    213–14, 217, 223–6, 228, 234
energy imperialism 3, 12–13, 21, 137,
    140
    see also frame: energy
        superpowerframe
energy intensity 50, 94, 97, 106, 214,
    217, 224–6
energy savings 4, 92, 104, 109, 225, 227
energy security 11, 13, 17–18, 28, 37,
    41, 96, 119–20, 124, 134, 160, 179,
    189, 204, 206, 209, 213–17, 228,
    232
    security of supplies 11, 28, 37, 63,
        117, 209, 217, 234
    security of transit 17, 117, 217
    see also frame: energy security frame
energy superpower 3, 16, 21, 34, 36, 96,
    98, 106, 108, 113, 120, 146, 149,
    153, 207
    see also frame: energy superpower
        frame
energy transit 3–4, 9–11, 17, 20–21, 33,
    36–7, 39, 64, 74–7, 80, 104,
    117–20, 122–3, 126, 128–30,
    134–42, 144–53
engineering 6, 25, 30, 73, 84–5, 122, 187
Eni 133, 190, 203
ERG 105, 195
Estonia 125–6
Europe 4–5, 8–9, 18, 24, 28, 36, 49, 55,
    59, 60, 64, 93, 104, 109, 118–20,
    122, 126, 129, 136, 142, 148, 150,
    152, 159, 178, 189, 195, 198, 200,
    202, 204, 211–12, 216, 232
    Central Europe 9, 12, 22, 64, 136
    Eastern Europe 3, 4, 9, 12, 22, 64,
        105, 117, 119, 130, 132, 136,
        166, 196
    North Europe 9, 123
    Western Europe 100, 118–9, 124, 130,
        138, 143, 148
European Bank for Reconstruction and
    Development (EBRD) 82, 84, 105
European Commission 120, 123–4, 132,
    213

European Council 123–4
European Parliament 123–4
European Union (EU) 11–12, 14, 23, 36,
    40, 54, 59–61, 104, 117, 124–5,
    131–4, 203, 211–14, 216–18, 224,
    226, 232, 234
events 6, 13, 15, 20, 28, 35–41, 113,
    127–8, 132–3, 147, 212, 227,
    229–31, 234–5, 238
Exxon 164, 190, 199, 202

Far East 16–18, 24, 65, 71–4, 82, 85, 88,
    100, 102, 110, 156–60, 163–4, 169,
    173–4, 177–8, 218–219, 233
    see also Asia
Finland 55, 120–22, 124–6, 130, 133
Former Soviet Union (FSU) 138, 146
    former Soviet republics 126, 142
    see also Soviet Union
Fortum 118, 122–3
frame 26–8, 35, 37, 40, 45, 47, 54, 125,
    191, 195, 238
    business frame 15, 17–18, 26–8, 31–2,
        37, 46–7, 59, 61, 120, 129, 134,
        137, 140, 148–50, 179, 232
    energy security frame 28, 120, 232
    energy superpower frame 15–16,
        27–8, 37, 46–8, 61, 108, 113,
        134, 136–7, 139, 146, 207, 232
    political frame 147, 151–2
    Soviet interdependence frame 15, 46,
        62, 232
    sustainability frame 27–8, 35, 37,
        92–3, 97–8, 103, 108, 110–12,
        232
    see also energy superpower; policy
        environment
Fridman, M. 24, 197

Gaddy, Clifford 10–11, 207–8
Gazprom 9, 17, 22–4, 32, 36, 46, 48–56,
    62, 80–85, 87–90, 118–19, 121–4,
    126, 128, 133, 135, 137–8, 140–46,
    148–53, 163, 165, 177–9, 191–2,
    194, 196–8, 200, 203–4, 213,
    218–19, 235–6
Gazpromneft 24, 48, 203
GDF SUEZ 133, 190
geography 6, 30–31, 185–6, 199, 211,
    216, 224

geology 6, 30
geopolitics 11–13, 127, 209, 237
geothermal power 10, 100
Germany 9, 37, 118–24, 126, 128, 133,
    134, 160, 187, 189, 196, 200, 211
Government of Russia 16, 23, 25, 31–2,
    39, 48, 50, 52, 54, 56, 59, 62, 84,
    94, 99, 104, 126, 128, 131, 137,
    141, 144, 156, 163–4, 166, 179,
    189, 196, 200, 201, 204, 214, 221
Greenhouse gas (GHG) 4, 93, 97, 234
Gulf of Mexico 214, 218

Hanson, P. 220–21
Hungary 12, 187
hydro(power) 10, 47, 75, 77, 79, 93–4,
    97–100, 102, 107, 111

Ickes, Barry 10–11, 207–8
Independent Institute of Social Politics
    71, 74
India 159, 164, 204, 211
Indonesia 100, 171, 193
Interdisciplinarity 20–21
    see also multidisciplinary
interest 17, 26–8, 34–5, 37, 47, 49–51,
    56, 58, 61–2, 66, 69, 80, 96, 98,
    103, 121, 123, 139–40, 151, 153,
    188, 192, 195–6, 199, 219
International Energy Agency (IEA) 6,
    7, 103, 108, 159, 213, 215, 217,
    229
International Monetary Fund (IMF) 151,
    207
International Oil Companies (IOCs)
    81–2, 84–5, 193, 199–200, 211,
    217–19
International Panel on Climate Change
    (IPCC) 29, 215
international political economy (IPE)
    32–3, 233
    see also economics
international relations (IR) 11–13, 30,
    32–3, 127
Iran 22, 186, 203
Iraq 186, 189, 193–4, 197, 199, 203
Irkutsk (Irkutskaia) oblast 9, 16–17,
    71–5, 78–9, 80–81, 83, 85, 88–9,
    157–8, 165–7, 169, 201–2
Itera 145, 149

Japan 4, 17, 59, 88, 100, 160, 162, 164–6,
    169–72, 177–8, 224, 227, 236

Kamchatka 100, 113
Kara Sea 7–8, 210, 212, 218, 228
Karachaganak 189–90
Karelian Republic 105, 113
Kazakhstan 22, 188–9, 193, 199, 204
KazMunaiGaz 190, 199
Khodorkovsky, M. 24, 55–6
Kjærnet, H. 96, 105
Kovytka 16, 56, 60, 63, 79–81, 83–5, 89,
    219, 236
Kozmino (Bay) 9, 165–6, 170, 176, 202
Krasnoiarsk krai 157–8, 167–9
Kumkol 188, 190
Kurdistan 197–8
Kyoto protocol (treaty) 4, 24, 108, 112,
    215, 226

Ledeneva, A. 57–8
Leuna-2000 189, 191
law 14, 33, 98, 105–7, 125, 143, 164–5,
    167–8, 213, 217
Libya 186, 197, 203
liquefied natural gas (LNG) 9–10, 76–7,
    81–2, 88, 159, 165, 169, 171–3,
    177, 212, 219
Lithuania 125, 131, 138, 194, 196
Liuhto, K. 49, 129
Lukarco 189, 190, 193
Lukoil 18, 24, 48, 53, 59, 105, 187–91,
    193–8, 200, 236

Malaysia 171, 193
Mashinoimport 186, 190
Mazeikiu Nafta 194, 196–7
Mediterranean Sea 167, 196
Medvedev, D. 24, 32, 48, 51, 64, 94,
    109, 119, 130–31, 195, 199, 207,
    222, 226–7, 234
Meleya 189–90
Middle East 9, 28, 160–63, 170, 179,
    189, 233
Miller, Aleksei 123, 144
Mitsubishi 82, 84, 164
Mitsui 82, 84, 164
modernization 18, 49, 59, 79, 83,
    112–13, 207–8, 217, 219, 222, 226,
    228, 236

MOL 196, 198, 201
multidisciplinary 14–15, 35
    see also interdisciplinarity

NAK Naftohaz 149, 150
national oil companies (NOCs) 84, 86,
    192–3, 200, 203, 211, 219
Nenets AO (Oil Company) 165, 167
Neste 122, 126
Netherlands 121, 123, 195
Nord Stream gas pipeline (NSGP) 9, 17,
    28, 62, 117–20, 122–6, 129–35,
    232, 234
North Russia 99, 101, 110, 192
North West Russia 99, 105, 233
Norway 9, 52–3, 193
Novatek 23, 195, 219
nuclear energy 10, 97

OECD 103, 108, 211, 214, 216–17
Okhotsk Sea 102, 210
OMV 198, 201
Organization of Petroleum Exporting
    Countries (OPEC) 7, 60, 210, 211
Øverland, I. 96, 105

Pacific 65, 166, 202, 235
Pakistan 198–9
PDVSA 195, 200
peat 9, 99, 102, 110
PetroChina 201–2
Petronas 193, 203
PetroVietnam 186, 198, 204
Poland 17, 124, 128, 133, 152, 187, 194
policy environment 15, 19–20, 26, 29,
    35–7, 39, 40, 48, 65, 69–72, 74, 83,
    85, 88–90, 92, 94, 98, 104, 106,
    108, 111–12, 145, 185, 189, 228,
    230, 232–3, 237–8
    resource geographic dimension 15–6,
        18, 30–31, 34, 38–9, 66, 72,
        75–7, 92, 98, 103, 111, 113,
        147, 156, 169, 185–6, 192, 204,
        206, 209–10, 218, 228, 230–31,
        233
    financial dimension 15–6, 18, 30–34,
        39, 55, 64, 72, 75–7, 92, 104–6,
        111, 113, 127, 147, 156, 169,
        177, 185–9, 191–2, 196, 198,
        202–6, 212, 228, 230–31, 233

institutional dimension 15–8, 30,
    32–4, 39, 48, 55, 64, 66, 69, 72,
    75–7, 92, 106, 108, 111, 113,
    117, 127, 144, 147, 160, 167,
    175, 185–6, 188–9, 194, 196,
    198–9, 202–4, 206, 228,
    230–31, 233, 237
ecological dimension 15–6, 30, 34–5,
    38–9, 64, 72–3, 75–7, 92,
    111–13, 166, 206, 214, 228,
    230–31, 234
political science 11, 33
Prigorodnoe 82, 169, 171
privatization 47–8, 52, 57, 64, 143, 191,
    220
production-sharing agreement (PSA) 23,
    81–2, 84, 164–5, 189, 203
Putin, V. 25, 32, 48, 64, 128, 131–2, 134,
    166, 194–5, 198, 200–202, 204,
    207, 218, 227

Qatar 171, 193

RAO UES 27, 48, 104, 191
rationality 26, 32, 139, 142
renewable energy 4, 5, 6, 10–11, 16, 21,
    92–9, 101–9, 111–13, 209–10
rent 16, 23, 32, 36, 63–6, 68, 71–7, 80,
    83–90, 140, 144–6, 149, 151,
    206–8
resource curse 3, 103, 146, 207–8
    see also Dutch disease
ressentiment 17, 117, 127–9, 131, 134–5,
    232
Roshydromet 227, 228,
Rosneft 18, 23–4, 48, 50–52, 55, 60, 81,
    84, 133, 144, 164, 166, 168, 175,
    179, 189, 191–3, 196–203, 218–19,
    236
RosUkrEnergo 149–50
Rotterdam 167, 194
Royal Dutch Shell 56, 82, 164
RusHydro 100–101
Rusia Petroleum 56, 80–81, 84, 219

Sakha 70–71, 74, 77–9, 83, 85, 88–9,
    169
Sakha Republic 16, 72, 74, 78, 80,
    157–8, 167–8, 175, 178

Sakhalin (Sakhalinskaia) 9, 12, 18, 23, 49, 56, 60, 63, 71–2, 74, 76, 78–9, 80–2, 84–5, 88–9, 100, 157–8, 163–5, 169–74, 177–8, 217–18, 233
Saudi Arabia 7, 193
Scandinavia 208, 225
schemata 26–31, 35–40, 140
    see also frame
Sea of Azov 101, 167
Sea of Okhotsk 74, 99
Sechin, I. 24, 51–2, 199–202
Serbia 203–4
Shell 81–2, 84, 123, 218–19
Shtokman 9, 17, 27, 120–21, 195, 213, 219
Siberia 65, 71, 85, 100, 206, 218–19
    East Siberia 7, 9, 17, 23, 56, 65, 71–4, 85, 100, 110, 156–60, 163–4, 165–9,175–8, 192, 202, 210, 213, 219, 233, 235–6
    West Siberia 7, 8, 17, 37, 64, 156, 166, 175–6, 178, 187–8, 196, 210, 218
Sibneft 24, 59, 191, 203
Sinopec 199, 202
Skovorodino 17, 165–6, 171
Slavneft 25, 48, 219
Slovakia 12, 196, 197
socialism 185–6
sociology 22, 33
Sokol 162, 170
Sokolov, A. 58–9
solar (power/energy) 10, 98–9, 102, 105, 107
Sonatrach 193, 199
South Korea 4, 17, 59–60, 80, 88, 160, 163, 169, 170–73, 178
South Stream pipeline 9, 130, 133, 203
Soviet Union 5, 15, 45–7, 50, 54, 57, 62, 64, 82, 85, 88, 98, 100, 108, 117, 122, 128, 134, 160, 186–7, 204, 206, 213–15, 223
Statoil 27, 190, 193, 195, 219
Stern, J. 7, 118
structuration 15, 20, 37–40, 45, 49, 65, 69, 72, 80, 84–5, 88, 228, 230, 235, 237–8
Surgutneftegas 24, 48, 57, 59, 83, 175, 189, 191, 198, 200

sustainability 16, 86, 92, 94, 96–7, 108, 112–13, 131, 216–17, 234
    sustainable development 92–5, 103, 215
    see also policy environment: ecological dimension; frame: sustainability frame
Sutela, P. 221, 223
Sweden 120–121, 123–6, 130, 135
Syria 186, 197, 204

Taishet 165, 176
Taiwan 170–71
Talakan 168–9
Tatneft 25, 48, 197
Tengiz 189–90, 193
Tianjin 201–2
tidal power 10, 102
Timan-Pechora 7, 8, 164
TNK-BP 23–5, 48, 53, 55–7, 80, 84, 175, 191, 197, 200, 203, 219
Total 27, 165, 190, 195, 219
TPAO 190, 203
Transneft 25, 48, 110, 166–7, 176–7, 196–7, 201–2, 219
Transpetrol 196–7
Turkey 230, 159
Turkmenistan 22, 145, 149, 204
Tyumen 156–9

Ukraine 4, 9, 17, 28, 36, 54, 118–19, 122, 126, 128–31, 133–4, 136–8, 143, 145, 147–52, 187, 189, 197, 204, 232, 235
UNDP Russia 210, 222, 226
United Arab Emirates (UAE) 171, 199
United Kingdom 121, 123
United Nations (UN) 189, 215
United Nations Development Programme (UNDP) 93, 95
Urals 100, 167
USA 4, 9, 11–12, 37, 53, 55, 60, 100, 160, 170, 177–8, 195–6, 198, 202, 212, 223–4
Uzbekistan 22, 193

Vankor 167, 168, 169, 202
Venezuela 193, 194, 197–8, 200
Verkhniaia Chona 168–9
Vietnam 186, 198, 204
Vladivostok 173, 177–8

Volga-Urals 8, 210
Vostok Energy 201–2
Vyakhirev, R. 122, 144

West Kurna-2 189–90, 193
White Sea 99, 102
wind (power/energy) 10, 98–9, 101, 103,
       107
World Bank 105, 221, 225
World Trade Organization (WTO) 213,
       226
WWF Russia 25, 111

Yakutia 72, 74, 178, 192
Yakutsk 71, 88
Yamal peninsula 9, 17, 49, 120–21,
       167, 212, 219, 228
Yanukovich, V. 148, 150
Yeltsin, B. 64, 207
Yukos 18, 24, 53, 55–6, 59, 131,
       189, 191, 196–7, 199–201, 217,
       236

Zabaikal 163, 173
Zarubezhneft 186, 190, 204